Conflict and Cohesion in Families

Causes and Consequences

THE ADVANCES IN FAMILY RESEARCH SERIES

Volumes published under Series Editorship of David Reiss:

Volumes published under Series Editorship of Martha J. Cox and Rand Conger:

Conflict and Cohesion in Families

Causes and Consequences

Edited by

Martha J. Cox
University of North Carolina at Chapel Hill

Jeanne Brooks-Gunn
Teachers College, Columbia University

 LAWRENCE ERLBAUM ASSOCIATES, PUBLISHERS

1999   Mahwah, New Jersey   London

Lawrence Erlbaum Associates, Inc., Publishers
10 Industrial Avenue
Mahwah, New Jersey 07430

Cover design by Kathryn Houghtaling Lacey

Library of Congress Cataloging-in-Publication Data

Conflict and cohesion in families : causes and consequences / edited
by Martha J. Cox, Jeanne Brooks-Gunn.
p.   cm. — (The advances in family research series)
Papers from the Second Family Research Consortium, Research
Consortium on Family Risk and Resilience's first Summer Institute,
June, 1994, in Santa Fe, N.M.
Includes bibliographical references and index.
ISBN 0–8058–2410–3 (cloth : alk. paper)
1. Family violence.   2. Interpersonal conflict.   3. Communication
in the family.   4. Family psychotherapy.   I. Cox, Martha J.
II. Brooks-Gunn, Jeanne.   III. Research Consortium on Family Risk
and Resilience. Summer Institute (1st : 1994 : Santa, Fe, N.M.)
IV. Series: Advances in family research.
RC569.5.F3C66   1998
362.82—dc21   98-28381
                                                         CIP

Books published by Lawrence Erlbaum Associates are printed on acid-free paper,
and their bindings are chosen for strength and durability.

Printed in the United States of America
10   9   8   7   6   5   4   3   2   1

To Mavis Hetherington and David Reiss
for their commitment and contribution to research on the family
and for their leadership in the Family Research Consortium

Contents

Preface

The Family Research Consortium was established with funding from the National Institute of Mental Health in 1985 to improve the quality of investigation, stimulate broader collaboration to enhance discussion across disciplines, and inform prevention efforts in the field of family research. The Family Research Consortium was funded for two successive 5-year periods. Since 1986, the consortium has held summer institutes, bringing together an interdisciplinary group of senior and junior researchers to focus each summer on a different, specific, and timely theme in family research. The Family Research Consortium also runs a multi-site postdoctoral training program in family research and sponsors a number of collaborative research projects among its members. The Second Family Research Consortium (The Research Consortium on Family Risk and Resilience), begun in 1993, consists of 12 scientists, each of whom has an active, funded program of longitudinal family research on biological, psychological, social, or social–structural factors involved in the developmental course of mental health or illness. The consortium group includes Mark Appelbaum, Ph.D. (University of California, San Diego), Jeanne Brooks-Gunn, Ph.D. (Columbia University), Linda Burton, Ph.D. (Penn State University), Ana Mari Cauce, Ph.D. (University of Washington), Lindsay Chase-Lansdale, Ph.D. (University of Chicago), Rand Conger, Ph.D. (Iowa State University), Martha Cox, Ph.D. (University of North Carolina at Chapel Hill), Marion Forgatch, Ph.D. (Oregon Social Learning Center), Stuart Hauser, M.D., Ph.D. (Harvard University), Ron Kessler, Ph.D. (Harvard University), Howard Markman, Ph.D. (University of Denver), and Steve Suomi, Ph.D. (National Institute of Child Health and Human Development). Disciplines represented in this group of scholars include developmental psychology, clinical psychology, sociology, epidemiology, psychiatry, animal behavior/ethology, and demography. Rand Conger and Martha Cox serve as Co-chairs of the current consortium.

The current Research Consortium on Family Risk and Resilience was preceded by an earlier Research Consortium on Family Process and Mental Health (1986–1991). The first consortium group had 10 members and included Elaine Blechman, Ph.D. (University of Colorado), Robert Cole, Ph.D. (University of Rochester), Philip Cowan, Ph.D. (University of California at Berkeley), John Gottman, Ph.D. (University of Washington), Mavis Hetherington, Ph.D. (University of Virginia), Sheppard Kellam, M.D. (Johns Hopkins University), Ross Parke, Ph.D. (University of California, Riverside), Gerald Patterson, Ph.D. (Oregon Social Learning Center), David Reiss, M.D. (George Washington University), and Irving Siegel, Ph.D. (Educational Testing Service).

The first Family Research Consortium published five volumes in the series by Lawrence Erlbaum Associates. They are:

- *Depression and Aggression in Family Interaction* (Gerald Patterson, Editor, 1990)
- *Family Transitions* (Philip Cowan & E. Mavis Hetherington, Editors, 1991)
- *How Do Families Cope With Chronic Illness?* (Robert Cole & David Reiss, Editors, 1993)
- *Exploring Family Relationships With Other Social Contexts* (Ross Parke & Sheppard Kellam, Editors, 1994)
- *Stress, Coping, and Resiliency in Children and Families* (E. Mavis Hetherington & Elaine Blechman, Editors, 1996)

The work of the current consortium is supported by two NIMH grants: Research Grant No. RO1MH49694 and Training Grant No. T32MH19734. The work of the first consortium was supported by similar NIMH grants.

This volume is based on the first summer institute of the second consortium (June 1994, Santa Fe, New Mexico). In keeping with our focus on family risk and resilience, the first institute was on "Family Conflict and Cohesion" and was chaired by Jeanne Brooks-Gunn and Martha Cox. Each summer, the consortium sponsors an institute focusing on a distinct aspect of current family research. The topics of the second through fifth summer institutes are: Adolescence and Beyond: Family Processes and Development; Continuity and Change: Family Structure and Process; Diversity and Families: Context and Process; and Prevention Programs for Families: Process and Outcome. Additional volumes are forthcoming from Lawrence Erlbaum Associates; these are:

- *Adolescence and Beyond: Family Processes and Development* (Ana Mari Cauce & Stuart Hauser, Editors)
- *Continuity and Change: Family Structure and Process* (Rand Conger, Editor)
- *Diversity and Families: Context and Process* (Linda Burton & Lindsay Chase-Lansdale, Editors)
- *Prevention Programs for Families: Process and Outcome* (Marion Forgatch & Howard Markman, Editors)

The aim of the summer institutes is to increase the quality of investigation and the level of collaboration in the field of family research by bringing together junior and senior family scientists using a format that provides high quality presentations and ample opportunity for exciting intellectual exchanges between those attending. Similarly, the goal of this volume is to stimulate theoretical and empirical advances in research on family processes.

The members of the first and second consortium groups owe much to Joy Schulterbrandt and Della Hann, the NIMH program officers for the first and second consortiums, respectively, as does the field of family research. We wish to extend our sincere thanks and grateful appreciation to them for initiating and nurturing this important effort that has done much to stimulate high quality research in the family field. We also wish to thank Donna Fleming and Kathy Meese, who served as the Project Managers for the second consortium group. It is to a good extent due to their efforts that the summer institutes have been so successful. Additionally, we wish to thank Mavis Hetherington and David Reiss, who served as Principal Investigators of the former training and consortium grants, respectively. Both served as advisors to the current consortium and were of significant help in getting us on our way. We are very grateful to them for their vast wisdom and their generous support.

Martha J. Cox
Jeanne Brooks-Gunn

List of Contributors

Jeanne Brooks-Gunn Teachers College, Columbia University, New York.
Margaret Burchinal Frank Porter Graham Child Development Center, University of North Carolina at Chapel Hill.
Linda Burton Department of Individual & Family Studies, The Pennsylvania State University.
Martha J. Cox Frank Porter Graham Child Development Center, University of North Carolina at Chapel Hill.
Rand D. Conger Center for Family Research in Rural Mental Health, Iowa State University, Research Park, Ames, Iowa.
E. Mark Cummings Department of Psychology, Notre Dame University, Indiana.
David S. DeGarmo Oregon Social Learning Center, Eugene.
Marion S. Forgatch Oregon Social Learning Center, Eugene.
Melinda S. Forthofer School of Public Health, University of South Florida, Tampa.
Xiaojia Ge Department of Human & Community Development, University of California, Davis.
John M. Gottman Department of Psychology, University of Washington, Seattle.
Julia A. Graber Teachers College, Columbia University, New York.
Lynn Fainsilber Katz Department of Psychology, University of Washington, Seattle.
Ronald C. Kessler Department of Health Care Policy, Harvard Medical School, Boston.

Howard J. Markman   Psychology Department, University of Denver, Colorado.

Dawn A. Obeidallah   Harvard School of Public Health, Department of Maternal and Child Health, Boston.

Blair Paley   NPI & H, University of California, Los Angeles.

Gerald R. Patterson   Oregon Social Learning Center, Eugene.

C. Chris Payne   University of North Carolina at Greensboro.

Sally I. Powers   Department of Psychology, University of Massachusetts, Amherst.

Lydia M. Prado   Center for Marital & Family Studies, University of Denver, Colorado.

Stephen J. Suomi   NICHD, National Institutes of Health, Poolesville, Maryland.

Deborah P. Welsh   Department of Psychology, University of Tennessee at Knoxville.

Amy Wilson   Department of Psychology, West Virginia University, Morgantown.

Beverly Wilson   Department of Psychology, University of Washington, Seattle.

1

▼▼▼▼▼▼▼

Studying Conflict and Cohesion in Families: An Overview

Martha J. Cox
University of North Carolina at Chapel Hill

Jeanne Brooks-Gunn
Teachers College, Columbia University

The Family Research Consortium on Risk and Resilience is interested in relationships within the family and their links with individual and contextual factors, as they are associated with development. In this volume, the Family Research Consortium takes a detailed look at two dimensions of family relationships, conflict and cohesion. Family research needs to specify the dimensions of relationships that are critical for healthy development and those that are linked to less healthy or psychopathological development. We explore the constructs of conflict and cohesion because they reflect critical dimensions of family process (although not the only dimensions of family process). What are these family processes, and when and how do they operate to support healthy or problematic development? This volume also reflects the importance of context for understanding individual development and the impact of family processes—from neighborhood effects on family relationships, to multigenerational family effects on dyadic relationships, to marital relationships' effects on parent–child relationships, to earlier marital relational effects on current marital relationships, to parent–child relationships on both parents and children.

Over the last several decades, a shift in thinking about normative and nonnormative development involved the recognition that individual behavior is regulated by social context. This view stands in contrast to a traditional medical model of disorder in which "identifiable somatic entities underlie specific disease syndromes" (Sameroff, 1989). Many different, although often complementary, perspectives, which emphasize the study of relationships, individuals, and contexts influenced the way we understand how normative development proceeds and how disorders arise and are maintained. These perspectives include developmental, organizational, and systems frameworks (Cicchetti, 1990; Cox & Paley, 1997; Sameroff, 1983; Sroufe, 1989), ecological theory (Brofenbrenner, 1979; Bronfenbrenner & Morris, 1998), person-oriented theory (Magnussen & Bergman, 1990; Magnussen & Stattin, 1998), social network theory (Granovetter, 1982), and social capital (Coleman, 1988).

A common thread in these perspectives is that development is seen as occurring in the context of relationships. Indeed, research in the past 25 years made it clear that we cannot study the developmental course of individuals separately from their relationships. Sroufe (1989) maintains that most problems in the early years, although evident in child behavior, are best conceptualized as relationship problems. A very different approach to research on the development of individual disorder or competence results when one views the individual as involving integrated systems of biological, psychological, and social functioning (Sameroff, 1983) embedded in and mutually regulated in a family system that is itself embedded in and mutually regulated in a community and cultural context. Clearly, this view makes the study of the individual a complicated business, but the contention is that research must embrace this complexity. Individuals are embedded in a series of relationships that are themselves often nested in contexts—relationships with parents in the context of household residence (or, in the case of divorced or unwed parents, sometimes several residences), relationships with siblings in the context of the family, relationships with kin in the context of extended families, relationships with peers in the context of the neighborhood, school, or work settings, and so on (Bronfenbrenner, 1989; Hinde & Stevenson-Hinde, 1988).

Social relationships and social experiences such as those provided in the repeated transactions within a family are critical to understand in order to illuminate ways to disorder or competence. Longitudinal, "life course" research, in which levels of variables from the biological, psychological, social, community, and cultural are combined within the same studies, is necessary if processes at all of these levels contribute to individual development. Such research requires the cooperation of multiple disciplines with varying expertise concerning measurement at these various levels. Several of the contributions to this volume attempt to cross disciplinary boundaries. These chapters provide examples of how measurement at several levels elucidates the development of disorder or competence.

Over the last decade, it became clear that, for many children and adults, the origin of behavioral problems or deviancies can be found in problematic relationships in conflicted or disorganized families. Consequently, the study of the family in relation to individuals' problem behavior burgeoned. We understand that conflicted marital and family relationships are associated with increases in the probability of many disorders in children (Cummings & Davies, 1994; Emery, 1982; Grych & Fincham, 1990). However, many questions remain. Though conflict in marital and other family relationships was targeted as a particularly damaging risk factor, conflict is a common part of family life. How and under what conditions is conflict damaging, and when is it more benign or even facilitative of healthy development? Cohesiveness or closeness of families was suggested as a source of resilience, but what exactly are these family processes, how do they operate, and what are their benefits? We know little about different points in development and what family processes either hinder or help adaptation at these different points. Transition times in development may be times of particular vulnerability for individuals and families because of the press for new behaviors and adaptations. Moreover, little data exist about family processes across different cultural groups. How the disorder or organization of communities is associated with children's development and behavioral problems is not well studied—is their influence mediated through their impact on families, or do communities have direct effects on disorder? The chapters in this volume begin to provide some answers to these important questions.

AN OVERVIEW OF THE VOLUME

The chapters in this volume encompass a wide array of topics all related to understanding family processes, particularly conflict and cohesion or closeness, and individual disorder or competence.

In chapter 2, Patterson considers the role of context in determining deviant behavior in children from both the micro- and macroperspective. The model suggested by Patterson illustrates an effort to cross disciplinary boundaries and measure variables at different levels in the same study. Patterson proposes that, as societal rates for juvenile crime fluctuate, so do the prevalence rates for young antisocial children (e.g., the greater the prevalence of 8- and 9- year-old antisocial boys, the greater the risk for high prevalence rates for juvenile delinquency in that setting). Patterson also hypothesizes that these prevalence rates for antisocial behavior and for delinquency are both determined by the prevalence of family units characterized by disrupted parenting skills. Drawing on social disorganization theory, he proposes, in turn, that the prevalence of disrupted families in a society varies directly as the function of changes in economic cycles. The model that is proposed would identify the risk factors associated with the individual family and with macrochanges in society itself that determine juvenile crime rates. The general model integrates psychological and sociological variables and provides a blueprint for the kind of research that is needed to explore phenomena at multiple levels (the family and the community level; see also Brooks-Gunn, Duncan, & Aber, 1997a, 1997b).

In chapter 3, Obeidallah and Burton examine conceptual issues concerning the study of conflict and closeness in multigeneration African American families with teenage mothers. Burton and Obeidallah argue that existing perspectives on the study of conflict and closeness in White or middle-class families may have limited applicability to African American families in which a teenage pregnancy occurs. Using insights from a 5-year ethnographic study of 150 urban, multigeneration families with teenage parents, this chapter highlights the need to understand adaptive family processes in different environmental contexts and what becomes normative in different socioeconomic, cultural, and ethnic groups.

In chapter 4, Prado and Markman add to the understanding of different family structures. They observe remarried couples that all contain one partner who was in their original longitudinal investigation during a first marriage. This research is unique in that the same individuals were followed from before their first marriages through their second marriages. Prado and Markman consider how communication deficits reflecting affect regulation (predictive of initial marital breakup) are transferred from one relationship system to another. Their thesis is that it is not the number or content of problem areas that is related to marital dissatisfaction and divorce, but rather how the problem areas and conflicts are managed. Interestingly, they find that for women, negative affect in the first relationship correlated negatively with negative affect in the second marriage. The negative affect of the husbands of these women also correlated negatively with the ex-husband's negative affect. Thus, women appear to be using different strategies for problem solving in their second marriages as compared to their first. Prado and Markman discuss the possible implications of such a finding.

In chapter 5, Cox, Paley, Payne, and Burchinal consider the relationship between marital processes and parenting interactions in young couples experiencing the transition to parenthood. There has been great interest in the linkage between marital disruption and child problems during the last 2 decades. One assumption about this link is that the effect is mediated by disturbances in parent–child relationships, that disrupted marriage results in disrupted parenting, which leads to child problems. Cox and colleagues focus on understanding how and when marital processes are associated with disrupted parenting. They note that although much of the earlier work was on global constructs like "marital quality," the focus of more recent work is on marital conflict and its impact on other family relationships. Prominent have been models that stress the "spillover" effects of marital conflict, resulting in the direct transfer of mood, affect, or behavior from one setting to another (Erel & Burman, 1995). However, Cummings and Wilson (this volume) noted that marital conflict may not always have negative effects on children. If marital disagreements are effectively resolved, then conflict may not have the same impact on parenting relationships and child development, even in families where parents have a lot of marital conflict. Conditions under which marital conflict undermines parenting relationships are poorly understood. Gottman (1994) noted that a particular sign of problematic marriages is the withdrawal of partners in interaction, and that withdrawal from marriage may be accompanied by withdrawal from children. These authors test this idea in their study of young couples followed longitudinally from the prenatal period through the first years of the child's life. They focus particularly on marital conflict and withdrawal and its association with parenting, indexed by whether parents showed warm, involved, sensitive responding to their infants. They find evidence that marital withdrawal, more than marital conflict, particularly undermines parenting processes that are important for supporting early emotional development. Their research also demonstrates the importance of understanding how negative family situations may differentially affect mothers' treatment of male versus female children.

In chapter 6, Cummings and Wilson also focus on the issue of when marital conflict is problematic for children, but consider more direct effects of conflict on children. They contend that although marital conflict is often viewed as a sign of family dysfunction, when appropriately handled, marital conflict is not pathogenic and may be beneficial for marriages and families. This chapter advances the perspective that contextual elements determine the effects of conflict on children. They provide evidence that conflict resolution, or parents' explanations of resolution, may ameliorate children's negative reactions to the conflict. Analyses suggest that any explanation, other than a message that there is no possibility that things can be worked out, is beneficial from the child's perspective (e.g., We haven't worked it out yet but we will; We agree to disagree, but its okay). Such explanations do not change children's negative emotional reactions to conflict, but leave the children more optimistic about long-term marital relations. The literature on contextual factors and children's reactions to marital conflict is discussed in terms of an emotional security hypothesis (Davies & Cummings, 1994). This theory emphasizes that children react to conflicts in terms of their assessment of the meaning of conflicts for family functioning and children's well being. With regard to the studies presented, the results suggest that, although optimistic explanations about unresolved marital conflict do not change children's immediate reactions, such endings do reduce negative emotional security implications from the children's perspective. Thus, any explanations about marital conflict, other than explanations that leave the possibility of dire consequences, are beneficial.

In chapter 7, Katz, Gottman, and Wilson introduce a new concept of parenting that they refer to as *parental meta-emotion philosophy*. By parental meta-emotion, they mean parents' emotions about their own and their children's emotions. They propose that parents have an organized set of thoughts and an approach to their own emotions and to their children's emotions. Parents who have an "emotion-coaching" philosophy are aware of both their own and their children's emotions, value their children's emotional expressions, can talk about their own and their children's emotions in a differentiated fashion, and assist their children with their emotions of anger and sadness. Essentially, these parents see their role as a "coach" during their children's emotional moments. This parental meta-emotion philosophy they call an *emotion coaching philosophy*. Parents who have a *dismissing philosophy* of emotion are unaware of their own and their children's emotions, are critical, disapproving and not empathic to their child's emotional experiences, and see emotion as a behavior that needs to be controlled or gotten over.

They report evidence that an emotion coaching philosophy (EC-philosophy) has broad implications for the emotional well being of all family members and familial subsystems. Meta-emotion philosophy was found to relate to marital and parent–child interaction when children were 5 years old. EC-philosophy parents had marriages that were less hostile, and parents were less negative and more positive during parent–child interaction. Their children showed less evidence of physiological stress, greater ability to focus attention, and had less negative play with their best friends. A longitudinal follow-up of these families when the children were 8 years old indicated that children with EC-philosophy parents showed higher academic achievement in mathematics and reading (even controlling for earlier IQ scores) had fewer behavior problems, and were physically healthier than children of non-EC parents. Social class variables, emotional expressiveness, or the greater happiness and stability of parents with an EC-type meta-emotion philosophy did not explain the relations between child outcome and parental meta-emotion philosophy. Katz, Gottman, and Wilson present a model in which they argue that parental meta-emotion structure is related to the inhibition of parental derogation toward children, the facilitation of scaffolding/praising parenting, and that it directly affects children's regulatory physiology. This, in turn, affects their children's ability to regulate their emotions, and has impact on a broad range of outcomes. Meta-emotion philosophy is discussed as an approach to emotion that guides the degree to which family members are able to make an emotional connection with each other. These ideas help us consider what may be important in families with strong cohesion or closeness.

In chapter 8, Forgatch and DeGarmo consider how cohesion and conflict function as predictors of boys' wanderings. As boys approach adolescence, they seek increasing time away from home without adult supervision. Unsupervised wandering, however, has been found to be associated with antisocial and delinquent behavior. The authors note that wandering is an ideal outcome to study because it represents the kind of collaboration required between parent and child to ensure effective supervision at a time when the boys are typically given increased freedom and autonomy. The basic hypotheses tested in this study were that conflict would have a negative impact and cohesion would have a positive impact on changing levels of boys' wandering and antisocial behavior. A multiagent, multimethod strategy was used to assess 206 boys and their families when the boys were in Grades 4 and 6. The boys were considered to be at risk for delinquency because their families lived in the community's highest crime neighborhoods. As expected, cohesion was associated with reduced changes in wandering from Grades 4 to 6, whereas conflict showed no association.

In chapter 9, Conger and Ge examine the changing nature of parent–adolescent interactions during the transition from early to middle adolescence. Most of the major theories of adolescent development suggest that the quality of interactions between parents and children will change during this time of life, toward greater conflict and less warmth and support. Despite these predictions, empirical studies produced inconsistent findings, some supportive and others not supportive of such theories. Conger and Ge suggest that methodological limitations in earlier studies, such as cross-sectional comparisons of age differences and confounds in measurement, failed to produce adequate theoretical tests of the major developmental models. The present research corrects for these deficiencies, and the reported findings offer strong support for the thesis that parent–adolescent relations undergo profound changes in the expression of positive and negative emotional affect during the early to middle adolescent years. Both boys and girls increase hostility toward parents, but especially those from homes earlier characterized as higher in hostility and lower in warmth and supportiveness.

In chapter 10, Graber and Brooks-Gunn also focus on the nature of parent–child relationships during the transition toward adolescence. Building on earlier work on the intersection of pubertal growth, family relationships, and the context in which both occur (Paikoff & Brooks-Gunn, 1991), they focus on conflict and closeness in mother–daughter relationships, and the ways in which these two relational dimensions are associated with girls' development, as a function of pubertal status and onset of sexuality. Their premise is that conflict in mother–daughter relationships is inevitable, given the normative demand for autonomy that girls make as they become more mature. They wish to understand the circumstances in which conflict is maladaptive and those in which it is not. Questions also are raised about the dimensions of conflict that might be associated with healthy development, the inference being that some conflict is not only normative, but may be growth enhancing. Conflict and disagreements may be the context in which girls learn negotiation and bargaining skills.

In chapter 11, Powers and Welsh continue the theme of understanding the period of adolescence for girls in considering mother–daughter interactions and adolescent girl's symptoms of depression. They consider the proposition that adolescent depression is associated with difficulties in interpersonal behaviors that facilitate individuation. They explore this proposition by considering the relation of mother–daughter interactions to daughter's symptoms. They find evidence that in interaction, daughters and mothers show difficulty in negotiating autonomy as reactions to daughter's internalizing symptoms, and that these interpersonal behaviors, in turn, predict increases in daughter's internalizing symptoms 1 year later. Their data nicely illustrate the transactional nature of these processes. They suggest that conflict may be a necessary occurrence for optimal outcomes during specific developmental phases of transitions.

In chapter 12, Suomi describes cases of conflict and patterns of closeness as they occur in families of rhesus monkeys. In considering general principles underlying these phenomena in monkeys, Suomi contributes to our understanding on conflict and cohesion in human families. Rhesus monkeys, like most advanced nonhuman primate species, are highly social animals that live in large, well-defined social groups characterized by complex kinship and dominance relationships. Rhesus monkey females spend their entire lives in the presence of multiple generations of female kin, whereas males stay in their families only until puberty, at which point they leave to join other established groups, never to return to the family fold. Monkeys growing up in these groups inevitably experience within-family conflicts at the time of weaning, conception and birth of younger siblings, and (for males) emigration at puberty. On the other hand, the birth of an infant brings adolescent and adult female family members closer together, and threats from predators or from other monkey groups clearly increase closeness in the multigenerational matrilines. There are marked and developmentally stable differences among rhesus monkeys in the manner and degree to which family conflicts disrupt and family closeness enhances individual developmental trajectories, and these differences in turn affect each family's capacity for coping with both short- and long-term challenges.

In chapter 13, Kessler and Forthofer report on findings that illuminate how disrupted family systems are formed. They summarize results showing that young people with early-onset psychiatric disorders are more likely than others to marry early, have a disrupted marriage, have a child too early, get divorced, and then either remain a single parent or a person who continues to get married and divorced several times. The critical period seems to be prior to the age of 18. If marriage and pregnancy can be postponed until after this age, psychiatric disorders seem to have less of an impact on family formation problems.

In the last chapter, Cox, Brooks-Gunn, and Paley reflect on the contributions in this volume, integrate the insights gained from this research, discuss implications for perspectives on mental health and development, and highlight issues that remain to be addressed. We argue for a more nuanced and less deficit-driven model of family conflict. Additionally, we discuss alternative ways of conceptualizing conflict and cohesion.

REFERENCES

Bronfenbrenner, U. (1979). *The ecology of human development: Experiments by nature and design.* Cambridge, MA: Harvard University Press.

Bronfenbrenner, U. (1989). The ecology of the family as a context for human development: Research perspectives. *Developmental Psychology, 22,* 723–742.

Bronfenbrenner, U., & Morris, P. A. (1998). The ecology of developmental process. In R. M. Lerner (Ed.), *Handbook of child psychology, fifth edition, volume one: Theoretical models of human development* (pp. 993–1028). New York: John Wiley & Sons, Inc.

Brooks-Gunn, J., Duncan, G. J., & Aber, A. L. (1997a). *Neighborhood poverty: Contexts and consequences for children (Volume 1).* New York: Russell Sage Foundation Press.

Brooks-Gunn, J., Duncan, G. J., & Aber, A. L. (1997b). *Neighborhood poverty: Policy implications in studying neighborhoods (Volume 2).* New York: Russell Sage Foundation Press.

Cicchetti, D. (1990). A historical perspective on the discipline of developmental psychopathology. In J. Rolf, A. S. Masten, D. Cicchetti, K. H. Nuechterlein, & S. Weintraub (Eds.), *Risk and protective factors in the development of psychopathology* (pp. 2–28). Cambridge: Cambridge University Press.

Coleman, J. S. (1988). Social capital in the creation of human capital. *American Journal of Sociology, 94,* S95–S120.

Cox, M. J., & Paley, B. (1997). Families as systems. *Annual Review of Psychology, 48,* 243–267.

Cummings, M. E., & Davies, P. (1994). *Children and marital conflict: The impact of family dispute and resolution.* New York: The Guilford Press.

Davies, P. T., & Cummings, E. M. (1994). Marital conflict and child adjustment: An emotional security hypothesis. *Psychological Bulletin, 116,* 387–411.

Emery, R. E. (1982). Interparental conflict and the children of discord and divorce. *Psychological Bulletin, 92,* 310–330.

Erel, O., & Burman, B. (1995). Interrelatedness of marital relations and parent–child relations: A meta-analytic review. *Psychological Bulletin, 118*(1), 108–132.

Gottman, J. M. (1994). *What predicts divorce: The relationship between marital processes and marital outcomes.* Hillsdale, NJ: Lawrence Erlbaum Associates.

Granovetter, M. (1982). The strength of weak ties: A network theory revisited. In P. V. Marsden & N. Lin (Eds.), *Social structure and network analysis* (pp. 105–130). Beverly Hills, CA: Sage Publications.

Grych, J. H., & Fincham, F. D. (1990). Marital conflict and children's adjustment: A cognitive–contextual framework. *Psychological Bulletin, 108,* 267–290.

Hinde, R. A., & Stevenson-Hinde, J. (1988). *Relationships within families: Mutual influences.* Oxford: Clarendon Press.

Magnusson, D., & Bergman, L. R. (1990). A pattern approach to the study of pathways from childhood to adulthood. In L. N. Robins & M. Rutter (Eds.), *Straight and devious pathways from childhood to adulthood* (pp. 101–115). New York: Cambridge University Press.

Magnussen, D., & Stattin, H. (1998). Person-context interaction theories. In R. M. Lerner (Ed.), *Handbook of child psychology, fifth edition, volume one: Theoretical models of human development* (pp. 685–760). New York: John Wiley & Sons, Inc.

Paikoff, R. L., & Brooks-Gunn, J. (1991). Do parent–child relationships change during puberty? *Psychological Bulletin, 110*, 47–66.

Sameroff, A. J. (1983). Developmental systems: Contexts and evolution. In W. Kessen (Ed.), *History, theory, and methods*. P. H. Mussen (Ed.), *Handbook of child psychology* (Vol. 1, pp. 237–294). New York: Wiley.

Sameroff, A. J. (1989). Principles of development and psychopathology. In A. J. Sameroff & R. N. Emde (Eds.), *Relationship disturbances in early childhood* (pp. 17–32). New York: Basic Books.

Sroufe, L. A. (1989). Relationship, self, and individual adaptation. In A. J. Sameroff & R. N. Emde (Eds.), *Relationship disturbances in early childhood* (pp. 71–94). New York: Basic Books.

2

▼▼▼▼▼▼▼

A Proposal Relating a Theory of Delinquency to Societal Rates of Juvenile Crime: Putting Humpty Dumpty Together Again

G. R. Patterson
Oregon Social Learning Center

JUVENILE CRIME

A Set of Problems to Be Explained

A major dilemma confronting decision makers concerns the problem of what can be done about the recent increases in juvenile violence (Reiss & Roth, 1993). In England and Wales, there were massive increases in rates of juvenile violence that began around 1987 and persisted at least through 1993 (James, 1995). What model accounts for these changes in international rates? Even more intriguing is the fact that in England and Wales, during the explosion in violence beginning in 1987, the rates for general juvenile offending were falling. We obviously require models that explain why societal rates of juvenile delinquency change and perhaps a different model to account for changes in societal rates of juvenile violence.

The traditional strain and social control models of juvenile delinquency do not explain these phenomena, nor do they account for the vexing problem of Black and White differences in rates of delinquency or differences in aggregated rates of violence (Reiss & Roth, 1993). I propose that an early-onset model that successfully accounts for individual differences in risk for early arrest and chronic offending (Patterson, Crosby, & Vuchinich, 1992; Patterson, Forgatch, Yoerger, & Stoolmiller, 1998; Patterson & Yoerger, 1997) may be extended to serve as a useful alternative in accounting for variations in societal rates of juvenile offending.

This chapter draws ideas and procedures both from recent developments in social disorganization theory and from developmentally oriented theories of delinquency. The a priori model has yet to be tested, but is currently part of a National Institute of Mental Health (NIMH) funded research project (Simons, 1994). The study is designed to pilot test some of the key features of the present model. In a very real sense then, the speculations in this chapter are designed as a blueprint for across-discipline studies focused on variations across setting and across time in societal rates of juvenile crime. In the discussion that follows, the dependent variable is juvenile forms of crime, rather than violence and homicide per se. The reason for this limited view is that most empirical work on the individual-difference model has focused on juvenile offending, rather than on lethal crimes. This is also in keeping with Zimring's (1996) careful distinction between models of general crime and models for lethal crime.

A Diaspora

Reviews such as Elliott, Huizinga, and Ageton (1985) attested to the longevity and variety of explanations given for juvenile delinquency. Their review of theories included Cloward and Ohlin's (1960) strain theory, Hirschi's (1969) social control theory, Akers' (1977) social learning theory, and Elliott's et al. (1985) integration of these points of view. More recent perspectives reflect a Glueck-type perspective with their emphasis upon the contribution of family as well as structural variables (Glueck & Glueck, 1950). Farrington and Hawkins (1991) and Thornberry (1990) are prominent examples. However, there are two important respects in which current theories failed in their mission. First and foremost, they failed to adequately predict which children became delinquents. A review of studies that purport to predict future juvenile offending based on childhood measures showed many significant predictions but invariably they were accompanied by high false positive errors (Loeber & Dishion, 1983). For example, the false positive error for one major longitudinal study was 85% (Glueck, & Glueck, 1950; Utting, Bright, & Henricson, 1993). The second and even more critical failure of these theories is that they do not effectively account for variations in societal rates of juvenile offending.

It is not surprising, of course, that theories about delinquency based on structural sociology might not fare well in accounting for individual differences in juvenile offending. Some of them—for example, strain theory—were not designed to address differences among individuals; they were designed to address differences between groups (Bernard, 1987). According to the historical account by Laub and Sampson (1991), the study of individual differences and family processes was to be left to others (such as psychologists) while sociologists concentrated on broader explanatory variables such as social disadvantage, deviant peers, employment, and divorce. This perspective reflected the views of Merton (1957), who dominated the field of sociology at that time.

One variable that did stand up across studies of aggregate crime rates required no sophisticated theory for its identification. The higher the proportion of young men in the population, the higher the rates of crime. Efforts to relate changes in divorce rates to crime rates do not fare so well. For example, during the past 30 years there was a seven-fold increase in divorce rates (Utting et al., 1993). Both crime and divorce rates increased during the 1960s and 1970s; however, during the 1980s divorce rates continued to climb although crime rates did not.

From a sociological macroperspective, one would assume that variations in prevalence for such variables as unemployment would play a key role in accounting for societal rates for juvenile offenders. However, Sampson's (1987) analyses of a sample of 171 metropolitan (population of 100,000 or more) areas showed nonsignificant correlations between unemployment for Black or White males and aggregated robbery rates. For example, Cloward and Ohlin (1960) hypothesized that crime would be generated by a major discrepancy between socially induced aspirations and the availability of socially approved means for realizing these aspirations. It was expected that lower class youth would experience the greatest strain and, therefore, be at greatest risk for employing delinquent means to satisfy these goals. From this view, unemployment rates would be expected to covary with crime rates. However, the Wilson and Herrnstein (1985, chap. 12) review showed that such a relationship was, at best, of borderline significance and that variables such as socioeconomic status (SES), unemployment, and divorce accounted for only limited amounts of variance in crime rates.

An extensive review by James (1995) showed that there were many countries with even more dramatic inequalities between rich and poor than in the United States, for example, India and China. However, their rates of juvenile offending were said to be lower than those for the United States. He hypothesized that family processes are less disrupted by poverty and unemployment in settings such as India and China, where family networks and the central role of family remain relatively intact. The hypothesis that family process may mediate the impact of poverty and inequality on juvenile offending was strongly supported by Junger's (1983) analyses of immigration into the Netherlands. Most immigrant groups (e.g., Moroccans) showed second generation increases in rates of juvenile offending. Chinese families did not show these increases, presumably because they managed somehow to keep their family processes relatively intact. There is increasing acceptability of the idea that a lack of economic opportunity does not function as a significant main effect in determining crime rates. However, it does play a key role in mediational models where the effects on crime are mediated by what happens to family process. I assumed that a lack of economic opportunity makes an indirect contribution to aggregate offending rates by increasing the prevalence of disrupted families.

The expanded perspective on the role of economic opportunity (or the lack of it) and crime has come about in large part because of the systematic studies by Wilson (1987), Sampson and Wilson (1995), and their colleagues. In these studies, *disrupted family* was defined as a single-parent household headed by a female (e.g., a broken home). In point of fact, such a simple model worked very well in predicting across-setting variations in violence for inner-city settings (Sampson, 1987). However, such a definition may not generalize to the population at large, where the single variable—female-headed households—does not significantly predict delinquent youth. For example, the review by Utting et al. (1993) showed inconsistent covariation of divorce or broken homes with offending. To account for societal rates of juvenile crime, the investigator must be able to identify *which* broken home or divorced family is at risk and which family is not. I believe it is at this juncture that the field of psychology can make a contribution. Developmental psychologists, including myself, have developed reliable models that relate family-process variables to juvenile offending (Patterson, Crosby, & Vuchinich, 1992; Patterson, Reid, & Dishion, 1992). In individual-difference studies, these measures were shown to account for from 30% to 50% of the variance in individual differences in antisocial behavior and juvenile offending (Forgatch, 1991; Metzler & Dishion, 1992; Patterson, Capaldi, & Bank, 1991). Presumably such measures could be used to assess the prevalence of disrupted family process in both single-parent and intact households. This point is discussed later in this chapter.

As a life-long student of human behavior, it has always remained a deep mystery to me as to how it was decided to divide social science into isolated territories. The boundaries defining such new-found academic disciplines as psychology, sociology, anthropology, and history are a case in point. Presumably, psychology would deal with small pieces of social behavior, whereas sociology was assigned the task of analyzing larger social contexts and society as a whole. However, some problems such as societal crime rates may require an understanding of how small pieces (e.g., differences among families) interact with larger contextual variables (e.g., unemployment). Unfortunately, these academic boundaries tend to become reified. The effect is similar in result to the 14th-century papal decree dividing the globe into "Spanish" and "Portuguese" segments. Any Portuguese found in areas of the map assigned to Spain were necessarily regarded with deep suspicion and no small amount of hostility. A similar fate awaits the psychologist who finds some of sociology's assigned territory to be intrinsically interesting. The problem of explaining societal crime rates is a case in point. The eventual solution to this problem is going to require a cooperative effort that contains both "Portuguese" and "Spanish" components. We need to put Humpty Dumpty together again.

For example, in Figure 2.1 the working model is informed by sociology's formulation about community disorganization and by psychology's measures of family process. In a later section, these variables are discussed in more detail. Suffice it to say here that disruptions in family process may also be associated with a drift into disorganized communities. Also, an otherwise intact family may, in turn, find its processes disrupted by the presence of a disorganized community. It is unknown at this early juncture whether the impact of the disorganized community is entirely mediated through disrupted family process or whether, in addition, the disorganized community may have a direct contribution to societal rates of crime.

How do we identify families at risk? Sampson and Wilson (1995) argue that families headed by single females are likely candidates. Most families disrupted in one way or another by economic downturns do not have adolescents who are arrested. Similarly, most single-parent families do not produce juvenile offenders. However, single-parent families and broken homes do contribute disproportionately to our pool of juvenile offenders. Capaldi and Patterson (1991) showed that a linear relation exists between the number of family-structure transitions (intact to divorce to stepparent) and the risk of child-adjustment problems. The data in Figure 2.2 show that a similar relationship holds for the risk of early police arrest, suggesting that transition frequency may be an important variable in understanding aggregated crime rates. In Figure 2.2, about 13% of boys from intact homes (all cases) have an early arrest as compared to 29% for single-parent and 32% for stepparent families. There is a clear relationship between the broken home and risk of early juvenile offending.

In the Oregon Youth Study (OYS), 80% of the early arrested boys came from homes that had been broken at some time or other during the child's lifetime. However, in the same sample, two thirds of the boys from broken

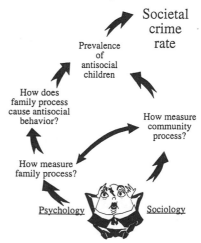

FIG. 2.1. Putting Humpty Dumpty together again.

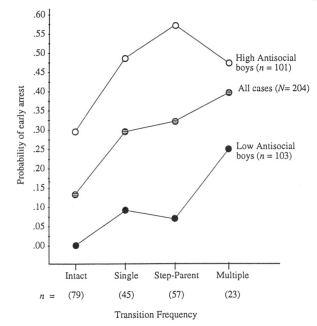

FIG. 2.2. Likelihood of early arrest conditional on antisocial child plus transition frequency.

homes *did not get arrested.* To make our societal-rate model work (e.g., explain a substantial proportion of the variance in societal rates), investigators must be able to specify *which* broken-home families will produce antisocial children and which will not. There are several ways of doing this. If measures of prevalence of parenting practices such as monitoring, discipline, and family problem are included, this would improve predictions. Including measures of prevalence for antisocial boys would further improve our predictions of societal rates.

A model that adequately accounts for changes in societal rates requires a team of investigators who can move across sociology and psychology. Certainly this is not to be a marriage arranged in heaven. Doubtless, the progeny will please neither its "Spanish"- nor its "Portuguese"-speaking parents. However, I assumed that the combined model would account for significant variance in juvenile crime rates across settings and time. The next section briefly outlines two important characteristics of the model to be constructed.

Mediated Models

During the 10 millennia since the rise of the city state, the majority of humankind has lived in conditions of extreme poverty. The conventional wisdom would have it that such a steady state for massive inequality in resources and opportunity might set the occasion for both frequent revolution and very high rates of crime. However, as is frequently the case with conventional wisdom, it tends to oversimplify the relationship between inequality and both crime and revolution. As documented by Mousnier (1970), peasant uprisings in 17th century Europe and China occurred only sporadically. This led him to search for mediating political and economic conditions to increase knowledge about when and where uprisings did occur. In *The Quality of American Life*, Campbell, Converse, and Rodgers (1970) empirically identified variables that differentiated between well being and satisfaction. Although a substantial proportion of the population reported themselves as not very happy, only 8% said they were dissatisfied. For the vast majority, life was pretty much as they expected it to be. Gurr (1970) carefully examined psychological variables looking for mediators that could be combined with information about inequality to better predict rebellions.

Researchers interested in crime also came to view the contribution of inequality as being indirect. The individual-difference models contain variables that mediate between measures of inequality such as unemployment, income, education, on the one hand, and measures of juvenile crime, on the other. For example, Larzelere and Patterson (1990) used data from the OYS to demonstrate that a latent construct for SES correlated significantly with a latent construct for early-onset offending. However, this relation is mediated by a construct for parenting practices. In Figure 2.3, the significant path coefficient (.66) showed that a significant proportion of socially disadvantaged parents were relatively ineffective in their monitoring and discipline practices.

Children were likely to have an early arrest (prior to age 14.0) only if parental discipline and monitoring practices were ineffective. The path coefficient of −.76 attested to the strength of the relationship between earlier measures of parenting and measures of juvenile offending. Notice that it was not social disadvantage per se that directly caused early police arrest. Prior to this study, Sampson and Laub (Laub & Sampson, 1988; Sampson & Laub, 1993) reanalyzed the Glueck and Glueck (1950) data sets and found support for a very similar model. The effects of contextual factors such as parent criminality and social disadvantage on juvenile crime were mediated through disrupted parenting practices. Bank, Forgatch, Patterson, and Fetrow (1993) replicated these findings for at-risk samples of recently separated and socially disadvantaged families. Additional evidence for a mediational model for contextual effects was reviewed in Patterson, Reid, and Dishion (1992).

A key assumption in the model is that the bulk of chronic and violent offending juveniles are drawn from an earlier pool of antisocial children (Capaldi & Patterson, 1996; Farrington, 1991; Patterson, Forgatch, & Stoolmiller, 1995). The prevalence of antisocial children 9 and 10 years of age should, therefore, be the most effective predictor for concurrent aggregate

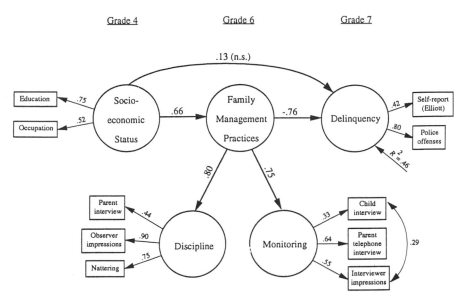

$$\chi^2_{(29)} = 35.92, p = .176, \text{GFI} = .963, \text{RMSR} = .022$$

FIG. 2.3.   Mediational model for contextual variables (from Larzelere & Patterson, 1990). Reprinted by permission.

rates of juvenile offending. The data in Figure 2.2 shows that, given an antisocial boy from a single-parent family, the likelihood of an early arrest was about .48, and given an antisocial boy in a stepparent family, the likelihood was about .57.

SOCIOLOGY'S CONTRIBUTION: MACROVARIABLES

The key components for the macroelements of the model draw heavily from Wilson's (1987) classic *The Truly Disadvantaged*. To test the Wilson thesis, Sampson (1987) analyzed the records of 152 large metropolitan areas for rates of robbery and homicide. The two-stage model showed a strong linkage between joblessness and prevalence rates for households headed by single women and between single-parent households and prevalence of juvenile robbery. By far the strongest predictor of single-woman-headed households was the proportion of employed young men. This finding held for both White and Black families. In keeping with the hypothesis, the R squared for disaggregated rates of juvenile robbery by Black males was .50 ($p < .01$); the largest contributor was the proportion of Black, single-female-headed households. The comparable value for White inner-city residents was .52 ($p < .01$).

An important note is that in all major respects, the models for Whites and Blacks were the same. They differed only in that the extent of unemployment for Blacks was much higher than for Whites. This is very strong support indeed for the Wilson-Sampson two-stage structural model. The model stands in sharp contrast to other explanations of the same phenomena such as "result of failed welfare programs," "result of racial differences in culture values," or "result of persisting values reflecting an enduring culture of poverty."

The two-stage model is summarized in Figure 2.4. Economic downturns lead to very high unemployment rates for inner-city males, and this, in turn, leads to an increase in the prevalence of single-female-headed households. As pointed out by Lykken (1995), there are, in fact, additional causes for the unavailability of young Black males for marriage. He notes that about one fourth of them have been incarcerated and 1 in 10 has died as the result of violent assault. In his analysis, Sampson (1987) also tested the possibility that violent crime further disrupted families. In Figure 2.4, the data showed the relevant path to be a nonsignificant .14.

As noted earlier in Figure 2.2, it would be possible to improve the "disrupted family" (single female-headed household) measure by taking into account the number of transitions. Oregon Social Learning Center's (OSLC) data also strongly suggest that mother's status as an antisocial adult would further increase risk. Measures, such as maternal driver's license suspension, arrests, drug use, and age at birth of first child were all shown to be linearly related to both transition frequency and to increased risk of child's early arrest (Patterson, 1996). Measuring frequency of transitions, frequency of households headed by antisocial women, and those households at greatest risk for disrupted parenting. This would identify the families most at risk to produce antisocial children.

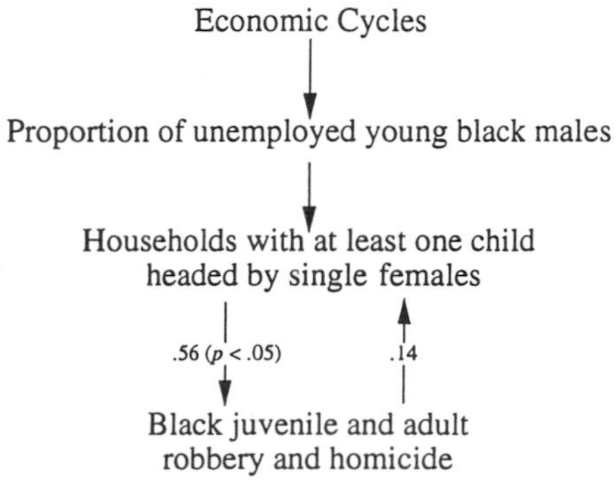

Economic Cycles

↓

Proportion of unemployed young black males

↓

Households with at least one child
headed by single females

.56 ($p < .05$)　　　.14

↓　　　↑

Black juvenile and adult
robbery and homicide

FIG. 2.4. A two-stage Wilson-Sampson structural model for violence.

Selective Vulnerability

As already noted, economic downturns selectively impact socially disadvantaged groups, such as inner-city Blacks and Whites. I hypothesized that
antisocial adults are members of the extremely vulnerable segments of the
society. In part, it is the behavior of the antisocial adults that creates this
vulnerability. Their obdurate noncompliance and abrasiveness make them
difficult to train. Most of them are lacking in the skills that most adults bring
with them to the job, such as showing up on time, not talking back, cooperat-
ing, complying, and not stealing. Lacking these skills makes it difficult for them
to find and hold a job. Their abrasive demeanor and argumentativeness make
it likely that they will not remain employed. In keeping with this formulation,
findings from the Berkeley cross-generational studies showed antisocial adults
to be downwardly mobile (Caspi & Elder, 1988; Caspi, Elder, & Bem, 1987;
Caspi, Elder, & Herbener, 1990). In that the antisocial adult was less likely to
be a skilled worker, he was also less likely to be hired during a sagging economy
(e.g., was selectively vulnerable). Robins (1966) found a similar set of relationships between childhood antisocial behavior and adult occupation level, job
stability, income level, and mobility. She concluded that the antisocial trait in
childhood was a better predictor of adult social status than social status was
as a predictor of antisocial behavior. Sampson and Laub's (1993) reanalyses
of the Glueck and Glueck data set showed that juvenile offenders were three
times more likely than nondelinquents to show an adult record of unstable
employment and were also significantly more likely to be on welfare as adults.
In a similar vein, Huesmann, Eron, and Yarmel (1987) found that a childhood
measure of antisocial behavior correlated negatively with adult intellectual
functioning. Note, this is just the reverse of the position taken by Wilson and
Herrnstein (1985) and Moffitt (1993) that low-verbal IQ is a cause for
antisocial behavior.

   As already noted, antisocial parents are at increased risk for disrupted
parenting and, in turn, to produce antisocial boys (Patterson & Capaldi,
1991; Patterson & Dishion, 1988). Presumably, prevalence rates of antisocial
children is a prime determinant for early-onset arrest data in Figure 2.2 that
showed roughly 50% of the high-antisocial boys from transition families were
arrested early.

Setting Selection

I hypothesized that during economic downturns both the antisocial and the
socially disadvantaged would become increasingly mobile as they seek either
cheaper quarters or better employment opportunities. A giant centrifuge
would be an appropriate metaphor for the function served by economic

FIG. 2.5. The spatial assignment centrifuge.

downturns in relocating families spatially. In Figure 2.5, given economic downturns, the disadvantaged and antisocial groups are all at risk of becoming relocated to less desirable living arrangements—the inner-city ghetto or the park bench. In small towns, the relocation is likely to be the unpaved section on the other side of the tracks or the sharecrop farm.

The review by Sampson and Lauritsen (as cited in Sampson and Wilson, 1995) showed that poverty and mobility were highly interactive. Bursik (1986) and others have also noted that mobility within a city or a society was significantly related to economic variables. In considering movement within cities, Burgess (1925, as cited in Bursik, 1986) pointed out that land values were the primary determinants for this process. In his concentric ring model, the transition area between one zone and another was the least attractive. The least attractive areas, in turn, became a haven for those searching for low-cost housing.

Although two areas may be of roughly equivalent economic value, they may still differ in the density of criminal activity. Presumably, antisocial parents would find high-crime areas to be more attractive than would nonantisocial parents of equivalent social status. This is in keeping with the selective shopping hypothesis, where each individual selectively shops for settings and activities that maximize the individual's payoffs (Patterson, Reid, & Dishion, 1992).

In a societal-rates model, the effect of the centrifuge process would be to create areas in society where the prevalence of ineffective parents and anti-social children would be higher than in other areas. The fact that prevalence for antisocial boys or juvenile offenders is not randomly distributed is hardly a surprise to any experienced probation officer. However, from my perspective, delineation of high-risk areas is indispensable to the prevention strategist because it directs attention to high densities of families with children at risk of juvenile offending. The next section considers the possibility that some of the communities to which disadvantaged families are consigned develop unique structural characteristics that, in turn, contribute directly to further disruptions in family process (Sampson, 1986).

Community Disorganization as Direct Cause of Family Disruption

I assumed that, given repeated downturns in the economy, certain areas would be characterized as having an increasing prevalence of disrupted families. These increases would, in turn, be followed by increases in the prevalence of antisocial children and, within a short time, by increases in the prevalence of early arrest.

Sampson (1992) emphasized two different characteristics of the disorganized setting that may have contributed directly to exacerbating disrupted family processes and thus indirectly to crime rates. The effectiveness of parenting activities is partially related to the support available from friends and extended family networks (DeGarmo & Forgatch, 1997). Disorganized communities are characterized by reduced support, partially as a function of the sparse network of friends and family. Other adults in disorganized communities are also unlikely to contribute effective supervision when the adolescent is on the street and free from immediate parental surveillance. In most individual-difference models of juvenile offending, the amount of un-supervised street time is a key variable contributing to the growth of ado-lescent delinquent behaviors (Osgood, Wilson, Bachman, O'Malley, & Johnston, 1996; Stoolmiller, 1994).

As shown in Figure 2.6, the effect of lack of support and the absence of supplementary adult supervision on disaggregated estimates of juvenile crime are thought to be indirect (i.e., mediated through the parenting variables). However, as shown in the figure, a community may also actively teach the adolescent a set of values about crime and provide opportunities that con-tribute directly to crime. McGahey's (1986) apt phrase for this situation was *crime prone environments.* In such an environment it is common knowledge that crime pays off and prosocial skills do not. If there are relatively few jobs available to anyone, then the process of acquiring work skills, academic credentials, or a solid work history becomes nonfunctional. The implication

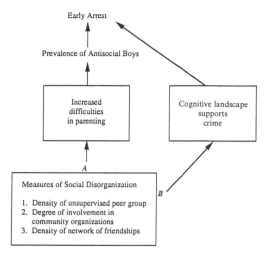

FIG. 2.6. Two models for the indirect contribution of social disorganization to juvenile crime.

is that society may inadvertently create an environment where nothing pays off except crime.

As shown on the right side of Figure 2.7, a disorganized community also may lack government investment in such general infrastructure as education, police surveillance, and medical care. For example, the absence of prenatal medical services indirectly increases the prevalence of antisocial children in that setting. In keeping with this idea, studies showed that settings with low medical coverage had higher crime rates. The direct effect of prenatal coverage was to increase the prevalence of low birth weight and otherwise difficult-to-raise infants. Sampson (1992) cited several studies that demonstrated the surprisingly high correlation between absence of prenatal services and disaggregated crime rates.

Given the antisocial dispositions of many of these mothers, substance abuse during pregnancy might be expected to contribute further to the prevalence of difficult-to-raise infants. This was in keeping with the findings from longitudinal studies of early development by Werner (1989), Sameroff and colleagues (Sameroff, Dickstein, Seifer, Schiller, & Hayden, 1993), and Belsky (1984). Each of these investigators interpreted their findings to show that the interaction between infant temperament and parenting skills determined long-term outcomes. As suggested in Figure 2.7, the increased prevalence of difficult-to-raise toddlers constituted an important contribution to disrupted parenting and indirectly to juvenile crime rates. A key tenet of the coercion model is that the interaction between maternal lack of skill and the difficult-to-raise toddler is the prime determinant in training of antisocial children (Patterson, Reid, & Dishion, 1992).

An alternate view is that social disorganization variables contribute directly to societal crime rates. Reiss (1986) holds that the structural characteristics of communities contributed directly to crime rates independent of

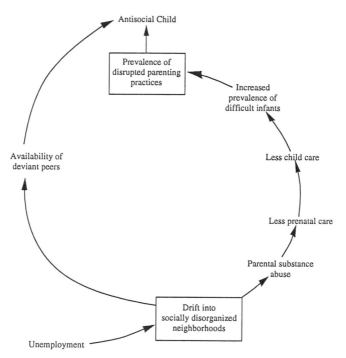

FIG. 2.7.   Further contribution of community disorganization to disrupted families.

the individual characteristics of the residents. For example, Taylor and colleagues (Taylor, Gottfredson, & Brower, 1984, as cited in Sampson & Wilson, 1995) sampled 687 households from 63 street blocks. They found that measures of the extent to which respondents were mutually involved in community organizations and the proportion feeling responsible for what happens in their community both covaried negatively with community levels of crime.

As shown on the left side of Figure 2.7, a major contribution of disorganized community is thought to be a high density of deviant peers. In studies of individual differences, this variable was shown to make a major contribution to accounting for variance in early arrest and chronic offending (Patterson, Forgatch, Yoerger, & Stoolmiller, 1998; Patterson & Yoerger, 1997). Sampson and Groves (as cited in Sampson, 1992) had access to data from 60 addresses in each of 238 ecological areas in Great Britain. They found that the prevalence of unsupervised peer groups and other measures of community disorganization covaried significantly with level of family disruption and with local crime rates.

Do social disorganizational variables contribute directly to societal rates of juvenile crime, or are these variables mediated through their disrupting effect on parenting practices? The answers are unknown, but both alternatives are eminently testable and form part of the agenda for the Simons (1994) study now underway.

PARENT PRACTICES AND CHILDHOOD ANTISOCIAL BEHAVIOR AS MEDIATORS

In the proposed model, the prevalence of families who use ineffective parenting practices would significantly predict the prevalence of antisocial boys. Families in frequent transition are at greatest risk for these disruptions, and, in turn, it is the antisocial parent who is most likely to be involved in frequent transitions. But it is parenting practices that are the driving mechanism for the model.

The initial correlational test of this model was based on data from a sample of normal families of adolescent boys (Patterson & Stouthamer-Loeber, 1984). As predicted, the findings showed that parental dysfunctions in discipline and monitoring composite scores correlated significantly with police arrest. A second test was based on data from a high-risk sample, the OYS assessed at Grade 4. A structural equation model (SEM) showed that both discipline and monitoring made significant contributions accounting for concurrent measures of an antisocial construct (Patterson, 1986). Eddy, Fagot, and Leve (1996) found an acceptable fit for both boys and girls in a normal sample of preschool children; Metzler and Dishion (1992) also found a good fit for a SEM based on a normal sample of adolescents. The findings demonstrated that the parenting model was replicable across both normal and at-risk samples, as well as across gender and age groups.

Experimental tests of the parenting model.   No matter how often replicated, correlational models cannot, by themselves, establish the causal status of parenting practices. This issue can only be addressed by a series of experimental manipulations. This section briefly reviews findings from studies of that address this issue.

In the early 1970s, both single-subject and group-design laboratory studies amply demonstrated the effect of parent-dispensed positive reinforcement and punishment in altering children's prosocial and coercive behaviors (Forehand, King, Peed, & Yoder, 1975; Powers & Witmer, 1951; Snyder, 1991). Several decades of intervention studies carried out in Oregon, Washington, Tennessee, and Georgia showed that training parents in these skills produced long-lasting and significant improvements in antisocial behavior for preadolescent children (Kazdin, 1987; Patterson, Dishion, & Chamberlain, 1993; Serketich & Dumas, 1996). For a comprehensive review, see the OSLC web site: http://www.oslc.org. These studies demonstrated that changes in contingencies supplied by parents produced changes in antisocial children's behavior. However, these early studies were not designed to demonstrate that the magnitude of improvement in parenting skills covaried with the magnitude of improvement in child adjustment. Recently, there were several tests of the magnitude-covariation hypothesis.

When Parent Training Therapy (PTT) was provided for a clinical group, the magnitude of improvement observed in parental discipline practices significantly predicted both arrest and out-of-home placement 2 years after termination of treatment (Patterson & Forgatch, 1995). Those parents who failed to improve were associated with a greater risk of negative outcomes. Although these findings supported the magnitude–covariation hypothesis, the design was such that we could not eliminate the possibility that there was some third variable, unrelated to PTT, that produced the changes in parenting practices. Dishion, Patterson, and Kavanagh (1992) tested the hypothesis using a random assignment longitudinal study of preadolescent boys and girls thought to be at risk of substance abuse. Families were assigned to either peer-group treatment, parent training, or videotape alone condition. The findings showed that only assignment to PTT was significantly associated with improved parental discipline. The findings also showed that parental discipline measured at termination covaried with the magnitude of change in teacher ratings of the child's antisocial behavior (Dishion et al., 1992). Three additional experimental tests of the hypothesis are currently underway. The findings all concur in showing that changes in parenting cause changes in child adjustment (Chamberlain & Reid, in press; DeGarmo, Forgatch, & Martinez, in press; Reid, Eddy, Fetrow, & Stoolmiller, in press).

Measurement. It is increasingly apparent in the study of family process and individual differences in child adjustment that if multimethod indicators are used to define the constructs, the models are more likely to replicate across samples (Bank, Dishion, Skinner, & Patterson, 1990). Recent across-site replication for a complex mediational model relating stress to child adjustment provides additional support for the assumption that multimethod constructs are more likely to be generalizable (Conger, Patterson, & Ge, 1995). I propose to follow the multiagent and multimethod strategy in assessing both the psychological and sociological variables.

Explorations of means for measuring parenting practices showed that interviews and questionnaires were totally inadequate for assessing two of the three central constructs (Patterson, Reid, & Dishion, 1992). The strongest measures of discipline were based on variables drawn from three observation sessions in the home. Videotaped family problem-solving interactions developed by Forgatch (1989) provided a basis for measuring both problem-solving outcomes and discipline practices. Repeated efforts to develop interview-based measures of these two constructs failed to load on the constructs and generally made only weak predictions to outside criteria. Separate interviews with the parents and child proved effective in defining parental monitoring.

In Ron Simons's study, the assumption was that the constructs defining disrupted parenting skills (discipline, monitoring, family problem solving) should be used to define the prevalence of disrupted parenting skills within each social unit. The cost of measuring parenting practices in a field study may be prohibitively high. For example, within a census-tract unit, it would be necessary to select a stratified sample of families of 9- and 10-year-old boys to participate in a 30-minute videotaped interaction as they attempt to solve several of their current problems. Each family member would also be asked to participate in a brief interview focused on monitoring and child antisocial behavior and to fill out some questionnaires.

Presumably, the social units with the highest rates of ineffectively parented families would also have the highest prevalence of antisocial 9- and 10-year-old boys, (ratings by teacher, peer, parent) as well as the highest prevalence rates for boys arrested (official records and self-report) prior to 14 years of age. Teachers and peers would also provide reports of the child's antisocial behavior.

Antisocial Trait as Mediator

There is a coherent progression from preschool aggression to chronic offending (Patterson, Reid, & Dishion, 1992). The coercion model details the steps by which these changes in form occur (Patterson, 1993; Patterson, Forgatch, Yoerger, & Stoolmiller, 1998). A key assumption of the coercion model was that the higher the frequency of coercive responses, the greater the risk of increasingly severe, high-amplitude reactions (Patterson, 1995; Reid, Bank, & Stoolmiller, 1992). During the toddler stages, the progression of child deviancy moves from noncompliance to temper tantrums to hitting (Patterson, 1992). At school age, this progression expands to include stealing, cheating, truancy, school failure, and rejection by normal peers (Patterson, Reid, & Dishion, 1992). During preadolescence the progression expanded again to include early time on the street, hanging out with deviant peers, and arrest prior to age 14.0. From there the progression moved to chronic offending, violence, and adult offending (Forgatch, Patterson, & Stoolmiller, 1994; Patterson et al., 1998).

A multivariate analysis would demonstrate that current prevalence rates for antisocial 9- and 10-year-old boys would be the most effective predictor for (disaggregated) early arrest over the next 4-year interval. If prevalence of single-mother-headed households were entered into the prediction equation first, it would be expected to yield a value that is of borderline significance. Entering prevalence of antisocial mothers and fathers as the second variable and transition frequency as a third variable should account for further variance in measures of socital rates for early arrest in these units. In designing such a study, we assume that it would be too expensive to assess parenting skills; however, if these variables were included, they would be expected to make a further increase in predictability. For example, in an individual-difference model, Patterson, Crosby, and Vuchinich (1992) showed that parenting practices made a significant contribution to predicting time to early arrest. However, as noted earlier, when appropriate measures of antisocial child behavior are entered, it is expected that all variables entered earlier became nonsignificant, and the primary contributor remaining is the trait score.

In the model proposed here, the key lies in an adequate measure of the prevalence of antisocial children. Given the central role insures the necessity for a multimethod-multiagent definition. The report by Patterson, Reid, and Dishion (1992) listed more than 20 measures that were explored in building the antisocial construct (see Fig. 2.8). The construct can be defined by indicators based on reports from participant agents such as mothers, fathers, peers, self-report, and teachers (Bank & Patterson, 1992). These indicators tend to converge very well. The factor loadings vary from .79 to .88. Our colleagues in Iowa showed that sibling reports of antisocial behavior in the

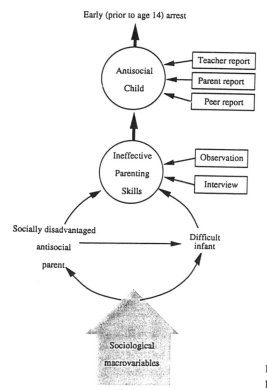

FIG. 2.8. Multiple mediators to predict early arrest.

target child are also a useful measure of this construct (Conger et al., 1995). In a societal-rates model, measures that tap both the home and the school setting would be desirable (e.g., ratings by mothers, and fathers if available, plus ratings by peers or teachers). If possible, it would include data from a random sampling of playground observation data for the third- and fourth-grade boys.

Early onset as a dependent variable. It was proposed that juvenile offenders do not constitute a homogeneous group. Patterson, DeBaryshe, and Ramsey (1989) suggested that boys arrested prior to 14.0 years of age could be differentiated from late starters in terms of the contexts in which they were raised, levels of social skill, child deviancy, and disruption in parenting skills. Data presented by Patterson (1994), by Capaldi and Patterson (1994), and by Patterson and Yoerger (1997) supported each of these hypotheses. Another hypothesis is that early and late police arrestees could be differentiated in terms of their adult outcomes. Findings presented for two samples by Forgatch et al. (1994) strongly supported these hypotheses by showing that early-onset boys accounted for most of the chronic offenders and for the majority of the violent offenders as well. For this reason, I proposed in this report that the criterion variable be prevalence of boys arrested prior to the age of 14.0.

As noted earlier in the chapter, the traditional sociological theories of juvenile offending were not very successful in accounting for individual differences in offending. Many of these very early studies were poorly designed in that self-report data were used to define both the dependent and the independent variables (Elliott et al., 1985). However, in the last decade a number of major efforts were made to predict general delinquency. The more recent studies corrected some of the major flaws that characterized the earlier work. For example, Farrington and Hawkins (1991) used child adjustment and family variables to account for about 20% of the variance in official records of delinquency. The analysis of data from the OYS with SEM demonstrated that a latent construct for antisocial behavior assessed at Grade 4 accounted for 44% of the variance in a latent construct for early offending (official records and self-report; Patterson, Capaldi, & Bank, 1991). The composite score for antisocial behavior predicts early arrest with false positive errors of 54% and false negative errors of 6%. In the present context, it was predicted that current estimates of prevalence of 9- and 10-year-old antisocial boys would predict prevalence of early arrests over the ensuing 4-year interval.

IMPLICATIONS

The general strategy is to dismantle components that were successful in models designed to account for individual differences in risk for early arrest, and to apply them to the task of accounting for aggregate rate. Presumably, the components will make a significant contribution when serving as mediators between sociological macrovariables and societal rates of juvenile offending. Simons's NIMH proposal has been funded; we should soon have data tell us whether this approach is feasible.

There are several questions of theoretical importance that investigators can begin to address with the Simons' study. Of particular interest are the direct and indirect contributions to be made by the variables from social disorganization theory. Are the effects of variables such as friendship networks, participation in community organizations, density of deviant peers, and prevalence of difficult-to-raise infants mediated through their disrupting effects on parenting practices as implied by the coercion model? Or do variables such as these contribute directly to juvenile crime rates? Does a model that accounts for significant variance for across-setting variations also function in accounting for variations in rates across time?

The general model is based on the idea that both sociological macrovariables (unemployment, mobility, social disorganization) and psychological variables (antisocial trait, parenting practices, parent traits) are required in order to understand variance associated with changes in rates across time and settings. The central focus is on what is happening to family processes. If they are totally disrupted, then violence and chaos are its products. For example, this was the effect that followed the disintegration of the Eek families under conditions of prolonged famine (Turnbull, 1972). However, Wilson (1980) documents the fact that even under the extreme conditions encountered in an inner-city ghetto, some families were so effective in their supervision of their adolescent children that their delinquency rates remained very low. Similarly, as noted earlier, Junger (1983) documented the successful adjustment of Chinese families to the challenges introduced by their status as immigrants. Although these findings support several plausible interpretations, they are also consistent with the thesis offered in this chapter. It is the interaction between macro- and family breakdown that determines crime rates. If researchers understand which variables disrupt parenting practices, then they should be in a position to understand changes in societal rates of crime and eventually to prevent their increase.

ACKNOWLEDGMENTS

I gratefully acknowledge the support provided by National Institute of Mental Health Grant Nos. MH 37940 (Center for Studies of Violent Behavior and Traumatic Stress, U.S. Public Health Service [U.S. PHS]), MH 38318 (Prevention Research Branch, Division of Epidemiology and Services Research, U.S. PHS), and MH 46690 (Behavioral Sciences Research Branch,

Family Processes Division, U.S. PHS). In some important measure, the paper reflects a series of brief meetings with sociology colleagues Rand Conger, John Laub, Robert Sampson, and Ron Simons. These exchanges also led to Simons' proposal submission to the National Institute of Mental Health that is designed to test many of the ideas outline here. I also wish to acknowledge the thoughtful critique by John Laub of an earlier draft of this chapter.

REFERENCES

Akers, R. L. (1977). *Deviant behavior: A social learning approach* (2nd ed.). Belmont, CA: Wadsworth Publishing Co.

Bank, L., Dishion, T. J., Skinner, M. L., & Patterson, G. R. (1990). Method variance in structural equation modeling: Living with "glop." In G. R. Patterson (Ed.), *Depression and aggression in family interaction* (pp. 247–279). Hillsdale, NJ: Lawrence Erlbaum Associates.

Bank, L., Forgatch, M. S., Patterson, G. R., & Fetrow, R. A. (1993). Parenting practices of single mothers: Mediators of negative contextual factors. *Journal of Marriage and the Family, 55,* 371–384.

Bank, L., & Patterson, G. R. (1992). Use of structural equation models in combining data from different levels of assessment. In J. Rosen & P. McReynolds (Eds.), *Advances in psychological assessment* (Vol. 8, pp. 41–74). New York: Plenum Press.

Belsky, J. (1984). The Pennsylvania infant and family development project: I. Stability and change in mother–infant and father–infant interaction in a family setting at one, three, and nine months. *Child Development, 55,* 692–705.

Bernard, T. J. (1987). Testing structural strain theories. *Journal of Research in Crime and Delinquency, 24,* 262–280.

Burgess, E. W. (1925). The growth of the city: An introduction to a research project. In R. E. Park, E. W. Burgess, & R. D. McKenzie with L. Wirth (Eds.), *The city* (pp. 47–62). Chicago: University of Chicago Press.

Bursik, R. J. (1986). Ecological stability and the dynamics of delinquency. In A. J. Reiss & M. Tonry (Eds.), *Communities and crime* (Vol. 8, pp. 35–66). Chicago: University of Chicago Press.

Campbell, A., Converse, P. E., & Rodgers, W. L. (1970). *The quality of American life.* New York: Sage.

Capaldi, D. M., & Patterson, G. R. (1991). Relation of parental transitions to boys' adjustment problems: I. A linear hypothesis. II. Mothers at risk for transitions and unskilled parenting. *Developmental Psychology, 27,* 489–504.

Capaldi, D. M., & Patterson, G. R. (1994). Interrelated influences of contextual factors on antisocial behavior in childhood and adolescence for males. In D. Fowles, P. Sutker, & S. Goodman (Eds.), *Progress in experimental personality and psychopathology research* (pp. 165–198). New York: Springer.

Capaldi, D. M., & Patterson, G. R. (1996). Can violent offenders be distinguished from frequent offenders: Prediction from childhood to adolescence. *Journal of Research in Crime and Delinquency, 33,* 206–231.

Caspi, A., & Elder, G. H. (1988). Childhood precursors of the life course: Early personality and life disorganization. In M. Hetherington, R. M. Lerner, & M. Perlmutter (Eds.), *Child development in life span perspective* (pp. 115–142). Hillsdale, NJ: Lawrence Erlbaum Associates.

Caspi, A., Elder, G. H., & Bem, D. J. (1987). Moving against the world: Life course patterns of explosive children. *Developmental Psychology, 23,* 308–313.

Caspi, A., Elder, G. H., Jr., & Herbener, E. S. (1990). Childhood personality and the prediction of life-course patterns. In L. N. Robins & M. Rutter (Eds.), *Straight and devious pathways from childhood to adulthood* (pp. 13–35). New York: Cambridge University Press.

Chamberlain, P., & Reid, J. B. (in press). Comparison of two community alternatives to incarceration for chronic juvenile offenders. *Journal of Consulting and Clinical Psychology.*

Cloward, R., & Ohlin, L. I. (1960). *Delinquency and opportunity: A theory of delinquent gangs.* Glencoe, IL: Free Press.

Conger, R. D., Patterson, G. R., & Ge, X. (1995). It takes two to replicate: A mediational model for the impact of parents' stress on adolescent adjustment. *Child Development, 66,* 80–97.

DeGarmo, D., & Forgatch, M. S. (1997). Determinants of observed confidant support for divorced mothers. *Journal of Personality and Social Psychology, 72,* 336–345.

DeGarmo, D. S., Forgatch, M. S., & Martinez, C. R., Jr. (in press). Parenting of divorced mothers as a link between social status and boys' academic outcomes: Unpacking the effects of SES. *Child Development.*

Dishion, T. J., Patterson, G. R., & Kavanagh, K. A. (1992). An experimental test of the coercion model: Linking theory, measurement, and intervention. In J. McCord & R. Tremblay (Eds.), *The interaction of theory and practice: Experimental studies of intervention* (pp. 253–282). New York: Guilford.

Eddy, J. M., Fagot, B. I., & Leve, L. (1996). *Sex differences in aggression: Myths, methods, and models.* Unpublished manuscript available from the Oregon Social Learning Center, Eugene, OR.

Elliott, D. S., Huizinga, D., & Ageton, S. S. (1985). *Explaining delinquency and drug use.* Beverly Hills, CA: Sage.

Farrington, D. P. (1991). Childhood aggression and adults' violence: Early precursors and later-life outcomes. In D. J. Pepler & K. H. Rubin (Eds.), *The development and treatment of childhood aggression* (pp. 5–29). Hillsdale, NJ: Lawrence Erlbaum Associates.

Farrington, D. P., & Hawkins, J. D. (1991). Predicting participation, early onset and later persistence in officially recorded offending. *Criminal Behaviour and Mental Health, 1,* 1–33.

Forehand, R., King, H. E., Peed, S., & Yoder, P. (1975). Mother–child interactions: Comparisons of a noncompliant clinic group and a nonclinic group. *American Journal of Sociology, 13,* 79–84.

Forgatch, M. S. (1989). Patterns and outcome in family problem solving: The disrupting effect of negative emotion. *Journal of Marriage and the Family, 5*(1), 115–124.

Forgatch, M. S. (1991). The clinical science vortex: A developing theory of antisocial behavior. In D. J. Pepler & K. H. Rubin (Eds.), *The development and treatment of childhood aggression* (pp. 291–315). Hillsdale, NJ: Lawrence Erlbaum Associates.

Forgatch, M. S., Patterson, G. R., & Stoolmiller, M. (1994, November). *Progressing toward violence: A replication.* Paper presented at the panel "Oregon Models for Early- and Late-Onset Delinquency" at the American Society of Criminology, Miami, FL.

Glueck, S., & Glueck, E. (1950). *Unraveling juvenile delinquency.* Cambridge, MA: Harvard University Press.

Gurr, T. R. (1970). *Why men rebel.* Princeton, NJ: Princeton University Press.

Hirschi, T. (1969). *Causes of delinquency.* Berkeley: University of California Press.

Huesmann, L. R., Eron, L. D., & Yarmel, P. W. (1987). Intellectual functioning and aggression. *Journal of Personality and Social Psychology, 52,* 232–240.

James, O. (1995). *The growth of juvenile violence in a winner-loser culture.* London: Free Association Books.

Junger, M. (1983). Maandstatistiek politie, justitie en brandweek mei 1983. [Monthly statistic of police, justice, and fire and rescue department, May 1983.] *Centraal Bureau Voor de Statistiek, 27*(5), 52–57.

Kazdin, A. (1987). Treatment of antisocial behavior in children: Current status and future directions. *Psychological Bulletin, 102,* 187–203.

Larzelere, R. E., & Patterson, G. R. (1990). Parental management: Mediator of the effect of socioeconomic status on early delinquency. *Criminology, 28,* 301–324.

Laub, J. H., & Sampson, R. J. (1988). Unraveling families and delinquency: A reanalysis of the Gluecks' data. *Criminology, 26,* 355–380.

Laub, J. H., & Sampson, R. J. (1991). The Sutherland-Glueck debate: On the sociology of criminological knowledge. *American Journal of Sociology, 96,* 1402–1440.

Loeber, R., & Dishion, T. (1983). Early predictors of male delinquency: A review. *Psychological Bulletin, 94,* (68–99).

Lykken, D. T. (1995). *The antisocial personalities.* Mahwah, NJ: Lawrence Erlbaum Associates.

McGahey, R. M. (1986). Economic conditions, neighborhood organization, and urban crime. In J. A. J. Reiss & M. Tonry (Eds.), *Communities and crime* (Vol. 8, pp. 231–270). Chicago: University of Chicago Press.

Merton, R. K. (1957). *Social theory and social success.* Glencoe, IL: Free Press.

Metzler, C. E., & Dishion, T. J. (1992, May). *A model of the development of youthful problem behaviors.* Paper presented at the 18th Annual Convention for Association for Behavior Analysis, San Francisco, CA.

Mousnier, R. (1970). *Peasant uprisings in seventeenth century France, Russia, and China.* New York: Harper & Row.

Osgood, D. W., Wilson, J. K., Bachman, J. G., O'Malley, P. M., & Johnston, L. D. (1996). Routine activities and individual deviant behavior. *American Sociological Review, 61,* 635–655.

Patterson, G. R. (1986). Performance models for antisocial boys. *American Psychologist, 41,* 432–444.

Patterson, G. R. (1992). Developmental changes in antisocial behavior. In R. D. Peters, R. J. McMahon, & V. L. Quinsey (Eds.), *Aggression and violence throughout the life span* (pp. 52–82). Newbury Park, CA: Sage.

Patterson, G. R. (1993). Orderly change in a stable world: The antisocial trait as a chimera. *Journal of Consulting and Clinical Psychology, 61,* 911–919.

Patterson, G. R. (1994). Some alternatives to seven myths about treating families of antisocial children. In C. Henricson (Ed.), *Crime and the family: Conference report: Proceedings of an international conference, Occasional Paper 20* (pp. 26–49). London: Family Policy Studies Centre.

Patterson, G. R. (1995). Coercion as a basis for early age of onset for arrest. In J. McCord (Ed.), *Coercion and punishment in long-term perspective* (pp. 81–105). New York: Cambridge.

Patterson, G. R. (1996). Some characteristics of a developmental theory for early onset delinquency. In M. F. Lenzenweger & J. J. Haugaard (Eds.), *Frontiers of developmental psychopathology* (pp. 81–124). New York: Oxford University Press.

Patterson, G. R., & Capaldi, D. M. (1991). Antisocial parents: Unskilled and vulnerable. In P. A. Cowan & E. M. Hetherington (Eds.), *Family transitions* (pp. 195–218). Hillsdale, NJ: Lawrence Erlbaum Associates.

Patterson, G. R., Capaldi, D., & Bank, L. (1991). An early starter model predicting delinquency. In D. J. Pepler & K. H. Rubin (Eds.), *The development and treatment of childhood aggression* (pp. 139–168). Hillsdale, NJ: Lawrence Erlbaum Associates.

Patterson, G. R., Crosby, L., & Vuchinich, S. (1992). Predicting risk for early police arrest. *Journal of Quantitative Criminology, 8,* 333–355.

Patterson, G. R., DeBaryshe, B. D., & Ramsey, E. (1989). A developmental perspective on antisocial behavior. *American Psychologist, 44,* 329–335.

Patterson, G. R., & Dishion, T. J. (1988). Multilevel family process models: Traits, interactions, and relationships. In R. A. Hinde & J. Stevenson-Hinde (Eds.), *Relationships within families: Mutual influences* (pp. 283–310). Oxford, UK: Clarendon.

Patterson, G. R., Dishion, T. J., & Chamberlain, P. (1993). Outcomes and methodological issues relating to treatment of antisocial children. In T. R. Giles (Ed.), *Handbook of effective psychotherapy* (pp. 43–88). New York: Plenum.

Patterson, G. R., & Forgatch, M. S. (1995). Predicting future clinical adjustment from treatment outcome and process variables. *Psychological Assessment, 7*, 275–285.

Patterson, G. R., Forgatch, M. S., Yoerger, K., & Stoolmiller, M. (1998). Variables that maintain an early-onset trajectory for juvenile offending. *Development and Psychopathology, 10*, 531–547.

Patterson, G. R., Reid, J. B., & Dishion, T. J. (1992). *A social interactional approach: Vol. 4: Antisocial boys.* Eugene, OR: Castalia.

Patterson, G. R., & Stouthamer-Loeber, M. (1984). The correlation of family management practices and delinquency. *Child Development, 55*, 1299–1307.

Patterson, G. R., & Yoerger, K. (1997). A developmental model for late-onset delinquency. In D. W. Osgood (Ed.), *Motivation and delinquency: Vol. 44 of the Nebraska Symposium on Motivation* (pp. 119–177). Lincoln: University of Nebraska Press.

Powers, E., & Witmer, H. (1951). *An experiment in the prevention of delinquency: The Cambridge-Somerville youth study.* New York: Columbia University Press.

Reid, J. B., Bank, L., & Stoolmiller, M. (1992). *The relationship of frequency and escalation in amplitude of aggression.* Unpublished manuscript available from the Oregon Social Learning Center, Eugene, OR.

Reid, J. B., Eddy, J. M., Fetrow, R. A., & Stoolmiller, M. (in press). Description and immediate impacts of a preventive intervention for conduct problems. *American Journal of Community Psychology.*

Reiss, A. J., Jr. (1986). Why are communities important in understanding crime? In J. A. J. Reiss & M. Tonry (Eds.), *Communities and crime* (Vol. 8, pp. 1–33). Chicago: University of Chicago Press.

Reiss, A. J., & Roth, J. (Eds.). (1993). *Understanding and preventing violence.* Washington, DC: National Academy of Sciences Press.

Robins, L. N. (1966). *Deviant children grown up: A sociological and psychiatric study of sociopathic personality.* Baltimore: Williams & Wilkins.

Sameroff, A. J., Dickstein, S., Seifer, R., Schiller, M., & Hayden, L. (1993, March). *Effects of family process and parental depression on children.* Paper presented at the biennial meetings of the Society for Research in Child Development, New Orleans, LA.

Sampson, R. J. (1986). Crime in cities: The effects of formal and informal social control. In A. J. Reiss & M. Tonry (Eds.), *Communities and crime* (Vol. 8, pp. 271–313). Chicago: University of Chicago Press.

Sampson, R. J. (1987). Urban black violence: The effect of male joblessness and family disruption. *American Journal of Sociology, 93*, 348–382.

Sampson, R. J. (1992). Family management and child development: Insights from social disorganization theory. In J. McCord (Ed.), *Facts, frameworks, and forecasts, Vol. 3 of advances in criminological theory* (pp. 63–91). New Brunswick, NJ: Transactions.

Sampson, R. J., & Groves, W. B. (1989). Community structure and crime: Testing social-disorganization theory. *American Journal of Sociology, 94*, 774–802.

Sampson, R. J., & Laub, J. H. (1993). *Crime in the making: Pathways and turning points through life.* Cambridge: Harvard University Press.

Sampson, R. J., & Wilson, W. J. (1995). Toward a theory of race crime and urban inequality. In J. Hagan & R. Peterson (Eds.), *Crime and inequality.* Stanford, CA: Stanford University Press.

Serketich, W. J., & Dumas, J. E. (1996). The effectiveness of behavioral parent training to modify antisocial behavior in children: A meta-analysis. *Behavior Therapy, 27*, 171–186.

Simons, R. (1994). *Proposal III. Rural communities, family processes, and child outcomes. In R. D. Conger's Grant Application: Research on mental disorders in rural populations.* Grant

Application to Department of Health and Human Services, Public Health Service: Iowa State University.

Snyder, J. J. (1991). Discipline as a mediator of the impact of maternal stress and mood on child conduct problems. *Development and Psychopathology, 3,* 263–276.

Stoolmiller, M. (1994). Antisocial behavior, delinquent peer association, and unsupervised wandering for boys: Growth and change from childhood to early adolescence. *Multivariate Behavioral Research, 29,* 263–288.

Taylor, R. S., Gottfredson, S., & Brower, S. (1984). Block crime and fear: Defensible space, local social ties, and territorial functioning. *Journal of Research in Crime and Delinquency, 21,* 303–331.

Thornberry, T. P. (1990). *Empirical support for interactional theory: A review of the literature* (Working Paper No. 5): Rochester Youth Development Study, Hindelang Criminal Justice Research Center, The University at Albany.

Turnbull, C. M. (1972). *The mountain people.* New York: Simon & Schuster.

Utting, D., Bright, J., & Henricson, C. (1993). *Crime in the family: Improving child rearing and preventing delinquency* (Vol. 16). London: Family Policy Studies Centre.

Werner, E. E. (1989). Children of the garden island. *Scientific American, 260,* 107–111.

Wilson, H. (1980). Parental supervision: A neglected aspect of delinquency. *British Journal of Criminology, 20,* 203–235.

Wilson, J. Q., & Herrnstein, R. J. (1985). *Crime and human nature.* New York: Simon & Schuster.

Wilson, W. J. (1987). *The truly disadvantaged: The inner city, the underclass, and public policy.* Chicago: University of Chicago Press.

Zimring, F. E. (1996). Kids, guns, and homicide: Policy notes on an age-specific epidemic. *Law and Contemporary Problems, 59*(1), 25–37.

Affective Ties Between Mothers and Daughters in Adolescent Childbearing Families

Dawn A. Obeidallah
Harvard Medical School

Linda M. Burton
The Pennsylvania State University

It's hard to explain about my relationship with my mother. Sometimes we fight like cats and dogs. Other times we love each other up like play-sisters. I can't speak for her, but there are times when I love her and hate her at the same time. I don't know if having my baby has changed our relationship much. It seems like we've both been trying to figure it out since I was a little girl . . . trying to make it work one day and then wishing we weren't even related the next.

—Kenya, a 16-year-old mother

I don't know what to say about my relationship with Kenya. It's very difficult to describe. Sometimes it is so volatile . . . . . like a volcano erupting. There are other days that I thoroughly enjoy her company. I wonder if we get along the way we do because we are almost like sisters? My mother raised us both . . . you know, I'm only 16 years older than Kenya. Sisters don't get along the same way that parents and children do. There is always friction and caring, competition and compassion, love and hate. Do you think that's why we have such a hard time working out our relationship?

—Sandra, Kenya's 32-year-old mother

Affective ties between mothers and daughters represent one of the most fundamental, yet complex forms of human bonds that exist among women (Chodorow, 1978; Fischer, 1991; Gilligan, 1982; Rossi & Rossi, 1990). As Kenya and Sandra note, the tenor of these ties can fluctuate over time and is occasionally contradictory in nature. Both mother and daughter indicate

37

that their relationship can be warm and caring one week and intensely conflictual the next. Moreover, this pair reports that they often experience a
"paradoxical web" of feelings in their relationship (Burton, 1997). Their
paradox is expressed in feelings of simultaneously "loving and hating each
other."

Given Kenya's and Sandra's descriptions of their relationship, one won-
ders whether their affective ties reflect normal levels of closeness and conflict
between mothers and daughters, or if perhaps the nature of their relationship
is characteristic of those experienced by pregnant and/or parenting teens and
their mothers who are "relatively close in age" (Burton, 1990; Ladner, 1971;
Obeidallah & Burton, 1995). Increasingly, empirical studies explored the
former issue (Cauce et al., 1996; Chodorow, 1978; Fischer, 1991; Smetana,
1989; Youniss & Smollar, 1985). However, relatively few studies addressed
the latter (Burton, 1996; Chase-Lansdale, Brooks-Gunn, & Zamsky, 1994;
Musick, 1993; Scott, 1993). What is the nature of affective ties (e.g., feelings
of closeness and conflict) between mothers and their adolescent childbearing
daughters? Does the relative age distance between mothers and daughters
impact the nature of their relationship?

In this chapter, we explore perceptions of closeness and conflict between
adult mothers and their teen parent daughters. We also assess the impact of
generational age distance on their relationships—that is, whether mothers
and daughters who are close in age have more conflictual and/or closer
relationships than those who are not. We begin our exploration with a brief
overview of relevant theoretical and empirical perspectives on closeness and
conflict in mother–teen parent daughter relationships. Using data from a
5-year, community-based study of teenage pregnancy in urban African
American multigeneration families, we then examine levels of closeness and
conflict in 73 mother–teen parent daughter dyads. We conclude our chapter
with a discussion of the implications of our research for future studies of
affective ties in teenage childbearing families.

THEORETICAL AND EMPIRICAL PERSPECTIVES
ON CONFLICT AND CLOSENESS IN MOTHER–TEEN
PARENT DAUGHTER RELATIONSHIPS

In exploring conflict, closeness, and generational age distance in mother–teen
parent daughter relationships, we draw on two theoretical perspectives—psychoanalytic (Freud, 1948; La Sorsa & Fodor, 1990) and neofreudian theories
(Chodorow, 1978; Smith & Forehand, 1986)—and the relatively small body
of existing empirical research on affective relationships between adolescent
mothers and their mothers (Kaplan, 1996; Oz, Tari, & Fine, 1992; Scott,
1993; Troester, 1984).

To begin, psychoanalytic theory contends that conflict in the mother–adolescent daughter relationship exists because daughters reach reproductive maturity at a time when mothers are typically ending their reproductive years. Conflict is believed to be a result of mothers' difficulty in accepting this menstrual asynchrony (Freud, 1948; La Sorsa & Fodor, 1990). The co-occurrence of menarcheal onset in daughters and menopause in mothers may be common among families in which women, across generations, bear children during their young adult years. Typically, the age distance between mothers and daughters in these families ranges from 25 to 32 years or more (Bengtson, Rosenthal, & Burton, 1990). This generational spread, however, may not be the case for many families that experience multiple generations of teenage pregnancy.

Families with multiple generations of early childbearing often have age-condensed family structures, a family form characterized by narrow age distances between generations (Burton, 1996). The typical generational span found in age-condensed families is 13 to 17 years between parent and child (Burton & Dilworth-Anderson, 1991). In an age-condensed family, a 14-year-old daughter may have a 30-year-old mother. Given the probability that most mothers and daughters at these ages are still having regular menstrual cycles, it stands to reason that young mothers of teen parents are not experiencing menstrual asynchrony with their daughters. Hence, the source of conflict in the mother–daughter relationship among families with multiple generations of early childbearing may be qualitatively different from that proposed by psychoanalytic theory.

Consider, for example the description of a four-generation, age-condensed family identified in Burton, Allison, and Obeidallah's (1995) ethnographic study of multigeneration, teenage childbearing families. In this family, the child generation included both a young mother (age 15) and her child (age 1), a young-adult generation comprised of a 29-year-old grandmother, and a middle-age generation that included a 43-year-old great-grandmother. As a result of the closeness in generational ages, chronological and developmental challenges often become inconsistent with generational positions in these families. This is evident by the fact that the adolescent mother, as a function of giving birth, is launched into the young-adult role status; however, she remains legally and developmentally a member of the child generation. Similarly, her young-adult mother has moved to the status of grandmother, a stage typically embodied by a midlife or older woman. This premature shifting of stages produced a blurring of developmental role boundaries in the family that often resulted in mothers and their adolescent daughters behaving like siblings toward each other. This sibling-like relationship created some dissonance and intense conflict with respect to how the mother and her teen daughter related to each other, particularly over issues of parental authority and adolescent autonomy.

Building on psychoanalytic approaches, neofreudians suggest that the mother–adolescent daughter dyad is characterized by conflict because mothers struggle with simultaneously maintaining emotional closeness with daughters while pushing them into adulthood. This process is believed to contribute to "tense" mother–daughter dyads (Chodorow, 1978). Smith and Forehand (1986) empirically tested this notion in a sample of 36 White mother–adolescent daughter dyads. They found that mothers' ratings of their daughters were more negative than were daughters' ratings of their mothers. They argued that mothers' negative ratings of their daughters were due to mothers' feelings of incompetence surrounding the negotiation of autonomy with their daughters.

Kaplan's (1996) study of mother–daughter relationships among African American childbearing teens offers additional support for this contention. Findings from her study suggest that adolescent daughters who become pregnant may threaten their mother's sense of control over their autonomy. One adolescent childbearer who participated in the study recalled her mother vocalizing this sentiment (Kaplan, 1996): "I know she was only 14 when she got pregnant and some of my church friends couldn't stop blaming me for what happened to my daughter. Like I can follow her around everywhere to stop her from getting pregnant" (p. 436).

Struggles with autonomy among families with multiple generations of adolescent pregnancy may also reflect the effects of caregiving needs and economic and contextual factors associated with early childbearing (Breakwell, 1996; Brooks-Gunn & Furstenberg, 1990; Kiernan, 1980; Upchurch & McCarthy, 1990). For example, adolescent mothers tend to turn to their mothers and other kin for instrumental help, particularly concerning the caregiving needs of their babies (Burton et al., 1995; Chase-Lansdale, Brooks-Gunn, & Zamsky, 1994; Furstenburg, Brooks-Gunn, & Chase-Lansdale, 1989; Stack & Burton, 1993; Williams, 1992). In addition to the need for child care assistance, as adolescents, teen mothers are also faced with the developmental challenge of establishing autonomy from their own caregivers (Wakschlag, Chase-Lansdale, & Brooks-Gunn, 1996). This contradictory position for the teen mother can potentially impact levels of closeness and conflict in the mother–daughter relationship (Kaplan, 1996; Williams, 1992).

Similarly, adult mothers' anticipation of additional responsibility of caregiving may impact perceptions of closeness and conflict in their relationship with their childbearing adolescent daughters. For example, the strains and joys that may accompany coparenting could potentially increase adult mothers' perceptions of closeness but also increase perceptions of conflict in this relationship.

Furthermore, the context in which teenage pregnancy emerges may complicate the relationship between mothers and their childbearing adolescents. For instance, higher rates of adolescent pregnancy are associated with economically impoverished neighborhoods (Brooks-Gunn, Duncan, & Aber, 1997). Generally, low resource or "poverty" contexts are associated with more physical and psychological dangers than are high resource contexts (Collins, 1990; Wilson, 1991). Some scholars defined the role of many mothers raising daughters in low income contexts as contradictory (Collins, 1987; Stack, 1974). The context demands that the mothers be overprotective of their daughters, yet at the same time they must foster a sense of self-reliance in them. Collins (1990) contends that mothers rearing their children in high-risk environments must be careful not to enhance daughters' self-reliance at the expense of their daughters' survival: "Black daughters with strong self-definitions and self-valuations who offer serious challenges to oppressive situations may not physically survive" (pp. 123–124). This contradictory position for mothers and daughters provides a challenging backdrop for the development of closeness and conflict among teen mothers and their mothers. In fact, the struggle over these issues in the mother–adolescent daughter relationship may lay the foundation for an emotionally intense relationship characterized by high conflict and variable closeness.

Responses to surviving in a socially and economically deprived context may also promote individuals' notions of an "accelerated life course," which is based on an individual's view that he or she has a foreshortened life expectancy (Burton, Obeidallah, & Allison, 1994). A truncated view of the length of one's life course reflects the realities of life expectancy and mortality rates in many low income populations, and may be linked to race as well (Farley & Allen, 1987). For example, in reference to low income African American youths' experiences, Cauce et al. (1996) state, "While the dangers for African American boys have received increasing attention, perhaps due to their elevated mortality rate, African American girls also receive a clear message that society places a low premium on their existence" (p. 113).

Internalization of the concept of a foreshortened lifespan may contribute to an intensification of relationships. Relationships characterized by emotional intensity are described as typical in Liebow's (1967) *Tally's Corner*. Liebow (1967) offers this description of inner-city community members who intensify their relationships: ". . . to get as much as he can from [personal relationships] while they last and perhaps hopefully to prolong them, the man hurries each relationship toward a maximum intensity, quickly upgrading casual acquaintances to friends, and friends to best friends and lovers" (p. 217).

Although Liebow describes the intensity involved in friendships, the general notion of intensification of relationships may be particularly salient in mother–teen parent daughter dyads (Horowitz, Klerman, Kuo, & Jekel, 1991; Peterson, 1983; Scott, 1993; Wakschlag et al., 1996). Musick (1993), reporting findings from a meta-analysis of nine studies of economically impoverished White, Hispanic, and Black teenage mothers (15 to 17 years old) underscores this point. She notes that the mother–adolescent daughter relationship tended to be characterized by emotional intensity. One adolescent daughter states, "When I'm angry at my father, I want to punch him; but when I'm angry at my mother, it's as though something is ripping me up inside" (p. 131). Musick (1993) also found that many daughters recall their mothers as "chronically worn out, depressed or totally preoccupied with their own lives . . . emotionally unavailable" (p. 101). One daughter comments about her relationship with her mother (Musick, 1993): "Now to my mother. I hate her so much. She has never been a mother to me. My mother used to treat me like shit, that's why I had a baby. So I can show the best possible love towards my baby than anyone has ever given me" (p. 15). From Musick's interpretation, some adolescent parent daughters seemed to perceive intense conflict in combination with a lack of emotional closeness in their relationship with their mothers.

Boxill's (1987) clinical study of twelve economically disadvantaged African American adolescent mothers (16 to 19 years old) provides yet another perspective on relationship intensity between mothers and their teen parent daughters. He reports that the majority of adolescent mothers in his study discussed fighting frequently with their parents. Despite the prevalence of conflict, most communicated that they "really" loved their mothers, suggesting the co-occurrence of high emotional closeness and conflict in this relationship similar to the affective ties described by Kenya and Sandra earlier in this chapter and research findings reported in other studies (Wakschlag et al., 1996; Scott, 1993).

Our review of relevant theoretical perspectives and the existing empirical research led us to examine two questions concerning affective ties between mothers and their teen parent daughters: What is the connection between levels of closeness and conflict in the mother–teen parent daughter relationship? Does the relative age distance between mothers and their adolescent daughters moderate the relationship between closeness and conflict, such that dyads closer in age experience stronger relationship between closeness and conflict that do dyads further apart in age?

The first question is based on the notion that mothers and daughters are expected to experience an emotionally intense relationship with one another—that is, although high levels of conflict may occur, it is likely to be experienced in the context of variably close relationships. Our assumption is that high levels of conflict will not necessarily preclude closeness between mothers and daughters, but rather the two dimensions will both be present. As noted by Liebow (1967), emotional intensity may reflect demanding and stressful experiences associated with low income contexts, a situation commonly experienced by many families with multiple generations of early childbearing. Thus, we hypothesize that mothers' and daughters' perceptions of conflict will be positively associated with perceptions of closeness.

With respect to the second question, we hypothesize that dyads closer in age will report higher levels of both conflict and closeness than will dyads further apart in age. This idea is in keeping with notions regarding blurred generational boundaries, a phenomena expected to typify the mother–daughter dyads with short age distances between the pair (i.e., age-condensed generations). That is, the relationship between mothers and daughters with age-condensed generations is expected to take on characteristics more similar to a sibling relationship than a parent–child relationship (Burton, 1990). As such, dyads closer in age are expected to report high levels of both dimensions.

MOTHER-PREGNANT ADOLESCENT DAUGHTER RELATIONSHIPS: INSIGHTS FROM THE IRAP STUDY

Description of the Study

We now explore our research questions using data from the Intergenerational Relationship and Adolescent Pregnancy Project (IRAP; Burton, 1990). IRAP is a 5-year, community-based study of the impact of teenage childbearing on multigeneration urban African American families (see Burton et al., 1995, for a more detailed description of the study). As part of the larger study, 121 pregnant African American teenagers and 73 of their mothers were interviewed regarding their relationship with each other. In order to compare responses from mothers and daughters, only daughters whose mothers also responded were included in the analyses, leaving a total of 73 mother–daughters dyads in the final analyses. The ages of the adolescents ranged from 12 to 19 years (X = 16.5 years, SD = 2.3) and the ages of their mothers from 28 to 51 years (X = 35.5 years, SD = 5.1). All respondents resided in economically disadvantaged urban communities.

Participants comprised a purposive sample and were recruited through a variety of sources including the metropolitan school district, local hospitals and clinics, churches, and teenage pregnancy programs. All participants were interviewed separately in their homes. Each interview averaged approximately 3 to 4 hours in length. Respondents were administered structured interviews comprising open- and closed-ended questions concerning their personal development and relationships with family members. The interviews were conducted by trained African American female interviewers.

Conflict was measured using a one-item five-point scale. Daughters and mothers were asked to rate the frequency of conflict/arguments they have with each other (1 = Never Argue, 2 = Rarely Argue, 3 = Sometimes Argue, 4 = Frequently Argue, and 5 = Always Argue).

Daughters and mothers rated emotional closeness with one another on a 10-item, three-point scale. Items were designed to tap emotional closeness and degree of solidarity in the mother–daughter relationship. Example items included: "How much do you trust your mother/daughter?"; "How important is your mother/daughter to you?"; and "How close do you feel to your mother/daughter?" Items were summed across each scale to create summary scores for mothers and daughters separately. Cronbach alpha reliability for each scale was .87 and .84, respectively.

Results

Approximately a third of both mothers and daughters reported a relatively high degree of conflict, and about half reported a moderate level of conflict (see Table 3.1). Analyses conducted on the emotional closeness scale revealed that, on average, both mothers and daughters felt emotionally close to one another ($M = 18.47$, $SD = 2.79$ and $M = 18.98$, $SD = 3.14$ for mothers and daughters, respectively). A one-way ANOVA revealed that mothers reported significantly more conflict than did daughters ($M = 3.18$ and $M = 2.98$, respectively; $F(1, 73) = 8.07$, $p < .01$). This finding parallels work by Paikoff, Carlton-Ford, and Brooks-Gunn (1993), who found that adolescent daughters reported higher levels of conflict in this relationship than did mothers. One explanation for this may be that, knowing that their mothers were also being interviewed, daughters were reluctant to rate their mothers critically (cf. Breakwell, 1996). Nonetheless, this pattern is consistent with findings from Smith and Forehands's (1986) study, which showed that mothers reported more negativity in their relationship with their daughters than did daughters about their relationship with their mothers.

Separate correlational analyses were conducted to determine the way in which mothers and daughters' reports of emotional closeness correlated with

TABLE 3.1
Frequency of Conflict Reported by Mothers and Daughters

	N = 74	*Percent*
Mothers' Reports of Conflict with Daughter		
Never Disagree	5	6.8%
Rarely Disagree	8	10.8%
Sometimes Disagree	35	47.3%
Frequently Disagree	20	27.0%
Always Disagree	6	8.1%
Daughters' Reports of Conflict with Mother		
Never Disagree	7	9.5%
Rarely Disagree	15	20.3%
Sometimes Disagree	32	43.2%
Frequently Disagree	12	16.2%
Always Disagree	8	10.8%

TABLE 3.2
Pearson Correlation Coefficients Between Mothers' and Daughters'
Reports of Closeness and Conflict in the Mother–Daughter Relationship

	Emotional Closeness	*Conflict*
Emotional Closeness		
Mothers' reports	1.0	−.58*
Daughters' reports	1.0	−.19

Note. *$p < .001$.

their reports of conflict. Mothers' reports of closeness with their daughters were inversely related to the amount of conflict they reported with their daughter ($r = -.57$, $p < .001$). An inverse but less pronounced trend was also found for daughters' reports of conflict and emotional closeness ($r = -.19$, $p = .09$; see Table 3.2).

In examining the second research question, we tested whether generational span between mothers and daughters influenced perceptions of closeness and conflict. Based on age spans between mother and daughter dyads used in previous work (Burton & Bengston, 1985), two groups were created: dyads who were less than 17 years apart, and dyads who were more than 17 years apart. Regression analyses were conducted to examine levels of closeness and conflict as a function of group membership. Results indicated that in dyads closer in age, mothers reported lower levels of closeness than did mothers in dyads further apart in age ($F = 3.89$; B = $-.03$, $p < .05$). This finding contradicts our hypothesis that dyads closer in age would report higher levels of closeness. Instead, results here are consistent with Kaplan's (1996) findings that younger adult mothers were less close to their childbearing adolescents. No significant differences were found for daughters' reports of closeness based on generational age span. Neither mothers' nor daughters' reports of conflict differed based on membership in generational span groups.

DISCUSSION AND CONCLUSION

Our chapter began with a brief profile of the affective ties between Kenya and Sandra. On the most general level, this excerpt illustrated some of the complexities involved in the mother–daughter relationship. More specifically, Kenya and Sandra revealed meaningful fluctuations in the tenor and temperament of affective ties among mothers and daughters. Our overview of theoretical and empirical perspectives on the mother–childbearing teen daughter relationship underscored paradigms traditionally used to explain the emotionally intense and sometimes contradictory nature of this relationship. According to some psychoanalytic theorists, high levels of conflict in the mother–childbearing teen daughter relationship are believed to be an outgrowth of menstrual asynchrony. Springing from the psychoanalytic tradition, some neofreudian theorists suggest that the conflictual characteristic of this relationship reflects tension experienced by mothers as they simultaneously push their daughters into adulthood while maintaining emotional closeness with them. Although these perspectives may be useful among many mother–childbearing daughter relationships, we propose that perspectives that take contextual and social characteristics into account would be more relevant for some families.

In contrast to traditional paradigms explaining mother–daughter relationships, insights garnered from ethnographic research suggest that families with multiple generations of teen childbearing may experience a very different relationship. First, as a function of being closer in age, mothers and daughters are less likely to experience menstrual asynchrony. Secondly, in age-condensed families, generational boundaries and explicit roles attributed to one's generational position may be blurred. Thus, the unique characteristics of families who experience multiple generations of teen pregnancy led us to re-examine the mother–daughter relationship in such contexts.

We explored the nature of affective ties among a sample of mother–daughter dyads from families with multiple generations of teen pregnancy. We hypothesized that mothers and daughters would experience high levels of conflict, but that this would emerge in the family context of high levels of closeness. We also investigated connections between affective ties among mother–daughter dyads as a function of generational span, hypothesizing that those dyads experiencing shorter generational span (i.e., age-condensed generations), would be more likely to experience a relationship typically characteristic of a sibling relationship—that is, high levels of conflict and variable levels of closeness. This was expected to result from blurred distinctions between generational positions.

Our results indicated, however, that the majority of mother–daughter pairs experienced moderate levels of conflict and moderate levels of closeness. Interpretations of this pattern draw on Collins' (1990) work, in which parenting is expected to contribute to increased hope. Increased hope, in turn, may attenuate perceptions of a foreshortened life span, perceptions that were believed to increase the intensity of relationships. Similarly, it is possible that the dual embrace of motherhood (i.e., adult and teen mother), although ushering in a shift in roles and responsibilities, may also bring in a greater feeling of a common experience. Such feelings may potentially reduce high levels of conflict. The moderate levels of closeness and conflict reported by mothers and daughters suggest that the majority of our families experience a more even-tone relationship than expected.

Most surprising from these analyses was the counterhypothesis finding that mothers in dyads closer in age reported lower levels of emotional closeness than did their dyadic counterparts further apart in age. Lowered emotional closeness in dyads shorter in generational span may reflect the idea that these mothers and daughters compete for similar resources (e.g., jobs, partners), a situation that may contribute to lowered emotional closeness. Notwithstanding, it is important to note that lowered emotional closeness was relative and that the absolute levels of closeness were in the moderate rate. As an aside, we discovered that mothers and daughters held divergent perspectives of their relationship with one another. Consistent with other findings, divergent perspectives are considered normative during periods of stress and transitional life events (Collins, 1990; Youniss & Smollar, 1985). Divergent perspectives found here echo the importance of considering the perspectives of both members of a dyad when examining relationship dynamics.

Regarding implications of our study, it is clear that the mother–teen daughter relationship should continue to be studied through the lens of both members. It would be especially valuable to conduct prospective studies of this relationship, to test the idea that the advent of pregnancy changes the nature of affective ties in this dyad. Further, additional nonself-report measures would be useful in unpacking the dynamics of this relationship. Nonetheless, these patterns lay the foundation from which to generate additional hypotheses and research questions regarding mothers and their parenting teen daughters, particularly within families of multiple generations of early childbearing. For example, how does extended kin (e.g., maternal grandmothers) contribute to perceptions of this relationship? Would patterns found here be different between relationships with fathers and sons, or between fathers and daughters within age-condensed generational families? In what way would difficult neighborhood circumstances (e.g., high mobility, high levels of crime) moderate levels of closeness and conflict in the mother–daughter relationship?

Although an initial step, the present chapter underscores the importance of examining both levels of closeness and conflict (rather than one or the other), and the value of exploring these affective ties with respect to generational span between mothers and daughters. Moreover, investigating such relationships among families that experience multiple generations of teen childbearing is key toward reevaluating and reformulating traditional theories surrounding this unique and special relationship.

ACKNOWLEDGMENTS

The research reported in this paper was supported by grants to Linda Burton from the William T. Grant Foundation, a FIRST Award from the National Institute of Mental Health (No. R29MH4605-01), and support services provided by the Population Research Institute, The Pennsylvania State University, which has core support from NICHD Grant 1-HD28263.

REFERENCES

Bengston, V. L., Rosenthal, C., & Burton, L. M. (1990). Families and aging. In R. Binstock & L. George (Eds.), *Handbook of aging and the social sciences* (pp. 263–287). New York: Academic Press.

Boxill, N. A. (1987). "How do you feel . . . ?": Clinical interviews with Black adolescent mothers. In S. F. Battle (Ed.), *The Black adolescent parent* (pp. 41–52). NY: Haworth.

Breakwell, G. M. (1996). Psychological and social characteristics of teenagers who have children. In A. Lawson & D. L. Rhode (Eds.), *The Politics of Pregnancy: Adolescent Sexuality and Public Policy* (pp. 159–173). New Haven, CT: Yale University Press.

Brooks-Gunn, J., Duncan, G. J., & Aber, L. J. (Eds.). (1997). *Neighborhood poverty: Policy implications in studying neighborhoods.* New York: Russell Sage.

Brooks-Gunn, J., & Furstenberg, F. F. (1990). Coming of age in the era of AIDS: Puberty, sexuality, and contraception. *The Millbank Quarterly, 68*, 59–84.

Burton, L. M. (1990). Teenage childbearing as an alternative life-course strategy in multigeneration black families. *Human Nature, 1(2)*, 123–143.

Burton, L. M. (1996). Age norms, the timing of family role transitions, and intergenerational caregiving among aging African American women. *The Gerontologist, 36(2)*, 199–208.

Burton, L. M. (1997). Ethnography and the meaning of adolescence in high-risk neighborhoods. *Ethos, 25(2)*, 208–217.

Burton, L. M., Allison, K. W., & Obeidallah, D. (1995). Social context and adolescence: Perspectives on development among inner-city African-American Teens. In L. J. Crockett & A. C. Crouter (Eds.), *Pathways through adolescence: Individual development in relation to social contexts* (pp. 119–138). New Jersey: Lawrence Erlbaum Associates.

Burton, L. M., & Bengston, V. L. (1985). Black grandmothers: Issues of timing and meaning in roles. In V. L. Bengston & J. F. Robertson (Eds.), *Grandparenthood: Research and policy perspectives* (pp. 61–77). Beverly Hills, CA: Sage.

Burton, L. M., & Dilworth-Anderson, P. (1991). The intergenerational family roles of aged Black Americans. *Marriage and Family Review, 16*, 311–330.

Burton, L. M., Obeidallah, D. A., & Allison, K. (1994). Ethnographic perspectives on social context and adolescent development among inner-city African American teenagers. In D. Jessor, A. Colby, & R. Shweder (Eds.), *Ethnography and human development: Context and meaning in social inquiry.* Chicago, IL: University of Chicago Press.

Cauce, A. M., Hiaga, Y., Graves, D., Gonzales, N., Ryan-Finn, K., & Grove, K. (1996). African American mothers and their adolescent daughters: Closeness, conflict and control. In B. J. R. Leadbeater & N. Way (Eds.), *Urban girls: Resisting stereotypes, creating identities* (pp. 100–116). New York: New York University Press.

Chase-Lansdale, P. L., Brooks-Gunn, J., & Zamsky, E. S. (1994). Young African-American multigenerational families in poverty: Quality of mothering and grandmothering. *Child Development, 65*, 373–393.

Chodorow, N. (1978). *The Reproduction of mothering: Psychoanalysis and the sociology of gender.* Berkeley, CA: University of California Press.

Collins, P. H. (1987). The meaning of motherhood in Black culture and Black mother/daughter relationships. *SAGE, 4*(2), 3–11.

Collins, P. H. (1990). *Black feminist thought: Knowledge, consciousness, and the politics of empowerment.* Cambridge, England: Harper Collins Academic.

Farley, R., & Allen, W. R. (1987). *The color line and the quality of the life in America.* New York: Russell Sage Foundation.

Fischer, L. R. (1991). Between mothers and daughters. In *Families: Intergenerational and generational connections.* NY: The Hawthorne Press.

Freud, A. (1958). Adolescence. *The Psychoanalytic Study of the Child, 13*, 255–278.

Furstenberg, F. F., Brooks-Gunn, J., & Chase-Lansdale, C. (1989). Teenaged pregnancy and childbearing. *American Psychologist, 44*(2), 313–320.

Gilligan, C. (1982). *In a different voice: Psychological theory and women's development.* Cambridge, MA: Harvard University Press.

Horowitz, S. M., Klerman, L. V., Kuo, H. S., & Jekel, J. F. (1991). Intergenerational transmission of school-age parenthood. *Family Planning Perspectives, 23,* 128–133.

Kaplan, E. B. (1996). Black teenage mothers and their mothers: The impact of adolescent childbearing on daughters' relations with their mothers. *Social Problems, 43*(4), 427–433.

Kiernan, K. (1980). Teenage motherhood—associated factors and consequences—The experiences of a British birth cohort. *Journal of Biosocial Science, 12,* 393–405.

La Sorsa, V. A., & Fodor, I. G. (1990). Adolescent daughter/midlife mother dyad: A new look at separation and self-definition. *Psychology of Women Quarterly, 14,* 593–606.

Ladner, J. A. (1971). *Tomorrow's tomorrow: The black woman.* New York: Anchor Books.

Liebow, E. (1967). *Tally's corner: A study of Negro street corner men.* Boston, MA: Little, Brown.

Musick, J. S. (1993). *Young, poor and pregnant.* New Haven, CT: Yale University Press.

Obeidallah, D. A., & Burton, L. M. (1995). Picking up the pace: The accelerated life course and developmental pathways for African American youth. Poster presented at *Society for Research in Child Development.* Indianapolis, IN.

Oz, S., Tari, A., & Fine, M. (1992). A comparison of the psychological profiles of teenage mothers and their nonmother peers: I. Ego development. *Adolescence, 27,* 193–202.

Paikoff, R. L., Carlton-Ford, S., & Brooks-Gunn, J. (1993). Mother–daughter dyads view the family: Associations between divergent perceptions and daughter well-being. *Journal of Youth and Adolescence, 22*(5), 473–492.

Peterson, D. R. (1983). Conflict. In H. H. Kelley, E. Berscheid, A. Christensen, J. H. Harvey, T. L. Huston, G. Levinger, E. McClintock, L. A. Peplau, & D. R. Peterson (Eds.), *Close relationships* (pp. 360–396). New York: W. H. Freeman and Company.

Rossi, A. S., & Rossi, P. H. (1990). *Of human bonding.* New York: Aldine de Gruyter.

Scott, J. W. (1993). African American daughter–mother relations and teenage pregnancy: Two faces of premarital teenage pregnancy. *The Western Journal of Black Studies, 17,* 73–81.

Smetana, J. G. (1989). Adolescents' and parents' reasoning about their actual family conflict. *Child Development, 60,* 1052–1067.

Smith, K. A., & Forehand, R. (1986). Parent–adolescent conflict: Comparison and prediction of the perceptions of mothers, fathers and daughters. *Journal of Early Adolescence, 6*(4), 353–367.

Stack, C. B. (1974). *All our kin: Survival strategies in a Black community.* New York: Harper & Row.

Stack, C. B., & Burton, L. M. (1993). Kinscripts. *Journal of Comparative Family Studies, 24*(2), 157–170.

Troester, R. R. (1984). Turbulence and tenderness: Mothers, daughters, and "other mothers" in Paula Marshall's *Brown Girl, Brownstones. SAGE, 1*(2), 13–16.

Upchurch, D. M., & McCarthy, J. (1990). The timing of first birth and high school completion. *American Sociological Review, 55*(2), 224–234.

Wakschlag, L. S., & Chase-Lansdale, P., & Brooks-Gunn, J. (1996). Not just "Ghosts in the nursery": Contemporaneous intergenerational relationships and parenting in young African American families. *Child Development, 67,* 2123–2147.

Williams, C. W. (1992). *Black teenage mothers: Pregnancy and child rearing from their perspective.* Lexington, MA: Lexington Books.

Wilson, W. J. (1991). Public policy research and the truly disadvantaged. In C. Jencks & P. E. Petersen (Eds.), *The urban underclass* (pp. 460–482). Washington, DC: The Brookings Institute.

Youniss, J., & Smollar, J. (1985). *Adolescent relations with mothers, fathers and friends.* Chicago, IL: The University of Chicago Press.

4

▼▼▼▼▼▼▼

Unearthing the Seeds of Marital Distress: What We Have Learned From Married and Remarried Couples

Lydia M. Prado
Howard J. Markman
University of Denver

Despite the fact that marital divorce rates decreased throughout the 1980s and into the 1990s, couples marrying for the first time continue to face a 50% chance of divorce during their lifetimes (National Center for Health Statistics, in press). Along with these divorce rates is a concomitant increase in remarriage. As evidence, one can point to the experience of persons 65 to 74 years old in 1980; about four of every five of those whose first marriage had ended in divorce had remarried by the survey date in 1980 (Glick, 1984). For men, the proportion was somewhat higher (84%) than for women (77%). Remarriages are more likely to fail than are first marriages (Glick, 1984; McCarthy, 1978), with approximately 60% ending in divorce. Approximately 40% of all children born in America today will belong to a stepfamily before they reach the age of 18 (Eckler, 1993). Many other couples never divorce, but remain in distressed and/or abusive relationships (Notarius & Markman, 1993). Clearly, marital distress and family disruption are among the most far-reaching problems in this country.

The aims of this chapter are to describe our longitudinal research program, summarize results from our investigation into the causes of marital distress, and address the vulnerability of remarriages to divorce from an interactive, communication-based perspective. Specifically, the focus is on how remarried couples negotiate conflict and how the nature of the couples' communication impacts satisfaction in the remarital relationship. The current study of remarital relationships was a natural outgrowth of our longitudinal project wherein a subsample of our engaged couples (1980) subsequently divorced and are now remarried. The remarriage study is unique given that it is longitudinal and the participants have been known *since before the first marriage.*

SUMMARY OF LONGITUDINAL RESEARCH

The foundation for our current research program was laid about 20 years ago when Howard Markman, working with John Gottman and Clifford Notarius at Indiana University, began investigating the causes of marital distress. These initial studies indicated that the quality of couples' communication clearly discriminated between distressed and nondistressed couples (e.g., Gottman, Markman, & Notarius, 1977). On the basis of these early studies, the group developed a treatment program for couples, summarized in *A Couple's Guide to Communication* (Gottman, Notarius, Gonso, & Markman, 1976).

At the same time, Markman began a series of longitudinal studies to test the hypothesis that the communication variables that discriminated between distressed and nondistressed couples would predict the development of marital distress and divorce. Longitudinal studies were deemed essential because of the possibility that the differences in communication between distressed and nondistressed couples were a result of distress caused by other factors, rather than communication itself being a significant etiological factor in the development of distress.

Since 1980, we have conducted a large-scale, longitudinal investigation of the development and early detection of marital distress. Next, we briefly describe this study and highlight some of the key results from the first 12 years of the project (for more depth, see Markman, Floyd, Stanley, & Storaasli, 1988; Markman & Hahlweg, 1993; Markman, Renick, Floyd, Stanley, & Clements, 1993).

We recruited 135 couples, who were planning to be married for the first time, from the Denver community in 1980 and 1981. We followed as many of these original 135 couples as possible from the beginning of the study, which allowed us to assess the potential of various premarital patterns to predict divorce. Since 1980, most of these couples who are still together have come in for research sessions approximately every 1½ years. To date, 25 of our original participants are in long-term, postdivorce relationships. We maintain contact with this group on a yearly basis. At various follow-up points, partners completed a variety of self-report measures and were asked to communicate about important marital issues, with their conversations being recorded on videotape.

RESULTS: CONFLICT MANAGEMENT AND FUTURE
MARITAL DISTRESS AND DIVORCE

This section provides a few key results relevant to the prediction of marital distress and divorce. Some of these findings were presented in other articles (e.g., Markman & Hahlweg, 1993; see also Markman et al., 1988, and Markman, Renick et al., 1993, for a detailed presentation of methods, measures, and design issues). Further, manuscripts in which we present the latest prediction analyses and findings in great detail are currently in preparation.

In one series of studies, we investigated the role of premarital communication quality in the development of divorce and marital distress. We compared those couples who remained happy and stable (using their premarital assessment data) with couples who developed marital distress (defined by having one or both partners score as distressed on the Locke–Wallace Marital Adjustment Test, Locke & Wallace, 1959, or by being separated or divorced.) We compared these two groups using data from observational coding of their premarital interaction (using the Couples Interactive Coding System, Notarius & Markman, 1983; see Notarius & Markman, 1989, for a discussion of objective coding of communication; and the Interactional Dimensions Coding System, Julien, Markman, & Lindahl, 1989, which we present in more detail later in this chapter). There were significant differences in problem-solving facilitation and in problem-solving inhibition—but only for the men. Men who subsequently became distressed or divorced had significantly lower levels of problem-solving facilitation (e.g., offering positive solutions) and significantly higher levels of problem-solving inhibition (e.g., withdrawal) compared to men who remained nondistressed.

Based on such findings, we tentatively conclude that how men handle conflict in a relationship is more important in terms of predicting the future than how women handle conflict (Markman, Silvern, Kraft, & Clements, 1993). Our conclusion in this regard parallels that of other researchers (e.g., Gottman, 1993) that men on average seem particularly wary of, and less skilled at handling, marital conflict. Overall, negative escalation cycles were found to be one of the most effective discriminators between distressed and nondistressed spouses, and also one of the strongest premarital predictors of future marital distress and divorce (Gottman & Levinson, 1986; Markman, 1989). *Negative escalation* is the process whereby one partner's expression of negative affect or behavior is reciprocated by negativity from the other partner. To reiterate, distressed couples have a propensity for entering into, and continuing, negative escalation cycles, much more so than nondistressed couples (Gottman, Markman, & Notarius, 1977; Notarius, Markman, & Gottman, 1983). This underscores the importance of preventive efforts that allow both genders to be equipped to handle potentially divisive issues well in the context of the dyad. In other words, if either partner feels less able to deal with conflict effectively, the couple will likely have significant problems handling their issues in ways that allow for the preservation of the quality of the relationship. To this end, we emphasize the concept of structure in our prevention program, The Prevention and Relationship Enhancement Program (PREP), because the rules presented can help both partners handle difficult issues well, using rules that both agree on. PREP was designed to teach partners skills and ground rules for handling conflict and promoting intimacy in six 2-hour sessions. The original PREP program is described in detail elsewhere (Markman, Floyd, Stanley, & Lewis, 1986). Although the program targets the enhancement of protective, positive aspects of relationships (e.g., commitment, friendship, fun, sensuality), research demonstrates that it is most crucial that couples have or learn ways to handle differences and negative affect (e.g., anger, frustration) constructively (Gottman, 1993; Markman, 1981; see Lindahl & Markman, 1990, for a discussion of our affect management model). Our longitudinal PREP data demonstrate promising results. Couples completing PREP had a significantly lower (8%) divorce/separation rate than the control group (19%) at the 5-year point (Markman, Renick et al., 1993). In terms of conflict management, pre/post analyses indicate that PREP couples showed significant improvement in conflict management skills compared to control couples who showed no such gains (Floyd & Markman, 1981). Follow-up results indicate that PREP couples maintained advantages on various dimensions of communication and conflict management at every follow-up point, including the most recent follow-up, 12 years after the intervention (see Markman et al., 1988, and Markman, Renick et al., 1993, for reports up through 5 years post intervention; reports on later follow-ups are in preparation.) We are currently conducting a large-scale outcome research project wherein PREP is disseminated through religious organizations to first-time engaged couples throughout central Colorado.

Structuring emotional conversations can help both men and women better tolerate a difficult exchange. For example, we believe it is helpful for couples to learn techniques and strategies for preventing or reducing the tendency for one partner to pursue talking about issues (usually the female) and one partner to avoid or withdraw from such talking (usually the male), which is clearly one of the most damaging and frustrating patterns for couples, a pattern that remarried partners recognize and consciously try to avoid in their remarriages.

Most theories of marriage suggest that a high level of validating interactions leads to sustained marital satisfaction. However, we observed no differences between distressed and nondistressed couples on the degree of validation in their premarital interactions. Of surprise to many who work with couples, levels of premarital *invalidation,* not validation, strongly differentiated couples who did well in the future from those who did not do well. Couples who would become distressed or divorced (at some point during the 12 years of participation in our research) had higher levels of invalidation in their premarital interaction than couples who remained nondistressed. Couples who later become distressed, compared to those who continue to be nondistressed, also demonstrate higher levels of negative affect reciprocity, higher levels of problem-solving inhibition and higher levels of negative communication behaviors such as mind-reading (Stanley, Markman, St. Peters, & Leber, 1995). Negative affect was predictive of distress for both husbands and wives, but it was much more strongly predictive for husbands. Positive affect was weakly associated with future distress and only for wives. Problem-solving facilitation and problem-solving inhibition were predictive of future distress only for husbands, whereas emotional invalidation was predictive of future distress for both, but more strongly for wives (Markman et al., 1993). These facets of communication are important for the management of negative affect and the resolution of conflict.

The longitudinal data demonstrate the importance of negative affect regulation. A tendency to enter into, and the inability to redirect, negative affect chains proceeds to development of marital distress. Further, the data reveal that indicators of communication quality generally increase in predictive power over time, and indicators of premarital relationship quality (i.e., relationship satisfaction) were not associated with divorce. Therefore, the quality of the couples' communication may be a more important determinant of long-term rather than short-term marital quality.

Markman and his colleagues (1993) also examined the consistency of communication patterns over time. The strongest evidence for consistency (over a 4-year period) emerged for negative communication dimensions (e.g., conflict), especially for men (Clements & Markman, in press). In addition, the frequency of positive communication cycles appears to decline over time. This suggests that couples need to learn to decrease the levels of negativity in their relationships, as well as maintain adequate levels of positive communication, if they want to maintain the integrity of their relationship.

The marital couples in the Markman, Renick et al. (1993) longitudinal study also indicated that problem areas change over time. In general, factors associated with communication and intimacy appear to become increasingly problematic for marital couples (Storaasli & Markman, 1990). As noted earlier, remarital couples also report problems involving communication and their interpersonal relationship as primary, problems that evidently persist over time (Koren, Lahti, Sadler, & Kimboko, 1983). To reiterate, it is not the number or content of problem areas that is related to marital satisfaction and divorce, but rather how the problem areas and conflicts are managed by the marital couple. We highlight such points in our preventive efforts because we think couples need to know that certain negative patterns do far more harm to their relationship than positive patterns can reasonably counteract. In layman's terms, "One zinger erases many positive acts of kindness" (Notarius & Markman, 1993, p. 28).

Another approach to assessing predictive patterns is through the use of discriminant function analyses. Such analyses, based on premarital indices of communication, problem intensity ratings, and demographics, correctly classified 90% of our sample as either married or divorced at 7 years following the first assessment (which is significantly greater than the prediction obtainable by base rates in the sample; Notarius & Markman, 1993). Similar findings were obtained in analyses of the 12-year outcome data, although the prediction rate is a little lower, yet still significantly exceeding base rates (Clements, Stanley, & Markman, 1995). These results suggest the sobering conclusion that, for many couples, the seeds of divorce are sown premaritally—ironically, at a time of great commitment and satisfaction (Stanley & Markman, 1992).

In sum, our analyses indicate that couples with dysfunctional premarital interaction patterns, especially a tendency to approach discussions of relationship issues with invalidation, negative affect, and withdrawal, are at risk for marital distress and divorce. When evaluated as a whole, studies strongly suggest that the negatives of how couples interact are much more predictive than the positives in predicting the future prospects of the relationship (Gottman, 1993; Markman & Hahlweg, 1993). In our view, these results highlight the need for partners to learn together how to adequately regulate negative affect arising from relationship conflict. Therefore, although the current version of PREP addresses many aspects of healthy marriages, it emphasizes key affect-management skills that enable difficult issues to be handled in a constructive manner (Markman, Stanley, & Blumberg, 1994).

EXPLORING THE ROLE OF COMMUNICATION
IN REMARITAL RELATIONSHIPS

The salience of negative communication patterns with regard to the development of distress and divorce in first marriages led us to consider the possibility that dysfunctional interaction patterns heavily impact satisfaction and distress in remarriages. It was hypothesized that communication deficits reflecting dysfunctional affect regulation, which are predictive of the initial marital breakup, are transferred from one relationship system to another. These dysfunctional patterns operate similarly within the second marriage, therefore putting the second marriage at risk for dissolution. In a preliminary study, Farrell and Markman (1984) found that remarital couples have lower levels of communication skills than once-married couples, suggesting that remarital pairs may be replicating dysfunctional interaction patterns.

There is additional evidence that interactional styles developed in one marriage may be repeated in subsequent marriages as a result of learning and environmental conditioning, influencing adjustment to remarriage (Aguirre & Parr, 1982; Furstenberg & Spanier, 1984; Kalmuss & Seltzer, 1986). Negative behavior learned in a first marriage can undermine later marriages as well (Bitterman, 1968; Cherlin, 1978; Kalmuss & Seltzer, 1986). Furstenberg and Spanier (1987) found that a majority of their sample of remarried people believed that mistakes from prior marriages are in fact repeated in remarriage. Further, Kalmuss and Seltzer (1986) found that spousal violence, if present in a first marriage, is likely to continue in subsequent marriages. If negative behaviors that contributed to the failure of a first marriage continue to cause difficulty in a remarriage, the dissolution of the second marriage may result. In addition, the evidence indicates that the main problem areas for remarried couples (which include communication) are the same as the main problem areas for once-married couples. However, as indicated in the marital research literature (Notarius & Markman, 1993), it is not the content or number of the problems that is the key to marital success, but how the problem areas are handled and negotiated by couple. All couples are inevitably confronted with conflicts that need to be resolved, and one important way that couples significantly impact each other and the quality of their relationship is through the process of handling differences and disagreements (Notarious & Markman, 1993).

The remarriage study presented here reflects the proposition that effective communication skills significantly impact the success of remarital relationships. Therefore, dysfunctional communication patterns contribute to the vulnerability of remarriages and negatively affect remarital satisfaction (as they do in first marriages). We addressed the vulnerability of remarriages to divorce from an interactive, communication-based perspective. Specifically, the focus is on how remarried couples negotiate conflict and how the nature of the couples' communication impacts satisfaction in the remarital relationship. Remarital communication patterns were explored in a recent study conducted at the Center for Marital and Family Studies at the University of Denver. The study is unique given that it is longitudinal and the participants have been known *since before the first marriage*. Therefore, assessment of differences and similarities between first and second marriages and first and second partners was possible.

Following a review of the relevant literature on remarriages, the current study is presented. The major findings from this study are then reviewed and implications of these findings for our current prevention work are discussed.

Satisfaction in Remarriage

A number of researchers examined the differential divorce rate between once-married couples and remarried couples. Fewer examined the factors that contribute to marital satisfaction or the primary issues faced by remarried couples. Although it is impossible to make conclusive statements regarding the value of the various theoretical explanations of remarriage vulnerability (Bergler, 1948; Cherlin, 1978; Furstenberg & Spanier, 1987; Halliday, 1980), a few consistent findings are apparent. It appears that remarried couples face a more complicated marital and family situation (Clingempeel & Brand,

1985; Mills, 1984; Visher & Visher, 1982), their prior marital history affects their attitudes toward marriage (Furstenberg & Spanier, 1987; Papernow, 1984), and that serial marriers are psychologically different from those who remarry once. The findings from the literature to date also indicate that individual difference variables (e.g., high expressiveness) are more strongly associated with relationship quality and satisfaction in remarriages than demographic variables (e.g., age, years divorced prior to remarriage).

The researchers who examined typical remarried families found that remarried couples consistently identify three distinct problem areas: the couple's interpersonal relationship and communication, children (specifically the discipline of children), and money and finances. In addition, problems that are apparent early in the relationship persist over time. It is noteworthy that the three main problem areas for remarried couples are consistently reported as problem areas for first-married couples. Thus, it appears that salient issues for first-married couples are similarly important to adjustment and satisfaction in remarital relationship.

Vemer, Coleman, Ganong, and Cooper (1989) suggest that rather than comparing types of households (simple vs. complex), researchers in the remarriage field might investigate the factors that contribute to marital satisfaction in each. Several authors have discussed a variety of ways for improving the quality of research on remarriage and stepfamilies (Esses & Campbell, 1984; Ganong & Coleman, 1984). All agreed that longitudinal research is required to understand the changes that occur in families as they experience the transition from divorce to singlehood to remarriage. Subsequently, adaptive as well as maladaptive processes can be identified over time.

The potential for conflict may be greater for remarriers than for first-married, given that remarried individuals are vigilant of the relationship and expect difficulties (Furstenberg & Spanier, 1987). The population of remarried individuals appears to include individuals who are reactive to any behavior and/or circumstance that is reminiscent of a failed marital relationship. Therefore, the ability to effectively communicate concerns, doubts, and feelings, as well as the ability to listen and validate without judging the other person's motives or reacting in a defensive manner, seems particularly important. For these reasons, adaptive conflict resolution and good communication are likely to be central in the development of satisfying remarital relationships. The current study focuses on communication variables across marriages and investigates the relationship between communication patterns and remarital satisfaction.

Communication in Remarriages

Given the complexity of remarital relationships (Koren et al., 1983; Visher & Visher, 1982), it is likely that remarital couples will encounter many difficult issues (e.g., relationships with former in-laws and ex-spouses) that require resolution early in the development of the new relationship. Adults in stepfamilies have almost twice as many stressors as those in other families (Bray, 1995). The need to negotiate significant issues early in the relationship puts additional emphasis on the quality of communication in remarital relationships, especially when the individuals involved are anticipating problems and vigilantly surveying the relationship for signs of deterioration (Furstenberg & Spanier, 1987). However, communication styles of remarital couples were largely ignored with regard to empirical work, and there is little consistency with regard to methodology.

Studies that used self-report about communication behaviors resulted in a variety of sometimes contradictory findings. Pasley, Ihinger-Tallman, and Coleman (1984) examined differences in consensus styles among happy and unhappy remarried couples. They found that happy remarried couples more often shared the same perceptions regarding the frequency of agreement, whereas unhappy remarried couples either shared similar perceptions regarding the frequency of disagreement or held dissimilar perceptions on the frequency of agreement or disagreement. Koren and his colleagues (1983), in their analysis of remarried families, found that supportive communication reported between husband and wife was negatively correlated with frequency of reported conflict and avoidance behavior. Hobart (1991), in a self-report study of first-married and remarried couples, found that remarried respondents report elevated levels of tension and disagreement in comparison to first-married respondents. Hobart (1991) noted that self-report marital adjustment scores are similar between groups and suggests that difficulties are negotiated by the remarried husband being more likely than once-married husbands to give in when spousal disagreements arise. Overall, self-report data indicate that communication is a critical aspect of remarried life and often associated with satisfaction in remarriage.

Studies that focused on specific aspects of communication demonstrated this trend as well. In a naturalistic study of successful stepfamily marriages, Burke (1993) found that a successful stepfamily marriage was governed by two major themes: individual efficacy and couple efficacy. Couple efficacy is achieved by attaining a balance in the spousal relationship through communication; a sharing of values, goals, and responsibilities; working on the parenting partnership, and giving and gaining support from one another.

Bograd (1992), in her analysis of self-disclosure and marital satisfaction, found that there is a positive relationship between self-disclosure and remarital satisfaction. Openness and honesty were an acknowledged presence in remarriages. In addition, no significant differences were found between men and women in the amount of self-disclosure shared in the remarriage.

With few exceptions (Clingempeel, 1981; Clingempeel & Brand, 1985, 1987), no published studies used behavioral ratings of remarital interaction. Clingempeel et al. (1985) employed the Marital Interaction Coding System

(Hops, Willis, Patterson, & Weiss, 1972), specifically positive and negative exchange behaviors, as a dependent measure of remarital quality. Clingempeel and Brand (1987) found that individuals in simple stepfather families exhibited lower rates of positive nonverbal behaviors than persons in simple stepmother families. These behaviors correlated significantly with the rate of negative nonverbal behaviors and dyadic adjustment.

Furstenberg and Spanier (1987) reported that almost all respondents in their longitudinal self-report study believe that they communicate better in their second marriages. Couples reported that they are much more likely to exchange ideas, to laugh together, to discuss issues calmly, and to confide in each other. The respondents reported that they have not changed significantly in their second marriages, but have simply found someone who understands them or who sees them as they really are.

The respondents in the Furstenberg and Spanier (1987) study also reported a different attitude toward conflict. All respondents reported lower levels of conflict in their second than in their first marriages. Both the men and women are more likely to see themselves as accepting conflict in their second marriage than in their first. The men were much less likely to report avoiding conflict in their second marriage than in their first; only 4% of the men report that they try to avoid conflict at all costs in their second marriage, whereas 25% report that they did so in their first marriages. Although the women were less likely than the men to avoid conflict in their first marriage, they did not report less avoidance in their second marriage. However, many of the women shifted their attitude from grudging to ready acceptance of conflict. The data indicate that the women assumed a less submissive stance in their second marriage and hence are more receptive to open controversy. The men responded by discussing differences of opinion more openly. It is important to keep in mind that the first to second marriage comparisons made by Furstenberg and Spanier (1987) are exaggerated by contrasting the communication at the end of the first marriage with the second marriage in its early stages. More importantly, the researchers did not obtain behavioral observations of interaction patterns.

Although the individuals reported that they did not change as a function of the divorce, another interpretation is that the respondents changed their communication skills as a result of marrying someone with communication skills very different from those of their first partner. This alternative interpretation was tested directly in the current study. The communication patterns of the partner in the longitudinal study were compared across relationships to determine whether she or he changed her or his communication behavior over marriages. In addition, the communication patterns of the individual's new partner were compared to the communication patterns of the ex-spouse to determine whether the remarried person is currently involved with an individual who demonstrates different communication skills from the first marital partner. It is also possible that the partner in the longitudinal study changed his or her communication behaviors in addition to having a partner with different communications skills from the first marriage partner.

To date, no studies have been conducted using observed interactional behavior as an independent measure, and none have followed divorced–remarried individuals longitudinally with regard to their observed communication patterns.

Given the importance of negative affect regulation and conflict management to individuals in first marriages, it is plausible that these same variables will be important and associated with remarital satisfaction for remarried couples. The available research on remarital communication to date suggests this is true (Bograd, 1992; Clingempeel & Brand, 1985; Koren et al., 1983; Pasley, Ihinger-Tallman, & Coleman, 1984). The results from the current study, which are presented next, provide further evidence that communication affects the quality of the remarital relationship.

COMMUNICATION IN REMARITAL RELATIONSHIPS: OVERVIEW OF CURRENT STUDY

The study presented here was an exploratory, empirical investigation of the communication-based explanation of the vulnerability of remarriages to divorce. Participants were 15 couples in joint remarital relationships. All the participants in the current study were married and divorced once. One person in each couple was involved in the longitudinal research program at the Center for Marital and Family Studies with his or her first marital partner. The average relationship satisfaction score was 117.46 ($SD = 17.74$) as measured by the Marital Adjustment Test (Locke & Wallace, 1959). This placed the sample of remarital couples in the nondistressed range of marital functioning.

A control group was included in the current study to address concerns regarding coder drift and to assist our understanding of the dynamics of the remarried group. The two groups are matched on the average length of time between the initial assessment (before the first marriage) and assessment as a remarried partner ($M = 10$ years). Accordingly, the remarried group is matched to the once-married group at Follow-up 6, which occurs approximately 10 years after the once-married participants were initially assessed. Participants in the control group were 45 once-married couples who are involved in the longitudinal research project at the University of Denver Center for Marital and Family Studies.

For the present study, the objective was to follow as closely as possible the procedures used with the index partner (the partner from the longitudinal study) at the initial assessment 10 years ago. All the couples had the opportunity to express their feelings about being at the center as remarital partners and were invited to share the history of their current relationship. There was a brief discussion addressing how each individual approached a new relationship after divorce. Next, the couples completed the same set of questionnaires and videotaped problem discussion tasks as those completed at the initial assessment session 10 years earlier. Last, the couples participated in a remarriage interview.

The primary objective of the current study was to evaluate communication patterns in second marriages of spouses who divorce and remarry, to determine the extent to which the communication patterns that predicted divorce in first marriages (e.g., negative escalation cycles and negative affect) are found in subsequent relationships. It was hypothesized that dysfunctional patterns of negative affect regulation would be consistent from one relationship to the next. Communication patterns were assessed through self-report and observational analyses. The Interactional Dimensions Coding System, a global, observational coding system, was used to study the remarriage interactions.

The Interactional Dimensions Coding System (IDCS)

The Interactional Dimensions Coding System (IDCS; Julien, Markman, & Lindahl, 1989), which we use to observe and assess marital interactions, is also used to code the problem discussions of our remarried participants. Given that observational data is central to our research program, a description of the IDCS is provided here (see Julien, Markman, & Lindahl, 1989, for a more detailed presentation). A description of the microanalytic Couples Interaction Coding System (CISS), which we have used in a series of our longitudinal studies, can be found in Gottman (1979) and in Notarius and Markman (1989).

The IDCS dimensions were selected on the basis of several theoretical and empirical considerations. First, Julien, Markman, and Lindahl (1989) included a set of core interactional dimensions that guided the development of the most prominent marital and family coding systems and that were consistent with most theories of family distress. Second, Julien, Markman, and Lindahl (1989), built on codes and behavior patterns that were shown to discriminate functional and dysfunctional communication processes in families. (For empirical reviews see Hetherington & Martin, 1972; Jacob, 1975; Schapp, 1984.) Based on these considerations, the IDCS assesses five negative dimensions (conflict, dominance, withdrawal, denial, negative affect) and four positive dimensions (communications skills, support–validation, problem-solving, positive affect) on an individual level. The IDCS also contains five dyadic codes wherein the dyad is rated as a specific unit. The five dyadic dimensions are positive escalation, negative escalation, commitment, future satisfaction, and future stability. The first two codes, positive and negative escalation, involve coding the entire behavioral stream of interaction, focusing on how each partner responds to the other. The latter three dyadic dimensions involve assessing the couple's commitment to the relationship, and the coder's estimation of the couple's future levels of satisfaction and stability. The definitions of the codes are presented in Fig. 4.1. The IDCS also employs guidelines that outline behavioral cues, both affect and content, to assist the coder when assigning values to the various codes.

Prior to assigning specific codes, however, a coder must become familiar with the specific coding units and standardized procedures. Each discussion is divided into thirds based on the number of thought units present in the interaction. A *thought unit* is any verbal phrase grammatically separated by a conjunction, subordinate clause indicator, question mark, or period. The transcripts are identified by couple code, type of session, and number of thought units. Each third section of the transcript is considered to be one "unit" of interaction to be coded using the IDCS.

Each of the individual and dyadic dimensions are rated separately. The ratings are determined by the observed strength or intensity of a particular code relative to a nine-point scale that ranges from low to high. Each category of intensity is associated with specific ratings: low = 1-2-3, moderate = 4-5-6, high = 7-8-9. The procedure used to code a complete interactional episode includes three steps:

1. The observer watches the first segment of an interaction, rates one spouse's behaviors on each of the first nine dimensions, and then rates the partner's behaviors similarly. If too much uncertainty remains for a scoring decision, the interaction segment is watched for a second or third time. The same procedure is used for coding the interaction in the second and third segments of the discussion.
2. Following this, the observer again rates partners' behaviors on the nine individual dimensions, using the total interaction as the coding unit.
3. Lastly, the observer rates the couple (as a unit) on the two dyadic dimensions, using the entire interaction as the coding unit.

Coders use inference rules to select a score on the nine-point scale. The score for a given dimension is based on the number of behavioral cues observed, their estimated frequency, their strength or intensity, and, when it applies, their duration. For example, in rating "male conflict," coders are instructed to attend to the number, the frequency, the intensity, and the duration (if appropriate) of content cues (e.g., making a critical comment directed at partner, putting down partner), and of affect cues (e.g., face displaying anger, speaking with a sarcastic voice, hands fidgeting). The individual dimensions defined with content and affect components receive a maximum of 4.5 points for each component. These dimensions are conflict, withdrawal, communica-

INDIVIDUAL CODES	*DEFINITIONS*
NEGATIVE	
1. Conflict	Conflict is globally defined as the level of tension, hostility, dissension, antagonism, or negative affect an individual displays.
2. Dominance	Dominance is defined as the control or influence an individual exerts in the interaction.
3. Denial	Denial is defined as the active rejection of a problem's existence or of personal responsibility for the problems discussed.
4. Withdrawal	Withdrawal is defined as an avoidance of the interaction or of the problems discussion in some way. The individual may evade the issue or may seem to "pull him or herself out of" the interaction. He or she may seem to retreat into a shell, back off, or try to displace the conversation.
5. Negative Affect	Negative affect is defined as the emotional tone or quality of the voice, the facial expression, and the position of the body during the interaction. Negative affect codes the degree to which an individual is negative in each of these dimensions.

INDIVIDUAL CODES	*DEFINITIONS*
POSITIVE	
6. Support Validation	Support validation is defined as appropriate and *positive* listening skills and speaking skills that convey supportiveness and understanding to the partner. For example, speaking skills that are supportive and validating positively reinforce the partner's preceding statements. Positive reinforcement means that the partner's statements seem to be registered, acknowledged, and encouraged.
7. Communication Skills	Communication skills are defined as appropriate and *positive* expressive skills. In rating this dimension, you only attend to the person's behavior while he or she is *speaking*.
8. Problem Solving	Problem solving is defined as the ability to define a problem (in the relationship) and work toward a mutually satisfactory solution for the problem. This needs to be done in a constructive manner.
9. Positive Affect	Positive affect is defined as the emotional tone or quality of the voice, the facial expression, and the position of the body during the interaction. Positive affect codes the degree to which an individual is positive on each of these dimensions.

FIG. 4.1.   Interactional Dimensions Coding System (IDCS).

tion skills, and support–validation. For the other dimensions, a maximum of nine points is based solely on content components (denial, dominance, and problem solving), or solely on affect components (positive and negative affect). A maximum of nine points is assigned to each of the dyadic dimensions, based on the likelihood that one spouse would respond in kind (positively or negatively) to the partner's previous behavior or behaviors. It is possible for the escalation dimensions to combine nonverbal and verbal behaviors (e.g., sneer in response to a put-down). Observers require approximately 6 hours to code an hour of interaction (in contrast to the 24 hours needed when using the

DYADIC CODES	DEFINITIONS
1. Positive Escalation	Positive escalation dimension is defined as a sequence in which a positive behavior of one partner is followed by a positive behavior of the spouse and so forth, creating a snowball effect. This is a measure of how often positive behaviors of one partner are responded to with positive behaviors from the other partner. Consecutive positive chains of behaviors are the essential ingredients that must be observed. This means that non-contingent positive behaviors in an interaction do not constitute a snowball or spiraling effect; such an interaction must be rated low on the positive escalation dimension, even though one or both partners may receive moderate or high scores on the positive affect dimension. To be rated very high on positive escalation, both partners would not only display a high frequency of positive verbal *and* non-verbal behaviors, but also give the impression of triggering each other's positive behaviors.
2. Negative Escalation	The same rationale that applies to positive escalation applies to negative escalation except that it refers to negative behaviors and not positive behaviors.
3. Commitment	Commitment is defined as the willingness of the couple to make their relationship a high priority, to work on improving their relationship. How personally dedicated are they to the relationship? Do they put their partner's needs or the relationship's needs above their own at times? Do they think of themselves as a team ("we" vs. "I")? Do you see a desire for them to continue their relationship because of a love for their partner?
4. Future Satisfaction	Future satisfaction is defined as how happy you predict the couple will be 5 years from now. How rewarding will this relationship be for the couple? How pleased will the couple be with the relationship?
5. Future Stability	Future stability is defined as how likely is it that this couple will be together 5 years from now. Base your answer on the following: Dedication, satisfaction, habit, and amount of constraints. Constraints are forces that keep people in relationships regardless of their desire to stay in the relationship. Examples of constraint include social pressure, religious beliefs, monetary investments, children, difficulties associated with ending the relationship, availability of alternatives to current relationship (and the attractiveness of these alternatives).

FIG. 4.1. *(Continued)*

CISS content and affect system; Notarius & Markman, 1989). On average, it takes two quarters of an academic year to train an observer in using the Interactional Dimensions Coding System. Cohen's Kappas for the codes average .60 and the codes discriminate between distressed and nondistressed couples (Julien, Markman, & Lindahl, 1989).

For the purposes of the current remarriage study, only the overall ratings were used because correlations between the overall ratings (Step 2) and the ratings of the three respective segments were high (range = .64–.94).

Before we present findings from the observational data for the remarried couples, we present participant reports of how these couples approached the second marriage. This qualitative data provides a context for evaluating the communication patterns of the remarried couples. Then, highlights from both the qualitative and quantitative findings regarding communication patterns are discussed.

The Remarriage Context

All the remarried individuals in this study report that they altered their views regarding marriage as a function of their divorce experiences. They appear to create a new relationship strategy whereby they are more cautious, pragmatic, and vigilant of their relationships. In general, many developed a different standard for their marriage such that they are more "grounded" and less influenced by the "fantasy" of the first marriage.

For example, approximately 80% of the participants noted that they had more realistic expectations of marriage the second time: "I'm not blind! I'm awake and can see both the good and the bad," "You wait for an enduring kind of love that can manage the rough spots," "I certainly don't believe in falling in love or the knight in shining armor." More than 75% reported that they were clear about the qualities they did and did not want in a partner. About three quarters of the respondents noted that they approached the relationship with greater caution and circumspection than their first marriage. One woman reported, "It takes longer to develop trust after being burnt." One man explained, "I thought relationships should be forever. Now, I know they don't always last. You really need to take some time to get to know yourself . . . self-knowledge is important. You're a little more guarded the second time." Another woman noted, "Of course you're more careful . . . you're a different person making a different kind of choice. It's more realistic."

Nevertheless, the majority of respondents in this study maintain that their realistic views of marriage make it more likely that their marriages will succeed. Almost 90% of the respondents in this study indicated that they understand the amount of "work" involved in a successful relationship, meaning that they realize they have to make an effort to understand their partner and help their partner understand them. If this type of "work" is central to the relationship, then good communication/conflict management skills could be critical to the success of the relationship.

Communication Patterns

Every remarried individual reported that he or she communicates differently in the second marriage. All of the couples noted that their communication is better the second time around. The majority of the couples stated that "honesty" and "openness" are primary ingredients of their second marriages. For example, couples often expressed the following sentiments: "I'm able to express myself and be who I am" or "I know myself well and I know my partner well." One couple noted that at the beginning of their relationship, they "had a discussion first of stipulations of a healthy relationship."

Overall, the remarried individuals accounted for the differences in communication by acknowledging differences in their partners, maturity in themselves ("knowing what you want and need and how to ask for it"), and identifying a different approach to conflict. Most of the couples reported that they were less avoidant of conflict and cite their "realistic" approach to the marital relationship as opposed to the "dreams and fantasies" of the first marriage. For example, "You have to talk . . . express negatives well. You can't be in a relationship just thinking about yourself." Another couple stated, "You have to be honest about dealing with the children. The children is (sic) the hardest part, an issue you live with and deal with it as it comes up, ongoing, don't focus on it though because it will destroy your marriage. You need to talk, talk, talk." These couples acknowledge that there will be issues and differences that need to be addressed. For instance, "There is conflict and there are differences. . . . differences that must be resolved. You have to talk about it . . . agree to disagree." One couple had the following advice: "Talk on the phone a lot before getting too serious. Phone conversations are really good. You learn a lot." The interview data cited gives one a sense of the subjective experiences of the couples in this study. The vast majority believe that they are communicating better in the second marriage, being less avoidant of conflict, and expressing negatives more constructively. The subjective experience of these couples reflects the idea that positive changes in communication styles are possible. Although the observational data are consistent with this idea of change being possible, even observable and measurable, the outcomes of these changes are not necessarily positive. The behavioral data obtained in this sample indicate that despite changes in an individual's management of conflict, mean levels of negative communication within the dyad remain the same across marriages. The observational data are presented next.

OVERVIEW OF OBSERVATIONAL DATA ANALYSES

The first set of analyses presented here addresses the question of communication patterns being transferred from the initial marriage to the remarriage. This question was addressed in multiple ways. First, to evaluate the consistency and transference of an individual's negative and positive affect regulation patterns, the variables contributing to the negative and positive affect regulation composites during the first marriage were correlated with those obtained from interactions during the second marriage for each individual index partner (the index partner is the partner from the longitudinal study who is currently remarried). Second, mean levels of negative and positive communication at remarriage were compared to mean levels of negative and positive communication at first marriage. The overall objective of this initial set of analyses was to determine if an individual's communication pattern is different in the second marriage as opposed to the first.

The communication skills of the nonindex partner were also evaluated, using the same statistical methods employed for the index partner. Analysis of the nonindex partner's communication skills addresses the issue of stability of communication style across marital partners. Specifically, the objective was to determine whether the communication patterns of the second marital partner are similar to or significantly different from the communication patterns of the first marital partner.

To examine potential gender differences, male and female data were analyzed together and then separately. For the separate gender analyses of index partners, the uneven number of index females and males in the sample (there were only four male index partners) limited the interpretations and conclusions that can be drawn from the findings. Therefore, results reported for the index males should be viewed with caution.

A control group was added to the analyses to better understand the results obtained. The control group was formed from the longitudinal data base of once-married individuals. The control group was matched to the remarried group on the basis of the mean number of years between initial participation with the Center for Marital and Family Studies and participation as a remarried individual ($M = 10$), rather than being matched on individual difference or demographic variables. Therefore, index and control group individuals are 10 years older than they were when they initially became involved with the longitudinal study. Consequently, the individuals in both groups had equal time to change their negative and positive communication behaviors.

The comparison of remarried couples with once-married couples provides a context for evaluating changes in the remarital couples. The once-married versus remarried comparison allowed for the evaluation of the correlations obtained from the initial set of analyses by employing the z-test. The group comparison also allowed for the evaluation of mean level changes over time of the individual negative and positive communication variables for the remarried individuals.

The second set of analyses presented here addressed the communication transference question by determining whether the dyadic communication system is different from first marriage to remarriage. The dyadic codes reflect the couple as a discrete communication system. A one-between, one-within ANOVA was used. Group (once-married or remarried) was the between-subjects factor, and time was the within-subjects factor. Time one (Time 1) was defined as time of entry into the longitudinal study for both groups. Time two (Time 2) was defined as the point 10 years following Time 1. Essentially, for the remarried group, the time factor compares first marriage and remarriage. For the once-married group, the time factor compares the couple at Time 1 and the same couple 10 years later. The group comparison allows for the evaluation of changes evident in the remarried group by comparing them to changes made in the once-married group.

RESULTS

As noted, in the following presentation of results, the individuals from the longitudinal study are identified as the index partners. The individuals who were not involved with the longitudinal study are identified as the first and second marital partners.

For the first set of analyses, the correlations were performed in the following order for both index partners and their first and second marital partners. First, collapsing across gender, individual communication at Time 1 (pre) was correlated with individual communication at Time 2 (remarriage for the remarried group, Follow-up 6 for the once-married group). Then, to examine potential gender differences, separate correlations were performed with male and female data. The same format was used for the mean level comparisons.

For all analyses, the following statistical parameters were employed. All correlations and t tests were two-tailed with significance defined as $p < .05$. A trend was defined as $p < .10$. For all measures, the data were evaluated to identify outliers. An outlier was defined as any data point that was a minimum of three standard deviations from the mean.

Negative Communication: Correlation Between Time 1 and Time 2

Collapsing across gender for index partners, individual negative communication in the first marriage was not significantly correlated to negative communication in remarriage ($r = .18$, $p = .53$). Thus, contrary to predictions, there was no relationship between negative communication at first marriage and remarriage. However, when male and female data were analyzed separately, a significant correlation was apparent for the index females.

Contrary to predictions, negative communication for female index partners in their first marriage was negatively correlated with their negative communication in remarriage ($r = -.74$, $p < .05$). If the female index partner demonstrated higher levels of negative communication in the first marriage, she demonstrated lower levels in the second marriage. If the female index partner demonstrated lower levels of negative communication in the first marriage, she demonstrated higher levels in the second marriage.

For once-married women in the comparison group, negative communication at time 1 was not correlated with negative communication at Follow-up 6, approximately 9 to 10 years later.

A z-test (Glass & Hopkins, 1984) was employed to determine if the correlation of negative communication of women in first marriages with the same women in second marriages was different from the correlation of negative communication of once-married women between Time 1 and Time 2 (Follow-up 6). Results indicated that the correlation of negative communication of women between first marriage and second marriage is significantly different from the correlation of negative communication of once-married women over a 10-year period (z-ratio = 2.49, $p < .05$).

Contrary to predictions, negative communication for male index partners in their first marriage was not correlated with negative communication in remarriage.

Correlation Between Negative Communication of First and Second Partners of Index Individuals. Collapsing across gender for the first marital partners and second marital partners, individual negative communication of the second marital partners was negatively correlated with the individual negative communication of the first marital partners ($r = -.67$, $p < .05$). If the first marital partner demonstrated higher levels of individual negative communication, the second marital partner exhibited lower levels of individual negative communication. If the first marital partner demonstrated lower levels of individual negative communication, the second marital partner exhibited higher levels of individual negative communication.

Examining this effect by gender for index females, the first husband's negative communication was negatively correlated with her second husband's individual negative communication ($r = -.67$, $p < .05$). If the first husband exhibited higher levels of negative communication, the second husband exhibited lower levels of negative communication. If the first husband exhibited lower levels of negative communication, the second husband exhibited higher levels of negative communication. This is the same correlational pattern that is demonstrated by the index females themselves.

For once-married men in the comparison group, individual negative communication at Time 1 is not correlated with individual negative communication at Time 2, approximately 10 years later ($r = .11$, ns).

A z-test was employed to determine if the correlation of negative communication between first husbands and second husbands was significantly different from the correlation of negative communication of once-married husbands over the same 10-year period. Results indicated that the correlation of negative communication between first and second husbands was significantly different from the correlation of negative communication between Time 1 and Time 2 for the once-married husbands (z-ratio = 2.38, $p < .05$).

For index males ($n = 4$), the first wife's individual negative communication was not correlated with the second wife's individual negative communication ($r = -.55$, ns). Clearly, the small number of first wives versus second wives limits the power of this analysis. With this sample, the individual negative communication of the second wife is not associated with the individual negative communication of the first wife. These findings are summarized in Table 4.1.

Positive Communication: Correlations Between Time 1 and Time 2

For each separate analysis (female index partners; male index partners; first marital partners with second marital partners; once-married men and once-married women) individual positive communication at Time 1 was not significantly correlated with individual positive communication at Time 2. These findings are summarized in Table 4.2.

Individual Negative and Positive Communication: Mean Comparisons

To further test the hypothesis that communication patterns are consistent from the first marriage to the second marriage, individual negative and positive communication levels were compared across marriages. It was expected

TABLE 4.1
Correlations Between Negative Communication at Time 1 and Time 2
for Index Partners, Nonindex Partners, and Once-Married Partners

Index Partners		
Collapsed Across Gender ($n = 15$)	Males ($n = 4$)	Females ($n = 11$)
−.17	.19	−.74*
Nonindex Partners		
Collapsed Across Gender ($n = 15$)	Males ($n = 11$)	Females ($n = 4$)
−.67*	−.67*	−.54
Once-Married Partners		
Males ($n = 45$)		Females ($n = 45$)
.11		.10

*$p < .05$.

TABLE 4.2
Correlations Between Positive Communication at Time 1 and Time 2
for Index Partners, Nonindex Partners, and Once-Married Partners

Index Partners		
Collapsed Across Gender (n = 15)	Males (n = 4)	Females (n = 11)
.21	.18	.16
Nonindex Partners		
Collapsed Across Gender (n = 15)	−.14	.11
Once-Married Partners		
Males (n = 45)		Females (n = 45)
.06		−.05

that individuals in the remarried group would exhibit similar levels of negative and positive communication in both marriages. The individual negative and positive communication of the first and second partners of the remarried individuals was also evaluated.

Mean levels of individual negative and positive communication were examined in separate t tests. For index partners, the t tests compared their individual communication behaviors in first marriages with their individual communication behaviors in second marriages. For the partners of the index individuals, the analyses essentially compared first husbands with second husbands and first wives with second wives. For the once-married group, these analyses compare husbands and wives with themselves 10 years later.

Negative Communication

Collapsing across gender for index partners, negative communication was found to be stable when comparing first marriage to second marriage ($t(14)$ = −.76, ns) as predicted. Overall, the degree of negative communication demonstrated in second marriages was similar to the degree of negative communication demonstrated in first marriages. This result was obtained when index men and women were analyzed separately.

The results obtained for once-married men and women are different. Individual negative communication was found to increase over 10 years for the once-married females ($t(44)$ = 10.85, $p < .05$). Individual negative communication was also found to increase over 10 years for the once-married males ($t(44)$ = 9.23, $p < .05$), as can be seen in Table 4.3.

Comparing First and Second Partners of Index Individuals. Collapsing across gender for first marital partners and second marital partners, the degree of negative communication exhibited by the first marital partner was

TABLE 4.3
Mean Negative Communication Over Time by Partner Type and Gender

	Index Partners	
	Males ($n = 4$)	Females ($n = 11$)
Time 1	5.18	3.36
	(1.36)	(1.18)
Time 2	4.75	4.11
	(1.92)	(1.27)
	Once-Married Partners	
	Males ($n = 45$)	Females ($n = 45$)
Time 1	2.63	2.34
	(.91)	(.76)
Time 2	4.73	4.72
	(1.32)	(1.27)
	Nonindex Partners	
	Males ($n = 11$)	Females ($n = 4$)
Time 1	3.59	3.06
	(1.29)	(.87)
Time 2	4.25	5.37
	(1.56)	(1.19)

similar to the degree of negative communication exhibited by the second marital partner ($t(14) = -1.71$, ns). A different result is obtained when first husbands and first wives are analyzed separately.

The first and second husbands of index females demonstrated a similar degree of negative communication. There was a trend for the negative communication of second wives to be higher than the negative communication of first wives of index males ($t(3) = -2.80$, $p < .10$). These findings are summarized in Table 4.3.

Positive Communication

Collapsing across gender, index partners had higher levels of positive communication in second marriages ($t(14) = -3.93$, $p < .05$). Positive communication increased for index females ($t(10) = -2.80$, $p < .05$) from first marriage to second marriage. There was a trend for the positive communication of index males to be higher in second marriages than in first marriages ($t(3) = -3.16$, $p < .10$).

The findings for once-married men and women are similar. Once-married women had higher levels of positive communication after 10 years of marriage ($t(44) = 3.55$, $p < .05$). Once-married men also had higher levels of positive communication after 10 years of marriage ($t(44) = 3.39, p < .05$), as shown in Table 4.4.

Comparing First and Second Partners of Index Individuals. Collapsing across gender for first marital partners and second marital partners, there was a trend for the positive communication of second marital partners to be higher than the positive communication of first marital partners ($t(14) = -1.74, p < .10$).

As shown in Table 4.4, second husbands of index females displayed higher levels of positive communication than first husbands ($t(10) = -2.33, p < .05$). Similar levels of positive communication were displayed by the first and second wives of index males ($t(3) = .21, p > .05$).

Negative and Positive Communication: Comparisons Between Groups at Time 1

To evaluate for possible selection effects with regard to the negative and positive communication variables, the remarried and once-married groups were compared at Time 1. As can be seen in Table 4.5, men in the remarried group had higher levels of negative communication than the once-married men at Time 1 ($t(17.61) = -3.46, p < .05$). Women in the remarried group

TABLE 4.4
Mean Positive Communication Over Time by Partner Type and Gender

	Index Partners	
	Males ($n = 4$)	Females ($n = 11$)
Time 1	3.50	5.06
	(.408)	(1.18)
Time 2	6.19	6.36
	(2.01)	(1.17)
	Once-Married Partners	
	Males ($n = 45$)	Females ($n = 45$)
Time 1	4.92	5.04
	(1.21)	(1.05)
Time 2	5.83	5.91
	(1.41)	(1.21)
	Nonindex Partners	
	Males ($n = 11$)	Females ($n = 4$)
Time 1	4.79	5.25
	(1.28)	(.54)
Time 2	6.22	5.00
	(1.40)	(2.41)

TABLE 4.5
Mean Communication at Time 1 by Group and Gender

	Remarried		Once-Married	
	Males	*Females*	*Males*	*Females*
Communication	(*n* = 15)	(*n* = 15)	(*n* = 47)	(*n* = 47)
Negative	4.01	3.28	2.64	2.34
	(1.45)	(1.09)	(.909)	(.75)
Positive	4.45	5.11	4.97	5.09
	(1.25)	(1.04)	(1.22)	(1.05)

had higher levels of negative communication than women in the once-married group at Time 1 ($t(18.42) = -3.13$, $p < .05$).

Comparisons of positive communication between remarried and once-married individuals revealed the following results. At Time 1, similar levels of positive communication were demonstrated by remarried and once-married men ($t(23.12) = 17$, *ns*). At Time 1, remarried and once-married women demonstrated similar levels of positive communication ($t(23.94) = -.08$, *ns*).

DYADIC COMMUNICATION

To further test the hypothesis that communication patterns are stable across marriages, a series of 2×2 (group × time) repeated measures ANOVAS were conducted using the dyadic codes. Group (once-married or remarried) was the between-subjects factor, and time (pre- to remarriage Follow-up 6) was the repeated measure. To further evaluate for selection effects, planned comparisons between groups at Time 1 were conducted within each ANOVA. The dyadic communication codes reflect the couple as a dyadic system; all the dyadic codes assess interactional behaviors. The couple's communication is observed and measured with regard to negative and positive escalation.

To review, negative escalation is a measure of how often negative behaviors of one partner are responded to with negative behaviors of the other partner and vice versa. Positive escalation is a measure of how often positive behaviors of one partner are responded to with positive behaviors of the other partner and vice versa.

Negative Escalation

The ANOVA with negative escalation as the dependent variable revealed a significant main effect for group ($f(1,58) = 8.46$, $p < .05$). The remarried group had higher levels of negative escalation than the once-married group.

TABLE 4.6
Mean Negative Escalation Over Time by Group

Time	Remarried	Once-Married
	(n = 15)	(n = 45)
Time 1	4.20	2.73
	(1.74)	(1.03)
Time 2	4.20	3.93
	(2.14)	(1.62)

A trend for a main effect for time emerged ($f(1,58,)$, $p < .10$). There was a trend for negative escalation at Time 2 to be higher than negative escalation at Time 1. A trend for group by time interaction emerged as well ($f(1,58) = 3.04$, $p < .10$). As can be seen in Table 4.6, there was a trend for negative escalation to be higher at Time 2 for the once-married group but not the remarital group. A planned comparison was conducted and revealed that the significant main effect for group can be accounted for by the significant difference between groups at Time 1 ($t(17.25) = -3.07$, $p < .05$).

Positive Escalation

The ANOVA with positive escalation as the dependent variable revealed a significant main effect for time ($f(1,58) = 12.28$, $p < .05$). Positive escalation was higher at Time 2 than at Time 1. A main effect for group was not found. A significant group x time interaction ($f(1,58) = 5.89$, $p < .05$) was found. As can be seen in Table 4.7, positive escalation increases from Time 1 to Time 2 for the remarried group but not the once-married group. The time main effect can be accounted for by the significant increase in positive escalation for the remarried group. Specifically, positive escalation in second marriages is higher than the positive escalation in first marriages. The planned comparison revealed a trend for the positive escalation demonstrated by the once-married group to be higher than the positive escalation demonstrated by the remarried group at Time 1 ($t(18.09 = 1.87$, $p < .05$).

TABLE 4.7
Mean Positive Escalation Over Time by Group

Time	Remarried	Once-Married
	(n = 15)	(n = 45)
Time 1	4.20	5.26
	(2.21)	(1.45)
Time 2	6.40	5.66
	(2.38)	(1.75)

TABLE 4.8
Correlations Between Communication and
Marital Satisfaction For the Remarried Group

Communication	Marital Satisfaction Remarried Group (n = 30)
Negative	−.34*
Positive	.11
Negative Escalation	−.38**
Positive Escalation	−.30*

*$p < .10$; **$p < .0$

SATISFACTION IN REMARRIAGE

Correlational analyses were conducted to determine whether the communication variables were related to remarital satisfaction as expected.

There was a trend for negative communication to be related to marital satisfaction for the remarried group ($r = −.34$, $p < .10$). Positive communication was not significantly correlated with remarital satisfaction.

A couple's level of negative escalation was negatively correlated with remarital satisfaction ($r = −.38$, $p < .05$). The lower the level of negative escalation, the higher the level of satisfaction. The higher the level of negative escalation, the lower the level of satisfaction. There was a trend for positive escalation to be related to satisfaction in remarriage ($r = .30$, $p < .10$), suggesting that increases in positive escalation are related to increases in remarital satisfaction.

DISCUSSION

The major quantitative finding of the present study is that there were significant changes in communication from the index partner's first to second marriage. Changes were evident in the index partner's communication, the nonindex partner's communication, and the couple system. Communication changes were found for both negative and positive communication.

Negative Communication

The strong negative correlation evident for remarital wives between negative communication in their first marriage and negative communication in their second marriage is probably the most striking finding from this study. If a woman had higher levels of negativity in her first marriage, she had lower levels of negativity in the second relationship. If a woman had lower levels of negativity in the first marriage, she had higher levels of negativity in the second marriage. A number of possible explanations for this finding can be considered.

First, one might hypothesize that the women are making a considerable effort to improve conflict management in their second marriage as opposed to their first marriage. If this were the case, one would expect lower level of negativity in the remarriage overall. However, this hypothesis is clearly not supported by the data. Although the women are changing communication behaviors, the behaviors level of negativity within the dyad remains the same across marriages. The negative correlation suggests that women are handling the negativity in the second marriage differently than they did in their first marriage. The negative correlation suggests that those women who were lowest in negativity in their first relationship are higher in negativity in the second relationship and those who were higher in negativity in the first relationship are lower in negativity in the second relationship.

The hypothesis that there is some conscious attempt to improve communication from one relationship to the next is consistent with the self-report results that indicate the women are making a conscious effort to work harder on the new relationship and do things differently. A high degree of motivation to improve communication, which is noted by previous research (Bograd, 1992; Furstenberg & Spanier, 1987; Koren et al., 1983; Smith, Goslen, Byrd, & Reece, 1991), is consistent with other remarital samples. As discussed next, there are positive changes in positive communication. However, any changes made have not resulted in decreased negativity.

Another possible explanation for the negative correlation obtained is that the women are selecting second partners whose pattern of handling negativity is maximally different from the first partner's pattern of handling negativity. The change in the partner's negative communication pattern could elicit different responses from the wife, thereby changing the couple's overall interaction. This hypothesis receives some support from the data that show a negative correlation between the negative communication of the index partner's first partner and the negative communication of the index partner's second partner.[1]

---

[1]A third explanation for the significant negative correlation finding is that the correctional results are simply a function of the changes in the International Dimensions Coding System. If this were true, then one would expect similar patterns in the comparison group. However, when one examines the correlation between negative communication from premarital to 10 years later for the comparison group of women, who were married to the same partner over time, different results are noted. There is no significant correlation between negative communication at pre and negative correlation 10 years later. The same is true for once-married husbands. The different patterns for the comparison group suggest that changes in the coding system do not explain the results obtained from the remarital group.

Taken together, these data suggest that there is a dynamic process operating such that the remarital relationship is maximally different from the old relationship in terms of how negative communication is managed. It is unclear how much the changes observed may be attributed to a conscious decision to do things differently or how much can be attributed to unconscious processes that compel individuals to select a partner who is maximally different on a key interactional dimension.

The family of origin literature (Boszormenyi-Nagy & Spark, 1973; Bowen, 1966), suggests that individuals select characteristics in a first marital partner that are opposite with regard to the key characteristics of one's family of origin. It is possible that similar processes are operating as an individual transitions from one significant relationship (marriage) to the next (remarriage). Therefore, divorced individuals might be choosing a second partner based on an important relationship dimension (i.e., negative communication) that is the opposite of the characteristic of the first partner on this dimension.

Regardless of the reason, the changes in the woman's negative communication style might mean that the experience of the second relationship in terms of negative communication is quite different when compared to the first. For women who were lower in negative communication in the first marriage, this might indicate that they were not calling attention to problematic issues or expressing much disagreement in the first relationship, and the relationship may have suffered as a result (Markman, Stanley, & Blumberg, 1994). Therefore, part of the difficulties experienced in the first relationship could be attributed to a lack of constructive arguing.

Thus, in comparison, the new relationship has a higher degree of negativity. Several studies suggest that higher levels of constructive negativity early in a relationship are predictive of higher satisfaction later in the relationship (Gottman & Krokoff, 1989). Therefore, it is possible that the increase in negativity for this set of couples might be positive. Alternatively, if the increase in negativity produces higher levels of destructive communication, the couple may be at risk for future problems. Clearly, a follow-up study of the current sample is needed to adequately address these questions.

Next, the focus is on the women who had higher levels of negativity in the first relationship. These women are currently in a relationship with lower levels of negativity. To the extent that the higher levels of negativity in the first relationship are indicative of destructive handling of conflict, the lower levels of negativity in the second relationship would bode well for the future of that relationship (Markman et al., 1994). Several longitudinal investigations of marital success reported that negative communication behaviors before marriage were predictive of marital distress and divorce. If this is the case for remarriage, the relationships with less negativity are less likely to experience distress and divorce. Once again, longitudinal follow-up of the current sample is necessary to assess ultimate risk of remarital distress and redivorce. Such follow-ups are planned as part of our overall research program. Given the small sample size in the current study, the results should be interpreted with caution as replications are needed to validate the current findings.

Positive Communication

An overall increase in positive communication from first marriage to second marriage is the second major finding in this study, reinforcing the belief of couples themselves that changes in communication patterns occur. The increases in positive communication also support the hypothesis that individuals can change communication patterns from one relationship to the next without intervention. The qualitative findings suggest that remarried individuals tend to focus on increasing positivity in their relationship instead of specifically addressing the level of negativity. For example, remarried individuals report that they "listen more" and are more "open" to communication in general. They also report that they are better able to express themselves and that their partners are more willing to listen. Several studies (Bograd, 1992; Smith, Goslen, Byrd, & Reece, 1991) similarly report that remarried individuals focus on positive dimensions (e.g., increasing self-disclosure and honesty) when making a conscious effort to make their second relationship better than the first.

Again, it is unclear from the current study how much the increase in positive communication from first to second marriage can be attributed to the individual's conscious effort to increase positivity and how much can be attributed to a more positive dyadic communication system resulting from the partner's greater positivity. Whatever the reason for the increase in positive communication, the finding indicates that the index partner's level of positive communication in the remarital relationship is significantly higher than the level of positive communication in the first marriage. All the remarried individuals believe that the cumulative effect of the changes they made is a better overall communication system. For positive communication, the increases may be a result of an individual's efforts to improve communication. In this case, the self-report data and the communication behaviors observed are consistent with each other, both indicating that increases in positive communication are occurring. However, the observational data do not support the perception of a better overall communication system with regard to negative communication. Although negativity is being handled differently, the level of negativity within each dyad is the same across marriages.

The self-report data from the Furstenberg and Spanier (1987) study suggest that remarried individuals have a different attitude toward conflict and experience lower levels of conflict in their remarriages than in their first marriages. The majority of the respondents in this study report that they are handling conflicts and problems better in the second relationship. Perhaps individuals in intimate relationships are simply not objective with regard to negative interactions within that relationship. It may be that people have a general tendency to minimize the negativity in their relationships while accentuating the positive. In fact, there is some evidence to suggest that nondistressed partners do exactly that; they minimize the negative (Markman et al., 1994). Clinically, it has been demonstrated that many psychological factors (e.g., denial, avoidance) combine to produce an inaccurate perspective with regard to the level of negativity expressed in intimate relationships, especially when one is currently invested in continuing the relationship (Walker, 1979). In contrast, distressed couples tend to minimize the positive and emphasize the negative (Markman et al., 1994). It is possible that increasing positivity, which certainly makes sense in terms of making the relationship more enjoyable, is psychologically more palatable for nondistressed partners than focusing on the possible destabilizing effects of negative interactions. Unfortunately, the remarried couples have not successfully reduced overall negativity on their own. This negativity is inversely related to remarital satisfaction and may be related to future distress and divorce.

Implications for Intervention

The implications for intervention are twofold. First, the negative correlation between negative escalation and remarital satisfaction suggests that addressing the negative interaction patterns of remarried individuals is crucial. Communication is identified as a major problem, and remarried individuals are dealing with crucial issues at the outset of their relationships. The need for effective conflict management skills is clear. For the subsample of couples with increased negativity, remarital satisfaction seems especially threatened. For the low negativity couples, the goal of intervention would be to maintain those low levels of negativity.

Interventionists might focus on systematically helping remarital couples develop constructive ways of handling conflict. The remarried individuals can then apply effective conflict management skills to the problems facing them. Because most current studies consistently find that remarital couples show more conflict and problem areas than do once-married couples (Booth & Edwards, 1992; Bray, 1995; Hobart, 1991), the need for intervention when couples are planning remarriage or are in the early stages of marriage is important. Clarke and Wilson (1994) note that remarriages are most at risk for divorce in the first 5 years of the relationship. To date, there has been surprisingly little attention paid to forming intervention programs for remarital couples (Bray, 1995). Our ultimate goal at the Center for Marital and Family Studies (CFMFS) is to modify PREP (Prevention and Relationship Enhancement Program) to address the specific issues and needs of remarital couples. As mentioned earlier, PREP is a research-based, skills building approach to helping couples communicate effectively. The PREP program has consistently demonstrated positive results (Markman, Renick, Floyd, Stanley, & Clements, 1993).

Directions for Future Research

First, with regard to the changes observed in negative communication for the index women, it is important to determine if the extreme changes in negative communication are ultimately constructive or destructive. To assess the eventual outcome, it is important to evaluate those who increase negativity separately from those who decrease negativity.

For those women who have increased negativity from the first marriage to the second marriage, it could be hypothesized that the increase in negativity is positive and related to remarital satisfaction later in the relationship, as suggested by Gottman & Krokoff (1989). It could also be hypothesized that this effect may be a function of this particular pattern of communication change. In other words, increases in negativity may be positive for those women who did not express disagreements enough in the first relationship.

For those women who have decreased negativity, it could be hypothesized that the decrease in negative communication is related to increased marital satisfaction as suggested by the longitudinal research of Markman, Silvern, Kraft, and Clements (1993). Again, one could hypothesize that the eventual outcome of the change is related to the particular pattern of negative communication change from the first marriage to second marriage. A decrease in negative communication for a woman who had been engaging in a lot of destruction arguing in the first relationship may be related to a positive outcome for her.

It is possible that both types of changes could have eventual positive outcomes. Given that the mean levels of negativity across marriages is the same, it is also possible that a similar level of negativity in the remarriage puts both types of relationships at risk for difficulties regardless of the changes made. Clearly, follow-up studies at the current sample are needed to adequately address these questions.

Replicating the current study with a larger, more representative sample is an important next step in this area of research. The current sample was relatively homogenous in terms of ethnicity and socioeconomic class, being primarily white middle class. The communication patterns of individuals in more diverse populations may be measurably different. The effects of culture, education, and income are expected to be important in negotiating remarital relationships.

In addition, to evaluate the development of remarital relationships as opposed to first marital relationships, it is important to include a control group that is matched to the remarried group on length of marital relationship.

Also, given that negative communication and negative escalation are related to remarital satisfaction, it is important to determine if remarried couples could benefit from communication skills training that focuses on conflict management. In fact, it is important to determine if participation by couples in primary intervention programs that focus on communication skills building has the desired effect of reducing negativity.

REFERENCES

Aquirre, B. E., & Parr, W. C. (1982). Husbands' marriage order and the stability of first and second marriages of white and black women. *Journal of Marriage and Family, 44,* 605–620.

Bergler, E. (1948). *Divorce won't help.* New York: Harper & Brothers.

Bitterman, C. M. (1968). The multimarriage family. *Social Casework, 49,* 218–221.

Bograd, R. (1992). *The relationship between self-disclosure and marital satisfaction in late-life remarriages.* Unpublished dissertation, University of Denver.

Booth, A., & Edwards, J. N. (1992). Starting over: Why remarriages are more unstable. *Journal of Family Issues, 13,* 179–194.

Boszormenyi-Nagy, I., & Spark, G. (1973). *Invisible localities: Reciprocity in intergenerational family therapy.* New York: Harper & Row.

Bowen, M. (1966). The use of family therapy in clinical practice. *Comprehensive Psychiatry, 7,* 345–374.

Bray, J. (1995). *What does family psychology have to contribute to marital and family therapy research?* Presented at the Marital and Family Therapy Outcome and Process Research State of the Science Conference, Philadelphia, PA.

Burke, B. (1993). *A naturalistic study of successful stepfamily marriages.* Unpublished dissertation, Northern Illinois University, DeKalb, IL.

Cherlin, A. (1978). Remarriage as an incomplete institution. *American Journal of Sociology, 84,* 634–650.

Clarke, S. C., & Wilson, B. F. (1994). The relative stability of remarriage. *Family Relations, 43,* 305–310.

Clements, M., & Markman, H. J. (in press). *The transition to parenthood: Is having children hazardous to marriage?* Lifetime of Relationships.

Clements, M., Stanley, S. M., & Markman, H. J. (1995). The seeds of divorce: Predicting marital failure from premarital patterns. Manuscript in preparation, University of Denver.

Clingempeel, W. G. (1981). Quasi-Kin relationships and marital quality in stepfather families. *Journal of Personality and Social Psychology, 41,* 890–901.

Clingempeel, W. G., & Brand, E. (1985). Quasi-Kin relationships, structural complexity, and marital quality in stepfamilies: A replication, extension, and clinical implications. *Family Relations, 34,* 401–409.

Clingempeel, W. G., & Brand, E. (1987). Interdependencies of marital and stepparent–stepchild relationships and children's psychological adjustment: Research findings and clinical implications. *Family Relations, 36,* 140–145.

Eckler, James D. (1993). *Step by step parenting.* Cincinnati, OH: Betterway Books.

Esses, L., & Campbell, R. (1984). Challenges of researching the remarried. *Family Relations, 33,* 415–424.

Farrell, J., & Markman, H. J. (1984). Individual and interpersonal factors in the etiology of marital distress: The example of remarital couples. In R. Gilmour & S. Duck (Eds.), *Personal relationships* (pp. 251–262). London: Academic Press.

Floyd, F., & Markman, H. J. (1981). *Inside's and outside's assessment of distressed and non-distressed marital interaction.* Paper presented at the annual meeting of the American Association for the Advancement of Behavior Therapy, Toronto, Canada.

Furstenberg, F., & Spanier, G. B. (1984). The risk of dissolution in remarriage: An examination of Cherlin's hypothesis of incomplete institutionalization. *Family Relations, 33,* 433–441.

Furstenberg, F., & Spanier, G. B. (1987). *Recycling the family remarriage after divorce.* Newbury Park, CA: Sage Publications, Inc.

Ganong, L. H., & Coleman, M. (1984). The effects of remarriage on children: A review of the empirical literature. *Family Relations, 33,* 389–405.

Glass, G., & Hopkins, K. (1984). *Statistical methods in education and psychology.* Englewood Cliffs, NJ: Prentice-Hall.

Glick, P. C. (1984). Marriage, divorce, and living arrangements: Prospective changes. *Journal of Family Issues, 5,* 7–26.

Gottman, J. M. (1979). *Empirical investigation of marriage.* New York: Academic Press.

Gottman, J. M. (1993). A theory of marital dissolution and stability. *Journal of Family Psychology, 7,* 57–75.

Gottman, J. M., & Krokoff, L. J. (1989). Marital interaction and satisfaction: A longitudinal view. *Journal of Consulting and Clinical Psychology, 57.*

Gottman, J. M., & Levinson, R. W. (1986). Assessing the role of emotion in marriage. *Behavioral Assessment, 8,* 31–48.

Gottman, J. M., Markman, H. J., & Notarius, C. I. (1977). The topography of marital conflict: A sequential analysis of verbal and nonverbal behavior. *Journal of Marriage and the Family, 39,* 461–478.

Gottman, J., Notarius, C., Gonso, J., & Markman, H. J. (1976). *A couple's guide to communication.* Champaign, IL: Research Press.

Halliday, T. C. (1980). Remarriage: The more complete institution. *American Journal of Sociology, 86,* 630–635.

Hetherington, E. M., & Martin, B. (1972). Family interaction and psychopathology in children. In H. C. Quay & J. S. Werry (Eds.), *Psychopathological disorders of childhood* (pp. 247–302). New York: John Wiley & Sons.

Hobart, C. (1991). Conflict in remarriage. *Journal of Divorce and Remarriage, 15,* 69–86.

Hops, H., Wills, T. A., Patterson, G. R., & Weiss, R. L. (1972). *Marital Interaction Coding System.* Unpublished manuscript, University of Oregon and Oregon Research Institute.

Jacob, T. (1975). Family interaction in disturbed and normal families: A methodological and substantive review. *Psychological Bulletin, 82,* 33–65.

Julien, D., Markman, H. J., & Lindahl, K. (1989). A comparison of a global and a microanalytic coding system: Implications of future trends in studying interactions. *Behavioral Assessment, 11,* 81–100.

Kalmuss, D., & Seltzer, J. A. (1986). Continuity of marital behavior in remarriage: The case of spouse abuse. *Journal of Marriage and the Family, 51,* 1053–1064.

Koren, P. E., Lahti, J. I., Sadler, C. A., & Kimboko, P. J. (1983). *The adjustment of new stepfamilies: Characteristics and trends.* Administration for Children, Youth, and Families, Office of Human Development Services, Department of Health and Human Services. Regional Research Institute, Portland, OR.

Lindahl, K., & Markman, H. J. (1990). Communication and negative affect regulation in the family. In E. Blechman (Ed.), *Emotions and families* (pp. 99–116). New York: Plenum Press.

Locke, H., & Wallace, K. (1959). Short marital adjustment and prediction tests: Their reliability and validity. *Marriage and Family Living, 21,* 251–255.

Markman, H. J. (1981). Prediction of marital distress: A five year follow-up. *Journal of Counseling and Clinical Psychology, 49,* 760–762.

Markman, H. J. (1989). *The prevention of marital distress.* Paper presented at the World Congress of Behavior Therapy, Edinburgh, Scotland.

Markman, H. J., Floyd, F., Stanley, S., & Lewis, H. (1986). Prevention. In N. Jacobson & A. Gurman (Eds.), *Clinical handbook of marital therapy* (pp. 174–194). New York: Guilford.

Markman, H. J., Floyd, F., Stanley, S., & Storaasli, R. (1988). The prevention of marital distress: A longitudinal investigation. *Journal of Consulting and Clinical Psychology, 56,* 210–217.

Markman, H. J., & Hahlweg, K. (1993). The prediction and prevention of marital distress: An international perspective. *Clinical Psychology Review, 13,* 29–43.

Markman, H. J., Renick, M. J., Floyd, F., Stanley, S., & Clements, M. (1993). Preventing marital distress through communication and conflict management training: A four and five year follow-up. *Journal of Consulting and Clinical Psychology, 61*(1), 70–77.

Markman, H. J., Silvern, L., Kraft, S., & Clements, M. (1993). Men and women dealing with conflict in heterosexual relationships. *Journal of Social Issues, 49,* 107–125.

Markman, H. J., Stanley, S., & Blumberg, S. (1994). *Fighting for your marriage: The PREP approach.* San Francisco, CA: Jossey-Bass.

McCarthy, J. F. (1978). A comparison of the probability of dissolution of first and second marriages. *Demography, 15,* 345–349.

Mills, D. (1984). A model for stepfamily development. *Family Relations, 33,* 365–372.

National Center for Health Statistics. (in press). *Vital statistics of the United States, 1988, Vol. VII, Marriage and divorce* (DHHS Pub. No. PHS 94-1103). Hyattsville, MD: Public Health Service.

Notarius, C., & Markman, H. J. (1989). Coding marital and family interaction: A sampling and discussion of current issues. *Behavior Assessment, 11,* 1–13.

Notarius, C. I., & Markman, H. J. (1993). *We can work it out: Making sense of marital conflict.* New York: Putnam.

Notarius, C. I., Markman, H. J., & Gottman, J. M. (1983). The couples interaction scoring system: Clinical issues. In E. Filsinger (Ed.), *Marital measurement sourcebook* (pp. 117–136). Beverly Hills, CA: Sage.

Papernow, P. (1984). The stepfamily cycle: An experiential model of stepfamily development. *Family Relations, 33,* 355–363.

Pasley, K., Ihinger-Tallman, M., & Coleman, C. (1984). Consensus styles among happy and unhappy remarried couples. *Family Relations, 33,* 451–457.

Schapp, C. (1984). A comparison of the interaction of distressed and nondistressed married couples in a laboratory situation: Literature survey, methodological issues and an empirical investigation. In K. Hahlweg & N. S. Jacobsen (Eds.), *Marital interaction: Analysis and modification* (pp. 133–158). New York: Guilford Press.

Smith, R. M., Goslen, M. A., Byrd, A. J., & Reece, L. (1991). Self-other orientation and sex-role orientation of men and women who remarry. *Comparison of gender differences* (pp. 3–32). New York: Haworth Press.

Stanley, S., & Markman, H. J. (1992). Assessing commitment in personal relationships. *Journal of Marriage and the Family, 54,* 595–608.

Stanley, S., Markman, H. J., St. Peters, M., & Leber, D. (1995). Strengthening marriage and preventing divorce. New direction in prevention research. *Family Relations, 44,* 392–401.

Storaasli, R. D., & Markman, H. J. (1990). Relationship problems in the early stages of marriage: A longitudinal investigation. *Journal of Family Psychology, 4*(1), 80–98.

Vemer, E., Coleman, M., Ganong, L. H., & Cooper, H. (1989). Marital satisfaction in remarriage: A meta-analysis. *Journal of Marriage and the Family, 51,* 713–725.

Visher, J. S., & Visher, E. V. (1982). Stepfamilies and stepparenting. In Froma Walsh (Ed.), *Normal family processes.* New York: Guilford Press.

Walker, Lenore (1979). *The battered women.* New York: Harper Colophon.

5

▼▼▼▼▼▼▼

The Transition to Parenthood: Marital Conflict and Withdrawal and Parent–Infant Interactions

Martha J. Cox
University of North Carolina at Chapel Hill

Blair Paley
University of California,
Los Angeles Neuropsychiatric Institute and Hospital

C. Chris Payne
University of North Carolina at Greensboro

Margaret Burchinal
University of North Carolina at Chapel Hill

MARITAL AND PARENT–CHILD INTERACTIONS

In this chapter, we explore the association between the marital relationship and each parent's relationship with the child in families. In order to investigate the interplay between these relationships within the family, we used the transition to parenthood as a beginning point to understand how marital relationships change, how parent–child relationships develop over time, and the way in which these relationships are mutually influential. Our emphasis is on the whole family, and we were interested in the role of men as well as women both as marital partners and as parents. In this chapter, we explore qualities of marital interactions and their association with parents' interactions with their infants. We are interested in couples who have difficulty resolving conflict and show either angry, negative interactions with each other or show withdrawn behavior in the context of trying to resolve a disagreement, and whether such relationships set the stage for more difficult parent–child relationships.

87

The Transition to Parenthood

For many years, we studied couples as they made the transition from a couple to "and baby makes three." The introduction of a child into a marital system has profound effects on that system, as any new parent will tell you. This period of family life has great potential for gaining insights into the mutual impact of marital relationships and other relationships in the family like the parent–child relationship. By studying couples before the birth of the child, some sense can be obtained of the marital relationship unaffected by the demands of parenting and the particular qualities of the child. By following couples longitudinally, our hope was to gain some insight into the way in which marriages were affected by the birth of the child (particularly how different marriages were affected differently) and how the marriage helped set the stage for parenting.

Early writing on the transition to parenthood was done mostly by family sociologists and focused on the "crisis" of parenthood for a young couple (i.e., Benedek, 1959; Hill, 1949; Hobbs, 1965). The debate generally centered on whether or not becoming a parent was a "crisis," whether it was instead a "normal crisis," and whether the crisis aspects had been overemphasized. Although this work focused attention on an important stage of family life, the studies involved mostly retrospective, self-reports of parents about the transition to parenthood. These methods are particularly prone to distortions of recall and the need to give socially desirable responses. Moreover, the concept of crisis is too simplistic to capture the complexity of a couple's adaptation to the addition of a child and the myriad interdependent influences between the couple relationship, parent–child relationships, and the child's development (Cox, 1985). Prospective, longitudinal studies were needed that involved observation as well as interview and self-report so that independent sources of data were available, some with the "insider" view of the couple and some with the "outsider" view of the observer. In the 1980s, my colleagues and I began an intensive study of a small sample of couples before and after the birth of a first child (see Cox, Owen, Henderson, & Margand, 1992; Cox, Owen, Lewis, & Henderson, 1989; Lewis, Owen, & Cox, 1989; Owen & Cox, 1988). This was followed by a second, larger-scale but equally intensive, study of couples in the 1990s. Data from this second study are reported here.

Insights From Family Therapy

Our interest in these issues was spurred partly by the observations of family therapists long concerned with the relationship between child disturbance, parent–child relationships, and marital problems. Therapists observed clinically that many child problems are associated with other family problems, particularly marital problems (Margolin, 1981). Even in the absence of adequate data to understand these relationships, observations such as these led therapists to switch their focus of intervention from individuals to the entire family. Framo (1965) and Haley (1967) made particularly strong statements concerning the importance of the marital relationship in the etiology of disturbances in children. Minuchin (1974) suggested that coalitions formed between parent and child in the absence of a strong marital coalition. The particularly damaging aspect of such coalitions and the breakdown of generation boundaries seems to us to be that parental behavior in parent–child interactions is likely to be in reaction to the parent's needs, not the child's needs. Thus, it seems that a lack of sensitivity to the child's needs would be seen in such family systems. However, these ideas are based primarily on clinical observation of families long after the child has manifested serious problems and less on observations in investigations of family development. We saw that there was a clear need for such investigations.

Redressing Limitations of Developmental Research

There was a peculiar division of interest among family sociologists and developmental psychologists concerning marriage and parenting (Aldous, 1977; Belsky, 1981). Family sociologists tended to focus on marriage without regard for the many relationships in the family (notably the parent–child relationship). Developmental psychologists, on the other hand, tended to focus on the child's development and parent–child relationships without an appreciation for the influence of qualities of the marital relationships. The result was, as Furstenberg (1985) noted, that the study of child development failed generally to consider how children are incorporated into marital systems, how different systems accommodate to the child, and the implications of that process for the development of the parent–child relationship. There have been recent breakdowns of this division of interest that resulted in important findings. Prominent among those projects that include a consideration of both marital and parenting process (in addition to our own work) are the projects of Cowan and Cowan (1992); Belsky (Belsky, Gilstrap, & Rovine, 1984); Conger and Elder (1994) and Katz and Gottman (Katz & Gottman, 1993; Katz, Wilson, & Gottman, this volume). These projects document the important interplay between marital and parenting processes and highlight the complexity of the mutual influence between marriage and parenting. Clearly, there is still much to know.

The Current Analyses

Over the last two decades, there has been increased interest in understanding the linkage between marital and parent–child relationships. This interest is driven in part by the early studies and insights of clinicians. However, it is driven also by the increased acceptance of systems and organizational theoretical views that stress the importance of relationships in the family for individual development as well as the interdependence of relationships within the family (e.g., Cox & Paley, 1997; Hinde & Stevenson-Hinde, 1988; Minuchin, 1988; Sameroff, 1989, Sroufe, 1989).

Numerous studies link marital disruption and problem behavior in children (for a summary see Crockenberg & Covey, 1991 or Cummings & Davies, 1994). One often stated assumption about this link is that the effect is mediated by disturbances in parent–child relationships; that is, disrupted marriages result in disrupted parenting, which leads to child problems (Crockenberg & Covey, 1991). Understanding the relation between marital and parenting processes is obviously important for intervention in families with disrupted relationships. However, we still have little specific information about the qualities of marital relationships that are important for parenting.

This was one of the major limitations of research on the link between marriage and parenting. The literature on marriage mostly involves nonspecific constructs like "marital quality" or "adjustment" (Grych & Fincham, 1990). These constructs are broad and leave us with a limited understanding of the specific marital behaviors or processes that are associated with problematic parenting or child maladjustment. In our current study, we address this limitation by investigating specific aspects of the marital relationships and parenting of couples in the transition to parenthood.

More recently, researchers moved beyond global constructs such as "marital quality" and began focusing on marital conflict and its impact on children and other family relationships (e.g., Cummings & Davies, 1994). Prominent are models that stress the "spillover" effects of marital conflict, resulting in the direct transfer of mood, affect, or behavior from one setting to another (Erel & Burman, 1995). However, Cummings and Wilson (this volume) note that if marital disagreements are resolved, then conflict may not have the same negative impact on parenting relationships and child development as conflict that is not resolved. Conditions under which marital conflict undermines parenting relationships are poorly understood. Katz, Wilson, & Gottman (this volume) note that there is no evidence that anger expression in marriage, if it is not blended with criticism, contempt, defensiveness, and withdrawal, is harmful to a marriage. In fact, they note that anger may be a necessary part of a couple living together and making the continual adjustments to keep a marriage close and intimate. Thus, anger and conflict, by themselves, may not be problematic, but other qualities of interaction often associated with conflict may be important to understand.

In this chapter, we focus specifically on conflict and withdrawal. Gottman (1994) noted that a particular sign of problematic marriages is the withdrawal of partners in interaction. He further suggested that withdrawal from marriage may be associated with withdrawal from children, especially for men.

In general, there is virtually no study of how withdrawal from the spouse influences parenting, although here we hypothesize that withdrawal may be more damaging than conflicted, but still engaged, marital behavior.

Why do we think that withdrawal may be more damaging than conflict? In agreement with Katz and her colleagues (this volume), we suggest that some conflict is a normal part of marriages. Some conflict may be necessary for couples to effect the repairs in marriages that allow individuals to continue to support each other in a close, intimate relationship. Withdrawal, however, may signal that the couple is unable to effect repairs in their marriage and that positive support for each other is not as likely. When conflicts are resolved, one would expect that the negative affect of the partners that may spill over into other family relationships might also be resolved. Withdrawal, however, may signal that there is not a resolution and that resolutions are precluded by the withdrawn behavior. Thus, the more negative affect that the marriage generates may not be resolved in couples who are withdrawn from each other and may be more likely to negatively influence interactions with children.

The way in which marital processes influence parenting may vary depending on the developmental stage of the child. Here we are concerned with the parenting of infants. Infancy may be a period when support from the spouse is particularly important to the quality of parenting, because it is a time of high demand and of transition (Goldberg & Easterbrook, 1984). The demands of caring for an infant who can do little for himself or herself are great; at the same time, variations in quality of care appear to have significant implications for later competence in the child. Research on attachment suggested that variation in regulation of the infant by caregivers results in variation in later social competence during the preschool and early school years (Sroufe, 1983). The role of the caregiver in soothing distress, enhancing alertness, and allowing the child the experience of self-regulation (by sensitively responding to the child's signals of need for soothing or increased stimulation) is critical to the development of infant adaptive self-organization (Sameroff, 1989; Tronick, 1989). We know little about what factors might support or contribute to a parent's ability to provide sensitive and responsive care of their infant. Several researchers (e.g., Belsky, Rovine, & Fish, 1989; Cox et al., 1989; Emery, 1982; Goldberg & Easterbrook, 1984) suggested that one key factor may be the marital relationship.

In the present study, we hypothesize that marital withdrawal, more than marital conflict, will be associated with less sensitive and responsive parenting behavior. As noted earlier, we think that the foreclosure of resolution of anger and conflict associated with withdrawal, in contrast to engaged conflict, will lead to more spillover of negative emotion into the parent–child relationship and will be associated with less support from the spouse for parenting.

Gottman (1994) suggested that withdrawal in marriage may lead to withdrawal of fathers from their children, but not withdrawal of mothers. Other research also suggests that the parenting of fathers is more influenced by the qualities of the marriage than is the parenting of mothers (Belsky, 1979; Gamble & Belsky, 1982; Goldberg & Easterbrook, 1984). This question of differential influence on mothers and fathers is unresolved by current research. In contrast to Gottman, we consider it likely that marital withdrawal may be more detrimental to the mother's parenting than to the father's during the infancy period or may at least influence their parenting differently. In the early months of life, there is evidence that it is the mother who more often soothes distress and responds to the infant's need for caregiver intervention to maintain self-regulation (Belsky et al., 1984; Lamb, 1981; Lamb & Elster, 1985; Yogman, 1982). We suspect that supportive marital processes may be particularly important for mothers during this demanding early parenting period, although at later developmental periods it may be that the father's parenting is influenced more by the marital relationship.

It is important that research on the link between marital processes and parenting consider factors that may provide alternative explanations for the relation between the two. For example, marital difficulties and depressive symptoms in parents are highly correlated (see Barnett & Gotlib, 1988; Beach, Sandeen, & O'Leary, 1990), and there is a broad literature on the impact of depression on parenting as well (see Cummings & Davies, 1994). Thus, the linkage between marital and parenting processes may be artifactual, wherein both discordant or withdrawn marriages and insensitive parenting may be accounted for by depressive symptoms in one or both spouses. Research is needed that examines whether parental depression may play a role in the relation between marital and parenting processes. That is, does the presence of depressive symptoms in the parent contribute independently of marital processes to parenting? Or perhaps depressive symptoms mediate the effects of marital processes (i.e., problematic marital processes lead to depressive symptoms in the spouse, and those depressive symptoms lead to insensitive, unresponsive parenting). Alternatively, depressive symptoms may moderate the impact of the marital process on parenting (problematic marital processes have a greater impact on the parenting skills of those parents who are experiencing depressive symptoms).

A further limitation of the work on marital processes and parenting is that much of the work done involves clinical samples and children at latency age. Longitudinal work is needed at earlier ages with community samples in which marital and parenting processes can be investigated prior to the child developing behavior problems to understand better the processes involved.

Another important consideration is that of the gender of the child. Boys develop behavior problems more often than do girls (Asher & Coie, 1990), and we know little about why. Are boys more vulnerable to adverse family circumstances, or are they treated differently when family circumstances are adverse? There has been little attempt to examine child gender in relation to parental conflict and parent–child relationships, especially during infancy.

In the current study, 136 young couples were followed longitudinally across the transition to parenthood with information about marital processes first obtained prior to the birth of the child, which allows for some inference about the direction of effects when looking at marriage and parenting. Couples were observed in marital interaction at the prenatal period and at 3 and 12 months. We were interested in marital conflict and withdrawal and its effect on parenting, specifically whether parents showed sensitive and involved responding to their infants at 3 and 12 months. In these analyses, we controlled for (a) the education of the parent (as a broad demographic control); (b) depressive symptoms and hostility of the parent, because these variables could be related to both marital processes and parenting processes and could account for the relation between them (both depressive symptoms and hostility were used because of the suggestion that depression measures don't capture negative affectivity for fathers); and (c) the negativity of the infant in the same interaction, because parents react to the child's behavior and we wished to understand parental behavior after child negativity was controlled. In this way, we hoped to get a sense of whether marital factors influenced parenting when we controlled for other factors that might account for this relation. Finally, we examined whether different patterns of association would be observed for boys and girls.

METHODS EMPLOYED IN THE CURRENT STUDY

Description of Research Subjects

Table 5.1 shows the characteristics of the sample.

The 136 families in this study were recruited from prenatal classes in a four-county, predominantly White, rural, mountainous area of western North Carolina. As can be seen in Table 5.1, the sample included a wide socioeconomic range of couples. This marriage was a first marriage for 88% of the men and 85% of the women. None of the husbands or wives had any other children except the child that they were expecting (this was a criterion for inclusion). Of the fathers at the prenatal visit, 71% said that the pregnancy was planned, while 64% of the mothers said the pregnancy was planned. Because the numbers of African American families are low in this mountainous, rural area of North Carolina (less than 10%), African American families constitute a small part of the sample (about 3%, which is close to the percentage of married couples having a first child who are African American in this area). Likewise, there are very few other minorities in this area. However, low education families are well represented in this sample.

TABLE 5.1
Sample Description

136 FAMILIES: 73 WITH A FEMALE CHILD; 63 WITH A MALE CHILD AT PRENATAL VISIT:		
	AVERAGE	*RANGE*
AGE OF FATHERS	28.3	19–41
AGE OF MOTHERS	27.2	18–35
SES (HOLLINGSHEAD)	44	24–63
YRS. ED. FATHERS	13.9	9–22
YRS. ED. MOTHERS	13.8	8–18
YRS. MARRIAGE	3.42	.5–17
INCOME (PER MONTH)	$2,450	$652–$5,002

Because rural families are vastly understudied, we consider this an important sample of families to study.

Of the 136 families in the study, 73 families had a female first-born child and 63 had a male first-born child. These children are the subject children. The births of the children in the study were concentrated in the period from March 1990 to August 1991 with fairly equal distribution through that period.

Procedures Used in the Study

Couples were seen during the 6th to 8th month of the prenatal period, before the birth of their first child. Spouses were interviewed and administered questionnaires separately, and then were videotaped together in a 10- to 15-minute marital interactions task, in which they were asked to discuss and attempt to resolve an issue that was a current source of disagreement in their relationship. This procedure was repeated at 3, 12, and 24 months. At 3 and 12 months after the birth, the couples also were videotaped individually interacting with their infant in a free-play situation.

Measures Used in the Study

Several measures collected from the couples were used in the current analyses. These are described in Table 5.2.

RESULTS OBTAINED

Logic of the Analyses

The logic of the analyses was as follows: Predictors were entered into the equation in steps. First, the education of the parent was entered as a broad, demographic control. Then the observed negative mood of the child in the

TABLE 5.2
Relevant Study Measures

---

1. Child Temperament: Early Infancy Temperament Questionnaire (Adaptability, Mood and Intensity Subscales; Medoff-Cooper, Carey, & McDevitt, 1993). These three subscales were highly intercorrelated, so they were combined for one index (both fathers and mothers completed). This questionnaire was collected at 3 and 12 months. This measure was removed from the hierarchical regression models because it never accounted for any variation. The observed negativity of the child in the observation was used as a control for child behavior instead.

2. Mother's and Father's depressive symptoms (CES–D, Radloff, 1977). This questionnaire was collected at prenatal, 3, 12, and 24 months. For the prediction of 3-month parenting, prenatal scores were used, for prediction of 12-month parenting, the mean of the prenatal and 3-month scores were used.

3. Neo-Personality Inventory: (Costa & McCrae, 1985). Hostility subscale of the Neuroticism Component. This subscale questionnaire was collected at the prenatal period.

4. Marital conflict and withdrawal. The couple was observed prenatally on a problem-solving task (discuss the major source of disagreement and try to reach some resolution). Global ratings using the Interactional Dimensions Coding System (Julien, Markman, Lindahl, & Johnson, 1987) were made later by independent coders from videotape. As an index of **conflict**, we used the ratings for conflict (level of tension and overt hostility), which uses both affect and content cues, plus the rating of negative affect, which uses face, voice, and body cues (i.e., cold, angry, furious, depressed, irritated, frown, sneer, mocking, etc.) for both husband and wives during the interaction. As an index of marital **withdrawal**, behaviors observed included: avoids eye contact while listening or speaking, body turned away from partner, increases/maintains physical distance, puts a physical barrier between, fidgeting, gives up discussion, clams up, low communication assertiveness, is unresponsive, rarely adds new information, low self-disclosure. Again, a separate score was derived for husband and wife.

For prediction of 3-month parenting, prenatal marital scores were used, for prediction of 12-month parenting, the mean of the prenatal and 3-month scores was used.

5. Parent–child interaction (3 months and 12 months; Cox, 1992). Each parent and the child were observed in 15-minute, videotaped, free-play interactions. The interactions were coded globally on 7-point scales from videotape. Based on factor analyses, sensitivity, detachment, stimulation, warmth, flat affect, and reciprocal play were combined in the current analysis as an index of parent behavior at 3 months. Thus, this variable reflected **positive, sensitive, responsive, engaged interaction**. At 12 months, the composite was the same except that the dyadic variable, reciprocal play, was replaced by a more age-appropriate dyadic variable, dyadic mutuality. At each time period, child negative affect was coded globally on a 7-point scale.

---

parent–child observation was entered as a conservative control for child behavior in the situation. Next, the depressive symptoms of the parent and the parent's score on the NEO–PI hostility subscale were entered to control for the parent's affective symptoms. Then the parent's negative, conflictual behavior in marital interaction was entered, followed by his or her score on withdrawal behavior. An interaction between the two was tested. Finally, gender interactions for all predictors were tested. The results of the hierarchical multiple regression can be seen in Tables 5.3 and 5.4. In follow-up analyses, depressive symptoms as moderators of marital processes were tested by entering depressive symptom by marital variable interactions. Tests for depressive symptoms as a mediator of marital variables were undertaken in

TABLE 5.3
Predicting Mother's Sensitive, Warm, Involved Interaction

SET		3 Months	12 Months
STEP 1: DEMOGRAPHIC	ΔR^2	.00	.04*
Education of mother (prenatal)	β	−.01	.20
STEP 2: CHILD CHARACTERISTICS	ΔR^2	.15***	.14***
Negative mood of child in interaction: 3 months	β	−.39	−.18
Negative mood of child in interaction: 12 months	β	—	−.35
STEP 3: SYMPTOMS/ADJ	ΔR^2	.01	.04†
Mother's symptoms of depression	β	−.06	−.16
Mother's hostility (prenatal)	β	−.04	−.15
STEP 4: MARITAL CONFLICT	ΔR^2	.01	.01
Mother's observed conflict plus negative affect	β	−.13	−.12
STEP 5: MARITAL WITHDRAWAL	ΔR^2	.21***	.03*
Mother's observed withdrawal from spouse	β	−.46	−.20
STEP 6: BY CHILD GENDER INTERACTIONS	ΔR^2	.10**	.08*
Sex of child			
Mother's education by sex			
3-month child negative mood by sex		***	
12-month child negative mood by sex		*	
Mother's depressive symptoms by sex			*
Mother's hostility by sex			
Mother's marital conflict by sex			
Mother's marital withdrawal by sex			
TOTAL MODEL R^2		.48***	.34***

Note: ΔR^2 = Increased R^2 at that step; β is standardized beta at point of entry; * denotes significance: $^{\dagger}p < .10$ *$p < .05$ **$p < .01$ ***$p < .001$; for 3-month parenting, prenatal predictor variables were used; for 12-month parenting, an average of prenatal and 3-month predictors was used unless otherwise noted.

regression analyses in which depressive symptoms were entered after marital variables.

Findings for Mothers

The hierarchical multiple regression findings for prediction of 3- and 12-month maternal behavior can be seen in Table 5.3.

In the prediction of 3-month interactions between mother and child, the child's negative mood during the parent–child interaction, the extent of the mother's withdrawal in earlier marital interaction, and a child negativity by child gender interaction were strong, unique predictors of the mother's sensitive and responsive parenting. That is, mothers who were more withdrawn from their husbands during the prenatal marital interaction were less sensitive and responsive to their children than were wives who were less

TABLE 5.4
Predicting Father's 3-Month Sensitive, Warm, Involved Interaction

SET		3 Months	12 Months
STEP 1: DEMOGRAPHIC	ΔR^2	.04*	.03*
Education of father (prenatal)	β	.19	.17
STEP 2: CHILD CHARACTERISTICS	ΔR^2	.11***	.10***
Negative mood of child in interaction: 3 months	β	−.34	−.18
Negative mood of child in interaction: 12 months	β	—	−.28
STEP 3: SYMPTOMS/ADJ	ΔR^2	.05*	.05*
Father's symptoms of depression	β	−.10	−.06
Father's hostility (prenatal)*	β	−.17	−.22
STEP 4: MARITAL CONFLICT	ΔR^2	.03*	.01
Father's observed conflict plus negative affect	β	−.16	−.10
STEP 5: MARITAL WITHDRAWAL	ΔR^2	.03*	.03*
Father's observed withdrawal from spouse	β	−.20	−.21
STEP 6: FATHER'S MARITAL CONFLICT BY MARITAL WITHDRAWAL	ΔR^2	.02†	.03*
NO SIGNIFICANT BY GENDER INTERACTIONS			
TOTAL MODEL R^2		.28***	.25***

Note: ΔR^2 = Increased R^2 at that step; β is standardized beta at point of entry; * denotes significance: $^\dagger p < .10$ $*p < .05$ $**p < .01$ $***p < .001$; for 3-month parenting, prenatal predictor variables were used; for 12-month parenting, an average of prenatal and 3-month predictors was used unless otherwise noted.

withdrawn in marital interaction. The addition of the withdrawal variable in the equation increased the prediction of parenting by an R^2 of .21, even after controlling for maternal education, child negativity, depressive symptoms, and marital conflict. Notably, mothers who had shown more conflictual, negative behavior during prenatal marital interactions did not show any less sensitive or responsive parenting than did mothers who had not exhibited negative, conflict behavior toward their husbands during the prenatal period. The child negativity by child gender interaction indicated that the child's negativity was only a significant predictor of less sensitive and responsive parent behavior for mothers interacting with sons.

At 12 months, earlier marital withdrawal again is a significant, albeit smaller, predictor of less sensitive and responsive parenting by mothers, whereas earlier marital conflict again is not a significant predictor. Maternal education also was a significant predictor, wherein more highly educated mothers were more sensitive and responsive when interacting with their children. Child negativity by child gender interactions and depressive symptoms by child gender interactions indicated that child's negativity and mother's earlier depressive symptoms also were predictive of mothers' less sensitive and responsive parenting, but only for the mothers interacting with sons.

Analysis of interactions between depressive symptoms and marital variables provided no support for the hypothesis that level of depressive symptoms moderates the impact of marital variables. Likewise, there was no support for the hypothesis that depressive symptoms mediate the effect of marital processes on parenting. Depressive symptoms appeared to be a predictor independent of marital processes.

Findings for Fathers

The hierarchical multiple regression findings for prediction of 3- and 12-month paternal behavior can be seen in Table 5.4.

For fathers, as for mothers, higher marital withdrawal at earlier time periods was a significant predictor of less sensitive and responsive interactions with their infants at both 3 and 12 months. However, at 3 months, marital conflict also was a significant predictor and the interaction between the marital conflict and withdrawal was nearly significant. At 12 months, the interaction between the conflict and withdrawal reached significance, so that it was the fathers who showed both withdrawal and angry, conflict behavior who were the least sensitive with their infants. Again, this is with a number of variables controlled, many of which were significant predictors of the father's sensitive responsiveness with his infant at both 3 and 12 months. These included education of father (fathers who were more highly educated were more sensitive), negative mood of child (when the child was more negative in the interaction, the father was less sensitive), and father's hostility (fathers who scored higher on the hostility subscale prenatally were less sensitive with their infants at both 3 and 12 months). There were no significant by-child gender interactions for fathers.

As with mothers, for fathers, the analysis of interactions between depressive symptoms and marital variables provided no support for the hypothesis that depressive symptoms moderate the impact of marital variables. Likewise, there was no support for the hypothesis that depressive symptoms mediate the effect of marital processes on parenting.

Discussion of Results

In these analyses, we wished to consider the longitudinal association between conflict and withdrawal in marriage and the presence of sensitive, responsive parenting behavior toward the infant. We found that whereas earlier marital conflict was not consistently associated with less sensitive, responsive behavior, earlier marital withdrawal was a consistently significant predictor of such parenting, even after accounting for the contribution of parental education, parental depressive symptoms, and the child's negativity. When parents had shown withdrawal in interaction with their spouses at earlier time periods (prenatally for the 3-month prediction and a mean of prenatal and 3 months for the 12-month prediction), both husband and wife were consistently less sensitive and responsive with their infants in interaction. The effect was particularly strong for mothers at 3 months, but was significant every time it was tested for mothers or fathers. For fathers, there was evidence at 12 months of an interaction between conflict and withdrawal, such that fathers were less sensitive and responsive to the infant when they showed *both* conflict and withdrawal in marital interaction. These findings fit with findings from Katz, Wilson, & Gottman (this volume), who report that there is no evidence that anger is problematic in a marriage when it is not blended with criticism, defensiveness, contempt, or withdrawal. Here we see that, for men, it is the combination of angry, conflict behavior with withdrawal that is predictive of less sensitive and responsive parenting. For women, it is simply marital withdrawal that is predictive of less sensitive and responsive parenting.[1]

For mothers, but not fathers, there were by-child gender interactions. At 3 months and 12 months, mothers were less sensitive and responsive with infants who showed more negative affect in the interaction, but this was only true for the mothers of boys, not for the mothers of girls. At 12 months, mothers with higher levels of depressive symptoms were less sensitive and responsive to their infants, but again this was only true for mothers of boys, not for mothers of girls.

These findings that negative affect in the child during parent–child interaction or in the mother in terms of depressive symptoms are associated with less sensitive and responsive behaviors in the mother with boys, but not with girls, is intriguing. One hypothesis in the literature concerning why boys show more behavior problems than girls is that boys may be more vulnerable to negative family circumstances. These findings suggest that boys may not be (or may not just be) more vulnerable to negative family circumstances, but rather that when mothers have depressive symptoms or infants are more negative, mothers are more negatively reactive to boys than to girls even at this young age. The findings for depression are consistent with findings by Hinde and Stevenson-Hinde (1987) with older children (50 months). In the work by Hinde and Stevenson-Hinde, mothers who scored high on depression were less friendly and solicitous with boys, but not with girls. Additionally, Hinde and Stevenson-Hinde found some interactions between child gender and child characteristics in predicting parent–child interaction, but for child shyness, not for child negativity, as is reported here. In their study, at 50

---

[1]It is interesting to note that fathers seem more likely to show both withdrawal and angry, conflicted behavior in the same interaction than mothers. The correlation between withdrawn behavior and angry, conflicted behavior for fathers for the prenatal predictor and the prental + 3 month predictor were .54 and .43, respectively. The corresponding correlations for mothers were .23 and .24. Thus, it appears that the withdrawn men are likely to alternate between withdrawn behavior and angry, conflicted behavior in the same interaction, whereas women are more likely to show one or the other pattern.

months, shy daughters tended to have warmer relationships with their mothers than did nonshy daughters, but the opposite was true for boys. It should be noted that in the current study, the mean level of negative affect in interaction of the group of boys when compared with the group of girls was not significantly different at either 3 or 12 months. As a group, the female infants showed just as much negative affect in the interactions as the male infants. This finding is consistent with findings that gender differences in temperament or negativity are generally not found in young children, but gender differences in the relation between individual characteristics and mother–child interaction are more common (Hinde & Stevenson-Hinde, 1987). These findings emphasize, as Hinde and Stevenson-Hinde noted, the importance of examining gender differences not merely in terms of means or frequencies, but in terms of different associations between variables for boys and girls.

Findings from the present study suggest that marital withdrawal may particularly undermine parenting processes that are important for supporting children's early emotional development. The effects of marital withdrawal can be seen for both men's and women's parenting and are more predictive than marital conflict. That is, there appears to be more "spillover" from the marital relationships to the parenting relationship when couples are withdrawn from each other than when they are just conflicted. For fathers, when they are both withdrawn *and* they are exhibiting conflictual and negative behavior toward their wives, their parenting appears to be especially compromised.

These analyses illustrate the importance of looking at specific qualities of marriages to understand how marital processes are associated with parenting processes. Global studies of marital "quality" or "disruption" fail to provide explicit information about this association, yet more explicit information is needed to inform intervention efforts. These findings support contentions by others that marital conflict may not always be problematic (Cummings et al., this volume) and that anger in marital relationships alone may not be destructive if not paired with withdrawal (Katz et al., this volume).

This study illustrates the importance of looking at specific behaviors and emotions in marital interaction. Ideally, studies of marriage and parenting should separate the specific emotions that Gottman and his colleagues note are important in marital processes (Gottman, 1994; Katz et al., this volume). Studies in which anger, contempt, criticism, defensiveness, and withdrawal are all coded separately are needed to illuminate even more specifically what marital behaviors are associated with problematic parenting. The current chapter makes an important contribution in illuminating the role of withdrawal as distinct from conflict. However, the question of whether anger can be constructive in a family when it is not associated with criticism, defensiveness, and contempt is still unresolved.

The current analyses are focused on a particular set of processes (the association between marital and parenting interactions) and a particular developmental period (infancy). As such, they are relevant to the issue of indirect influences on very young children of marriage as mediated by parenting, but only look at the marriage–parenting link. Marital anger, even when not paired with withdrawal or other qualities, may have direct effects on children. Emery, Fincham, and Cummings (1992) highlighted the importance of considering the direct impact of marital conflict on children. Especially when children are older, parents likely serve as models of adult relationships, and, in particular, of male–female relationships for their children, providing them with examples of how emotions are communicated and how problems are resolved between adults (Minuchin, 1988). Cummings and O'Reilly (in press) note that "There is considerable evidence that adults' conflicts can have direct 'exposure effects' on children's emotionality, physiological functioning, and social behavior" (p. 13). With an earlier longitudinal sample, Owen and Cox (1997) found that marital conflict was directly associated with disorganization of attachment in the infant. The work by Cummings et al. (this volume) speaks more specifically to this issue of when and under what circumstances marital conflict has direct effects on children. Thus, it is important to look beyond indirect effects of marital conflict on children (through parenting) and consider direct effects. Although we find here that marital withdrawal is associated with less sensitive parenting more strongly than is marital conflict, it may be that the direct effects of marital conflict on children are stronger than the direct effects of marital withdrawal. Such a hypothesis may be reasonable, in that one might expect that the display of anger is frightening to children, especially very young children. However, it is also very likely that children even at older preschool ages understand the meaning of marital withdrawal, and in considering the "security hypothesis" of Cummings and his colleagues (this volume), children may consider marital withdrawal as much of a threat to their security as marital conflict.

The findings with regard to depressive symptoms were surprisingly weak given the wealth of studies that indicate that depression is associated with less sensitive parenting. It should be noted that here we were considering self-reported depressive symptoms, not clinical depression, among a community sample, not a clinical sample. It may be that we simply do not have the range of problems with depression represented in this sample where one would find strong relations between depression and parenting. It also may be that depressive symptoms have a greater impact on some aspects of parenting than on others. Affect with the child may be influenced more by depressive symptoms than is a parent's ability to read and respond to the baby's cues. The composite variable used in this study included both sensitivity to cues and warm and flat affect. In fact, when we looked at individual correlations of depressive symptoms and each of these parenting variables, depressive symptoms were most highly associated with flat affect with the baby for mothers. Thus, it may be important in considering the impact of depression on parenting to separate affect with the infant from sensitive responding to cues.

In these analyses, we did not look at child adjustment as an outcome, but rather focused on the link between marriage and parenting. Future analyses will test models of the association between marital withdrawal and child adjustment as mediated by parent–child interactions. The analyses reported here support the importance of looking at specific marital processes such as marital withdrawal as they influence parenting and child adjustment.

ACKNOWLEDGMENTS

This research was supported by a grant from the National Institute of Mental Health (R01MH44763) to Martha Cox. Partial support for preparation of this chapter for Martha Cox was provided by Department of Education Grant R307A60004 (for the National Center for Early Development and Learning) and by the National Institute of Mental Health Grant P50MH52429 (for the Center for Developmental Science Research). Partial support for the preparation of this chapter for Blair Paley was provided by NIMH Grant MH19734 (Multisite Research Training in Family Risk and Resilience).

REFERENCES

Aldous, J. (1977). Family interaction patterns. *Annual Review of Sociology, 3*, 105–135.
Asher, S. R., & Coie, J. D. (1990). *Peer rejection in childhood.* Cambridge, England: Cambridge University Press.
Barnett, P. A., & Gotlib, I. H. (1988). Psychosocial functioning and depression: Distinguishing among antecedents, concomitants, and consequences. *Psychological Bulletin, 104,* 97–126.
Beach, S. R., Sandeen, E. E., & O'Leary, K. D. (1990). *Depression in marriage.* New York: Guilford Press.
Belsky, J. (1979). The interrelation of parental and spousal behavior during infancy in traditional nuclear families: An exploratory analysis. *Journal of Marriage and the Family, 41,* 749–755.
Belsky, J. (1981). Early human experience: A family perspective. *Developmental Psychology, 17,* 3–23.
Belsky, J., Gilstrap, B., & Rovine, M. (1984). The Pennsylvania Infant and Family Development Project I: Stability and change in mother–infant and father–infant interaction in a family setting at one, three, and nine months. *Child Development, 55,* 692–705.
Belsky, J., Rovine, M., & Fish, M. (1989). The developing family system. In M. Gunnar & E. Thelen (Eds.), *Systems and development* (pp. 119–166). Hillsdale, NJ: Lawrence Erlbaum Associates.
Benedek, T. (1959). Parenthood as a developmental phase. *Journal of the American Psychoanalytic Association, 7,* 389–417.

Conger, R. D., & Elder, G. H. (1994). *Families in troubled times: Adapting to changes in rural America.* New York: Aldine de Gruyter.

Costa, P. T., & McCrae, R. R. (1985). *The NEO Personality Inventory Manual.* Odessa, FL: Psychological Assessment Resources.

Cowan, C. P., & Cowan, P. A. (1992). *When partners become parents: The big life changes for couples.* New York: Basic.

Cox, M. J. (1985). Progress and continued challenges in understanding the transition to parenthood. *Journal of Family Issues, 6,* 395–408.

Cox, M. J. (1992). Qualitative ratings for Parent–Child Interaction. (Available from author at Frank Porter Graham Child Development Center, University of North Carolina at Chapel Hill, CB #8180, Chapel Hill, NC 27599).

Cox, M. J., Owen, M. T., Henderson, V. K., & Margand, N. A. (1992). Antecedents of infant–father and infant–mother attachment. *Developmental Psychology, 28*(3), 474–483.

Cox, M. J., Owen, M. T., Lewis, J. M., & Henderson, V. K. (1989). Marriage, adult adjustment, and early parenting. *Child Development, 60,* 1015–1024.

Cox, M. J., & Paley, B. (1997). Families as systems. *Annual Review of Psychology, 48,* 243–267.

Crockenberg, S., & Covey, S. L. (1991). Marital conflict and externalizing behavior in children. In D. Cicchetti & S. L. Toth (Eds.), *Rochester symposium on developmental psychopathology: Models and integrations* (Vol. 3, pp. 235–260). Rochester, NY: University of Rochester Press.

Cummings, M. E., & Davies, P. (1994). *Children and marital conflict: The impact of family dispute and resolution.* New York: Guilford.

Cummings, M. E., & O'Reilly, A. W. (in press). Fathers in family context: Effects of marital quality on child adjustment. In M. E. Lamb (Ed.), *The role of the father in child development* (3rd ed.). New York: Wiley.

Emery, R. E. (1982). Interparental conflict and the children of discord and divorce. *Psychological Bulletin, 92,* 310–330.

Emery, R. E., Fincham, F. D., & Cummings, E. M. (1992). Parenting in context: Systemic thinking about parental conflict and its influence on children. *Journal of Consulting and Clinical Psychology, 60,* 909–912.

Erel, O., & Burman, B. (1995). Interrelatedness of marital relations and parent-child relations: A meta-analytic review. *Psychological Bulletin, 118*(1), 108–132.

Framo, J. L. (1965). Personal reflections of a family therapist. *Journal of Marriage and Family Counseling, 1,* 15–18.

Furstenberg, F. F. (1985). Sociological ventures in child development. *Child Development, 56,* 281–288.

Gamble, W. C., & Belsky, J. (1982, May). *The determinants of parenting within a family context: A preliminary analysis.* Paper presented at the Third International Conference on Infant Studies, Austin, TX.

Goldberg, W. A., & Easterbrook, M. A. (1984). The role of marital quality in toddler development. *Developmental Psychology, 20,* 504–514.

Gottman, J. M. (1994). *What predicts divorce: The relationship between marital processes and marital outcomes.* Hillsdale, NJ: Lawrence Erlbaum Associates.

Grych, J. H., & Fincham, F. D. (1990). Marital conflict and children's adjustment: A cognitive–contextual framework. *Psychological Bulletin, 108,* 267–290.

Haley, J. (1967). Experiments with abnormal families. *Archives of General Psychiatry, 17,* 53–63.

Hill, R. (1949). *Families under stress.* New York: Harper.

Hinde, R. A., & Stevenson-Hinde, J. (1987). Implications of a relationship approach for the study of gender differences. *Infant Mental Health Journal, 8,* 221–236.

Hinde, R. A., & Stevenson-Hinde, J. (Eds.). (1988). *Relationships within families: Mutual influences.* Oxford: Clarendon Press.

Hobbs, D. F. (1965). Parenthood as crisis: A third study. *Journal of Marriage and the Family, 27,* 367–372.

Julien, D., Markman, H., Lindahl, K., Johnson, H. M., & Van Widenfelt, B. T. (1987, October). *Interactional dimensions coding systems: Coders manual.* (Available from Howard Markman, Department of Psychology, University of Denver, Denver, CO).

Katz, L. F., & Gottman, J. M. (1993). Patterns of marital conflict predict children's internalizing and externalizing behaviors. *Developmental Psychology, 29,* 940–950.

Lamb, M. E. (1981). The development of father–infant relationships. In M. E. Lamb (Ed.), *The role of the father in child development* (pp. 459–488). New York: Wiley.

Lamb, M. E., & Elster, A. B. (1985). Adolescent mother–infant–father relationships. *Developmental Psychology, 21,* 768–773.

Lewis, J. M., Owen, M. T., & Cox, M. J. (1989). Incorporation of the child into the family. In J. M. Lewis, *The birth of the family* (pp. 76–88). New York: Bruner/Mazel.

Margolin, G. (1981). The reciprocal relationship between marital and child problems. In J. P. Vincent (Ed.), *Advances in intervention, assessment, and theory* (Vol. 2, pp. 131–182). Greenwich, CT: JAI Press.

Medoff-Cooper, B., Carey, W. B., & McDevitt, S. C. (1993). Early Infancy Temperament Questionnaire. *Journal of Developmental and Behavioral Pediatrics, 14,* 230–235.

Minuchin, P. (1988). Relationships within the family: A systems perspective on development. In R. A. Hinde & J. Stevenson-Hinde (Eds.), *Relationships within families: Mutual influences* (pp. 7–26). Oxford: Clarendon Press.

Minuchin, S. (1974). *Families and family therapy.* Cambridge: Harvard University Press.

Owen, M. T., & Cox, M. J. (1988). Maternal employment and the transition to parenthood: Family functioning and child development. In A. E. Gottfried & A. W. Gottfried (Eds.), *Maternal employment and children's development: Longitudinal research* (pp. 85–119). New York: Plenum Press.

Owen, M. T., & Cox, M. J. (1997). Marital conflict and the development of infant-parent attachment relationships. *Journal of Family Psychology, 11,* 152–164.

Radloff, L. (1977). The CES–D scale: A self-report depression scale for research in the general population. *Applied Psychological Measurement, 1,* 385–410.

Sameroff, A. J. (1989). Principles of development and psychopathology. In A. J. Sameroff & R. N. Emde (Eds.), *Relationship disturbances in early childhood* (pp. 17–32). New York: Basic Books.

Sroufe, L. A. (1983). Infant–caregiver attachment and patterns of adaptation in the preschool: The roots of maladaptation and competence. In M. Perlmutter (Ed.), *Minnesota symposia on child psychology* (Vol. 16, pp. 41–81). Hillsdale, NJ: Lawrence Erlbaum Associates.

Sroufe, L. A. (1989). Relationships and relationship disturbances. In A. J. Sameroff & R. N. Emde (Eds.), *Relationships disturbances in early childhood: A developmental approach* (pp. 97–124), New York: Basic.

Tronick, E. Z. (1989). Emotions and emotional communication in infants. *American Psychologist, 44,* 112–119.

Yogman, M. W. (1982). Development of the father–infant relationship. In H. Fitzgerald, B. Lester, & M. W. Yogman (Eds.), *Theory and research in behavioral pediatrics* (Vol. 1, pp. 221–229). New York: Plenum.

6

▼▼▼▼▼▼▼

Contexts of Marital Conflict and Children's Emotional Security: Exploring the Distinction Between Constructive and Destructive Conflict From the Children's Perspective

E. Mark Cummings
Notre Dame University

Amy Wilson
West Virginia University

Links have long been reported between marital discord and children's adjustment problems (e.g., Baruch & Wilcox, 1944; Hubbard & Adams, 1936; Towle, 1931), with children from high conflict homes more vulnerable to both externalizing and internalizing disorders (Emery, 1982; Fincham & Osborne, 1993; Grych & Fincham, 1990; Katz & Gottman, 1993). Increased risk is due to the "direct effects" of repeated exposure to interspousal and familial negativity and conflict (Cummings & Davies, 1994; Davies & Cummings, 1994; Emery, Fincham, & Cummings, 1992), and "indirect effects" of diminished parenting induced by marital discord (Cox & Owen, 1993; Cox, Owen, Lewis, & Henderson, 1989; Cummings & O'Reilly, 1997; Katz & Gottman, 1995a). Marital conflict is also linked to children's increased vulnerability to adjustment problems in families experiencing divorce (Amato & Keith, 1991; Amato, Loomis, & Booth, 1995; Booth & Amato, 1994), parental depression (Downey & Coyne, 1990), and sexual or physical abuse (Browne & Finkelhor, 1986; Jouriles, Barling, & O'Leary, 1987).

However, the effects of marital conflict on children and families may be overpathologized. Conflict is inevitable in relationships, and it is not necessarily a negative event for children to observe, particularly when conflicts are resolved (Cummings, Ballard, El-Sheikh, & Lake, 1991) or are otherwise expressed constructively (Easterbrooks, Cummings, & Emde, 1994). Conflict can be necessary, even beneficial, for the optimal functioning of relationships under certain circumstances. For example, conflict can be a vehicle for working out differences that would otherwise foster resentment, anger, or negative emotionality or withdrawal between the spouses (Gottman, 1994; Gottman & Krokoff, 1989; Notarius & Markman, 1993). Constructive conflict can also teach the children invaluable lessons about appropriate versus inappropriate ways to handle interpersonal differences with friends, peers, and loved ones (Beach & Cummings, 1996).

Thus, although the focus was on marital conflict as family dysfunction, marital conflict may serve useful functions for families. Moreover, some contexts of marital problem solving may even act as a protective factor and a source of resilience for children when effective interpersonal coping skills are modelled. Accordingly, an important question is to distinguish which types of marital conflict are constructive and which are destructive, from the children's perspective. This topic is significant to a theoretical understanding of relations between family functioning and child development, and to practitioners and others concerned with improving family functioning for the sake of the children (Cummings & Davies, 1994).

A broad range of contextual factors, including individual (e.g., children's temperament; their family histories of marital conflict) and environmental (e.g., dimensions of conflict expression) variables, are relevant to the distinction between constructive and destructive conflict from the children's perspective (Cummings & Cummings, 1988; Cummings & Davies, 1996). The present chapter focuses particularly on dimensions of conflict expression that affect children's reactions. First, we briefly review evidence of the impact of exposure to adults' conflict on children. Second, theoretical models—in particular, an emotional security hypothesis—and methodological considerations for the study of the distinction between constructive and destructive conflict are considered. Third, a new study is presented that examines a particular contextual aspect of marital conflict, that is, the effects of parental explanations of their resolved and unresolved conflicts on children's reactions. Although parental explanations of conflict *resolutions* were shown to ameliorate children's negative reactions (Cummings, Simpson, & Wilson, 1993), there is no information on how children react to parental explanations that conflicts are *not* resolved. The central hypothesis is that the short term and longer term emotional security implications of parental explanations importantly affect their reactions. Finally, the findings are discussed in terms of an emotional security hypothesis and also considered in terms of practical implications for those concerned about marital conflict and the well-being of children.

CHILDREN ARE HIGHLY SENSITIVE TO ADULTS' CONFLICTS

Throughout childhood, interadult and marital conflicts are distressing for children (Cummings, 1994). Children cry, express anger, freeze, evidence facial distress or bodily distress reactions (e.g., children covering their ears with their hands), make requests to leave, or describe feelings of discomfort, anxiety, or concern (e.g., Cummings, Zahn-Waxler, & Radke-Yarrow, 1981; Cummings, Pellegrini, Notarius, & Cummings, 1989). Children report feelings of anger, sadness, fear, guilt, shame, or worry (e.g., Grych & Fincham, 1993). Physiological reactions also occur, including changes in heart rate, blood pressure, skin conductance, or vagal tone (e.g., El-Sheikh, Cummings, & Goetsch, 1989; El-Sheikh, Ballard, & Cummings, 1994; Gottman & Katz, 1989; Katz & Gottman, 1995b). Exposure to conflict also increases children's aggressiveness (e.g., Cummings, Iannotti, & Zahn-Waxler, 1985; Cummings, 1987), and children's involvement in parental conflicts increases when there are high levels of marital conflict (e.g., Cummings et al., 1981; Cummings et al., 1989; O'Brien, Margolin, John, & Krueger, 1991). A history of marital conflict in the home is linked with children showing greater emotional and behavioral reactivity, greater involvement in parental disputes, and more negative representations (see Davies & Cummings, 1994).

CONTEXTS OF CONFLICT EXPRESSION THAT INCREASE CHILDREN'S DISTRESS

Although high frequencies of unresolved marital conflict are associated with adjustment problems in children (e.g., Davies & Cummings, 1994; Jouriles et al., 1991), certain forms of conflict appear to be particularly destructive from the children's perspective and linked with the development of adjustment problems. Interspousal aggression and abuse have repeatedly been associated with the development of behavioral and emotional problems in children. In the home, physical aggression between parents elicits more distress from children than verbal anger (Cummings et al., 1981). Emotional responses to physical forms of anger expression are more negative than to other forms (Cummings, Vogel, Cummings, & El-Sheikh, 1989; Cummings, Ballard, & El-Sheikh, 1991). Children who witness interparental violence are more vulnerable to a wide range of problems (Hershorn & Rosenbaum, 1985; Holden & Ritchie, 1991), even after statistically controlling for the general level of marital discord (Jouriles, Murphy, & O'Leary, 1989), with effects greater than those for children exposed to verbal conflict alone (Fantuzzo et al., 1991). Children's distress may also be increased when conflicts involve child-related themes or are more negative in affect expression (Grych & Fincham, 1993).

CONTEXTUAL ELEMENTS THAT REDUCE CHILDREN'S DISTRESS: CONFLICT RESOLUTION

Resolution ameliorates the deleterious impact of conflict on children's emotions and behavior. Children's aggression and distress reactions to interadult anger return to baseline levels after children observe a complete resolution

(Cummings, 1987; Cummings et al., 1985; see Davies & Cummings, 1994, for an extended review). Even when adults resolve their differences "behind closed doors," children may obtain beneficial effects (Cummings, Simpson, & Wilson, 1993). These studies suggest that children do not just react to the fact of conflict, but assess the overall meaning and message of how adults feel toward each other and how well they are getting along. Children engage in an appraisal that continues after the argument has ended, which includes an accounting of the end result of the interaction, even if some information comes later.

AN EMOTIONAL SECURITY HYPOTHESIS
FOR THE EFFECTS OF SPECIFIC CONFLICT
CONTEXTS ON CHILDREN

The emotional security hypothesis specifies a *particular* meaning against which children appraise the implications of marital and family conflict for themselves and their families, suggests how that meaning is personal, and indicates why children respond emotionally (Davies & Cummings, 1994). In important respects, this model builds on and complements the cognitive–contextual model proposed by Grych and Fincham (1990), which stresses how children's cognitive processing and coping behaviors are shaped by the characteristics of marital conflict and contextual factors such as past experience with conflict, gender, expectations, and mood. However, although cognition is acknowledged as important to coping processes, this model places greater emphasis on emotionality in the very emotion-laden domain of family conflict and, specifically, the significance of emotional security to children's reactions to marital conflict.

Emotional security is a latent construct that can be inferred from the overall organization and meaning of children's emotions, behaviors, thoughts, and physiological responses, and serves as a set goal by which children regulate their own functioning in social contexts, thereby directing social, emotional, cognitive, and physiological reactions. (Cummings & Davies, in press, p. 126)

Thus, whereas recent theory stresses that children react to conflict in terms of their assessment of the meaning of conflict for family functioning and their own well-being (e.g., Crockenberg & Forgays, 1996; Feldman & Downey, 1994; Grych & Fincham, 1990; Wilson & Gottman, 1995), the emotional security hypothesis proposes that a particular meaning is especially important, that is, the emotional security implications of conflicts. Building on attachment theory (Sroufe & Waters, 1977), emotional security is seen as a paramount factor in children's regulation of emotional arousal and organization and in their motivation to respond in the face of marital conflict.

Emotional security is conceptualized from a contextualistic perspective, emphasizing the interplay between socioemotional and biological processes (Cummings & Davies, 1996). Although emotional security is described as the set goal of regulatory functioning, various specific regulatory systems are conceptualized to be subsumed within emotional security as an operating process, that is, emotional regulation, regulation of exposure to family affect, and internal representations of family relations (see Cummings & Davies, in press; Davies & Cummings, 1994). An important implication for the study of the distinction between constructive versus destructive conflict from the children's perspective is that contexts of marital conflict are evaluated by children in terms of their emotional security implications for the child and the family, and these appraisals, in turn, serve to motivate and regulate children's emotional regulation, regulation of exposure to marital conflict, and internal representations of marital relations. In other words, children do not react just to the occurrence of marital conflict, but to whether marital conflict has destructive or constructive implications for personal and family functioning from the child's point of view.

THE ROLE OF EXPERIMENTAL AND ANALOGUE RESEARCH IN THE STUDY OF THE IMPACT OF CONTEXTS OF CONFLICT EXPRESSION ON CHILDREN

Advancing the study of the distinction between constructive and destructive conflict from the children's perspective requires the identification of the significant categories of marital conflict expression, and the isolation of the specific effects of specific forms of conflict on children. These issues are inherently difficult to study from a methodological perspective. Children's exposure to marital conflict typically occurs outside the view of observers, and may be significantly altered by the presence of observers. Although parents can be trained to record children's reactions to marital conflict in the home (e.g., Cummings, Zahn-Waxler, & Radke-Yarrow, 1981, 1984), causal relations may be impossible to disentangle given the complexity and variability of social interactions in the home and possible biases in the parents' choice of events to report and memories for those events. Questionnaires may be used to tap dimensions of emotionality, but parents may not accurately remember their own emotional behavior, or critical elements in their sometimes long interaction sequences (e.g., the terms and emotions of resolution; Cummings, Vogel, Cummings, & El-Sheikh, 1989; Simpson & Cummings, in press), and they may not notice or remember children's emotional responses, particularly at key points in the conflict (e.g., reactions to violence or conflict resolution). Inducing marital conflicts that may become intense and hostile in front of children in the laboratory raises ethical concerns pertinent to the well-being of the parents' marriage and the children. Analogue and experimental methods that follow scripts and use actors (and perhaps include one parent, e.g., Cummings et al., 1989) provide alternative avenues toward the rigorous study of the impact of emotional and interpersonal aspects of interadult conflicts on children's emotional response processes and other elements of responding relevant to their emotional security concerns when faced with marital conflict.

The significant role of emotionality in children's reaction to marital conflict (Cummings & Davies, 1994; Davies & Cummings, 1994), as well as in the adult partners' expression of conflict, requires the use of methods that adequately represent and record emotionality in family interactions. Experimental and analogue methods are useful for exploring the constructiveness or destructiveness of contexts of conflict, including the role of specific contextual aspects of conflict expression that (a) may be quite brief but highly important, for example, brief physical contact or a final resolution of conflict at its end, (b) occur later, such as explanation of resolution, or (c) may be difficult to remember, such as the emotional contents of adults' conflict expression (i.e., negative vs. nonnegative emotional expression; Simpson & Cummings, 1996), or children's emotionality in response to adults' conflicts (Cummings & Davies, 1994). Although questions of generalizability always pertain to experiments, it is less often recognized that similar questions pertain for questionnaires and other more commonly used methods in family research. Experiments can also lay the groundwork for the subsequent, more expensive process of instrument development surrounding focal constructs of family interactions by exploring which variables of social interaction do, and do not, carry substantial variance in interpersonal interaction and reaction, and thus merit more extensive treatment and study. It should further be recognized that, to be useful, the burden of proof with regard to the utility of experiments is primarily to induce significant response processes that occur in family contexts, *not* to recreate actual family interactions and contexts in a mundane sense (see Cummings, 1995, for an extended discussion of the strengths and limitations of the experiment for family research).

A STUDY OF THE EFFECTS OF PARENTAL
EXPLANATIONS OF RESOLVED AND UNRESOLVED
CONFLICTS ON CHILDREN

The emotional security hypothesis specifies that children's reactions to marital conflict are based on their appraisals of emotional and personal security concerns. Children have realistic reasons for their sense of emotional security to be based, in part, on the course of marital and family conflict. Day-to-day, intense marital conflict makes family life unpleasant. Furthermore, marital conflict may cause breakdowns in discipline and reduced sensitivity and responsivity by parents to children's needs. Over the long term, intense marital conflict has negative implications for the future intactness of the family and the children's general emotional, social, physical, and financial security, safety, and well-being (Emery, 1988; Hetherington & Clingempeel, 1992).

Findings that the resolution of conflict greatly reduces children's distress reactions supports the notion that children evaluate the meaning, and not simply the occurrence, of conflict between adults (see Davies & Cummings, 1994). Consistent with an emotional security hypothesis, children do not seem to react so much to the fact that adults are fighting as to the implications of adults' fights for relationships. Children's representations of conflict are changed when conflicts are resolved (Simpson & Cummings, 1996). The significance of conflict resolution as a constructive element of conflict is supported by several specific findings: (a) conflict resolution reduces children's distress reactions even when actors, scripts, degree, and manner of anger expression are controlled (Cummings, Vogel, Cummings, & El-Sheikh, 1989); (b) conflict resolution reduces distress reactions even when the resolution is brief in duration in relation to the much longer duration of anger expression (Cummings, Ballard, & Sheikh, 1991; Cummings, Ballard, El-Sheikh, & Lake, 1991); and (c) conflict resolution reduces distress reactions even when conflict intensity is high (verbal–physical conflict; Cummings et al., 1993). Children's observations of conflict resolution is not the only way in which children may obtain information that the sequelae of conflict are constructive rather than destructive. Parental explanation provides another possible means for parents to communicate to children about the implications of conflicts outside of the immediate contexts of conflict expression, and may be an especially flexible and adaptable way for parents to reduce the negative impact of marital conflicts.

A recent study (Cummings et al., 1993) supports the notion that parental explanation of conflicts can reduce their negative impact on children. In this study, children were presented with videotaped analogues of interparental conflicts and friendly interactions, and, for some conflict scenarios, a "parent" later explained how the conflicts were resolved. Later parental explanations about marital conflict resolution greatly reduced children's negative emotional reactions in comparison to unresolved conflict, eliciting reactions that were comparable to those to resolved conflicts and even entirely friendly interactions for some dimensions of responding. Further, parental explanation of resolution was also associated with children's reports of more positive representations of the status of interparental relations in comparison to representations following unresolved conflict.

However, parents do not always fully resolve their conflicts, but may only make partial progress towards resolution. When the degree of conflict resolution is only partial, the amelioration of negative reactions is partial rather than complete (Cummings, Ballard, El-Sheikh, & Lake, 1991). Similarly, parental explanations may not necessarily describe conflict resolution, but may describe continuing problems in the relationship, that is, explanations may be about conflicts that are not yet resolved or that are partially resolved. Parents may wish to try to reduce children's emotional security concerns by explaining that parental disagreement and fighting is okay or normal, that parental fighting does not necessarily have dire consequences, or in other ways communicate reassuring messages about parental conflicts. That is, even when fights aren't resolved, parents may use explanation as a vehicle to help children understand that an unresolved conflict doesn't mean that the parents don't love each other, that the parents are optimistic things will eventually work out, that disagreements from time to time are natural, and that it's okay for parents to sometimes disagree. On the other hand, parental explanations may also make things worse for children, increasing their distress, anxiety, and general emotional security concerns. For example, a parent may explain that interparental conflicts are serious, reflect long standing differences, may well never be resolved, and might ultimately lead to divorce.

The emotional security implications for children of such different types of parental explanations may be quite different. Thus, the effects on the components of emotional security as a regulatory system, that is, emotional regulation, regulation of exposure to marital affect (e.g., leaving, intervention), and internal representations of interparental relations (Cummings & Davies, in press; Davies & Cummings, 1994), may vary as a function of the specific contents of parental explanations. However, it remains an unknown in the absence of research directed at the issue.

Moreover, children's emotional security concerns can be conceptualized as short term versus long term. Children's *immediate* reactions *during* any conflict situation, and before the occurrence of resolution or explanation, might be expected to reflect some distress. Furthermore, parental explanations of unresolved conflicts that acknowledge that the parents remain upset with each other, even if phrased in reassuring terms, are less likely to mitigate children's immediate negative reactions. On the other hand, children ought to be able to cope with exposure to short-term family stressors without necessarily incurring any lasting negative effects, and should be able to cope with acknowledging that parents or other loved ones don't always get along well. A more significant issue is the longer term implications of conflict from the child's point of view. Children's appraisal of the *future* or longer term status of the interparental relationship is likely to be more significant to their emotional security and psychological adjustment. In sum, the longer term implications of marital conflict are more likely than shorter term implications to be pertinent to children's stable representations of emotional security and their general functioning and adjustment.

Thus, if optimistic parental explanations of unresolved conflicts succeed in at least increasing the child's sense of emotional security in the longer term sense, such explanations might be regarded as a constructive element from the children's perspective, in comparison to unresolved conflicts or parental conflicts followed by less optimistic explanations. The present study examines the impact of various forms of parental explanations about resolved and unresolved conflicts on the various components of emotional security as a regulatory system, and differentiates between children's shorter and longer term reactions pertinent to their sense of emotional security.

The specific contents of conflicts may also affect children's reactions, especially whether the themes of conflicts are child-related (e.g., conflicts over the child's sports activities or spending money on toys) or adult-related (e.g., conflicts over housekeeping or in-laws). The valence of the explanations of child-related conflicts may be more significant than the valence of explanations of adult-related conflicts, since the former may be perceived by children to have more personal implications for their emotional relationships within the family. Grych and Fincham (1993) reported that child-related themes elicited greater shame, self-blame, and fears of becoming involved than those not related to the child (also see review in Davies & Cummings, 1994). On the other hand, Davies, Myers, and Cummings (1996) did not find support for this relation, although the discrepancy between the two studies might have reflected some differences in the dimensions studied. The present study revisits this issue, examining the reactions of children to parental explanation about child-related and adult-related conflicts as a dimension of conflict contexts.

Children's reactions to conflict resolution and explanation were repeatedly found to vary as a function of age. The relative sophistication of children's understanding of conflicts is found to increase with age, particularly when conflict contexts are relatively complex in terms of the information presented (e.g., mixed-message resolutions; Simpson & Cummings, 1996). Thus, it might be expected that children's understanding of discriminations between relative fine differences between parental explanations would also increase with age. For example, although even 5- to 6-year-olds were shown to benefit from parental explanations about the resolution of conflicts, 9- to 10-year-olds were found to make sharper, more precise discriminations about the information communicated with regard to the constructiveness of conflicts (Cummings et al., 1993).

Further, some components of emotional security may be more age sensitive than others; that is, the extent of age differences may depend on the component of emotional security examined. For example, Simpson and Cummings (1996) reported that 5- to 7-year-olds and 9- to 12-year-olds both made relatively fine, similar discriminations between conditions in their representations of whether marital problems were worked out as a function of different conflict endings, but that the younger children evidenced substantially less discrimination between conditions in their self-reported emo-

114 CUMMINGS AND WILSON

tional reactions and in their responses to regulate their exposure to parental emotion. It might be anticipated that these effects would be even greater in instances of parental explanations of *nonresolved* conflicts, which presents children with relatively complex messages about the short- and long-term consequences of marital conflict and its implications for children's emotional security. The present study examines the reactions of 6 to 8, 10 to 12, 14 to 16, and 18 to 21-year-olds to different parental explanation conditions, with the expectation that discriminations between parental explanation conditions will increase with age, particularly for children's attempts to regulate exposure to parental emotions (e.g., see also Cummings et al., 1993), and, to a lesser extent, their self-reported emotional responding.

Finally, even after more than a decade of study, the literature on sex differences in responding remains complex and sometimes contradictory (Cummings & Davies, 1994). Previous studies of children's responses to contexts of adults' conflicts revealed relatively few differences; in fact, no differences between the responding of boys and girls are reported in numerous studies (Cummings & Davies, 1994). Accordingly, although this question is again examined in the present study, no hypotheses or predictions about sex differences are made.

Thus, the resolution of conflict, or even explanation of the resolution of conflict, may not be necessary for parents to be able to increase children's sense of felt-security about marital conflicts. Optimistic parental explanations of *un*resolved conflicts may also serve to increase children's sense of security, at least with regard to the longer term implications of conflict. That is, parents may be able, through sanguine explanations, to diminish the threat of unresolved marital conflict to children's appraisals of the stability and positive emotionality of family functioning, and thus appraisals of personal safety and security.

In this study, the relative constructiveness of parental explanations of conflicts varies from explanations with relatively constructive implications to explanations with relatively destructive implications for marital functioning. Specifically, the explanations presented are:

1. an explanation that the conflict has been resolved (explain resolution, EXOK).
2. an explanation that the conflict is not worked out yet, but everything will somehow be okay (explain no resolution yet, EXYET).
3. an explanation that the conflict has not been worked out, and might not be due to parental differences, but that, in general, it's okay to disagree (explain ok to disagree, EXDISOK).
4. an explanation that the conflict is not worked out yet, but that parents still love each other despite that fact and are working on it (explain no resolution ok, EXNOK).

5. an explanation that conflict is not worked and may possibly lead to dire consequences such as the parents' divorce (explain no resolution, EXNO).

It is expected that the longer term implications of explanations for children's sense of emotional security, that is, their representations of longer term expectations regarding parental relations, will be a direct function of the relative constructiveness of explanations, and that older children will be more sensitive than younger children to the nuances of explanations. For comparison purposes, children were also presented with scenarios depicting unresolved conflicts (NO), resolved conflicts (RES), and entirely friendly interactions (HAPPY) between marital partners.

ANALOGUE METHODOLOGY FOR EXAMINING CHILDREN'S REACTIONS TO PARENTAL CONFLICT EXPLANATIONS

The participants were children (18 6- to 8-year-olds, 10 girls and 8 boys), preadolescents (20 10- to 12-year-olds, 10 girls and 10 boys), adolescents (20 14- to 16-year-olds, 10 girls and boys), and adults (26 18- to 21-year-olds, 14 girls and 12 boys). The participants were all from White, middle to upper-middle class, intact households. The 18- to 21-year-old subjects were recruited from psychology classes at WVU; other subjects were recruited from area schools and subject files from past research.

This study was conducted in the Developmental Research Suites in Oglebay Hall on the West Virginia University campus in Morgantown, WV. Research sessions with younger children were conducted in a room sparsely equipped with a table, two chairs, and a tape recorder to minimize distractions and focus the children on the task of the session. Parents of children in the three youngest age groups waited in an outer area of the research suites. Sessions with the 18- to 21-year-olds were conducted in a group format in a classroom.

Participants listened to 12 audiotaped scenes of marital interactions. Three scenes involved friendly interaction between a couple, whereas the remaining nine involved mild verbal conflict. Of the nine conflict scenes, two were resolved, two were unresolved, and five were unresolved but followed by an explanation by one "parent." Approximately half of the children in each age group were presented with child-centered themes and half with adult-centered themes. Conflict stems were allowed to vary in specific contents to maintain children's interest, but were constructed to reflect similar levels of anger expression. Graduate students rated these scenes, and any necessary adjustments were made to ensure that scripts were similar in intensity.

Following each scene, the participants were asked a series of questions and their answers were recorded verbatim for later coding. The following analyses focus on the questions pertinent to the three components of children's emotional security during exposure to marital conflict: emotional regulation, regulation of exposure to parental emotion, and representations of the short and longer term status of marital relations (Cummings & Davies, in press; Davies & Cummings, 1994).

The design of the study included three between-subjects factors (age, sex, theme) and one within-subjects factor (scene). The factor of age had four levels (6-8, 10-12, 14-16, 18-21), sex had two levels (boys and girls), and theme had two levels (adult and child). Mean scores were used in analyses for responding to the multiple friendly, resolved, and unresolved conflict conditions. Thus, the factor of scene had eight levels: friendly (HAPPY), resolved (RES), unresolved (NO), explain resolution (EXOK), explain no resolution (EXNO), explain ok to disagree (EXDISOK), explain no resolution ok (EXNOK), explain no resolution yet (EXYET)). Preliminary analyses indicated no statistically significant effects for sex. Thus, sex was dropped as a factor to increase cell sizes, and $4 \times 2 \times 2 \times 8$ mixed design ANOVAs were conducted for each dependent variable.

The dependent variables were (a) children's felt-emotion while listening to the interactions, with children asked to react as if the actors were their parents (0 = no negative emotion to 3 = highly negative emotion, e.g., anger, sadness, distress); (b) children's responses to regulate their exposure to adults' emotions (0 = no response indicated to regulate exposure; 1 = some response indicated, e.g., leave the room, mediate the conflict); (c) children's representations of whether "everything was ok between the adults" at the end of the interaction (1 = yes, 2 = no); and (d) children's representations of "what will happen next time the adults talk about this" (1 = will fight again; 2 = maybe will fight or will fight but then makeup; 3 = will *not* fight). Most responses to regulate adults' emotions reflected dispositions to become involved or takes sides in the conflicts, although some responses indicated a desire to leave the room. The friendly interaction was excluded from this particular analysis because reactions were not comparable; that is, children reacted to join in the fun rather than to regulate exposure. For each variable, responses to 360 scenes were coded by two independent raters to determine interobserver reliability, with reliabilities ranging from kappa = .97 to 1.0.

Finally, additional analyses were performed to advance precise interpretation of the results. Significant main effects were followed by Tukey tests making comparisons between all possible pairs of means. Significant interactions were followed by simple effects tests (Keppel, 1973) and, when significant, by Tukey tests making comparisons between all possible pairs of means. To foster the accessibility of this text, statistical levels but not statistical values (e.g., *F* values, degrees of freedom, Tukey values) are reported for these additional analyses. These values are available from the first author.

Statistics for significant result from omnibus analyses for each variable are shown in Table 6.1, with subsequent tables showing the means and statistical levels for follow-up tests. Parental explanations did little to reduce children's *immediate* emotional security concerns *during* marital conflicts (see Table 6.2). That is, children evidenced relatively high rates of distress, at levels comparable to unresolved conflicts, in response to most explanation conditions at most ages. An important qualification is that children were asked how they would feel during, not at the end of, conflicts (i.e., "If these were your parents, how would you feel listening to them?"), so that responses may not have reflected possibly ameliorative effects of explanations for reactions at the time of the end of conflicts, which is when explanations were given. In past research on the effects of resolution (e.g., Cummings, Ballard, El-Sheikh, & Lake, 1991), children were scored for how they would feel *after* any resolution or explanation. On the other hand, the results deriving from the present wording of the question does make the important point that exposure to conflict does affect children's felt-security, at least until a positive or relatively positive ending is added.

Moreover, further supporting the notion that children's immediate sense of emotional security is not entirely ameliorated by endings, children's dispositions to regulate their exposure to parental emotions, which primarily took the form of involvement in parental interactions, were generally comparable in response to explained and unresolved conflicts. For younger children (6- to 8- and 10- to 12-year-olds) the greatest reactions were to the scene in which parents said that they still disagreed but that it was okay and they were working on it (EXNOK; see Table 6.3). One interpretation is that this explanation, because it both identified the fact that further work was needed but also made the context seem safe, was more salient and inviting for younger children's involvement than the other explanation conditions.

TABLE 6.1
Significant ANOVA Results of Omnibus Tests

	Dependent Variable							
	Negative Emotionality		Disposition to Regulate		Current Representations		Future Representations	
Source	df	F	df	F	df	F	df	F
Scene	7,525	84.81***	6,450	4.52***	7.511	129.07***	7,511	65.62***
Scene × Age	21,525	2.35***	18,450	3.63***	21,511	1.80*	21,511	3.72***
Age	—	—	3.75	6.42***	—	—	3.73	9.04***
Theme × Age	3.75	4.22***	—	—	—	—	—	—

*p < .05; **p < .01; ***p < .001

TABLE 6.2

Age × Scene Variations in Children's Negative Emotionality in Response to Interparental Interactions

Scene	Age				Simple Effects of Age	Tukey Tests
	a 6–8	b 10–12	c 14–16	d 18–21		
1. HAPPY	0.00	0.45	0.00	0.00	—	
2. RES	1.91	1.40	0.88	0.94	**	* a > b-d; * b > c, d
3. EXOK	2.41	1.71	1.75	1.76	—	
4. EXNOK	2.06	1.81	2.50	2.28	—	
5. EXDISOK	2.05	2.43	2.30	2.20	—	
6. EXYET	1.88	1.76	2.20	2.48	—	
7. EXNO	2.41	2.52	2.80	2.72	—	
8. NO	2.50	2.19	2.77	2.28	*	* a > b; ** c > b, d
Scene Simple Effects	***	***	***	***		
Tukey Tests	** 2 – 8 > 1	** 2 – 8 > 1 ** 5, 7, 8 > 2	** 2 – 8 > 1 – 2 * 2 > 1 * 7, 8 > 3	** 3 – 8 > 1, 2 * 2 > 1 * 7 > 3		

*p < .05; **p < .01; ***p < .001

TABLE 6.3

Age × Scene Variations in Childrens's Dispositions to Regulate Their Exposure To Marital Conflict

| Scene | Age | | | | Simple Effects of Age | Tukey Tests |
	a 6–8	b 10–12	c 14–16	d 18–21		
1. RES	.47	.60	.55	.62	—	** c, d > a, b
2. EXOK	.35	.33	.80	.76	***	** b-d > a; ** c, d > b
3. EXNOK	.71	.90	.70	.84	—	
4. EXDISOK	.24	.52	.75	.76	**	** b-d > a
5. EXYET	.24	.76	.75	.88	***	** d > a
6. EXNO	.53	.57	.55	.88	*	** d > a-c
7. NO	.62	.45	.92	.76	***	*** c > a, b, d; * d > a, b; * a > b
Scene Simple Effects	**	***	**			
Tukey Tests	** 3 > 4, 5	** 3 > 2, 7 * 3 > 4 * 5 > 2	* 7 > 1, 6			

*p < .05; **p < .01; ***p < .001

On the other hand, parental explanations of resolution, or at least that conflict was okay or that it was okay to disagree, did positively affect children's immediate representations of the current status of interparental relations. As is shown in Table 6.4, for all ages, any form of explanation, other than that the conflict was not worked out and might lead to the dire consequence of divorce (EXNO), improved children's representation of interparental relations. This finding lends weight to the contention that a more reliable, sophisticated interpretation of children's emotional security results when interpretation is based on multiple components of emotional security (i.e., emotional regulation, regulation of parental emotion, representation of parental relationships) rather than a single component (e.g., emotional security; Cummings & Davies, 1996). Furthermore, explanation of resolution (EXOK) was understood as reflecting more positive relations between parents than conditions of explanation of nonresolution, with all comparisons statistically significant for children 10 to 12 years of age and older.

However, the constructive effects of resolution were most evident in terms of children's appraisals of the future or longer term implications of marital conflict to children's sense of emotional security. Children of all ages quite markedly distinguished between positive explanations—the explanation of resolution (EXOK), the explanation that conflicts were unresolved but that it *would* be okay (EXNOK), or explanations that conflict was nonthreatening for family relations (EXDISOK; EXYET)—and negative explanations—the explanation that the conflict might lead to long term negative consequences for the family (i.e., divorce; EXNO). Moreover, positive explanations led to representations of the longer term prospects for interparental relations as decidedly positive (see Table 6.5), whereas the EXNO condition was associated with a negative appraisal of the marital relationship for the longer term. As already noted, the longer term implications of marital conflict to children's sense of emotional security is likely to be more pertinent to their general functioning and adjustment over time than immediate responding. Given that stress is a normal part of life, and that coping with short term stresses are likely to be within most children's coping capacities, immediate negative reactions to marital conflict, in themselves, may well not have significant implications for adjustment problems. Thus, the present findings suggest that even explanations of unresolved conflicts, provided that such explanations are positive with regard to the meaning of conflicts for the marital relationship in the long run, might be regarded as a constructive element of conflict process from the children's perspective.

The only evidence that the specific themes of conflict (i.e., child-centered vs. adult-centered) affected children's responding to explanation conditions pertained to the negative emotionality component of emotional security (see Table 6.1). These effects are further qualified by the fact that only 6- to 8-year-olds ($p < .01$) and 10- to 12-year-olds ($p < .01$) year-olds distinguished

TABLE 6.4

Age × Sex Variations in Children's Representations of Current Interparental Relations

Scene	Age				Simple Effects of Age	Tukey Tests
	a 6–8	b 10–12	c 14–16	d 18–21		
1. HAPPY	1.00	1.00	1.00	1.00	—	
2. RES	1.00	1.00	1.05	1.00	—	
3. EXOK	1.35	1.09	1.00	1.33	**	** a, d > b, c
4. EXNOK	1.47	1.55	1.47	1.75	—	
5. EXDISOK	1.47	1.68	1.52	1.71	—	
6. EXYET	1.64	1.68	1.89	1.67	—	
7. EXNO	2.00	2.00	2.00	1.96	—	
8. NO	2.00	2.00	2.00	2.00	—	
Scene Simple Effects	***	***	***	***		
Tukey Tests	** 7 – 8 > 1 – 6 ** 3 – 6 > 1 – 2 * 6 > 3 – 5	** 7 – 8 > 1 – 6 ** 4 – 6 > 1 – 3	** 6 – 8 > 1 – 5 ** 4, 5 > 1 – 3	** 7 – 8 > 1 – 6 ** 4 – 6 > 1 – 3 ** 3 > 1, 2		

$*p < .05; **p < .01; ***p < .001$

121

TABLE 6.5
Age × Sex Variations in Children's Representations of Future Interparental Relations

| Scene | Age | | | | Simple Effects of Age | Tukey Tests |
	a 6-8	b 10-12	c 14-16	d 18-21		
1. HAPPY	2.94	2.97	3.00	3.00	—	
2. RES	2.83	2.68	2.89	2.77	—	
3. EXOK	2.76	2.63	2.79	2.67	—	
4. EXNOK	2.71	2.77	2.84	1.75	***	** a-c > d
5. EXDISOK	2.64	2.18	2.31	1.79	*	** a-c > d
6. EXYET	2.65	2.59	1.95	1.58	***	** a-b > c-d; * c > d
7. EXNO	1.65	1.91	1.53	1.17	*	** a-c > d; * b > c
8. NO	1.65	1.52	1.29	1.46	—	
Scene Simple Effects	***	***	***	***		
Tukey Tests	** 1 - 6 > 7, 8	* 1 > 2 - 8; ** 2 - 6 > 7; * 7 > 8	** 1 - 4 >; 5 - 8; ** 5 > 6 - 8; ** 6 > 7; * 7 > 8	** 1 - 3 >; 4 - 8; * 4 - 6 >; 7		

*p < .05; **p < .01; ***p > .001

between these conditions in responding. Interestingly, 6- to 8-year-olds responded more negatively to child-centered themes than to adult-centered themes (2.15 vs. 1.69, respectively), whereas 10- to 12-year-olds reacted with more negative emotions to adult-centered themes than to child-centered themes (2.13 vs. 1.44, respectively). The results indicate, at least in terms of this one dimension of responding, that younger children have greater emotional security concerns when they themselves are drawn into the discussion, implicating shame and self-blame as possible mediating processes (Grych & Fincham, 1993), whereas the older children have more concerns about the parents not getting along on adult issues, suggesting they are more concerned about the status of the interadult relationship than about its implications for themselves. However, the pattern of results across all analyses suggests that theme per se is not a central issue in terms of children's appraisals of the emotional security implications of conflicts (e.g., Davies et al., in press).

The findings also make clear that any assessment of the emotional security implications of marital conflicts must take into account both the age of the children and the component of emotional security studied (Davies & Cummings, 1994). As in past research, older children made finer discriminations between conditions than did younger children, particularly with regard to the representation of the future implications of marital conflicts (Simpson & Cummings, in press). The youngest group assessed any explanation as highly constructive in terms of its implications for future relations, that is, as equivalent to observing a resolution or even an entirely friendly interaction (see Table 6.5). The preadolescent group, on the other hand, distinguished between friendly interactions and conflicts with resolution or any positive explanation, between positive and negative explanations, and between negative explanation and unresolved conflict. Although viewing any positive ending as essentially an index of relatively constructive conflict, adolescents drew even finer discriminations than did preadolescents, making distinctions between (a) explanations of resolution and explanations that the specific conflict will be okay versus explanations that generally reassured children about the marital relationship, (b) the explanation that it is okay to disagree versus the parents generally love each other, (c) the explanation that the parents love each other versus the parents may divorce, and (d) an explanation that parents may divorce versus no explanation at all for unresolved conflict. Interestingly, adults were far more pessimistic about the longer term implications of explanations of unresolved conflicts than were the younger groups, although positive explanations (EXNOK, EXDISOK, EXYET) were still regarded as more sanguine than the negative one (EXNO). The results for the other dimensions of emotional security, that is, findings on current representations of marital conflicts and immediate reactions of negative emotionality, affirm this general ordering among scenes in terms of their relative constructiveness from the children's perspective, although the patterns of findings differed in important specific elements (see prior discussion and Tables 6.2 and 6.3).

Also consistent with past research, children became more likely to intervene in marital conflicts with increasing age (Table 6.3; e.g., Cummings, Ballard, & El-Sheikh, 1991; Cummings, Ballard, El-Sheikh, & Lake, 1991). Interestingly, individuals also became *less* discriminating between conditions in terms of dispositions to react behaviorally with increasing age, perhaps reflecting that the link between age and an impulse to regulate exposure to marital conflicts is stronger than the link between specific contexts and the impulse to respond. In any case, data on regulation of exposure to marital conflict are difficult to interpret with regard to their implications for the relative constructiveness of endings.

Consistent with previous studies (Cummings & Davies, 1994), there were no sex differences in responding.

GENERAL DISCUSSION

Parental Explanations as an Element
of Constructive Conflict

The present study extends the findings of past work that resolutions of conflict and explanations of resolution allay children's distress due to exposure to adults' conflicts. Thus, whereas partial resolution of conflict, or any progress towards resolution, is constructive relative to lack of resolution (Cummings, Vogel, Cummings, & El-Sheikh, 1991), similarly, explanations that conflicts are not resolved but that "it is okay to disagree" are constructive relative to lack of resolution or explanation. The results underscore that children do not simply respond to the fact of exposure to a negative, unpleasant event, (i.e., conflict) as emotional contagion. On the contrary, the findings again suggest that children appraise information about the conflict and any postconflict information, and formulate responses based on the implications for interpersonal and personal relationships.

The Effects of Different Parental Explanations:
Interpretation in Terms of an Emotional
Security Hypothesis

Interestingly, explanations did relatively little to reduce children's experiences of negative emotionality *during* conflicts, which suggests that explained conflicts may still affect children's sense of emotional security in an immediate sense. The effects of exposure to marital conflicts on children's reports of negative emotionality again affirms that these contexts are highly relevant to children's feelings of emotional well-being and security (see Cummings & Davies, 1994; Davies & Cummings, 1994). However, the significance of immediate distress reactions to children's long term emotional security and psychological adjustment in the absence of implications for continuing emotional reactions or representations of relationships may be minimal.

Longer term or continuing effects are more likely to matter for children's continuing sense of emotional security and adjustment. Children were generally more optimistic about the future of marital relationships following explanations. Thus, parental explanations may be a positive factor in the impact of marital conflict on children's sense of emotional security and adjustment.

Children's representations of marital relationships following explanations provided a window into the relative constructiveness of different endings from an emotional security perspective, with the precise nature of explanations mattering to children's responding. The most constructive explanation for all ages, of course, was explanation of resolution. For 6- to 12-year-olds, *any* explanation of nonresolution that was optimistic was more or less equivalent, and better than an explanation that suggested dire consequences, or the fact of unresolved conflict. Children between 14 and 21, on the other hand, differentiated between various explanations of nonresolution in terms of their relative constructiveness. Explanations that were seemingly more realistic about conflicts (EXNOK, EXDISOK) were perceived as more constructive than explanations that were relatively vague about how parents would work things out (EXYET). The 14- to 16-year-olds responded more favorably to the explanation that was specifically optimistic about the parental relationship (EXNOK) versus the explanation that was more pessimistic about differences in the relationship (EXDISOK), whereas 18- to 21-year-olds did *not* make this distinction. However, this primarily reflected that 18- to 21-year-olds were less sanguine than 14- to 16-year-olds about the future implications of *any* explanation of nonresolved conflicts. Perhaps experience has taught the adult group that conflicts are not so easily resolved over time, despite the participants' best intentions. Finally, in terms of the future implications for interparental relations, 10- to 12- and 14- to 16-year-olds reacted to the negative explanation (EXNO) as more constructive than no explanation at all (NO). One interpretation is that the fact that a parent was willing to talk about the conflict, albeit negatively, was perceived as more hopeful than no talk at all.

Practical Implications

As with any methodology, certain limitations accrue to the interpretation of results for analogue studies (see Cummings, 1995) and this particular presentation format (see Cummings et al., 1993). One function of analogue research is to stimulate follow-up studies using more costly and time-consuming research directions. Hopefully, these results provide encouragement for instrument development, field research, and other follow-up studies on the effects of parental explanations on children's reactions to marital conflicts.

With these considerations in mind, an instructive, and perhaps hopeful, message is that parents can reduce children's emotional security concerns about marital conflict through a variety of channels of information, including explanations of parental conflicts. In particular, it would appear that it is not necessary for conflicts to be resolved, or for parents to wait for conflict resolution, before talking to children about parental conflicts. Children seem to benefit from any discussion by the parents that communicates that the marital relationship is not threatened by the conflict, that conflict is normal, and that future expectations for the interparental relationship are positive, despite the fact that the conflict is not yet resolved. Further, children may even benefit from relatively pessimistic explanations, as opposed to no explanation at all for unresolved conflicts. This research thus further widens the conceptualization of contextual factors surrounding marital conflict that may enhance the constructiveness of conflicts from the children's perspective.

REFERENCES

Amato, P. R., & Keith, B. (1991). Consequences of parental divorce for children's well-being: A meta-analysis. *Psychological Bulletin, 110,* 26–46.

Amato, P. R., Loomis, L. S., & Booth, A. (1995). Parental divorce, marital conflict, and offspring well-being during early adulthood. *Social Forces, 73,* 895–915.

Baruch, D. W., & Wilcox, J. A. (1944). A study of sex differences in preschool children's adjustment coexistent with interparental tensions. *Journal of Genetic Psychology, 64,* 281–303.

Beach, B., & Cummings, E. M. (1996). *The relation between marital conflict and child adjustment: An examination of parental and child repertoires.* Unpublished manuscript.

Booth, A., & Amato, P. R. (1994). Parental marital quality, parental divorce, and relations with parents. *Journal of Marriage and the Family, 56,* 21–34.

Browne, A., & Finkelhor, D. (1986). Impact of sexual abuse: A review of the research. *Psychological Bulletin, 99,* 66–77.

Cox, M. J., & Owen, M. T. (1993, March). Marital conflict and conflict negotiation: Effects on infant–mother and infant–father relationships. In M. Cox & J. Brooks-Gunn (Chairs), *Conflict in families: Causes and consequences.* Symposium conducted at the meeting of the Society for Research in Child Development, New Orleans, LA.

Cox, M. J., Owen, M. T., Lewis, J. M., & Henderson, V. K. (1989). Marriage, adult adjustment and early parenting. *Child Development, 60,* 1015–1024.

Crockenberg, S. B., & Forgays, D. (1996). The role of emotion in children's understanding and emotional reactions to marital conflict. *Merrill-Palmer Quarterly, 42,* 22–47.

Cummings, E. M. (1987). Coping with background anger in early childhood. *Child Development, 58,* 976–984.

Cummings, E. M. (1994). Marital conflict and children's functioning. *Social Development, 3,* 16–36.

Cummings, E. M. (1995). The usefulness of experiments for the study of the family. *Journal of Family Psychology, 9*, 175–185.

Cummings, E. M., Ballard, M., & El-Sheikh, M. (1991). Responses of children and adolescents to interadult anger as a function of gender, age, and mode of expression. *Merrill-Palmer Quarterly, 37*, 543–560.

Cummings, E. M., Ballard, M., El-Sheikh, M., & Lake, M. (1991). Resolution and children's responses to interadult anger. *Developmental Psychology, 27*, 462–470.

Cummings, E. M., & Cummings, J. S. (1988). A process-oriented approach to children's coping with adults' angry behavior. *Developmental Review, 3*, 296–321.

Cummings, E. M., & Davies, P. T. (1994). *Children and marital conflict: The impact of family dispute and resolution*. New York: Guilford.

Cummings, E. M., & Davies, P. T. (1996). Emotional security as a regulatory process in normal development and the development of psychopathology. *Development and Psychopathology, 8*, 123–139.

Cummings, E. M., Iannotti, R., & Zahn-Waxler, C. (1985). The influence of conflict between adults on the emotions and aggression of young children. *Developmental Psychology, 21*, 495–507.

Cummings, E. M., & O'Reilly, A. (1997). Fathers in family context: Effects of marital quality on child adjustment. In M. E. Lamb (Ed.), *The role of the father in child development*. (3rd ed., pp. 49–65). New York: Wiley.

Cummings, E. M., Simpson, K., & Wilson, A. (1993). Children's responses to interadult anger as a function of information about resolution. *Developmental Psychology, 29*, 978–985.

Cummings, E. M., Vogel, D., Cummings, J. S., & El-Sheikh, M. (1989). Children's responses to different forms of expression of anger between adults. *Child Development, 60*, 1392–1404.

Cummings, E. M., Zahn-Waxler, C., & Radke-Yarrow, M. (1981). Young children's responses to expressions of anger and affection by others in the family. *Child Development, 52*, 1274–1282.

Cummings, E. M., Zahn-Waxler, C., & Radke-Yarrow, M. (1984). Developmental changes in children's reactions to anger in the home. *Journal of Child Psychology and Psychiatry, 25*, 63–75.

Cummings, J. S., Pelligrini, D., Notarius, C., & Cummings, E. M. (1989). Children's responses to angry adult behavior as a function of marital distress and history of interparent hostility. *Child Development, 60*, 1035–1043.

Davies, P. T., & Cummings, E. M. (1994). Marital conflict and child adjustment: An emotional security hypothesis. *Psychological Bulletin, 116*, 387–411.

Davies, P. T., Myers, R. L., & Cummings, E. M. (1996). Responses of children and adolescents to marital conflict scenarios as a function of the emotionality of conflict endings. *Merrill-Palmer Quarterly, 42*, 1–21.

Downey, G., & Coyne, J. C. (1990). Children of depressed parents: An integrative review. *Psychological Bulletin, 108*, 50–76.

Easterbrooks, M. A., Cummings, E. M., & Emde, R. N. (1994). Young children's responses to constructive marital disputes. *Journal of Family Psychology, 8*, 160–169.

El-Sheikh, M., Ballard, M., & Cummings, E. M. (1994). Individual differences in preschoolers' physiological and verbal responses to videotaped angry interactions. *Journal of Abnormal Child Psychology, 22*, 303–320.

El-Sheikh, M., Cummings, E. M., & Goetsch, V. (1989). Coping with adults' angry behavior: Behavioral, physiological, and self-reported responding in preschoolers. *Developmental Psychology, 25*, 490–498.

Emery, R. E. (1982). Interparental conflict and the children of discord and divorce. *Psychological Bulletin, 92*, 310–330.

Emery, R. E. (1988). *Marriage, divorce, and children's adjustment*. Newbury Park, CA: Sage.

Emery, R. E., Fincham, F. D., & Cummings, E. M. (1992). Parenting in context: Systemic thinking about parental conflict and its influence on children. *Journal of Consulting and Clinical Psychology, 60,* 909–912.

Fantuzzo, J. W., DePaola, L. M., Lambert, L., Martino, T., Anderson, G., & Sutton, S. (1991). Effects of interparental violence on the psychological adjustment and competencies of young children. *Journal of Clinical and Consulting Psychology, 59,* 258–265.

Feldman, S., & Downey, G. (1994). Rejection sensitivity as a mediator of the impact of childhood exposure to family violence on adult attachment behavior. *Development and Psychopathology, 6,* 231–247.

Fincham, F. D., & Osborne, L. N. (1993). Marital conflict and children: Retrospect and prospect. *Clinical Child Psychology, 13,* 75–88.

Gottman, J. M. (1994). *Why marriages succeed or fail.* New York: Simon & Schuster.

Gottman, J. M., & Katz, L. F. (1989). Effects of marital discord on young children's peer interaction and health. *Developmental Psychology, 25,* 373–381.

Gottman, J. M., & Krokoff, L. J. (1989). Marital interaction and satisfaction: A longitudinal view. *Journal of Consulting and Clinical Psychology, 57,* 47–52.

Grych, J. H., & Fincham, F. (1990). Marital conflict and children's adjustment: A cognitive–contextual framework. *Psychological Bulletin, 108,* 267–290.

Grych, J. H., & Fincham, F. (1993). Children's appraisals of marital conflict: Initial investigations of the cognitive–contextual framework. *Child Development, 64,* 215–230.

Hershorn, M., & Rosenbaum, A. (1985). Children of marital violence: A closer look at the unintended victims. *American Journal of Orthopsychiatry, 55,* 260–266.

Hetherington, E. M., & Clingempeel, W. G. (1992). Coping with marital transitions: A family systems perspective. *Monographs of the Society for Research in Child Development, 57,* Nos. 2–3, Serial No. 227.

Holden, G. W., & Ritchie, K. L. (1991). Linking extreme marital discord, child rearing, and child behavior problems: Evidence from battered women. *Child Development, 62,* 311–327.

Hubbard, R. M., & Adams, C. F. (1936). Factors affecting the success of child guidance clinic treatment. *American Journal of Orthopsychiatry, 6,* 81–103.

Jouriles, E. N., Barling, J., & O'Leary, K. D. (1987). Predicting child behavior problems in maritally violent families. *Journal of Abnormal Child Psychology, 15,* 165–173.

Jouriles, E. N., Murphy, C. M., Farris, A. M., Smith, D. A., Richters, J. E., & Waters, E. (1991). Marital adjustment, parental disagreements about child rearing, and behavior problems in boys: Increasing the specificity of the marital assessment. *Child Development, 62,* 1424–1433.

Jouriles, E. N., Murphy, C. M., & O'Leary, K. D. (1989). Interspousal aggression, marital discord, and child problems. *Journal of Consulting and Clinical Psychology, 57,* 453–455.

Katz, L. F., & Gottman, J. (1993). Patterns of marital conflict predict children's internalizing and externalizing disorders. *Development Psychology, 29,* 940–950.

Katz, L. F., & Gottman, J. M. (1995a). Vagal tone predicts children from marital conflict. *Development and Psychopathology, 7,* 83–92.

Katz, L. F., & Gottman, J. M. (1995b). Marital conflict and child adjustment: Father's parenting as a mediator of children's negative peer play. Paper presented at the Meetings of the Society for Research in Child Development, Indianapolis.

Keppel, G. (1973). *Design and analysis.* Englewood Cliffs, NJ: Prentice Hall.

Notarius, C., & Markman, H. (1993). *We can work it out: Making sense of marital conflict.* New York: Putnam.

O'Brien, M., Margolin, G., John, R. S., & Krueger, L. (1991). Mothers' and sons' cognitive and emotional reactions to simulated marital and family conflict. *Journal of Consulting and Clinical Psychology, 59,* 692–703.

Simpson, K., & Cummings, E. M. (1996). Mixed message resolution and children's responses to interadult conflict. *Child Development, 67,* 437–448.

Sroufe, L. A., & Waters, E. (1977). Attachment as an organizational construct. *Child Development, 48,* 1184–1199.

Towle, C. (1931). The evaluation and management of marital status in foster homes. *American Journal of Orthopsychiatry, 1,* 271–284.

Wilson, B. J., & Gottman, J. M. (1995). Marital interaction and parenting: The role of repair of negativity in families. In M. H. Bornstein (Ed.), *Handbook of parenting, Vol. 4,* Applied and practical considerations of parenting. Hillsdale, NJ: Lawrence Erlbaum Associates.

7

▼▼▼▼▼▼▼

Meta-Emotion Philosophy and Family Adjustment: Making an Emotional Connection

Lynn Fainsilber Katz
University of Washington

Beverly Wilson
Oregon State University

John M. Gottman
University of Washington

Recent advances in the study of family relationships emphasized the importance of understanding how emotions are experienced, expressed, and communicated within the family. For example, family emotional expressiveness was identified as important in predicting peer relations (Parke et al., 1989). In the marital literature, there is evidence that the single best predictor of whether a couple will separate or divorce is the wife's contemptuous behavior during marital interaction (Gottman, 1994). Emotional communication within the family also provides some understanding of how marital conflict leads to childhood adjustment problems. Katz and Gottman (1993) found that specific forms of emotional communication within the marriage differentially predict internalizing and externalizing behavior problems in children. Marital hostility characterized by contempt and belligerence predicted teacher ratings of child externalizing behavior 3 years later, and marital withdrawal predicted teacher ratings of child internalizing behavior 3 years later.

Given empirical data supporting the importance of emotional communication in understanding family relationships, the important next step is to develop a theory that can explain how emotional communication is related to the psychological well-being of family members. In this chapter, we propose that successful emotional communication between family members forms the basis for intimacy. We argue that this is achieved through the awareness of one's own emotional state and that of other family members, and through the ability to talk about feelings. We present a new concept of parenting referred to as parental *meta-emotion philosophy*. By introducing this concept, we suggest that parents have an organized set of feelings and thoughts about their own emotions and their children's emotions. The notion we have in mind parallels metacognition, which refers to the executive functions of cognition (Allen & Armour, 1993; Bvinelli, 1993; Flavell, 1979; Fodor, 1992; Olson & Astington, 1993). In an analogous manner, meta-emotion philosophy refers to executive functions of emotion.

In this chapter, we describe the evolution of the "meta-emotion" construct and describe its relationship to various aspects of family and child functioning. We present a parsimonious theoretical model of the role of parental meta-emotions in children's emotional development, and present data suggesting that families in which parents have a meta-emotion philosophy that values emotion have less negative marital relations, inhibit displays of parental rejection toward their children, and are more scaffolding and praising of children during teaching tasks. As a result, children in these families have greater physiological regulatory abilities, which affects their ability to regulate their emotion, and thus has an impact on a variety of child outcomes, including peer relations, academic achievement, behavior problems, and physical health. We also discuss the importance of parental meta-emotion philosophy in families with developmentally delayed children.

HISTORICAL ORIGINS OF THE CONCEPT
OF META-EMOTION

Research in developmental psychology on the effects of parenting focused on parental affect and discipline, selecting variables such as warmth, control, authoritarian or authoritative styles, and responsiveness to describe important qualities in the parent–child relationship (see Ainsworth, Bell, & Stayton, 1971; Baumrind, 1967; Becker, 1964; Cohn, Cowan, Cowan, & Pearson, 1992; Cowan & Cowan, 1992; Maccoby & Martin, 1983; Patterson, 1982; Schaefer, 1959). Little attention was placed on examining the parents' feelings and cognitions about their own affect or their feelings and cognitions about their child's affect.

Our informal review of popular parenting guides also reveals that the overwhelming majority of these parenting guides are based on obtaining and maintaining child discipline. However, one genre of parenting guides focuses on children's emotions and on how to make immediate and everyday emotional connections with a child that are not critical and contemptuous but accepting. These kinds of parenting guides can be traced to the seminal influence of one child psychologist, Hiam Ginott (Ginott, 1965, 1971, 1975). Although many psychological systems of thought (attachment theory, psychoanalysis) dealt with the importance of the child's affect, Ginott (1965, 1971, 1975) emphasized intervening with a child's strong negative emotions while the child is having the emotions. This difference was so important that it amounted to a revolution in dealing with children.

The Work of Haim Ginott

Ginott's work represents a major departure and innovation in the popular parenting guide literature because it is the first parenting guide to focus entirely on the processes of parent–child interaction, to focus on the child's emotions, and to alter parents' views of the emotional world of the child. Ginott suggested that what matters in the moment-to-moment interactions parents have with their child is emotion, and that it is essential that parents look for it, listen to it, and respond genuinely and empathically with real understanding. He suggested that the most important thing a parent can do is to listen for the emotion behind the words. Ginott did not contend that this listening is a social skill, and did not attempt to provide social skill training to enhance its development. He instead assumed that most parents already have this skill, and he proposed a way to feel about and respond to the child's affect, and a strategy for reading the child's emotions. Whether this form of listening is a trainable social skill is an empirical question. Ginott also suggested a "new code of communication" in which there are only two principles: that the messages preserve both the child's as well as the parent's self-respect, and that statements of understanding precede statements of advice. He suggested that these principles can be applied to mitigate the power struggles parents and children frequently encounter.

Take the following example. Suppose a parent is driving on a hot summer day with a child and gets caught in unrelenting bumper-to-bumper traffic. The child says, "Dad, I want some cold milk." Dad says very sweetly, "Honey, there's nothing I can do until we get home. Then I'll get you some milk." Not mollified, the child repeats the request more insistently: "I want some cold milk now!" Dad repeats himself, explaining why he cannot get the milk now. This exchange continues, with the child escalating, adding whining and crying as the exchange continues. Eventually the father is upset and threatening. An oppositional struggle has erupted. Ginott suggested that this battle might have been avoided if the father had originally said something like, "Yeah, cold milk sounds great. I wish I had some myself right now." The child, whose feelings are understood, would have said "Yeah," and the father might have added "Some ice cream would be nice, too," and the child might have continued, "Yeah, an ice cream sundae." Dad: "Yum."

Ginott said that when a child is in the midst of strong emotion, he or she cannot listen to anyone, and he or she certainly cannot process good advice. The child wants us to understand the feelings and thoughts going on inside at this very moment. Ginott pointed out that it is critical not to rush in and judge the child's reactions or discount the child's feelings. He suggested that a child's feelings do not disappear when he is told not to feel that way, or that it's not nice to feel that way, or that he has no proper justification for feeling that way. Ginott discouraged parents from telling children what they ought to feel, because it makes children distrust what they do feel. Statements like "You don't mean what you say. You love your little brother," or "This is not you. This is the devil in you acting up," or "If you mention that word 'hate' one more time, you'll get the spanking of your life," or "You don't really hate your brother. Maybe you dislike him. You should rise above such feelings" convey the message to the child not to trust his or her emotions, but instead to rely on what parents say he or she is feeling. This acceptance of a child's feelings does not imply that parents have to accept all of a child's *behavior*. He suggested that while all feelings are real and acceptable, not all actions are, and parents must set limits on destructive or harmful behavior.

Although it is important to set limits on a child's misbehaviors, Ginott also cautioned against doing so using contemptuous or derogatory remarks. He suggested that children will internalize a negative view of themselves that a parent communicates, either directly ("You'll break it. You're always breaking things." "You're clumsy.") or indirectly with a look of contempt or disgust. He suggested that these moments are times when the parent should try to repair the internalized self-image conveyed to the child or it will become a self-fulfilling prophecy. That is, children may internalize global parental disapproval as contempt, and contempt as their own characteristic trait of failure.

Ginott also distinguished between being angry with children and being contemptuous. In recent years it has become common to suggest that anger and its expression are destructive (e.g., Tavris, 1982), that anger is related to spousal violence (e.g., Walker, 1984), and that it is the expression of anger that is predictive of coronary artery disease (e.g., Siegman & Smith, 1994). However, we dispute this negative view of anger, and suggest instead that it is contempt and defensiveness, not anger, that is destructive in family relationships. Surprisingly, Ginott agreed with this perspective. He did not suggest that a parent avoid becoming angry toward a child. Indeed, he suggested that a parent's anger and specific displeasure can become the very type of emotional communication that can be the basis of effective discipline. Ginott suggested that the expression of anger be specific, direct, a statement of our inner feelings, perhaps with a reason for our anger, and a statement of what we would wish for.

A NEW APPLICATION OF GINOTT'S THINKING:
META-EMOTION PHILOSOPHY

Our initial interest was in this concept of parents' awareness of their children's emotional lives and their attempts to make an emotional connection with their children. This interest led to the development of our "meta-emotion interview" (Katz & Gottman, 1986). Each parent was separately interviewed about their own experience of sadness and anger, their philosophy of emotional expression and control, and their attitudes and behavior about their children's anger and sadness.

We discovered a great variety in the emotions, experiences, philosophies, and attitudes that parents had about their own emotions and the emotions of their children. For example, one parent said that she viewed anger as "from the devil," and that she would not permit herself or her children to express anger. Some parents were not disapproving of anger, but instead ignored anger in their children. Other parents were accepting of anger, but did not problem-solve with their child. Still other parents encouraged the expression and exploration of anger. There was similar variation with descriptions of sadness. Some parents minimized sadness in themselves and in their children, saying such things as, "I can't afford to be sad," or "What does a child have to be sad about?" Other parents thought that emotions like sadness in their children were opportunities for intimacy.

Our pilot data suggested that there were two main meta-emotion philosophies. Some parents have an *emotion-coaching* philosophy. These parents are aware of the emotions in their own and their children's lives, can talk about them in a differentiated manner, and act like an emotion coach in assisting their children with their negative emotions. An emotion-coaching meta-emotion philosophy had five components: Parents were aware of low intensity emotions in themselves and in their children, they viewed the child's negative emotion as an opportunity for intimacy or teaching, they validated their child's emotion, they assisted the child in verbally labeling the child's emotions, and they problem-solved with the child, setting behavioral limits and discussing goals and strategies for dealing with the situation that led to the emotion. We hypothesized that these parents have a greater ability than other parents to maneuver in the world of emotions and are better able to regulate emotions.

In contrast, a *dismissing* meta-emotion philosophy was one in which parents felt that the child's negative emotions were potentially harmful to the child. They viewed their job as needing to change these toxic negative emotions as quickly as possible and to convey to their children that these negative emotions would not last, were not very important, and that their children could "ride out" these negative emotions without damage. Emotion dismissing families could be sensitive to their children's feelings and want to be helpful, but their approach to emotion was to ignore or deny it. They tended to perceive a child's strong emotion as a demand to fix everything and make it better. They hoped that the dismissing strategy would make the emotion go away quickly, and they often used distraction to move the child along. They did not present an insightful description of their child's emotional experience and did not help the child problem-solve. Instead of helping the child during angry moments by listening and problem-solving, many dismissing families saw their child's anger, independent of any misbehavior, as deserving punishment.

It is important to point out that the term "meta-emotion" is being used in its broadest sense. Metacommunication is communication about communication, and meta-cognition is cognition about cognition. "Meta-emotion" in the narrow sense refers to emotions about emotion. For example, we might only be studying how parents feel about getting angry at their children (e.g., feel guilty about getting angry). However, the term is used broadly here to encompass feelings and thoughts about emotion. As the examples provided suggest, the construct being tapped involves parents' feelings and thoughts about their own and their children's emotions, their responses to their child's emotions, and their reasoning about these responses (i.e., what the parenting is trying to teach the child when responding to the child's anger). We think this broader construct indexes a fundamental attitude or approach to emotion. For some people, emotions are a welcome and enriching part of their lives, whereas for others, emotions are dangerous and to be avoided and minimized.

The concept of meta-emotion represents a significant departure from current conceptualizations of parenting. In the next section, we discuss how this concept differs from previously described parenting dimensions.

WHAT IS NEW IN THE CONCEPT OF META-EMOTION PHILOSOPHY?

Parenting was classified and studied primarily in terms of parental discipline techniques and parental affects displayed toward the child. What we think is missing is how the parent feels about and relates to specific emotional displays by the child, and how this might relate to the parent's feelings about his or her own emotions. This area of family functioning is likely to be more general than a focus on parental affect or discipline techniques. Since parental meta-emotion philosophy is likely to be embedded in a set of parenting skills, we briefly review the parenting research literature. We will not provide a thorough review of this large literature, but instead outline the kinds of variables that were considered to date. Our purpose in this limited review is to suggest that there is something new in considering meta-emotion as part of parenting.

In early multidimensional parenting research that employed factor analysis, two major independent dimensions emerged (Maccoby & Martin, 1983). They are (a) a *permissive/restrictive dimension,* which refers to the amount of autonomy parents permit their children to have, and (b) a *warm/cold-hostile dimension,* which refers to affect (Schaefer, 1959; Becker, 1964). Restrictive parents characteristically make many demands on their children, set limits, and monitor their children to ensure that they meet these demands. Permissive parents characteristically make relatively few demands and give their children much greater freedom in exploring and making decisions for themselves. Warm parents characteristically display affection and approval, whereas hostile parents are critical and likely to belittle and punish their child.

Baumrind (1967, 1971) subsequently distinguished three parental styles based on the two dimensions: authoritarian (restrictive and cold), authoritative (restrictive and warm), and permissive. Authoritarian parents characteristically impose many demands and limits and expect strict obedience, usually without giving the child an explanation. Authoritative parents also set limits on their child's behavior, but are considerably more flexible, providing explanations and lots of warmth. Permissive parents characteristically make few demands, encourage emotional expression in the children, rarely exert firm control, and are warm. Baumrind identified three groups of preschool children: energetic–friendly, conflicted–irritable, and impulsive–aggressive. Authoritarian parents tended to have children who were conflicted–irritable (fearful, apprehensive, moody, unhappy, easily annoyed, passively hostile, vulnerable to stress, aimless, sulky, and unfriendly). Authoritative parents tended to have children in the energetic–friendly category (self-reliant, self-controlled, cheerful, friendly, coping well with stress, cooperative with adults, curious, purposive, and achievement-oriented). Permissive parents tended to have children who were impulsive–aggressive (rebellious, low in self-reliance and self-control, impulsive, aggressive, domineering, aimless, and low in achievement). The children of authoritative parents were high in both social and cognitive skills, but children of permissive parents were relatively unskilled in both. These patterns, observed when the children were 8 to 9 years old, tend to persist into adolescence.

The work of attachment theorists (Bowlby, 1973; 1980; 1982; Ainsworth, Blehar, Waters, & Wall, 1978) added a focus on parental responsiveness, which is related to but not identical with the warmth/hostility dimension. According to attachment theorists, sensitive and responsive parenting provides the child with a secure base from which to explore his or her environment, and the establishment of a secure attachment relationship during the infancy period guides the development of self-regulation and effective socioemotional functioning.

One quality of parental responsiveness described by infancy and attachment theorists is the temporal linkage or contingent responding of the parent's behavior with the child's. In normal caregiver–infant interactions, about 30% of face-to-face interaction is spent in coordinated states (Tronick, 1989). Infants who habitually experience miscoordinated states, such as infants with depressed or otherwise unresponsive caregivers, exhibit difficulties in their regulatory patterns (Gianino & Tronick, 1988). Normal interactions are disrupted and infants employ self-regulatory behaviors in an automatic, inflexible, and indiscriminate way (Field, Healy, Goldsstein, & Perry, 1988).

As can be seen from this brief review, one of the main threads that run through the literature on parenting is the importance of parental discipline techniques and gaining child compliance. The concept of parental responsiveness emphasizes the notion of contingent responding to child behavior, but does not focus specifically on how parents deal with children's emotional displays. When the world of emotions has been brought into the realm of parenting, the emphasis has been placed on the emotions parents display towards their children (typically affection/praise or hostility/coldness). Ginott's main thesis was the importance of making and maintaining an emotional connection with the child, which he argues is achieved through listening, validating, and understanding the child's feelings. Thus, according to Ginott, one of the main goals of parenting is intimacy. It was Ginott's contention that having this type of intimate emotional relationship functions to obtain the child's compliance and minimize power struggles, although obtaining compliance is certainly not Ginott's idea of the goal of parenting.

The concept of parental meta-emotion philosophy is an attempt to operationalize and bring the spirit of Ginott's thinking into the research realm. We believe that such an integration will enrich the parenting literature. However, we believe that parental meta-emotion philosophy is embedded in a web of parenting skills. In the following section, we describe our efforts to build a theoretical model to explain how parental meta-emotion philosophy might function to affect children's adjustment.

META-EMOTION AND CHILD ADJUSTMENT: BUILDING A THEORETICAL MODEL

What mechanisms explain how meta-emotions affect the functioning of families and come to affect child outcomes? We are particularly drawn to theories that attempt to integrate behavior and physiology, and so our theorizing is oriented toward approaches that emphasized the importance of balance and regulation, the developing children's abilities in the regulation of emotion (Garber & Dodge, 1991), in the development of children's abilities to self-soothe strong, potentially disruptive emotional states (Dunn, 1977), focus attention, and organize themselves for coordinated action in the service of some goal.

Meta-Emotion and the Development
of Emotion Regulation Abilities

The ability to regulate emotion is probably learned by infants, to some degree, through interactions with parents. Some writers suggested that these abilities are also, to some extent, temperamental. Rothbart and Derryberry (1981) suggested that individual differences in reactivity and self-regulatory processes underlie much of an infant's affective, cognitive, and social behavior. Reactivity refers to the threshold, intensity, and latency of an infant's reactions to changes in the environment. Individual differences in reactivity may also influence interactions with caregivers (Porges, 1991). For example, irritable reactive infants may initiate more interactions with caregivers than more placid infants. In addition, infants who are more reactive to both negative and positive events may provide caregivers with more information about their optimal level of stimulation and preferred modes of interaction (Rothbart & Derryberry, 1981).

Self-regulatory processes develop at both the behavioral and physiological levels. The development of physiological homeostasis, which develops in the very first few months of life, is considered a crucial task for infants because it enables them to shift their energy and attention from the inner to the outer world. It also provides an optimal state for the reception of sensory and social information. This state was referred to as one of alert inactivity (Stern, 1985). During these times, infants are physically quiet, yet alert and apparently able to take in information from the outside world.

During the first 2 to 3 months of life, the infant's major task is one of achieving physiological homeostasis. Attentional and other emotion regulatory processes play a central role in this process as they provide multiple strategies for self-soothing and should increase the ability of infants to be soothed by others. Caregivers play a vital role by helping infants achieve this state before they are able to do this for themselves. In the way caregivers interact with their infants, they can influence the child's basic regulatory abilities, and, in part, lay the groundwork for later abilities the child will have in self-soothing, repairing interaction, and focusing attention. In addition, some infants are more physiologically able to accomplish this task.

Porges (1984) reviewed evidence that suggests that a child's *baseline vagal tone* is related to the child's capacity to react and to self-regulate. Vagal tone refers to the tonic firing of the vagus nerve, which is the main nerve of the parasympathetic nervous system. Vagal firing slows down many physiological processes, including the heart's rate. Porges' research in the early 1970s (Porges, 1972, 1973) demonstrated a link between heart rate reactivity and spontaneous base-level heart rate variability. Initially the demonstration was that among college students baseline heart rate variability was related to heart rate reactivity and to reaction time (higher variability was related to faster reaction times). This was extended to newborn infants' heart rate variability and their reaction to simple visual and auditory stimuli (Porges, Arnold, & Forbes, 1973); newborns with greater heart rate variability had shorter latency responses, and only the infants with high heart rate variability responded to the stimuli as the illumination was lowered. Because heart rate variability is related to many factors other than the functioning of the vagus nerve (respiratory, blood pressure changes, thermoregulatory influences), Porges and his colleagues developed a more precise measure of the tonic functioning of the vagus (*vagal tone*) by using only that portion of heart rate variability that is related to respiration (known as *respiratory sinus arrhythmia*). It is well known that the heart rate increases when we inhale and decreases when we exhale, and this induces a rhythmic respiratory component into heart rate variability, which can be extracted statistically with the methods known as time-series analysis (e.g., Gottman, 1981; Williams & Gottman, 1981).

Porges (1984) showed that baseline vagal tone is related to reactivity as well as to regulatory processes. During circumcision, infants with a higher vagal tone showed larger heart rate accelerations and lower fundamental cry frequencies (Porter, Porges, & Marshall, 1988). Behavioral reactivity and irritability on the Neonatal Behavioral Assessment Scale were also associated with higher basal vagal tone. DiPietro and Porges (1991) found that vagal tone was related to reactivity to gavage feeding. Fox (1989) found that infants who had higher basal vagal tone were more likely to cry during mild arm restraint than infants lower in vagal tone.

However, this relationship of basal vagal tone to reactivity is also usually associated with greater regulatory abilities as well. Linnemeyer and Porges (1986) found that infants with higher vagal tone were more likely to look longer at novel stimuli. Richards (1985, 1987) found that infants with higher basal vagal tone were less distractible. Infants with higher vagal tone habituate to novel stimuli more rapidly than infants with a lower vagal tone (Huffman, Bryan, Pederson, & Porges, 1988). Hofheimer and Lawson (1988) found that basal vagal tone with premature infants was significantly correlated with the percentage of focused attention they exhibited while with the mother; the high vagal tone infant's higher reactivity may predispose the infant to receive greater caretaking responses, and this ability to maintain attention when with the mother may also predispose these infants to be able to elicit more face-to-face positive interaction from the mother as well. Huffman et al. also found a relationship between higher vagal tone and greater soothability. Children with high vagal tone required little soothing and distress was easily relieved. Fox (Fox, 1989; Stifter & Fox, 1990; Stifter, Fox, & Porges, 1989) also found that the same infants who at 5 months had higher basal vagal tone were more reactive at 5 months to mild arm restraint; by 14 months they were better at self-soothing, higher in exploring a potentially scary novel stimulus, and more likely to approach a stranger.

There is another dimension of vagal tone that also needs to be considered, namely, the ability to suppress vagal tone. In general, vagal tone is suppressed during states that require focused or sustained attention, mental effort, focusing on relevant information, and organized responses to stress. Thus, the child's ability to perform a transitory suppression of vagal tone in response to environmental and, particularly, emotional demands is another index that needs to be added to the child regulatory physiology construct. Some infants with a high vagal tone who were unable to suppress vagal tone in attention-demanding tasks exhibited regulatory disorders (e.g., sleep disorders; Porges, 1991). Children with attentional deficits also exhibit an inability to suppress heart rate variability or vagal tone during task demands (Porges, 1991). In comparing hyperactive to developmentally delayed children, Porges, Walter, Korb, and Sprague (1975) found that developmentally delayed children do not suppress vagal tone and have a lower baseline heart rate variability, whereas hyperactive children were more likely to have normal levels of baseline heart rate variability but a deficit in suppression during task demands. Using the Garcia-Coll Behavioral Responsiveness Paradigm (BRP) with 3-month-old infants, Huffman, Bryan, Pederson, and Porges (1992) found that infants who suppressed vagal tone during the BRP were rated by their mothers as having longer durations of orienting, more frequent laughing and smiling, and greater ease in soothability as compared to infants who failed to suppress vagal tone. The ability to suppress vagal tone during infancy was also found to predict children's later adjustment. Portales, Doussard-Roosevelt, and Porges (1991) found that 9-month-old infants who had lower baseline vagal tone and less vagal tone suppression during the Bayley examination had the greatest behavioral problems at 3 years of age, as measured by the Achenbach & Edelbrock Child Behavior Checklist.

We know little about the mechanisms that contribute to variation in children's vagal tone. Porges and Doussard-Roosevelt (1997) argue that vagal tone represents a physiological substrate of a temperamental characteristic. The degree to which this physiological substrate represents genetic influences or an interaction between genetic and environmental factors remains unclear. Given the plasticity of the nervous system of the developing child, environmental conditions ranging from nutrition and health care behavior to social interaction may influence the child's physiological status. There is growing evidence that the social environment can influence children's autonomic nervous system. For example, infants of depressed mothers show higher heart rate during social interactions with both their mother and an unfamiliar adult than infants of nondepressed mothers (Dawson, Hessl, & Frey, 1994; Field et al., 1988). This heightened level of physiological arousal appears to be specific to social situations and does not occur under baseline or nonsocial conditions (Dawson, Hessl, & Frey, 1994). Field et al. (1988) also found that infants of depressed mothers had higher salivary cortisol levels than infants of nondepressed mothers following face-to-face interactions. To the extent that social interaction can affect physiological reactivity, we raise the intriguing hypothesis that parental meta-emotion philosophy may influence the child's ability to regulate emotion, as indexed by physiological measures of vagal tone and suppression of vagal tone. By coaching children during strong emotional events, parents may be teaching children how to physiologically self-soothe and calm themselves down after upsetting events. This may be one mechanism by which having an emotion-coaching meta-emotion philosophy results in more positive adjustment for children. In the next section, we explore the hypothesis that parental meta-emotion philosophy influences children's well-being through its effects on parenting skills.

Meta-Emotion and Parenting

Parents' philosophy about emotion is likely to be related to their parenting practices. The question, however, is exactly what type of parenting skills would be associated with an emotion-coaching philosophy? Two sets of hypotheses seemed plausible. The first hypothesis was that an emotion-coaching meta-emotion philosophy might be nested within a web of positive parenting. Emotion-coaching parents might show high levels of warmth, both toward their child and toward each other. To measure parental warmth, we employed the Cowans' observational system, which codes parental coldness and parental warmth, both toward the child, and toward one another (called "co-parenting" warmth and coldness). Another possibility was that emotion-coaching parents are not simply warm toward their child, but are structuring, enthusiastic, engaged, affectionate, and limit-setting, as is characteristic of Baumrind's authoritative parenting, and also show the responsive style that attachment theorists have identified. Within the context of a teaching task in our lab, we call this dimension *scaffolding/praising parenting*. To measure the scaffolding/praising dimension, we used our laboratory's Kahen engagement and affect coding systems. We computed the sum of five variables selected from the Kahen Engagement and Affect Coding Systems, which we called scaffolding/praising. There are three positive engagement codes: (a) engaged, which consisted of parental attention toward the child; (b) responds to child's needs, in which parents responded to a child's question or complaint; and (c) positive directiveness, in which parents issued a directive in a positive fashion. The sum also included two positive affect codes: (a) affection, which consisted of praise and physical affection, and (b) enthusiasm, which was coded as cheering and excitement at the child's performance. We omitted the father's enthusiasm code from this sum, because we found that, for the father alone, our enthusiasm code was significantly correlated with his criticism. This was not the case for the mother.

The hypothesis that this form of positive parenting should be related to a coaching meta-emotion structure is implicit in the writing of Ginott. Ginott also wrote strongly about the importance of understanding and validating the child's emotions, and avoiding criticism, contempt, and disapproval. Most of the examples from Ginott's books have to do with the importance of emotion coaching in avoiding escalating negativity, frustration, disapproval, and increasing emotional distance between parents and children. It appears to have been suggested foremost as a mechanism for obtaining extensive relief from spiraling negativity. Consistent with this stance, we hold that meta-emotion performs its major function by inhibiting parental derogation toward the child. To measure this form of negativity, we use the codes of our Kahen coding systems that tap parental intrusiveness, criticism, and mockery of the child. In a teaching task, as some of the parents in our laboratory instruct their children, they mix in a blend of frustration, taking over for the child as soon as the child has trouble with the task (intrusiveness), criticism, and derisive humor (mockery, humiliation, belittling the child). Although parents who display these behaviors do not desire to inflict harm, their behavior is detrimental to their children's development. In fact, we think that this dimension of parenting represents the microsocial processes characteristic of parental rejection.

The Theoretical Model

In building our theoretical model, we sought to explain how meta-emotion philosophy might be related to a variety of child outcomes. The theoretical model is depicted in Fig. 7.1. Two main pathways through the model can be seen. First, we expected that parental meta-emotion philosophy would have some effect through parenting practices. As already described, we examined whether meta-emotion philosophy would be related to scaffolding/praising parenting or to the inhibition of parental derogation. Second, we examined whether parental meta-emotion philosophy would directly af-

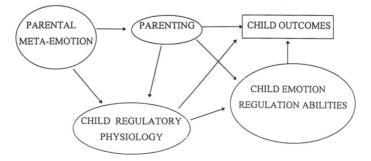

FIG. 7.1. Theoretical Model.

fect emotion regulation abilities, as assessed by parasympathetic nervous system functioning and parental report. That is, we fundamentally believe that these physiological variables are not entirely engraved in stone even if they are biological, but are instead malleable and shaped in part by parents through their emotional interactions with the child. This conceptual pathway enables us to assess whether meta-emotion philosophy is in some way related to the child's regulatory physiology, or, conversely, if the child's regulatory physiology is related to meta-emotion philosophy. Indirect effects of parental meta-emotion philosophy on emotion-regulation abilities that might occur through parenting were also examined. We also predict that there will be statistically significant path coefficients connecting the child physiology variables to the child outcome variables, suggesting that the child physiology at age 5 predicts child outcome at age 8. We also predict the physiological variables will predict the emotion regulation variable, and that the regulation and the parenting variables will relate to child outcomes. We predict that parenting will also have a direct effect on child regulation.

We proposed that the parents' meta-emotion coaching philosophy will be related to a variety of child outcomes. We hypothesized that a parental meta-emotion coaching philosophy would be related to the child's developing social competence with other children. We expect that the child's peer social competence will hold in the inhibition of negative affect (Guralnick, 1981), particularly negativity such as aggression, whining, oppositional behavior, fighting requiring parental intervention, sadness, and anxiety with peers. We also expected that an emotion-coaching meta-emotion philosophy would predict the development of superior *cognitive* skills of the child (through superior vagal tone and greater ability to focus attention). Finally, we examined the child's physical health as an outcome variable. Since the vagus innervates the thymus gland (Bulloch & Moore, 1981; Bulloch & Pomerantz, 1984; Magni, Brushi, & Kasti, 1987; Nance, Hopkins, & Bieger, 1987), a central part of the immune system that is involved in the production of T-cells, we also expected that basal vagal tone would be related to better child physical health.

RESULTS OF MODEL DEVELOPMENT

Separate sets of theoretical models were constructed to examine hypotheses related to each child outcome, and for hypotheses related to derogation and scaffolding/praising.

Model building using our theory was generally successful, and we were able to find linkages for the major pathways we proposed (for a complete presentation of results, see Gottman, Katz, & Hooven, 1996, 1997; Katz, Gottman, & Hooven, 1996). Several consistencies were observed across models. In all models, coaching the child's emotions was negatively related to the negative parenting variable, suggesting the hypothesis that coaching is an inhibitor of parental derogation of the child. Parental meta-emotion philosophy was also positively related to parents' use of scaffolding/praising. Parental meta-emotion philosophy was also directly and significantly related in all the models to the child's physiology. This suggests the intriguing hypothesis that parents can influence a child's physiology by emotion coaching, although we cannot differentiate directionality of effects without an experiment. It was interesting that in all models, the child's ability to suppress vagal tone at age 5 was a significant predictor of the child's emotion regulation at age 8. The greater the child's ability to suppress vagal tone at age 5, the less the parents had to down-regulate the child's negative affects, inappropriate behavior, and over-excitement at age 8.

Interestingly, our observational measures of parent–child interaction did not directly relate to child physiology, or to maternal ratings of emotion regulation ability at age 8. Only the parent's philosophy of emotion was related to the child's emotion regulation system. However, parenting was related to child outcomes in three of the six models. For derogatory parenting, there was a direct link with child academic achievement and child peer relations, whereas for scaffolding/praising there was a direct link only with academic achievement.

The data suggest, then, that parental meta-emotion philosophy affects different child outcomes via different pathways. When predicting teacher ratings of *peer relations*, parents who are aware of their children's emotions and coach their children during emotional moments have children who are better able to physiologically self-soothe. Children who are able to physiologically self-soothe showed an improved ability to calm themselves down when they were upset (as indexed by maternal ratings of emotion regulation ability), and, in turn, were rated by their teachers as showing better peer relations. Awareness and coaching of emotion were also directly related to teacher ratings of peer relations. When predicting *academic achievement*, parental meta-emotion philosophy had its effects through parenting abilities. Parental awareness and coaching of emotion were related to the inhibition of parental derogation and to scaffolding/praising during parent–child interaction. Parents who were less derogatory and more scaffolding/praising had children who showed better academic achievement. Finally, when predicting *child illness*, parents who were aware of their children's emotions and coached their children during emotional moments had children who were better able to physiologically self-soothe. The ability to physiologically self-soothe was directly related to child illness: children with higher basal vagal tone showed less physical illness. Parental meta-emotion philosophy was also directly related to child illness. Parents who coached their children during emotional moments had children who exhibited fewer physical illnesses.

Given that parental meta-emotion philosophy is related to the parent–child relationship, we wondered whether meta-emotion philosophy represents an approach to emotion that is unique to the parent–child relationship or theoretically represents a level of social skills that is applied to the marriage as well. In the next section, we explore the relation of meta-emotion philosophy and marital adjustment and conflict.

META-EMOTION PHILOSOPHY
AND MARITAL QUALITY

Research on marriage consistently demonstrated that the way couples resolve conflict is important in differentiating between happily and unhappily married couples. Happily married couples have been found to display higher ratios of agreement to disagreement (Gottman, 1979), exhibit more positive nonverbal cues (Birchler, 1977; Haynes, Follingstad, & Sullivan, 1979), more agreement and approval (Vincent & Friedman, 1979), and less coercive and attacking behaviors (Billings, 1979) than unhappily married couples. One of the most consistent discriminators between happily and unhappily married couples is the degree of negative affect expressed during conflict resolution. Unhappily married couples show more negative affect and negative affect reciprocity than happily married couples (e.g., Gottman, 1979; Revenstorf, Vogel, Wegener, Hahlweg, & Schindler, 1980).

However, not all negative affect is equally corrosive to relationships. In a series of papers based more on observational methods, our laboratory identified interactive processes that longitudinally predict which couples will separate and divorce (Buehlman, Gottman & Katz, 1992; Gottman, 1993a, 1993b, 1994; Gottman & Levenson, 1992). Despite the volumes of research on divorce, only a few studies have been longitudinal, prospective studies attempting to predict which couples will separate and divorce. These studies are reviewed elsewhere (Gottman 1993a; 1994). These studies have not done very well in prediction, nor have they been able to lead the way toward the development of a theory of marital dissolution.

Our laboratory approached the problem as follows. First, recognizing both the need for and the limitations of short term longitudinal research, we were able to identify an *outcome cascade* of events that form a Guttman-like scale of precursor events that lead to separation and divorce. It is important to be able to identify such a cascade because in our laboratory in any short term study only 2.5% to 5% of the sample divorces each year. Hence, divorce, a common event within the lifetime of a set of marriages, is a relatively rare event in any particular year of a longitudinal study. A similar problem faces any high risk research, such as the study of heart attacks. Heart attacks are rare in any particular sample in a short time period, and it would be helpful to be able to predict a cascade of events, with precursor events such as chest pain, that are more frequent. Such an outcome cascade exists for marriage. Second, we searched for *process cascades* that described the processes of marital interaction and change over time. We discovered these cascades in three domains: (a) behavior, interactive marital behavior and sequences of interaction in various types of conversations (events of the day, conflict resolution, positive conversations); (b) thought, self-report, thoughts about the interaction, attributions about the partner and the marriage; and (c) physiology, particularly indices of autonomic arousal. These predictor cascades were organized into a theory about the mechanism of marital dissolution.

Probably the clearest prediction is the presence of four processes that Gottman (1994) called "The Four Horsemen of the Apocalypse": Criticism, Contempt, Defensiveness, and Stonewalling. The best single predictor of dissolution across studies tends to be contempt, particularly the wife's contempt. Contempt is the single clearest index of the disintegration of affectionate and empathetic emotional connection in the marriage. The behavior of defensiveness is an essential element in this process cascade, and it fuels the process of emotionally distancing the couple. There is ample evidence across several laboratories that the antidote for defensiveness is validation (see Notarius & Markman, 1994).

Interestingly, anger in marital interaction is not predictive of marital dissolution. The damaging variables tap the dimensions of criticism, contempt, defensiveness, and withdrawal. Unfortunately, in many recent writings about marriage, there is an equation of anger with hostility and even violence (Cummings & Davies, 1994). There is no evidence that anger, if unblended with criticism, defensiveness, contempt, or stonewalling, is harmful to a marriage. No one likes to have a loved one angry with him or her. However, it may be a necessary part of living together and making the continual adjustments necessary to keep a marriage close and intimate. We think, in fact, that anger is a natural part of the *irritability system* (Wilson & Gottman, 1995), which is balanced with the *affectional system* to create a set point for each couple. Gottman and Krokoff (1989) reached a similar conclusion in predicting longitudinal changes in marital satisfaction. We think it is important for process researchers to be precise about which factors are harmful and which are protective to a marriage. It is also important to know which factors are harmful and protective to marriages because of the implications of destructive processes in marriages for negative child outcomes. Grych and Fincham's (1990) provocative integrative model is quite helpful in this regard. However, although we agree that both destructive marital conflict and violence are harmful to children, we think it was unfortunate that Grych and Fincham (1990) lumped domestic violence with marital conflict to review effects on children. The effects on children of these two variables are likely to be quite different.

There were no consistent gender differences in defensiveness and contempt across studies, although when there was a difference, men were found to be more defensive than women, but this difference declined dramatically with the length of marriage (Carstensen, Gottman, & Levenson, 1995). Criticism and stonewalling show consistent gender differences, with women consistently higher than men in criticism and men consistently higher than women in stonewalling. A related marital interaction pattern, called the *demand–withdraw pattern*, was identified by Christensen and his associates (Christensen & Heavey, 1990; Christensen & Shenk, 1991; Heavey, Layne, & Christensen, 1993). Gottman and Levenson (1988) reviewed research literature and speculated about the possible biological roots of gender differences, and Gottman (1994) reviewed research literature and speculated about the possible developmental roots of these gender differences. The Gottman–Levenson hypothesis about the biological roots of these gender differences is that men have a lower threshold of negative affect for physiological reactivity than women, and that their physiological recovery is slower. This hypothesis was recently modified (Levenson, Carstensen, & Gottman, 1994) with results that suggest that men are somewhat more aware of their own states of physiological arousal than are women, that when negative affect increases in a marital interaction, men are tuned into their bodies and respond to their physiological arousal with social withdrawal, whereas women, who are less aware of their own states of physiological arousal, respond to the negative affect in the marital interaction by becoming more engaged, responding to the social cues. The developmental hypothesis is that women have been socialized to code and decode emotion and have developed an expertise in emotion within relationships that is far greater than that of men. Maccoby (1980) proposed the idea that the cross-culturally universal sex-segregation effect in children's play is due primarily to the fact that girls will accept influence in play from both sexes, whereas boys will accept influence only from other boys. It is quite likely that women have also been socialized to take responsibility for keeping marriages in good repair, whereas men have been socialized not to accept influence from women. There is no evidence that this differential influence effect changes with increasing age to adulthood, although it may change in the elderly (Carstensen, Gottman, & Levenson, 1995).

In a marriage, the fact that most of the "business" of a marriage is emotional communication, the fact that women hold the greater expertise in the expression, decoding, and management of emotion in relationships, and the fact that men are socialized to not accept influence from women makes for a particularly volatile set of initial conditions for any marriage. There is a great deal of evidence to suggest that women are relentless in their pursuit of emotional intimacy and respect in marriages, and that they take the role of emotional managers in families (see Gottman, 1994, for a review). Thus, the critical dimension in understanding whether a marriage will work or not becomes the extent to which the man can accept the influence of the woman he loves and become socialized in emotional communication.

Given the importance of emotional communication within the marriage, the dimensions of meta-emotion that we are discussing may have critical implications for the marriage itself, as well as for the child. We are interested in several aspects of the parents' marriage. We want to see if the meta-emotion variables can be thought of as social skills that can be applied to the marriage as well as to parenting. In approaching this question, we examined whether meta-emotion philosophy is related to marital interaction during conflict resolution, and to variables that tap the longitudinal stability and happiness of the marriage. We also wish to assess whether the meta-emotion variables are related to the couple's overall philosophy of the marriage, particularly about how best to resolve conflict.

Meta-Emotion Philosophy and Resolving Marital Conflicts

Couples were observed while they engaged in a 15-minute high-conflict marital discussion. Self-identified problem areas were identified and explicated through the course of a play-by-play interview; then the interviewer left the room while the marital discussion occurred. We found that the father's awareness of his own emotions, particularly his sadness, was related to more positive means of resolving marital disputes. Fathers who are aware of their own sadness are more affectionate in the marital interaction, and their wives are significantly less contemptuous and belligerent. Fathers who accept their own sadness are also less likely to stonewall. Fathers who coach their children's sadness are less disgusted, less defensive, and more affectionate toward their wives; their wives are also less defensive and more affectionate.

Fathers who coach their children's anger are more affectionate, and their wives are less contemptuous, less belligerent, less defensive, and more affectionate. However, fathers who are aware of their own anger and aware of their child's anger were more defensive, so the father's awareness of his own anger may not be such a positive quality, viewed from the standpoint of the marital interaction.

The mother's awareness and coaching of emotion was also related to the way in which conflicts are resolved in the marriage. Mothers who are aware of their own sadness are less contemptuous and belligerent and have husbands who are less belligerent toward them. Mothers who are aware of their children's sadness have husbands who are less disgusted, and they are themselves less disgusted and less contemptuous. Mothers who coach their children's sadness have husbands who are less disgusted and less belligerent, and they themselves are less disgusted and less belligerent. Thus, we have preliminary evidence that meta-emotion philosophy is related to how couples resolve marital disputes.

Meta-Emotion and Marital Satisfaction and Stability

Gottman and his colleagues (Gottman, 1994; Gottman & Levenson, 1992) described a cascade toward marital dissolution. The cascade consists of precursor variables that predict divorce. Essentially, the cascade describes two trajectories couples take in their marriages, a happy and stable trajectory and another headed toward dissolution. The structural equation model for this cascade links research on the correlates of marital dissatisfaction with research on divorce, showing that there is a Guttman scale of precursor variables in divorce prediction. Couples headed for divorce are unhappily married for some time, seriously consider separation and divorce, and then actually do separate and divorce. In this section, we examine whether meta-emotion variables predict this cascade.

We found that the meta-emotion codes are uniformly related to higher marital satisfaction at Time 1 and at Time 2, to fewer serious considerations of separation and divorce, less actual separation, and, if separation did occur, to shorter separations, and less likelihood of divorce. Hence an emotion coaching meta-emotion philosophy is related to greater marital stability and to greater marital satisfaction.

Meta-Emotion Variables and the Parents' Philosophy
of Marriage

We found that the meta-emotion variables are not isolated and limited to only the parent–child family subsystem, but are also related to the couple's philosophy of marriage. Parents who were aware of their own emotions and were aware of or coached their children's emotions were more likely to spontaneously express fondness for their spouses, to talk about the importance of we-ness or a companionate philosophy of marriage, to say that it is important to discuss emotional issues in the marriage, to believe that marital conflict is worth the struggle, and to feel less chaotic and out of control of their lives.

Meta-Emotion Discrepancy

We noted in examining the transcripts of couples' meta-emotion interviews that a discrepancy between husband and wife in meta-emotion structure appeared to be strongly related to problems in the marriage. We computed two variables to index this discrepancy, the squares of the differences between spouses in coaching anger (a variable we called x) and coaching sadness (a variable we called y). These two variables alone were able to predict divorce or marital stability in a discriminant function analysis with 80% accuracy. These effects were unrelated to social class variables (nonsignificant correlations with occupational status, education, and income). They were also not mediated through marital interaction (i.e., they were uncorrelated with the marital interaction codes). They were not mediated through the husband's considering separation or divorce, but they were correlated with the wife's considerations of separation and divorce.

Discrepancies between husband and wife in how they ought to deal with emotion seems to be fundamental to the character of the marriage. This is an area that warrants further exploration. Using a mathematical model of marital interaction, we discovered (Cook et al., 1995) that a discrepancy in influence functions between husband and wife predicted divorce. It may be that influence pattern discrepancies are related to meta-emotion discrepancies (for details, see Gottman, 1994).

Summary

These data provide some preliminary evidence that meta-emotion philophy is related to the quality of both the parent–child relationship and the marriage. However, they also raise several important questions. From these correlational data, we cannot discover what comes first, a particular orientation toward one's own and others' emotions and then the quality of the marriage, or the converse. Without true experiments, we can only speculate. Our hypothesis is that meta-emotion precedes marital quality, for the reasons we gave in our earlier review of the processes predictive of marital stability and the gender differences we observed.

At this point in our work, we can only conclude that not only do the meta-emotion variables have validity in terms of the quality of the parent–child interaction, but amazingly, they are related to the quality of the marital interaction, marital satisfaction, and marital stability as well. The oral history variables provide some insight into these relationships. The meta-emotion variables are related to the couple's entire philosophy of emotional communication. Couples who have an emotion coaching meta-emotion structure are also more validating and affectionate during marital conflict, they are less disgusted, belligerent, and contemptuous during marital conflict, and the husbands are less likely to stonewall. They express a philosophy of marriage that emphasizes companionship and we-ness, and they express fondness and admiration for one another. They say spontaneously that they believe in expressing their negative feelings about the marriage and discussing them rather than avoiding them, they believe the pain and struggle of working on the marriage is worth it, and they feel less chaotic and out of control in their lives together.

Perhaps the meta-emotion variables tap a fundamental quality about emotional connection in the marriage as well as in the parent–child system. Perhaps some of the fundamental incompatibilities in marriage come from having divergent views about emotion, that is, disparate meta-emotion structures. We think this is a real possibility, and hypothesize that spouses who have different meta-emotion philosophies will have unstable marriages and their interaction will be characterized by disappointment, negativity, criticism, contempt, defensiveness, and by eventual emotional withdrawal. This meta-emotion compatibility may be the fundamental dynamic that operates to make marriages work.

META-EMOTION PHILOSOPHY AND FAMILIES
WITH DEVELOPMENTALLY DELAYED CHILDREN

To understand how parents' beliefs and philosophies concerning emotion may influence children's social and emotional development, it will be important to examine different groups of children who are at risk for social difficulties. Children with developmental delays are at particular risk for these problems. Observational and sociometric measures indicate that developmentally delayed children are the least preferred play partners of nondelayed children (Guralnick & Groom, 1987). They are more likely than nondelayed children to spend significant time in solitary play and spend less time in group play (Guralnick & Groom, 1985, 1987; Guralnick & Weinhouse, 1984). Researchers and educators are concerned by these difficulties because peer relationships serve important functions throughout development. We know that peers contribute to the socialization of children and encourage language as well as cognitive and moral development (Garvey, 1986; Hartup, 1978, 1983; Piaget, 1932/1965). Evidence also suggests that children who have difficulty in their peer relations, especially in making friends, are at considerable risk for later problems (Parker & Asher, 1987).

The peer-related social deficits evidenced by developmentally delayed children, especially the mildly delayed, far exceed that which can be attributed solely to their cognitive delay (Field, 1980; Guralnick & Groom, 1985, 1987; Guralnick & Weinhouse, 1984) or general communicative competence (Guralnick & Paul-Brown, 1986). Reputational bias and the unavailability of responsive social interactants are also unlikely candidates for explanation (Guralnick & Groom, 1987). One underlying process known to support effective peer relationships is the ability to regulate negative emotions and behavior (Cole, Zahn-Waxler, & Smith, 1994; Eisenberg et al., 1995; Sroufe, Schork, Motti, Lawroski, & LaFreniere, 1984).

Work by Kopp, Krakow, and Johnson (1983) indicates that delayed children have deficits in their ability to effectively regulate their behavior in frustrating situations. They found that Down syndrome children (with developmental ages between 24 and 40 months) had more difficulty with tasks requiring behavioral delay than did nondelayed children of the same developmental age. Kopp et al. suggested that a primary factor in the difficulties of these children was their lack of attention–distraction strategies. Selective attention provides a number of avenues for the regulation of negative emotion (Rothbart & Posner, 1985). During one task, children were shown an attractive play telephone and told that they could play with it after the experimenter returned from the next room. To cope with the frustration of having to wait, nondelayed children looked away from the telephone, watched their hands, gazed at the ceiling and around the room. The delayed children, on the other hand, rarely turned away from the telephone and were less able to resist touching it.

Wilson (1994) investigated the emotion regulation abilities of developmentally delayed children by observing their behavior during a challenging social task, entry into the on-going play of two other children. Parents were also interviewed concerning their meta-emotion system. The following sections present this research and discuss the central role of emotion regulation in children's ability to succeed at relevant social tasks such as entry, and the role of language in the regulation of affect and behavior. Speculations are made regarding the association between children's emotion regulation abilities and their parents' awareness and involvement in their emotional experiences.

Entry and Emotion Regulation

The entry situation provides an especially relevant context for examining emotion regulation, because research with nondelayed children indicates that this is a difficult and frustrating task (Dodge, McClaskey, & Feldman, 1985). Young children are frequently presented with the need to enter a new play group. Most of the play episodes of these children last less than 5 minutes (Corsaro, 1979). We also know that failure is a frequent event in entry situations. Groups tend to protect their play interactions by discouraging the initial entry attempts of others; consequently, over 50% of young children's initial attempts fail (Corsaro, 1979). Furthermore, it is likely that this figure underestimates the proportion of failures experienced by children with developmental delays. Low status nondelayed children typically encounter more resistance when attempting to enter groups; they require more time and more bids to achieve entry than more popular nondelayed children do (Putallaz & Gottman, 1981). Consequently, developmentally delayed children need to be especially patient yet persistent to succeed at entry. If they lack effective strategies for coping with entry failure, they may resort to inappropriate entry behaviors such as aggression. The expression of negative affect and behavior decreases the probability of group acceptance and may contribute to negative evaluations by peers and teachers (Eisenberg et al., 1995; Sroufe, Schork, Motti, Lawroski, & LaFreniere, 1984).

Wilson (1994) compared the responses of developmentally delayed and nondelayed children to having their entry attempts ignored. She found that delayed children were less likely than nondelayed children to avert their gaze away from the play area after their attempts failed. After experiencing failure, delayed children were more likely than nondelayed children to increase their use of disruptive entry strategies.

These results support the hypothesis that a primary social skill deficit of developmentally delayed children is an inability to effectively regulate their negative affect and behavior in challenging social situations. A number of mechanisms may help to explain these differences. One potential mechanism is children's ability to recognize and label affective states.

Language: A Mechanism for Regulating Negative Affect

With the development of symbolic thought, children have at their disposal a powerful tool for soothing negative affect during challenging situations. This is especially true when we consider talk that is directed to the self, that is "self-talk." Vygotsky (1962) observed that by 3 or 4 years of age, children begin to use egocentric speech, talking to themselves as they engage in activities. At this point, language provides a way for children to solve problems. The ability to symbolically represent internal states such as emotions also provides children with new ways to regulate these states. Verbal mediation was described by Pine (1985), who suggested that, "Words provide a moment of recognition and delay in which discomfort over feeling might have a chance of being handled in ways other than denial or immediate discharge through action" (p. 139). The use of language to express affective states may also facilitate control over nonverbal expressions of emotion and help the child regulate his or her affective experiences (Hesse & Cicchetti, 1982).

Another way that language helps children gain control of their affective experiences is through communicating these internal states to others. For example, preschool children's fantasy play often contains emotional themes. Children may act out situations that are upsetting to them, thus enabling them to understand and cope with them (Gottman, 1986). The following episode involves two cross-sex friends aged four and five. Eric pretends to be a skeleton.

E: (Screams) A skeleton, everyone, a skeleton?
N: I'm your friend. The dinosaur.
E: Oh, hi, dinosaur. You know, no one likes me.
N: But I like you. I'm your friend.
E: But none of my other friends like me. They don't like my new suit. They don't like my skeleton suit. It's really just me. They think I'm a dumb dumb.

N: I know what. He's a good skeleton.

E: (yelling): I am not a dumb dumb.

N: I'm not calling you a dumb dumb. I'm calling you a friendly skeleton. (Gottman, 1986, p. 160)

The skeleton expresses Eric's fear that people do not like him. This is a safe context for voicing these concerns because the feeling belongs to the skeleton, not Eric. The act of rehearsing emotional situations may help children experiment with ways of dealing with these experiences. In this example, it also provides a context for Eric's friend to give him support and solace. She reassures him that she likes him, that he is ". . . a friendly skeleton." Children who are able to talk about feelings with peers in fantasy or other contexts may have different developmental histories regarding emotions than children who do not verbalize these experiences. Parents who label affective states for their children before they are able to do this for themselves and who become involved in these states, such as coaching them regarding how to regulate these states, may provide essential scaffolding for their children's emotional development.

Several studies demonstrated a positive association between children's understanding of emotions and children's competence with peers. Goldman, Corsini, and DeUrioste (1980) had children match emotional expressions with hypothetical social situations. Children who were popular with peers were better at this task than children who were less popular. Cassidy, Parke, Butkovsky, and Braungart (1992) found that children's understanding of emotions, including recognition of emotion in self and others, was predictive of their social status with peers.

Emotion language is also related to children's ability to engage in self-control. In a study of normal 5-year-old children, Greenberg, Kusche, and Speltz (1991) assessed children's ability to tolerate having to wait before opening a gift. Researchers assessed "emotional openness" by having children view photographs of stressful events such as the parent leaving and identify relevant emotional reactions of the main characters. The quality of the parent–child attachment relationship was also assessed by observing the child's reunion behavior after a short separation from the mother. Children's ability to generate relevant emotional words was significantly related to their ability to tolerate frustration and to cope adaptively during the waiting period. In addition, emotional openness and the ability to tolerate frustration were positively associated with the attachment ratings of these children.

This study indicates that the development of emotion-related language skills aids children in tolerating frustrating events and that these variables are also related to the quality of interactions between caregivers and children.

To gain a better understanding of the role of parents in developmentally delayed children's emotional regulation abilities, Wilson (unpublished data) compared the responses of parents of these children to parents of nondelayed children during the meta-emotion interview. Initial analyses revealed some interesting findings. Parents of children with developmental delays were more likely to say that their child had never experienced either the emotion of sadness or anger or did not understand these affective states. Four out of twenty parents of developmentally delayed children made these comments, whereas none of the parents of nondelayed children did. Comparisons to a small group of children matched on mental age ($N = 9$) to the delayed sample also revealed no parents who made statements concerning their children not experiencing these emotions.

One father of a developmentally delayed child suggested that his son J did not experience anger, at least not real anger. He noted, "J likes to pretend he is angry a lot, but he's never really angry. He does this for manipulation and to be a 'ham'." This father also noted that he doesn't like it when J pretends to be angry. The mother of one developmentally delayed child said she didn't think her child had ever been sad, at least she couldn't remember this happening. Another father also said that he didn't know if his son had ever been sad. "I don't think he's ever been sad. Maybe he's too young. . . . He pouts to get away with things, but he really isn't sad." When asked how his child gets over being angry, this same father noted that when his son is angry or reluctant to do something, like go to school, the father physically directs him in the right direction. "I don't know if he gets over anger." When asked what he was trying to teach his child about the world of emotions, this father said that his son ". . . should respect other people. Mostly we are teaching him motor skills."

Before discussing the possible implications of these belief and philosophies regarding emotion, it is important to note that these parents represent only a minority of parents with developmentally delayed children in the current sample. The majority of parents of these children recognized different affective states in their child and talked to their children about these states. One mother with a Down syndrome child said her son says, "I'm sad," when he is down and that this has helped him deal more effectively with this emotion. She also noted that she is trying to teach him to recognize and verbalize his anger. She wants him to learn to talk about these feelings and not hit or punch things or people. Another father noted that his son will at times tell him that he is sad and that he usually wants a hug and to talk about it. He added that he thought it was alright for his son to be angry, but he doesn't want him hitting his brother. A number of these parents also stated that although their child experienced and understood the emotions of sadness or anger, they had difficulty verbalizing their experiences with these emotions.

Parents of delayed children who were unaware of their children's affective experiences may be misled by their children's lack of verbal competence regarding emotions. This could lead these parents to the conclusion their children do not have these experiences or do not understand them. Evidence indicates, however, that children's understanding of internal states precedes their ability to talk about them (Tingley, Berko Gleason, & Hooshyar, 1994). Tingley et al. found that mothers of Down syndrome children tend to use fewer internal state words with their children than mothers of children matched on their level of adaptive functioning (i.e., Vineland scale scores). This work suggests that parents of children with developmental delays may underestimate their children's ability to understand terms relating to affective states. According to Vygotsky (1978), a caregiver's role is to structure the experiences of children so that they are able to accomplish with the parent's assistance those tasks that are just beyond their ability to do on their own. By failing to recognize their children's affective experiences and not involving themselves in these experiences, these parents may not provide the basic scaffolding their children need for learning to recognize and deal with these experiences.

SUMMARY AND CONCLUSIONS

In 1965, Haim Ginott wrote about the importance of making an emotional connection with children. He stressed the value of listening for the emotions behind the words, responding genuinely and empathically during emotionally upsetting moments, and validating rather than judging the child's feelings. Our research begins to place Ginott's clinical intuition on strong empirical footing. We have preliminary evidence that parental meta-emotion philosophy is a pervasive social skill that impacts parenting behavior and child regulatory physiology, which in turn are related to children's peer relations, academic achievement, and physical illness. Parental meta-emotion philosophy is also related to marital satisfaction and stability, to conflict resolution within the marriage, and to the couple's philosophy of marriage. Furthermore, parental meta-emotion philosophy appears to be an important dimension of family life both in families with normally developing children and in families with developmentally delayed children.

Meta-emotion philosophy can be seen as an index of the degree of intimacy within the family. In contrast to emotion-dismissing parents, parents who are emotion-coaching appear to provide a safe environment in which to express feelings, thoughts, and concerns. They do not criticize or belittle their child when they are interacting, but convey a sense of appreciation and respect for the child's feelings and behavior. This same family atmosphere that respects and responds to others' fears and concerns is also characteristic of the marital relationship. Whereas emotion-dismissing couples are contemptuous, belligerent, domineering, and stonewalling when their partners articulate the changes they would like to see in the relationship, emotion-coaching couples see the importance in discussing emotional issues in the marriage and believe that marital conflict is worth the struggle. By valuing emotion, emotion-coaching couples provide a positive, supportive atmosphere in which emotional issues can be aired, bringing them one step closer to resolution.

Given that meta-emotion philosophy is broadly related to both parenting and marital processes, and positively impacts the quality of family relationships, it is important to determine the extent to which an individual's meta-emotion philosophy can be changed. Ginott's writings imply that he considered the central skills of listening to and empathizing with children to be trainable. Whether this is true or not remains an empirical question. Furthermore, it is unclear whether teaching parents and couples to listen and empathize will be sufficient to change their basic philosophy about emotion.

The models we developed have interesting implications about the relationship between social and biological processes. The relationship between parental meta-emotion philosophy and the child's regulatory physiology suggests that coaching the child's emotions has a soothing effect on the child that may change some key aspects of the child's parasympathetic nervous system. If this were true, then the child's ability to self-soothe, to regulate negative emotion, and to focus attention may be a result not only of temperament, but it may be affected by the parents' meta-emotion philosophy. However, the data also support the hypothesis that parents may be selecting emotion coaching as a good strategy of parenting with children who have higher basal vagal tone. An experimental test of the effects of training parents in emotion coaching on basal vagal tone would help sort out these alternatives.

A major goal of the research we undertook was to predict peer social relations in middle childhood from variables descriptive of the family's emotional life in preschool. We should explain what the theoretical challenge here is in predicting peer social relations across these two major developmental periods, from preschool to middle childhood. In middle childhood, some of the correlates of peer acceptance and rejection change dramatically, particularly with respect to the expression of emotion. One of the most interesting changes is that the socially competent response to a number of salient social situations such as peer entry and teasing is to be a good observer, somewhat wary, but basically to be "cool" and emotionally unflappable. The child in middle childhood being teased needs to act as if he or she had undergone an emotion-ectomy, and, indeed a major concern of children in this developmental period is avoiding embarrassment (see Fine, 1987; Gottman & Parker, 1986). Thus we can see that the basic elements and skills a child learns through emotion coaching (labeling, expressing one's feelings, and talking about one's feelings) become liabilities in the peer social world in middle childhood, if they were to be simply transferred by the child from the home to the school. Thus, the basic model linking emotion coaching in preschool to peer relations in middle childhood cannot be a simple social learning or modeling theory model in which an isomorphic transfer of social skills is proposed. Instead, it becomes necessary to identify a mechanism operative in the preschool period that makes it possible for the child to learn something in the preschool period that underlies the development of appropriate social skills across this major developmental shift in what constitutes social competence with peers.

As an alternative, we suggest that a set of *general abilities* underly the development of social and emotional competence with peers, and that these abilities form the basis of what Salovey and Mayer (1990) called *emotional intelligence.* While Salovey & Mayer's idea of emotional intelligence is a very long list of skills, we simplify the nature of the skills involved to suggest that the child's ability to regulate emotions and to self-soothe and focus attention during salient emotionally trying peer situations is the central component of emotional intelligence. In middle childhood, we suggest that the child who has been emotion coached by parents has developed a general set of skills that appear to have nothing to do with expressing and understanding one's own feelings. However, they have to do with the ability to inhibit negative affect, with being able to self-soothe, with being able to focus attention (including social attention), and with being able to regulate one's own emotions. These are the skills children learn with emotion coaching parents, but they are not applied isomorphically to the peer world. In middle childhood, these abilities are manifest by inhibiting displays of distress and inhibiting aggression when teased and instead acting emotionally unflappable, and in being able to enter an ongoing peer group with ease and awareness.

Much is left to learn about how meta-emotion philosophy impacts the quality of family relationships. Naturalistic samples of parents interacting with their children during emotional moments are needed to see how emotion-coaching families actually talk to their children during times of heightened emotion. It is also important to examine gender differences in meta-emotion philosophy as a function of gender of both parent and child. We also need to assess the stability of parental meta-emotion philosophy over time, and examine whether changes (if any) to parent's meta-emotion philosophy varies across developmental level of the child. Changes to the meta-emotion interview are also needed, including an expansion to include other emotions (particularly fear, guilt, and shame). We also are interested in developing a measure of child meta-emotion philosophy to see the ways in which parental meta-emotion philosophy transfers to the child. With these and other new developments, we hope to better understand the ways in which this new dimension of family functioning fosters intimacy and impacts children's adjustment.

REFERENCES

Ainsworth, M. D. S., Bell, S. M., & Stayton, D. J. (1971). Individual differences in the strange situation behavior of one-year-olds. In H. R. Schaffer (Ed.), *The origins of human social relations.* London: Academic Press.

Ainsworth, M. D. S., Blehar, M. C., Waters, E., & Wall, S. (1978). *Patterns of attachment: A psychological study of the strange situation.* Hillsdale, NJ: Lawrence Erlbaum Associates.

Allen, B. A., & Armour, T. E. (1993). Construct validation of metacognition. *Journal of Psychology, 127,* 203–211.

Baumrind, D. (1967). Child care practices anteceding 3 patterns of preschool behavior. *Genetic Psychology Monographs, 75,* 43–88.

Baumrind, D. (1971). Current patterns of parental authority. *Developmental Psychology Monograph, 1971, 4.*

Becker, W. C. (1964). Consequences of different kinds of parental discipline. In M. L. Hoffman & L. W. Hoffman (Eds.), *Review of child development research (Vol. 1).* New York: Russell Sage Foundation.

Billings, A. (1979). Conflict resolution in distressed and nondistressed couples. *Journal of Consulting and Clinical Psychology, 47,* 368–376.

Birchler, G. (1977, April). *A multimethod analysis of distressed and nondistressed marital interaction: A social learning approach.* Paper presented at the meeting of the Western Psychological Assocation, Seattle, WA.

Bowlby, J. (1973). *Attachment and loss: Vol 2. Separation.* New York: Basic Books.

Bowlby, J. (1980). *Attachment and loss: Vol. 3. Loss, sadness and depression.* New York: Basic Books.

Bowlby, J. (1982). *Attachment and loss: Vol. 1. Attachment.* New York: Basic Books. (Original work published 1969)

Buehlman, K., Gottman, J. M., & Katz, L. F. (1992). How a couple views their past predicts their future: Predicting divorce from an oral history interview. *Journal of Family Psychology, 5,* 295–318.

Bulloch, K., & Moore, R. Y. (1981). Innervation of the thymus gland by brain stem and spinal cord in mouse and rat. *American Journal of Anatomy, 162*(2), 157–166.

Bulloch, K., & Pomerantz, W. (1984). Autonomic nervous system innervation of thymic-related lymphoid tissue in wildtype and nude mice. *Journal of Comp. Neurol. 228*(1), 57–68.

Bvinelli, D. J. (1993). Reconstructing the evolution of mind. *American Psychologist, 48,* 493–509.

Carstensen, L. L., Gottman, J. M., & Levenson, R. W. (1995). Emotional behavior in long-term marriage. *Psychology and Aging, 10,* 140–149.

Cassidy, J., Parke, R. D., Butkovsky, L., & Braungart, J. M. (1992). Family-peer connections: The roles of emotional expressiveness within the family and children's understanding of emotions. *Child Development, 63,* 603–618.

Christensen, A., & Heavey, C. L. (1990). Gender and social structure in the demand/withdraw pattern. *Journal of Personality and Social Psychology, 59,* 73–81.

Christensen, A., & Shenk, J. L. (1991). Communication, conflict, and psychological distance in distressed, clinic, and divorcing couples. *Journal of Consulting and Clinical Psychology, 59,* 458–463.

Cohn, D. A., Cowan, P. A., Cowan, C. P., & Pearson, J. (1992). Mothers' and fathers' working models of childhood attachment relationships, parenting styles, and child behavior. *Development & Psychopathology, 4,* 417–431.

Cole, P. M., Zahn-Waxler, C., & Smith, K. D. (1994). Expressive control during a disappointment: Variations related to preschoolers' behavior problems. *Developmental Psychology, 30,* 835–846.

Cook, J., Tyson, R., White, J., Rushe, R., Gottman, J., & Murray, J. (1995). The mathematics of marital conflict. *Journal of Family Psychology, 9,* 110–130.

Corsaro, W. (1979). We're friends, right?: Children's use of access rituals in a nursery school. *Language in Society, 8,* 315–336.

Cowan, C. P., & Cowan, P. A. (1992). *When parents become partners.* New York: Basic Books.

Cummings, E. M., & Davies, P. (1994). *Children and marital conflict: The impact of family dispute resolution.* New York: Guilford.

Dawson, G., Hessl, D., & Frey, K. (1994). Social influences of early developing biological and behavioral systems related to risk for affective disorder. *Development and Psychopathology, 6,* 759–779.

DiPietro, J. A., & Porges, S. W. (1991). Relations between neonatal states and 8-month developmental outcome in preterm infants. *Infant Behavior & Development, 14,* 441–450.

Dodge, K., McClaskey, C. L., & Feldman, E. (1985). A situational approach to the assessment of social competence in children. *Journal of Consulting and Clinical Psychology, 53,* 344–353.

Dunn, J. (1977). *Distress and comfort.* Cambridge, MA: Harvard University Press.

Eisenberg, N., Fabes, R. A., Murphy, B., Mask, P., Smith, M., & Karbon, M. (1995). The role of emotionality and regulation in children's social functioning: A longitudinal study. *Child Development, 66,* 1360–1384.

Field, T. M. (1980). Self, teacher, toy, and peer-directed behavior of handicapped preschool children. In T. M. Field, S. Goldberg, D. Stern, & A. M. Sostek (Eds.), *High-risk infants and children: Adult and peer interactions* (pp. 313–326). New York: Academic Press.

Field, T., Healy, B., Goldsstein, S., & Perry, S. (1988). Infants of depressed mothers show "depressed" behavior even with nondepressed adults. *Child Development, 59,* 1569–1579.

Fine, G. A. (1987). *With the boys.* Chicago: University of Chicago Press.

Flavell, J. H. (1979). Metacognition and cognitive monitoring: A new area of cognitive-developmental inquiry. *American Psychologist, 34,* 906–911.

Fodor, J. A. (1992). A theory of the child's theory of mind. *Cognition, 44,* 283–296.

Fox, N. A. (1989). The psychophysiological correlates of emotional reactivity during the first year of life. *Developmental Psychology, 25,* 364–372.

Garber, J., & Dodge, K. A. (Eds.) (1991). *The development of emotion regulation and dysregulation.* New York: Cambridge University Press.

Garvey, C. (1986). Peer relationships and the growth of communication. In E. C. Mueller & C. R. Cooper (Eds.), *Process and outcome in peer relationships* (pp. 329–345). Orlando, Florida: Academic Press.

Gianino, A., & Tronick, E. Z. (1988). The mutual regulation model: The infant's self and interactive regulation and coping and defensive capacities. In T. M. Field, P. M. McCabe, & N. Schneiderman (Eds.), *Stress and coping across development* (pp. 47–70). Hillsdale, NJ: Lawrence Erlbaum Associates.

Ginott, H. G. (1965). *Between parent and child.* New York: Avon Books.

Ginott, H. G. (1971). *Between parent and teenager.* New York: Avon Books.

Ginott, H. G. (1975). *Teacher and child.* New York: Avon Books.

Goldman, J. A., Corsini, D. A., & DeUrioste, R. (1980). Implications of positive and negative sociometric status for assessing the social competence of young children. *Journal of Applied Developmental Psychology, 1,* 209–220.

Gottman, J. M. (1979). *Marital interaction: Experimental investigations.* New York: Academic Press.

Gottman, J. M. (1981). *Time-series analysis: A comprehensive introduction for social scientists.* New York: Cambridge University Press.

Gottman, J. M. (1986). The observation of social process. In J. Gottman & J. Parker (Eds.), *Conversations of friends: Speculations on affective development.* New York: Cambridge University Press.

162   KATZ, WILSON, GOTTMAN

Gottman, J. M. (1993a). The role of conflict engagement, escalation, or avoidance in marital interaction: A longitudinal view of five types of couples. *Journal of Consulting and Clinical Psychology, 61*, 6–15.

Gottman, J. M. (1993b). A theory of marital dissolution and stability. *Journal of Family Psychology, 7*, 57–75.

Gottman, J. M. (1994). *What predicts divorce?* Hillsdale, NJ: Lawrence Erlbaum Associates.

Gottman, J. M., Katz, L. F., & Hooven, C. (1996). Parental meta-emotion structure and the emotional life of families: Theoretical models and preliminary analyses. *Journal of Family Psychology, 10*, 243–268.

Gottman, J. M., Katz, L. F., & Hooven, C. (1997). *Meta-emotion: How families communicate emotionally.* Hillsdale, NJ: Lawrence Erlbaum Associates.

Gottman, J. M., & Krokoff, L. (1989). Marital interaction and satisfaction: A longitudinal view. *Journal of Consulting and Clinical Psychology, 57*, 47–52.

Gottman, J. M., & Levenson, R. W. (1988). The social psychophysiology of marriage. In P. Noller & M. A. Fitzpatrick (Eds.), *Perspectives on marital interaction* (pp. 183–200). Philadelphia: Multilingual Matters.

Gottman, J. M., & Levenson, R. W. (1992). Marital processes predictive of later dissolution: Behavior, physiology and health. *Journal of Personality and Social Psychology, 63*, 221–233.

Gottman, J. M., & Parker, J. (Eds.) (1986). *Conversations of friends: Speculations on affective development.* New York: Cambridge University Press.

Greenberg, M., Kusche, D. A., & Speltz, M. (1991). Emotion regulation, self-control and psychopathology: The role of relationships in early childhood. In D. Cicchetti & S. Toth (Eds.), *Rochester symposium on developmental psychopathology. Vol. 2: Internalizing and externalizing expressions of dysfunction.* New York: Cambridge University Press.

Grych, J. H., & Fincham, F. D. (1990). Marital conflict and children's adjustment: A cognitive-contextual framework. *Psychological Bulletin, 108*, 267–290.

Guralnick, M. J. (1981). Peer influences on the development of communciative competence. In P. Strain (Ed.), *The utilization of classroom peers as behavior change agents* (pp. 31–68). New York: Plenum.

Guralnick, M. J., & Groom, J. M. (1985). Correlates of peer-related social competence of developmentally delayed preschool children. *American Journal of Mental Deficiency, 90*, 140–150.

Guralnick, M. J., & Groom, J. M. (1987). The peer relations of mildly delayed and nonhandicapped preschool children in mainstreamed and specialized classrooms: A comparative analysis. *Exceptional Children, 54*, 415–425.

Guralnick, M. J., & Paul-Brown, D. (1986). Communicative interactions of mildly delayed and normally developing children at different developmental levels. *Child Development, 55*, 911–919.

Guralnick, M. J., & Weinhouse, E. M. (1984). Peer-related social interactions of developmentally delayed young children: Development and characteristics. *Developmental Psychology, 20*, 815–827.

Hartup, W. W. (1978). Peer interaction and processes of socialization. In M. J. Guralnick (Ed.), *Early intervention and the integration of handicapped and nonhandicapped children* (pp. 27–51). Baltimore: University Park Press.

Hartup, W. W. (1983). Peer relations. In E. M. Hetherington (Ed.), *Handbook of child psychology: Vol. 4, Socialization, personality, and social development* (pp. 103–196). New York: Wiley.

Haynes, S. N., Follingstad, D. R., & Sullivan, J. C. (1979). Assessment of marital satisfaction and interaction. *Journal of Consulting and Clinical Psychology, 47*, 789–791.

Heavey, C. L., Layne, C., & Christensen, A. (1993). Gender and conflict structure in marital interaction: A replication and extension. *Journal of Consulting and Clinical Psychology, 47*, 789–791.

Hesse, P., & Cicchetti, D. (1982). Perspectives on an integrated theory of emotional development. In D. Cicchetti & P. Hesse (Eds.), *New directions for child development: Number 16, Emotional development* (pp. 3–48). San Francisco: Jossey-Bass.

Hofheimer, J. A., & Lawson, (1988). Neurophysiological correlates of interactive behavior in preterm newborns. *Infant Behavior and Development, 11,* 143.

Huffman, L. C., Bryan, Y. E., Pederson, F. A., & Porges, S. W. (1988). Infant temperament: Relationships with heart rate variablility. Unpublished manuscript, National Institute of Mental Health, Rockville, MD.

Huffman, L. C., Bryan, Y. E., Pederson, F. A., & Porges, S. W. (1992). Autonomic correlates of reactivity and self-regulation at twelve weeks of age. Unpublished manuscript, National Institute of Mental Health, Rockville, MD.

Katz, L. F., & Gottman, J. M. (1986). The meta-emotion interview. Unpublished manual. University of Washington, Department of Psychology, Seattle, WA.

Katz, L. F., & Gottman, J. M. (1993). Patterns of marital conflict predict children's internalizing and externalizing behaviors. *Developmental Psychology, 29,* 940–950.

Katz, L. F., Gottman, J. M., & Hooven, C. (1996). Meta-emotion philosophy and family functioning: A reply to Cowan and Eisenberg. *Journal of Family Psychology, 10,* 284–291.

Kopp, C. B., Krakow, J. B., & Johnson, K. L. (1983). Strategy production by young Down syndrome children. *American Journal of Mental Deficiency, 88,* 164–169.

Levenson, R. W., Carstensen, L. L., & Gottman, J. M. (1994). Influence of age and gender on affect, physiology, and their interrelations: A study of long-term marriages. *Journal of Personality and Social Psychology, 67,* 56–68.

Linnemeyer, S. A., & Porges, S. W. (1986). Recognition memory and cardiac vagal tone in 6-month-old infants. *Infant Behavior and Development, 9,* 43–56.

Maccoby, E. E. (1980). *Social Development.* New York: Harcourt, Brace, & Jovanovitch.

Maccoby, E. E., & Martin, J. A. (1983). Socialization in the context of the family: Parent-child interaction. In E. M. Hetherington (Ed.), *Handbook of child psychology: Vol. 4, Socialization, Personality, and Social Behavior.* New York: Wiley.

Nance, D. M., Hopkins, D. A., & Bieger, D. (1987). Re-investigation of the innervation of the thymus gland in mice and rats. *Brain Behavior and Immunology, 1*(2), 134–147.

Notarius, C., & Markman, H. (1994). *We can work it out.* New York: Putnam.

Olson, D. R., & Astington, J. W. (1993). Thinking about thinking: Learning how to take statements and hold beliefs. *Educational Psychologist, 28* (1), 7–23.

Parke, R. D., MacDonald, K., Burks, V., Carson. J., Bhavnagri, N., Barth, J., & Beitel, A. (1989). Family and peer systems: In search of the linkages. In K. Kreppner & R. M. Lerner (Eds.), *Family systems and life-span development* (pp. 65–92). Hillsdale, NJ: Lawrence Erlbaum Associates.

Parker, J. G., & Asher, S. R. (1987). Peer relations and later personal adjustment: Are low-accepted children at risk? *Psychological Bulletin, 102,* 357–389.

Patterson, G. R. (1982). *Coercive family process.* Eugene, OR: Castalia.

Piaget, J. (1965). *The moral judgement of the child.* New York: Free Press. (Original work published 1932)

Pine, F. (1985). *Developmental theory and clinical process.* New Haven: Yale University Press.

Porges, S. W. (1972). Heart rate variability and deceleration as indices of reaction time. *Journal of Experimental Psychology, 92,* 103–110.

Porges, S. W. (1973). Heart rate variability: An autonomic correlate of reaction time performance. *Bulletin of the Psychonomics Society, 1,* 270–272.

Porges, S. W. (1984). Heart rate oscillation: An index of neural mediation. In M. G. H. Coles, J. R. Jennings, & J. A. Stern (Eds.), *Psychophysiological perspectives: Festschrift for Beatrice and John Lacey.* New York: Van Nostrand Reinhold.

Porges, S. W. (1991). Autonomic regulation and attention. In B. A. Campbell, H. Hayne, & R. Richardson (Eds.), *Attention and information processing in infants and adults* (pp. 201–223). Hillsdale, NJ: Lawrence Erlbaum Associates.

Porges, S. W., Arnold, W. R., & Forbes, E. J. (1973). Heart rate variability: An index of attentional responsivity in human newborns. *Developmental Psychology, 8,* 85–92.

Porges, S. W., & Doussard-Roosevelt, J. A. (1997). The psychophysiology of temperament. In J. D. Noshpitz (Ed.), *Handbook of child and adolescent psychiatry.* New York: Wiley.

Porges, S. W., Walter, G. F., Korb, R. J., & Sprague, R. L. (1975). The influence of methylphenidate on heart rate and behavioral measures of attention in hyperactive children. *Child Development, 46,* 727–733.

Porter, F. L., Porges, S. W., & Marshall, R. E. (1988). Newborn pain cries and vagal tone: Parallel changes in response to circumcision. *Child Development, 59,* 495–505.

Putallaz, M., & Gottman, J. M. (1981). An interactional model of children's entry into peer groups. *Child Development, 52,* 986–994.

Revenstorf, D., Vogel, B., Wegener, R., Hahlweg, K., & Schindler, L. (1980). Escalation phenomena in interaction sequences: An empirical comparison of distressed and nondistressed couples. *Behavior Analysis and Modification, 2,* 97–116.

Richards, J. E. (1985). The development of sustained visual attention in infants from 14 to 26 weeks of age. *Psychophysiology, 22,* 409–416.

Richards, J. E. (1987). Infant visual sustained attention and respiratory sinus arrhythmia. *Child Development, 58,* 488–496.

Rothbart, M. K., & Derryberry, D. (1981). Development of individual difference in temperament. In M. E. Lamb & A. L. Brown (Eds.), *Advances in developmental psychology* (Vol. 1). Hillsdale, NJ: Lawrence Erlbaum Associates.

Rothbart, M. K., & Posner, M. I. (1985). Temperament and the development of self-regulation. In C. L. Hartledge & C. R. Telzrow (Eds.), *The neuropsychology of individual differences: A developmental perspective.* New York: Plenum.

Salovey, P., & Mayer, J. D. (1990). Emotional intelligence. *Imagination, Cognition and Personality, 9,* 185–211.

Schaefer, E. S. (1959). A circumplex model for maternal behavior. *Journal of Abnormal and Social Psychology, 59,* 226–235.

Siegman, A. W., & Smith, T. W. (Eds.) (1994). *Anger, hostility, and the heart.* Hillsdale, NJ: Lawrence Erlbaum Associates.

Stern, D. N. (1985). *The interpersonal world of the infant: A view from psychoanalysis and developmental psychology.* New York: Basic Books.

Stifter, C. A., & Fox, N. A. (1990). Infant reactivity: Physiological correlates of newborn and 5-month temperament. *Developmental Psychology, 26,* 582–588.

Stifter, C. A., Fox, N. A., & Porges, S. W. (1989). Facial expressivity and vagal tone in 5- and 10-month-old infants. *Infant Behavior and Development, 12,* 127–137.

Sroufe, A. L., Schork, E., Motti, F., Lawroski, N., & LaFreniere, P. (1984). The role of affect in social competence. In C. E. Izard, J. Kagan, & R. B. Zajonc (Eds.), *Emotions, cognition, and Behavior.* New York: Cambridge University Press.

Tavris, C. (1982). *Anger: The misunderstood emotion.* New York: Simon & Schuster.

Tingley, E. C., Berko Gleason, J., & Hooshyar, N. (1994). Mother's lexicon of internal state words in speech to children with Down syndrome and to nonhandicapped children at mealtime. *Journal of Communication Disorders, 27,* 135–155.

Tronick, E. Z. (1989). Emotions and emotional communication in infants. *American Psychologist, 44,* 112–119.

Vygotsky, L. S. (1962). *Thought and language.* Cambridge, MA: MIT Press.

Vygotsky, L. S. (1978). *Mind in society.* Cambridge, MA: Harvard University Press.

Walker, L. E. (1984). *The battered woman syndrome.* New York: Springer.

Williams, E., & Gottman, J. M. (1981). *A user's guide to the Gottman-Williams time-series programs*. New York: Cambridge University Press.

Wilson, B. J. (1994). *The entry behavior and emotion regulation abilities of developmentally delayed children*. Unpublished doctoral dissertation, University of Washington, Seattle.

Wilson, B. J., & Gottman, J. M. (1995). Marital interaction and parenting. In M. H. Bornstein (Ed.), *Handbook of Parenting, Volume 4: Applied and Practical Parenting*. Mahwah, NJ: Lawrence Erlbaum Associates.

8

▼▼▼▼▼▼▼

Two Faces of Janus:
Cohesion and Conflict

Marion S. Forgatch
David S. DeGarmo
Oregon Social Learning Center

The dynamic system of contexts and relationships that affect the quality of family life and adjustment of family members defies casual study. Certain contexts impact how well family members function, and their performance in turn affects the family context. An example of this is the shared influence of the family's emotional ambiance and the quality of parenting that children receive, so that effective parenting increases good feelings and good feelings make it easier to parent competently (Dix, 1991). The family's emotional context also changes and is changed by children's contributions. In positive atmospheres, children tend to cooperate with parenting (Parpel & Maccoby, 1985). In negative emotional contexts, ineffective parenting is more probable and increases the likelihood that children will develop adjustment problems, which in turn increases the negative emotional environment and the difficulty of parenting (Forgatch, Patterson, & Ray, 1996; Patterson & Forgatch, 1995; Patterson, Reid, & Dishion, 1992).

To add yet another dimension to the complexity of families as systems, there are important changes that must take place in the balance of power between parents and their children (Maccoby & Martin, 1983). In the early stages of life, most children rely primarily on their parents for care and socialization. As part of the normal developmental process, children become increasingly autonomous, and parents have less and less control over the reinforcers that affect their children's behavior. These changes take place gradually through a series of relatively small transitions, each one requiring adaptation by parent and by child. As Maccoby and Martin (1983) point out, adult relationships that require such significant shifts in the balance of power rarely survive, although the parent–child relationship usually does. We think that successfully negotiating changes in the amount of youngsters' autonomy requires both competent parenting and a healthy emotional environment at home. Neither by itself is sufficient to the task.

In this chapter, we study how cohesion and conflict function as predictors of boys' wandering. Cohesion and conflict have enjoyed popular usage in the family literature as measures of emotional contexts that are related to family functioning and children's adjustment. In our model, cohesion and conflict are hypothesized to influence youngsters' cooperation with parenting processes, which results in changing levels of wandering (Stoolmiller, 1994). Wandering is an intermediary child outcome that straddles parental supervision and more serious adjustment outcomes that develop over time, such as increases in antisocial behavior or delinquency. We assume that cohesion serves as a kind of emotional adherent that enhances youngsters' cooperation with supervision and prevents undue wandering, whereas conflict intensifies resistance to supervision and leads to increased wandering.

Wandering is an ideal outcome to study within this framework because it represents the kind of collaboration that is required between parent and child to ensure effective supervision in the face of increasing autonomy. Measures of this construct contain information from both parent and youngster and describe the knowledge parents have about their son's whereabouts and activities, the difficulty they have in keeping track of him, and the extent to which the youngster provides this kind of information to his parents (Stoolmiller, 1994). We chose to study change in wandering from Grade 4 to Grade 6. This time frame bridges the transition from elementary to middle school, a passage characterized by emerging adolescence and increasing independence. This is a time when parental supervision becomes increasingly important to prevent boys' antisocial behavior (Patterson et al., 1992), but it is also more difficult to keep track of youngsters who spend more and more time away from home. If adolescents sabotage their parents' monitoring efforts, the task can become formidable (Dishion, Andrews, & Crosby, 1995). Wandering is the result of failed supervision.

The two-faced Roman god Janus, guardian of doorways, is shown in Fig. 8.1. Janus seemed a fitting metaphor to describe how cohesion and conflict may be related to the wandering of young male adolescents. His positive visage symbolizes cohesion, a quality found in families in which people share positive feelings and cooperate in the tasks of family living. We expected these qualities to characterize parents who monitor carefully and youngsters who cooperate with this effort. Janus's more negative side represents conflict. Even though conflict cannot always be avoided, nor would it be good to do so, some families regularly resort to arguments when change is desired or needed. If the outcomes of these disputes are unresolved, conflicts may

FIG. 8.1. The two-faced Roman god Janus, guardian of doorways.

multiply and intensify, and home may become a place to be avoided, which may further disrupt parenting and interfere with cohesion.

A PARENT-BASED DEVELOPMENTAL MODEL FOR DELINQUENCY IN MALES

A model for delinquency emerged during the past 15 years that provides a sound basis for the study of family functioning across multiple levels (Patterson, 1982; Patterson & Bank, 1986; Patterson & Forgatch, 1995). As a performance model, its validity was tested and replicated in correlational studies using longitudinal design, multiple method and agent assessment, and sophisticated data analytic techniques (Conger, Patterson, & Ge, 1995; Simons, Wu, Conger, & Lorenz, 1994). Recent tests of the model include experimental manipulations of the parenting variables thought to cause child adjustment problems (Dishion, Patterson, & Kavanagh, 1992; Forgatch, 1991; Reid, 1993). The findings clearly identify parenting practices such as discipline, problem solving, and supervision as critical to children's early adjustment.

The delinquency model adapts to developmental changes as was demonstrated in a study of boys at risk for delinquency (Patterson, 1993). Patterson studied this sample when boys were in Grades 4, 6, and 8. As boys moved from childhood into early and middle adolescence, there were changes in the topography of constructs for adjustment. In Grade 4, a deviancy construct for preadolescent boys included significant indicators for antisocial behavior and school failure. For adolescent boys, (Grades 6 & 8) these indicators remained relevant, but additional indicators were required to describe deviancy (i.e., substance abuse, delinquent activity, and police arrests). Within this model, parents were seen as the primary socializing agents in early childhood, and ineffective discipline and poor supervision were the facets of parenting that contributed to boys' antisocial behavior. With the onset of adolescence, deviant peer association and wandering were added as significant predictors. These two variables were seen as intermediary steps between parenting practices and child adjustment outcomes.

MEASURING COHESION AND CONFLICT

There is an extensive literature using measures designed to evaluate bonding within families under the rubric of cohesion/adaptability. Cohesion has been defined to reflect emotional bonding among family members and adaptability to reflect the family's ability to change in response to situational and developmental stress (Olson, Russell, & Sprenkle, 1983). Several investigators developed similar sets of variables (e.g., coordination/closure, Oliveri & Reiss, 1981; Reiss, 1971; and cohesion/control, Moos & Moos, 1981). Measures include self-report instruments (Epstein, Bishop, & Levin, 1978; Moos & Moos, 1981; Olsen, Portner, & Lavee, 1985) and behavioral observations of family interactions (Oliveri & Reiss, 1981; Reiss, 1971). Although robust measures draw on multiple perspectives that converge with each other and are distinct from variables assumed to be dissimilar (Campbell & Fiske, 1959), previously developed measures of cohesion demonstrate neither convergent nor discriminant validity.

The problems with convergent validity begin with the failure of people in the same family using the same self-report instrument to agree with each other (Cole & Jordan, 1989; Dickerson & Coyne, 1987; Doherty & Hovander, 1990). Measures obtained from observations of family interactions correlate sometimes with global ratings made by other outsiders, such as family therapists, but they do not correlate well with measures provided by family members (Balck, Jantschek, & Wietersheim, 1991; Dickerson & Coyne, 1987; Kog, Vertommen, & Vandereysken, 1987; Reiss, 1971). Cohesion and adaptability tend to have strong positive correlations with each other and consequently do not meet the requirements of discriminant validity (Cole & Jordan, 1989; Dickerson & Coyne, 1987; Kog et al., 1987; Perosa & Perosa, 1990). Consequently, valid measures of these variables are as rare as robins in Minnesota in January.

We developed our own measures of cohesion and conflict, which draw on multiple methods, agents, and settings and pass the test of convergent, discriminant and predictive validity. We employed a bootstrapping approach to develop the measures, which was described by Bank and his colleagues:

> This metaphor, originally introduced by Cronbach and Meehl (1956), defines a process of formulating the assessment of constructs that proceeds from the conception of the construct to its measurement, from its measurement to

validation, from validation back to redefinition and reconceptualization of the construct, and then returning to improving the measurement once again. At the present time, there is no definitive end to this process of successive approximation, simply a gradual, increased measurement fidelity. (Bank, Dishion, Skinner, & Patterson, 1990, p. 255)

This bootstrapping approach was successfully employed to develop constructs for parental discipline and monitoring, wandering, and child antisocial behavior in a series of methodological and substantive papers written by our colleagues at Oregon Social Learning Center (OSLC; Bank et al., 1990; Capaldi & Patterson, 1989; Patterson & Bank, 1986, 1987; Stoolmiller, 1994, 1995).

Our measure of cohesion taps three dimensions that reflect a positive style of parenting: encouraging prosocial behavior, directing positive affect toward the child, and general enjoyment of parenting. The data come from two settings, a minimum of four agents and up to five (depending on whether there are one or two parents in the family), and five methods. Five types of data are employed to form the construct: observations at home of the whole family, observations in the laboratory of parent(s) and target child, parent interview, ratings made by the parent interviewer, and parent questionnaires. Conflict was designed to reflect a negative parenting style in which parents initiate aversive interactions with their children or direct intense negative behaviors toward their children. The measure of conflict is based on observations of family interactions in two settings, the home and the laboratory. To alleviate method bias, the observation data for cohesion are observer ratings, and for conflict they are microsocial measures that are scored in real time.

In the present chapter, the multiple method measures of cohesion and conflict were developed and tested for convergent and discriminant validity using confirmatory factor analysis within structural equations models. Once their construct validity was evaluated, the constructs were employed in a model predicting change in boys' wandering. We expected that cohesion would be associated with parents who carefully monitored their children's activities and children who cooperated in this enterprise, resulting in relatively small increases in wandering in the transition from elementary to middle school. On the other hand, in families with frequent or intense conflicts, we expected greater increases in wandering. The hypotheses were tested in a sample of families with boys at risk for delinquency.

It may be that certain parent and child attributes make supervision more difficult. In the present study, we assumed that antisocial parents might not think it important to supervise their youngsters' activities carefully, or they might not take appropriate action to do so. Furthermore, antisocial children may have more activities to hide, making it more likely that they will be less cooperative with their parents' attempts to supervise. For this reason, we used measures of antisocial parent and child behavior as control variables in the models.

METHODS

Sample

Participants were from the Oregon Youth Study (OYS), a longitudinal study
designed to test a family-based theory that explains the development and
maintenance of antisocial behavior and delinquency in boys. Families were
recruited from elementary schools with a high incidence of delinquency in
the neighborhood. All participants lived in a Pacific Northwest metropolitan
area of approximately 150,000. The participation rate of eligible families was
74%, with a 98% retention rate over 10 years. At Time 1, there were two
successive Grade 4 cohorts of boys, with 102 in Cohort 1 and 104 in Cohort
2. The cohorts were similar in demographic characteristics and were combined for the analysis. The boys' mean age in Grade 4 was 10.04, with a
range of 9.2 to 11.5. The sample was 86% White. A large portion of the
sample was characterized by lower socioeconomic status, with 33% receiving
public assistance and 20% of the families having both parents unemployed.
By the end of Grade 10, 42% of the boys had been arrested. Of the 206
families in the analyses, there were 66 single-parent, 59 stepfather, and 81
biological two-parent families. All participants were paid $10 an hour, with
additional bonuses for timely assessment completion. The sample and procedures were described more fully in Patterson et al. (1992).

   This report is based on family data contributed when the boys were in
Grades 4 (T1) and 6 (T2). This period was seen as ideal for the study of the
effect of family cohesion and conflict on changes in boys' wandering given
the backdrop of the transition from elementary to middle school and the
boys' entry into adolescence.

Procedure

Extensive multiagent assessments were obtained every other year. Parents
and their sons completed structured interviews, family interaction tasks,
structured telephone interviews, and questionnaires. At T1 and T2, families
also were observed in their homes. Detailed information for the procedures,
measures, constructs, and analyses in this study are in ODS technical report
96-13, obtainable from Dr. Forgatch.

Family Interaction Task

   Following office interviews, parent(s) and their sons participated in videotaped problem-solving discussions. They spent 10 minutes on each of two
conflicts chosen from the Issues Checklist (adapted from Prinz, Foster, Kent,
& O'Leary, 1979), which listed frequent family disputes, (e.g., chores, cur-

fews, allowance, and school problems). Families were asked to address and attempt to resolve issues occurring in the prior month that they had rated as "hottest." Parent- and child-identified issues were counterbalanced for order. These sessions were scored with the Solving Problems in Family Interactions coding system (SPI-FI: Forgatch, Fetrow, & Lathrop, 1985). After each coding session, coders completed questionnaires rating family process, affect, and problem-solving outcome.

Home Observations

Families were observed in their homes in a series of three 1-hour observations. All family members were requested to be present, and the same family members were present for each observation. Home observers coded interactions using the Family Process Code (FPC: Dishion, Gardner, Patterson, Reid, & Thibodeaux, 1983) and completed questionnaires rating the family process, affect, and behavior after each observation.

Structured Telephone Interviews

Each family was called six times over approximately 3 weeks to complete the telephone interview. Items consisted of the occurrence of behaviors of interest either in the last 24 hours or the last 3 days. In all cases, the average score from the six calls was used as the basic item.

Measures

Constructs were formed through a process of identifying a priori variables and forming scales. Scales were required to have internal consistency and alphas of .60 or higher and to converge with other construct indicators. When there was more than one scale for a respondent in a construct, scores were averaged from a respondent-specific indicator. In two-parent families, reliability analyses were performed separately for each parent for each scale. The mother and father scales were then averaged to form a parent-respondent score for each family. Construct scores were computed by averaging over all the respondents.

Cohesion Construct

Five scales comprised the cohesion construct. Items within scales were recoded as necessary so that high scores indicated cohesion. After the scale scores were computed, they were standardized to have equal variances and a mean of zero. The scales were combined to form three indicators: parent report, observer report, and interviewer report. A mean score of the standardized indicators was computed for the cohesion construct.

Parent Report Indicator. For this indicator, scales were derived from a questionnaire and an interview. There were four items from the Family Environment questionnaire (Moos & Moos, 1981), with an alpha reliability of .60 for mothers and .72 for fathers. Sample items were: "Family members help and support each other" and "Feeling of togetherness in family." There were six items from the structured laboratory interview, with alpha reliabilities of .67 for mothers and .63 for fathers. Sample items were: "Has your son been pleasant to raise?" and "How much time did you spend doing fun things with your son?".

Observer Report Indicator. Two scales were formed, one from ratings made after home observations and one from ratings made after coding the laboratory interactions. From the home observations, 12 items evaluated parental positive affect and encouragement of prosocial behavior. Sample items were "Was physically affectionate with child" and "Specifically encouraged positive social behaviors." Scale alphas were .72 for ratings of mothers and .82 for fathers. From the lab tasks, there were six bipolar ratings of adjectives describing parental characteristics. Example items were: "humorless to humorous" and "cold to warm." The reliabilities were .91 for mothers and .89 for fathers.

Interviewer Report Indicator. After conducting the structured interview, interviewers rated parents on the following three items: "seemed to enjoy parenting," "seemed accepting of child," and "rating on positive reinforcement." The alpha reliability was .84 for mothers and .82 for fathers.

Conflict Construct

The conflict construct was a measure of contentious parental behaviors based on microsocial scores from home observations and from lab task family interactions. The indicators from these two settings were standardized and averaged for mothers and fathers. The correlation between the mother and father conflict scores was .42.

Home Observations. This indicator was computed from two microsocial scores, nattering and abusive cluster. *Nattering* was defined as the probability that a parent used nonabusive "negative behavior" when interacting with the child. *Abusive cluster* was defined as the probability that the parent was verbally or physically abusive when interacting with the child. Abusive behavior included yelling, humiliating, threatening, and hitting. Intercoder agreement was .66 for the parental nattering score and .74 for the parental abusive cluster. The zero-order correlation between these two scores was .43 for the mother and .50 for the father.

Lab Observations.   This indicator was a microsocial score obtained from the Family Interaction Task. This score was the frequency with which a parent started and ended negative process chains as scored with SPI-FI.

Wandering Construct

This construct, assessed when the boys were in Grades 4 and 6, is a measure of boys' unstructured, unsupervised time and his willingness to make his whereabouts and activities known to his parents. Two methods were employed to obtain information from the parents and the boy, repeated telephone interviews and structured lab interviews. The alpha reliabilities for wandering indicators were .50 at Grade 4 and .68 at Grade 6. In spite of the low alpha reliability for the Grade 4 measure, all items were retained because they were developmentally appropriate in Grade 6. The raw scores were rescaled to a common metric, in this case 0 to 2, in order to assess the change in these behaviors over time.

Child Report Indicator.   For this indicator, four items were used, three from the child structured interview and one from the child telephone interview. Sample items were: "How often, before you go out, do you tell your parents when you will be back?" and "If your parents or a sitter are not at home, how often do you leave a note for them about where you are going?" The alpha reliabilities for the child report indicator were .56 at both Grades 4 and 6.

Parent Report Indicator.   For this indicator, four items were used, three from the parent telephone interview and one from the structured interview. Sample items were: "During the last 24 hours, how many hours did your son spend at home unsupervised?"; and "Within the last 24 hours, how many hours was your son involved in activities outside the home, activities in which he was on his own or with children only?"; "Is it hard to keep track of your son?". The alpha reliabilities for the indicator were .45 and .65 at Grades 4 and 6, respectively.

Parent Antisocial Construct.   This construct was computed as the mean of the mother and father. Both parent scores included department of motor vehicle (DMV) records of license suspensions, number of arrests, substance use, and the MMPI subscales of hypomania and psychopathic deviate. The mother's risk score also included age at birth of first child. Mother and father indicators were standardized prior to computation of the parent antisocial construct. Detailed information on the psychometric properties of the indicators are in Capaldi and Patterson (1989).

Family Structure.   The family structure variable was an ordinal variable indicating the number of parental family transitions (Capaldi & Patterson, 1991). The variable was scored 0 for biological intact families, 1 for single parent families, and 2 for stepfamily status.

FINDINGS

Convergent and Construct Validity

A latent variable confirmatory factor analysis was chosen for evaluating the measurement of cohesion, conflict, and wandering. The use of structural equation modeling (SEM) is particularly advantageous when modeling multi-method, multiagent data (Bank & Patterson, 1992). In SEM, measurement can be further refined to partial out variance attributed to monomethod bias (e.g., agent, setting, method). One advantage, for example, is the ability to control for shared agent variance that may inflate the true relationship between two factors. In this case, variance between cohesion and conflict attributed to the home observer as the same source of data can be partialled from the true covariance of cohesion and conflict. For example, the observers' ratings of cohesion and the observers' microsocial coding of conflict are specified to be free in the model. The results of the confirmatory factor model are displayed in Fig. 8.2 in the form of standardized coefficients.

The measurement model had an acceptable fit to the data ($\chi^2 = 30.49$, $p > .05$). Cohesion and conflict were significantly correlated with each other($r = -.45$) and in the expected directions with child wandering ($r = -.67$ and .61, respectively). Three residual covariances were specified a priori. The first

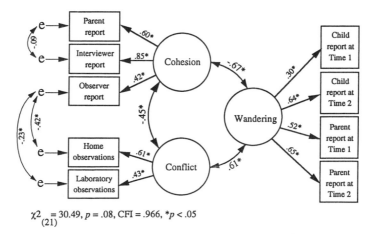

$\chi^2_{(21)} = 30.49$, $p = .08$, CFI = .966, $*p < .05$

FIG. 8.2.   Measurement model cf Cohesion, Conflict, and Wandering.

two pairs were the observers' ratings of cohesion and the observers' coding of conflict. The third pair was the error variance between the parent interviewer and the parents' report in the interview. The rationale for this path was to control for any setting or situational variance attributed to the lengthy amount of time the structured interviewer spends interacting with the families (up to 2 hours). Any variance shared variance from the situational context due to mood or setting can be partialled out. An alternative model that freed error variance between the parent report of wandering and the parent report of cohesion provided no significant improvement in fit.

The external associations of cohesion and conflict with child wandering in the expected directions indicate construct validity. A test of one factor versus two factors of cohesion and conflict was conducted (Zeller & Carmines, 1980) because wandering had opposite signed associations of similar magnitude with cohesion and conflict. This would indicate whether the measurement of cohesion and conflict was tapping one unipolar dimension or two separate dimensions of the family's emotional atmosphere. The nested models supported a separate factor solution for cohesion and conflict. The two factor model adequately fit the data ($\chi^2 = .15$, $df = 1$, $p = .69$), whereas a one-factor model did not ($p < .001$).

Predictive Validity

A more critical test of the separate dimensions of cohesion and conflict as family contexts is a test of predictive validity. For this analysis, we employed latent variable growth curve modeling (LGM) to test the hypotheses that cohesion would reduce change in wandering and that conflict would lead to growth in wandering. Construct scores combining the child report and parent report were computed for LGM.

The growth models specified two factors of child wandering: the intercept factor or initial status of child wandering in Grade 4, and the change or growth in wandering from Grade 4 to Grade 6. For identification of LGM factors using two time points, the error variance for the Grade 4 and Grade 6 wandering were fixed at 20% of their observed variances. For a discussion of modeling strategy and estimation procedures, see Stoolmiller (1994,1995).

We hypothesized that cohesion would lead to decreases in child wandering and conflict would lead to increases in wandering. The results of the factor model testing the predictive validity of cohesion and conflict are displayed in Fig. 8.3.

The growth model showed an adequate fit to the data ($\chi^2 = 7.68$, $p = .65$), with cohesion and conflict predicting 13% of the variance in the initial status of wandering and 18% of the variance in change. The disturbance term for the latent factors in structured mean estimation procedures represents the factor variance. The mean level of wandering for the group at Time 1 was

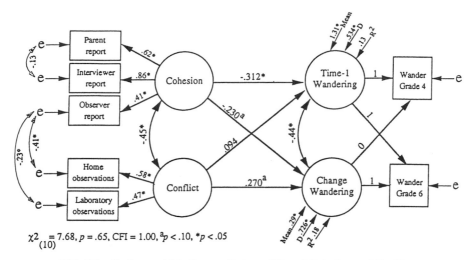

$\chi^2_{(10)} = 7.68, p = .65,$ CFI $= 1.00, {}^a p < .10, {}^* p < .05$

FIG. 8.3.   Factor model testing predictive validity of Cohesion and Conflict.

significantly different from zero, and there was significant variation among individual intercepts. The change factor showed a significant mean level increase in wandering from Grade 4 to Grade 6 and significant variation among individual slopes.

The paths from cohesion and conflict to change in wandering marginally supported our hypotheses. Cohesion was associated with reduced changes in wandering ($\beta = -.230$, $p < .10$) and conflict with increased changes ($\beta = .270$, $p < .10$). Both of the constructs showed lagged effects. However, cohesion at Grade 4 was synchronously associated with reductions in wandering at Grade 4 ($\beta = -.312$, $p < .05$). Conflict was not associated with initial status of wandering. Therefore, in terms of predictive validity, cohesion and conflict had differing synchronous effects with child wandering.

The final model introduced control variables that may account for the explained variation in child wandering. Boy antisocial, parent antisocial, and family structure were entered in the model. The results of the final model are displayed in Fig. 8.4. For the sake of clarity, the correlations between the factors and the control variables are presented in a matrix below the model, the indicators for the factors are not displayed, and only significant paths from the control variables are displayed.

The final model adequately fit the data ($\chi^2 = 24.4$, $p = .14$), with approximately 30% of the variance explained in the intercept factor and 20% of the variance explained in change. Some of the hypothesized paths for cohesion and conflict were changed in the presence of controls. First, boy antisocial entered the model as a strong predictor of Grade 4 wandering ($\beta = .463, p < .05$). Neither parent antisocial nor family structure significantly predicted the wandering factors. Second, the effect of cohesion on the intercept factor and the effect of conflict on change became nonsignificant. The effect of cohesion on change in

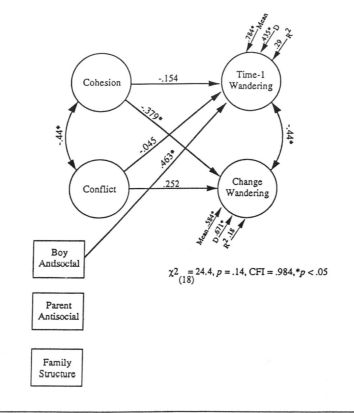

$\chi^2_{(18)} = 24.4, p = .14, CFI = .984, *p < .05$

	Cohesion	Conflict	Boy Antisocial	Parent Antisocial	Family Structure
Cohesion	1.00				
Conflict	-.44*	1.00			
Boy Antisocial	-.57*	.52*	1.00		
Parent Antisocial	-.20*	.62*	.27*	1.00	
Family Structure	-.36*	.23*	.18*	.28*	1.00

FIG. 8.4.   Control variables for variation in Wandering.

wandering, however, became stronger ($\beta = -.379, p < .05$). This meant that the association of conflict with child wandering was somewhat redundant with the control variables, whereas the effect of cohesion with change in wandering was slightly suppressed by the control variables.

Cohesion as a family context was uniquely related to change in wandering after partialling out the variance shared with the control variables. Inspection of the correlation matrix gives us some clues for these findings. Both cohesion and conflict are correlated in the expected direction with boy antisocial, parent antisocial, and family structure. Conflict, however, had stronger correlations with both parent antisocial than did cohesion ($r = .62$ and $-.20$, respectively). Parental antisocial qualities were related more to the measurement of conflict than they are with the measurement of cohesion.

In summary, the SEM factor model showed convergent and construct validity for the measurement of conflict, cohesion, and child wandering. SEM provided an analytic tool to partial out error variance to refine the covariance between the latent factors. LGM demonstrated the predictive validity of cohesion and conflict. Conflict as an emotional tone to the family environment was related more to the parental antisocial qualities, whereas cohesion had unique effects predicting the growth in wandering from Grade 4 to Grade 6.

IMPLICATIONS

In this chapter, we set out to develop two distinct measures that would evaluate affective dimensions of parenting style using multiple method, agent, and setting perspectives and a bootstrapping approach. The measures were tested for their construct and predictive validity using SEM. In a confirmatory factor analysis, a two-factor model fit the data and was preferable to a one-factor model, indicating acceptable convergent and discriminant validity for the two constructs. Next, the measures were tested for predictive validity. The hypothesis was that cohesion and conflict would contribute to changing levels of boys' wandering from Grades 4 to 6. Cohesion was expected to be associated with relatively small increases in wandering, whereas conflict was expected to predict increased wandering. The hypotheses were partially supported. Cohesion and conflict were related to wandering in the expected directions, with cohesion having unique effects predicting growth in wandering over and above boy and parent antisocial behaviors. Conflict did not contribute to change in wandering.

The findings are generally in keeping with those of other studies that examined the relationship between affective expression and parenting process (Dix, 1991). Some investigators believe that emotional expression has a direct effect on children's adjustment (e.g., Cummings, Pellegrini, Notarius, & Cummings, 1989; Gottman & Katz, 1989). Our position is that emotional expression operates primarily by influencing parenting practices, parent–child relationships, and intermediary child outcomes, which in turn influence youngsters' adjustment problems. Forgatch and Stoolmiller (1994) tested this hypothesis in a delinquency model. The model hypothesized that the effect of emotional expression on boys' delinquency would be mediated by its impact on parental monitoring. Boys' neutral affect and maternal humor facilitated monitoring; mutual contempt between mothers and sons interfered with monitoring. Monitoring and deviant peer association both accounted for variance in delinquency. There was no direct effect of emotional expression on deviant peer association or delinquency.

A set of studies examined the impact of emotional expression on the outcomes of problem-solving discussions about current family conflicts. Basically, positive and neutral affects were found to be associated with positive outcomes, whereas negative affects were associated with poor problem-solving outcomes (Capaldi, Forgatch, & Crosby, 1994; Forgatch, 1989; Rueter & Conger, 1995). When our measure of conflict failed to contribute to change in wandering, we tested an alternative hypothesis. The hypothesis was that families who resolved conflict by negotiating satisfactory problem-solving outcomes would have boys who showed little increase in wandering from Grades 4 to 6. The data did not support the hypothesis.

When testing models that attempt to understand how closely-related variables operate together, we must be particularly careful about measurement. Otherwise our findings may simply reflect method biases that come from one agent's vision, patterns of behavior common to a single setting, unreliability of the measurement approach, and other problems. These shortcomings can be alleviated to some degree by employing measures that draw on multiple perspectives, settings, and methods. To the extent that these measures converge, the information may be particularly salient—if the model fits.

Discriminant validity is also essential to disentangle cause and effect relationships. Variables tapping affective dimensions of parenting style are so close to parenting practices themselves that it sometimes becomes difficult to say where one concept ends and the other begins. If there is too much variance shared in common because of the measurement approach, then both constructs may be assessing the same thing. If there is no shared variance between constructs, then the model may be at fault.

In our study, we attempted to address these problems with constructs built on multiple agent, setting, and method approaches. Despite the richness of our assessment battery, there were, nevertheless, limitations. Sometimes there is less information about some constructs than others. Furthermore, one construct's strength may come at the expense of another. This was true with respect to cohesion and conflict. Studies using this dataset have emphasized coercive processes and given less attention to the more positive dimensions of parenting, which is why we focused on cohesion. However, the breadth of the cohesion construct resulted in a narrower measure of conflict. This may in part explain the failure to obtain the hypothesized relationship between conflict and increases in wandering. The construct was based on observational methods alone, although the data were obtained in two settings, the home and the laboratory. Within the observational method, we also defined the indicators to be aversive behaviors directed parents toward their youngster. Does this constitute conflict? We think it may not be the strongest measurement. Future studies call for more attention to the development of a more balanced construct for conflict.

ACKNOWLEDGMENTS

The authors thank Judy Ray, who conducted the analyses forming the Cohesion and Conflict Constructs; Mike Stoolmiller, whose tutelage and seminal work in Wandering and LGM guided these analyses; and Jerry Patterson, whose challenging discussions helped us put the theory and findings in perspective. Support for this project was provided by the following Grants: R01 MH38318 and R01 MH54703 from the Child and Adolescent Treatment and Prevention Intervention Research Branch, Division of Services and Intervention Research, National Institute of Mental Health (NIHM), U.S. Public Health Service (PHS); PH50 MH46690 awarded by the Prevention and Behavioral Medicine Research Branch, Division of Epidemiology and Services Research; NIMH, U.S. PHS; MH37940 from the Antisocial and Other Personality Disorders Program; Prevention, Early Intervention and Epidemiology Branch, NIMH, U.S. PHS; and MH19734, Division of Epidemiology and Services Branch, NIMH.

REFERENCES

Balck, F., Jantschek, G., & Wietersheim, J. (1991). Diagnostics with families: A comparison of FACES—II and SYMLOG. *Small Group Research, 22*(1), 115–123.

Bank, L., Dishion, T., Skinner, M., & Patterson, G. R. (1990). Method variance in structural equation modeling: Living with "glop." In G. R. Patterson (Ed.), *Depression and aggression in family interaction* (pp. 247–279). Hillsdale, NJ: Lawrence Erlbaum Associates.

Bank, L., & Patterson, G. R. (1992). The use of structural equation modeling in combining data from different types of assessment. In J. Rosen & P. McReynolds (Eds.), *Advances in psychological assessment* (Vol. 8, pp. 41–74). New York: Plenum.

Campbell, D. T., & Fiske, D. W. (1959). Convergent and discriminant validation of the multitrait and multimethod matrix. *Psychological Bulletin, 56*, 82–105.

Capaldi, D. M., Forgatch, M. S., & Crosby, L. (1994). Affective expression in family problem-solving discussions with adolescent boys: The association with family structure and function. *Journal of Adolescent Research, 9*(1), 28–49.

Capaldi, D. M., & Patterson, G. R. (1989). *Psychometric properties of fourteen latent constructs from the Oregon Youth Study.* New York: Springer-Verlag.

Capaldi, D. M., & Patterson, G. R. (1991). Relation of parental transition to boys' adjustment problems: Mothers at risk for transitions and unskilled parenting. *Developmental Psychology, 27*(3), 489–504.

Cole, D. A., & Jordan, A. E. (1989). Assessment of cohesion and adaptability in component family dyads: A question of convergent and discriminant validity. *Journal of Counseling Psychology, 36*(4), 456–463.

Conger, R. D., Patterson, G. R., & Ge, X. (1995). It takes two to replicate: A mediational model for the impact of parents' stress on adolescent adjustment. *Developmental Psychology, 66*, 80–97.

Cronbach, L. J., & Meehl, P. E. (Eds.). (1956). *Construct validity in psychological tests.* (Vol. I). Minneapolis: University of Minnesota Press.

Cummings, J. S., Pellegrini, D. S., Notarius, C. I., & Cummings, E. M. (1989). Children's responses to angry adult behavior as a function of marital distress and history of interparent hostility. *Child Development, 60*, 1035–1043.

DeGarmo, D. S., & Forgatch, M. S. (in preparation). *Emotional contexts of the family and their impact on intermediary and child adjustment outcomes.* Eugene, OR: Oregon Social Learning Center.

Dickerson, V. C., & Coyne, J. C. (1987). Family cohesion and control: A multitrait-multimethod study. *Journal of Marital and Family Therapy, 13*(3), 275–285.

Dishion, T. J., Andrews, D. W., & Crosby, L. (1995). Antisocial boys and their friends in early adolescence: Relationship characteristics, quality, and interactional processes. *Child Development, 66*, 139–151.

Dishion, T. J., Gardner, K., Patterson, G. R., Reid, J. B., & Thibodeaux, S. (1983). *Family process code: A multidimensional system for observing family interaction* (unpublished technical report). Eugene, OR: Oregon Social Learning Center.

Dishion, T. J., Patterson, G. R., & Kavanagh, K. A. (1992). An experimental test of the coercion model: Linking measurement theory, and intervention. In J. McCord & R. Tremblay (Eds.), *The interaction of theory and practice: Experimental studies of intervention* (pp. 253–282). New York: Guilford.

Dix, T. (1991). The affective organization of parenting: Adaptive and maladaptive processes. *Psychological Bulletin, 110*(1), 3–25.

Doherty, W. J., & Hovander, D. (1990). Why don't family measures of cohesion and control behave the way they're supposed to? Special Issue: Marital and family measurements. *American Journal of Family Therapy, 18*(1), 5–18.

Epstein, N. B., Bishop, D. S., & Levin, S. (1978). The McMaster model of family functioning. *Journal of Marriage and Family Counseling, 4*, 19–31.

Forgatch, M. S. (1989). Patterns and outcome in family problem solving: The disrupting effect of negative emotion. *Journal of Marriage and the Family, 51*, 115–124.

Forgatch, M. S. (1991). The clinical science vortex: Developing a theory for antisocial behavior. In D. Pepler & K. H. Rubin (Eds.), *The development and treatment of childhood aggression* (pp. 291–315). Hillsdale, NJ: Lawrence Erlbaum Associates.

Forgatch, M. S., Fetrow, B., & Lathrop, M. (1985). *Solving problems in family interactions.* Eugene, OR: Oregon Social Learning Center.

Forgatch, M. S., Patterson, G. R., & Ray, J. A. (1996). Divorce and boys' adjustment problems: Two paths with a single model. In E. M. Hetherington (Ed.), *Stress, coping, and resiliency in children and the family* (pp. 67–105). Hillsdale, NJ: Lawrence Erlbaum Associates.

Forgatch, M. S., & Stoolmiller, M. (1994). Emotions as contexts for adolescent delinquency. *Journal of Research in Adolescence, 4*(4), 601–614.

Gottman, J. M., & Katz, L. F. (1989). Effects of marital discord on young children's peer interaction and health. *Developmental Psychology, 25*(3), 001–009.

Kog, E., Vertommen, H., & Vandereysken, W. (1987). Minuchin's psychosomatic family model revised: A concept-validation study using a multitrait-multimethod approach. *Family Process, 26*(2), 235–253.

Maccoby, E. A., & Martin, J. A. (1983). Socialization in the context of the family: Parent–child interaction. In P. H. Mussen (Ed.), *Handbook of child psychology* (4th ed., Vol. IV, pp. 1–101). New York: Wiley.

Moos, R. H., & Moos, B. W. (1981). *Family environment scale and preliminary manual.* Palo Alto, CA: Consulting Psychologists Press.

Oliveri, M. E., & Reiss, D. (1981). A theory-based empirical classification of family problem-solving behavior. *Family Process, 20,* 409–418.

Olson, D. H., Portner, J., & Lavee, Y. (1985). *FACES III.* St. Paul, MN: Family Social Science, University of Minnesota.

Olson, D. H., Russell, C. S., & Sprenkle, D. H. (1983). Circumplex model of marital and family systems: VI. Theoretical update. *Family Process, 22,* 69–83.

Parpal, M., & Maccoby, E. E. (1985). Maternal responsiveness and subsequent child compliance. *Child Development, 56,* 1326–1334.

Patterson, G. R. (1982). *A social learning approach: Coercive family process.* (Vol. III). Eugene, OR: Castalia Publishing.

Patterson, G. R. (1993). Orderly change in a stable world: The antisocial trait as a CHIMERA. *Journal of Consulting and Clinical Psychology, 61,* 911–919.

Patterson, G. R., & Bank, L. (1986). Bootstrapping your way in the nomological thicket. *Behavioral Assessment, 8,* 49–73.

Patterson, G. R., & Bank, L. (1987). When is a nomological network a construct? In D. R. Peterson & D. B. Fishman (Eds.), *Assessment for decision* (pp. 249–279). New Brunswick, NJ: Rutgers University Press.

Patterson, G. R., & Forgatch, M. S. (1995). Predicting future clinical adjustment from treatment outcome and process variables: Special Edition "Methods and Problems in Clinical Assessment Research." *Psychological Assessment, 7*(3), 275–285.

Patterson, G. R., Reid, J. B., & Dishion, T. J. (1992). *Antisocial boys.* (Vol. 4). Eugene, OR: Castalia.

Perosa, L. M., & Perosa, S. L. (1990). Convergent and discriminant validity for family self-report measures. *Educational and Psychological Measurement, 50*(4), 855–868.

Prinz, R. J., Foster, S., Kent, R. N., & O'Leary, D. K. (1979). Multivariate assessment of conflict in distressed and nondistressed mother–adolescent dyads. *Journal of Applied Behavior Analysis, 12*(4), 691–700.

Reid, J. B. (1993). Prevention of conduct disorder before and after school entry: Relating interventions to development findings. *Journal of Development and Psychopathology, 5,* 243–262.

Reiss, D. (1971). Intimacy and problem-solving. *Archives of General Psychiatry, 25,* 442–445.

Rueter, M. A., & Conger, R. D. (1995). Interaction style, problem solving behavior, and family problem solving effectiveness. *Child Development, 66,* 98–115.

Simons, R. L., Wu, C., Conger, R. D., & Lorenz, R. O. (1994). Two routes to delinquency: Differences between early and late starters in the impact of parenting and deviant peers. *Criminology, 32*(2), 247–276.

Stoolmiller, M. (1994). Antisocial behavior, delinquent peer association, and unsupervised wandering: Growth and change from childhood to early adolescence. *Multivariate Behavioral Research, 29*(3), 263–288.

Stoolmiller, M. (1995). Using latent growth curve models to study developmental processes. In J. M. Gottman & G. Sackett (Eds.), *The analysis of change* (pp. 105–138). Hillsdale, NJ: Lawrence Erlbaum Associates.

Zeller, R., & Carmines, E. (1980). *Measurement in the social sciences: The link between theory and data.* New York: Cambridge University Press.

9

▼▼▼▼▼▼▼

Conflict and Cohesion in Parent–Adolescent Relations: Changes in Emotional Expression From Early to Midadolescence

Rand D. Conger
Iowa State University

Xiaojia Ge
University of California, Davis

Most theories of adolescent development propose that the quality of inter- actions between parents and their children changes during the transition from late childhood to early or middle adolescence. More specifically, several researchers proposed that conflict between the two generations systematically increases with the onset of puberty, peaks during early or midadolescence, then declines toward the end of the adolescent years (e.g., Montemayor, 1983). Laursen and Collins (1994), however, argued that this perspective rests more on theoretical than empirical grounds. Indeed, they suggested that the research evidence for this hypothesized developmental trend is rather weak and may not accurately reflect reality.

In response to the need for additional research on this issue, this chapter provides new evidence regarding changes in emotional expression between parents and adolescents during the early to midadolescent period and, thus, tests the adequacy of theoretical arguments that propose that such changes should occur. The study was concerned with three major issues. First, we sought to investigate over time increases, decreases, and stability in conflict and cohesion in parent–adolescent relations, operationalized as observed demonstrations of positive and negative emotional expression. Second, the study examined earlier qualities of parent–child interaction expected to pre- dict change in conflict and cohesion. Finally, we employed methodological procedures that improve on the research strategies used in many earlier studies so as to strengthen the inferences that might be drawn from the present findings. The following discussion considers the theoretical, empirical, and methodological issues addressed in the present study.

THEORETICAL PERSPECTIVES AND STUDY HYPOTHESES

In a recent review of the literature on interpersonal conflict during adolescence, Laursen and Collins (1994) proposed that most theories of adolescent development predict significant alterations in parent–child interactions as a function of maturation. They noted, for example, that psychoanalytic models hypothesize that physical maturation during adolescence reawakens Oedipal tensions that are resolved by emotional distancing between parents and adolescents (e.g., Blos, 1979). Similarly, sociobiological models suggest that puberty increases conflicts between parents and children because these conflicts assure that adolescents will turn their attention from family members to peers. The theory posits that this shift in social priorities increases the likelihood of the selection of sexual partners from the peer group (e.g., Steinberg, 1990). Finally, Laursen and Collins note that cognitive–developmental models also predict discontinuity in parent–adolescent interactions. According to this perspective, increasing mental abilities during the adolescent transition lead teenagers to reevaluate the prerogatives of parents and children. As young people question the authority of parents on a number of issues, conflict ensues until differing expectations can be renegotiated (e.g., Smetana, 1988).

Thus, Laursen and Collins (1994) argue that the major theoretical perspectives on adolescent development predict increasing conflict and withdrawal between parents and adolescents during the early to midadolescent years. In contrast to these views, however, they propose that social relational models of adolescent development predict greater continuity than change in the quality of parent–child and parent–adolescent interactions. They note that "social relational perspectives emphasize developmental continuity resulting from the inherent stability of close relationships" and that "change, when it occurs, will be gradual." This proposed continuity in parent–adolescent interactions suggests that, contrary to the sharp disjunctions hypothesized in earlier perspectives, change in parent–adolescent interactions occur slowly and primarily reflect qualities of the relationship present at earlier points in time.

Drawing on these insights, we proposed that parent–child interactions would be marked by increasing conflict and decreased cohesion over the period from early to midadolescence, consistent with psychodynamic, sociobiological, and cognitive–developmental perspectives. We also hypothesized, however, that these changes would occur gradually over time, as suggested by a social relational view of adolescent development. Also consistent with this perspective, we proposed that the affective tone of the parent–adolescent relationship early in this process would predict later changes in emotional expression between parents and children. That is, we expected that changing relations between parents and adolescents would actually represent continuing themes from their earlier relationships. Empirical support for this predicted process would be consistent with social relational models that propose that changes in parent–adolescent relations derive not only from biological or cognitive imperatives but also from the social–interactional histories of parents and adolescents.

EMPIRICAL AND METHODOLOGICAL ISSUES

Although we hypothesized that conflict (operationalized as overt hostility or negative affect) would increase and cohesion (operationalized as observable warmth and support or positive affect) would decrease between parents and their children during the transition from early to middle adolescence, earlier research findings are quite mixed regarding such developmental trajectories. From their review of earlier research, for example, Paikoff and Brooks-Gunn (1991) conclude that there is some, but not overwhelming, evidence that emotional closeness between parents and children declines during early adolescence as conflict increases. Laursen and Collins (1994), however, suggest that research findings are too inconsistent to draw any firm conclusions. Moreover, both sets of reviewers note that previous research varies greatly in terms of the methods employed and the strength of the inferences that can be drawn from any particular study. In the following discussion, we briefly review some of the major findings from this literature and also note many of the most significant methodological limitations in previous research. We then discuss the methodological strengths of the present study that help to overcome some of these limitations.

Earlier Findings

Even a cursory review of the research on parent–adolescent interactions reveals a sometimes confusing array of methodological approaches to the issue (Laursen & Collins, 1994; Paikoff & Brooks-Gunn, 1991). For instance, some studies employ self-report measures of behavioral interactions, others use reports from trained observers. Even when the same method is used to generate interactional variables, the focus of the measures often varies (e.g., overt disagreements over specific issues vs. conversational interruptions). Some studies examine changes across time, others investigate differences in cross-sectional comparisons of study participants. Finally, several studies relate parent–adolescent interactions to variations in age, and others investigate the association between interactional processes and pubertal status. With such a multitude of research procedures, it is not surprising that there are inconsistencies in the research findings.

Because the present study focuses on the changing nature of parent–child interactions over the period from early to midadolescence, this review considers only previous research that examined variations in parent–child relationships as a function of chronological age or grade level. In this study, we use grade level as a proxy variable for the complete set of biological, cognitive, and social forces predicted by the theories reviewed earlier to influence the parent–adolescent relationship during this period. Because the following analyses do not address specifically the connection between pubertal status and parent–child interactions and, thus, are not directly comparable to previous studies that used that methodology, we do not review this earlier work on biological maturation and the parent–adolescent relationship. As noted, however, we believe that biological change is one of the elements captured by our primary predictor variable, grade level or age change.

Studies that relate age-of-adolescent to parent–child interactions generally focus on conflict behaviors. They demonstrate a variety of findings ranging from increases to decreases in parent–adolescent strife during the early adolescent years. For example, Galambos and Almeida (1992) studied a cohort of 112 sixth graders and assessed both child and parent reports of conflicts over 44 specific issues such as household chores and finances. Over a 2.5 year period involving 4 measurement occasions, they found no evidence for an overall increase in conflict between these parents and their children. Indeed, their results indicated that conflicts decreased in most of the domains assessed. Some studies of age differences in conflict, on the other hand, found the expected trends for increased conflict during early and middle adolescence (e.g., Furman & Buhrmester, 1992); however, others provide contrary findings consistent with the Galambos and Almeida (1992) study (e.g., Smetana, 1989).

These data suggest, then, that the expected age differences regarding conflict and reduced closeness between parents and adolescents often are not found. Such findings run contrary to the theories reviewed earlier, which suggest that such changes should occur, and they also are inconsistent with research on pubertal status, which is associated with increased contentiousness and decreased emotional closeness in parent–adolescent relationships (e.g., Steinberg, 1981, 1988). We expect that methodological and measurement problems likely account for these inconsistent research findings (see also Laursen & Collins, 1994). For example, most of this research involves cross-sectional comparisons of adolescents of different ages, rather than investigation of changes in the same parents and adolescents across time (for an important exception, see Galambos & Almeida, 1992). This research strategy does not rule out the possibility that changes in parent–adolescent interactions actually occurred across time for same-aged adolescents. Thus, additional longitudinal research is required to increase confidence in empirical findings in this area of inquiry.

A second methodological problem involves the usually small sample sizes, and typically nonrepresentative samples, employed in previous research. For example, in the Galambos and Almeida study (1992), families were recruited through schools and newspaper advertisements, and the authors provided no information regarding the degree of success in recruiting from some known population. That is, we do not know whether 10% or 90% of families with the opportunity to participate in the study actually completed the mailed questionnaires used in the project; nor do the authors indicate the qualities of the target population from which the sample was drawn (e.g., poor, rich, lower class, middle class, etc.).

Without knowing something about the initial sampling frame, or the success in recruiting from that frame, we cannot easily interpret the meaning of the findings. For example, were these all highly cooperative families who represented a small proportion of the population that would readily participate in the study and who also were especially harmonious in their family interactions? Were they exceptions to families in general and does that account for the theoretically unexpected trends in their patterns of conflict? Finally, the sample in this study began with only 112 cases that dwindled to fewer than 70 families with complete data for the longitudinal analyses. How did this rate of over 30% attrition affect the findings? Did families in which conflict was most likely to increase across early adolescence drop out of the study? Thus, even though this study overcomes the problem of a cross-sectional research design by following families across time, its small, nonrepresentative sample and significant attrition rate raises many questions about the generalizability of its findings.

Another difficulty with studies of the relationship between adolescent age and parent–child interactions is their frequent reliance on self-report methodology (Laursen & Collins, 1994; Paikoff & Brooks-Gunn, 1991). The difficulty with family member reports of interactional processes is that they may reflect the emotional dispositions of the informant more than they indicate the quality of the behaviors exchanged between family members. A recent study by Tein, Roosa, and Michaels (1994) illustrates this problem. Their findings revealed very little agreement between parents and children in their assessments of parental behavior. Indeed, these family member reports demonstrated very poor convergent and discriminant validity and also were systematically biased by personal characteristics of the reporters. These perturbations in family member reports are also revealed in the Galambos and Almeida (1992) study in which there were statistically significant differences between parents and children in their assessments of levels of family conflict.

These difficulties with self-report measures led several investigators to call for the increased use of trained observer reports in studies of parent–child interactions (Galambos & Almeida, 1992; Laursen & Collins, 1994; Paikoff & Brooks-Gunn, 1991). Laursen & Collins (1994) note, for instance, that observational measures may more adequately evaluate the overt behaviors of interest in such studies and also help to reduce problems of method variance confounds. We also expect that trained observer reports of family interactional processes will be more sensitive to the actual changes in affective tone predicted by the various theoretical frameworks reviewed in this chapter. That is, the theories do not necessarily suggest that there will be increases in specific conflicts about chores, money, etc., but rather that there should be emotional distancing between parents and adolescents as captured both by increased negative affect (e.g., expressions of hostility that may or may not be tied to specific disagreements or conflicts) and by decreased positive affect (e.g., emotional closeness or warmth/supportiveness that, again, may or may not be tied to specific instances of conflict or disagreement).

Methodological Strengths of the Present Study

The present study sought to improve on the methodological limitations of earlier research in several ways. First, we employed a longitudinal rather than cross-sectional research design. The families who participated were assessed on three separate occasions when the adolescents in the study were in the seventh, eighth, and ninth grades. This time period reflects the transitional period from early to middle adolescence. Second, a carefully defined sample of rural adolescents was employed. All adolescents in intact families who were (a) enrolled in the seventh grade, (b) living in towns of less than 6,500 population or in the countryside, (c) attending a public or private school, and (d) residing in an eight-county area in a midwestern state were eligible to participate. Of those eligible, 78% agreed to be interviewed. This recruitment rate assured that the final sample was representative of the population of interest and that it included families with a broad range of social and demographic characteristics.

Third, the present study also addressed concerns regarding sample size and retention. In the present case, 451 families were recruited into the study and 90% of them continued to participate in the third year of data collection (ninth grade). Fourth, to overcome the noted difficulties with family report measures, this study relied on observer assessments of parent–adolescent interactions related to conflict and cohesion. Finally, these observational variables were not confined to behaviors that involved conflicts or discussions only about specific issues. Again, none of the theories reviewed earlier predicts that distancing between parents and children during this period will be manifested only during disagreements or quarrels about particular topics. Instead, the expression of negative or positive affect may occur in relation to almost any interaction such as mealtime discussions about the events of the day. Thus, a strength of the present investigation is its use of measures that will reflect growing hostility or conflict and declining cohesion or warmth/support in parent–adolescent relations regardless of the issues being discussed by the participants in the interaction.

With these theoretical, empirical, and methodological issues in mind, we now turn to a discussion of the specific procedures followed in the conduct of the study. The next section on study methods is followed by an examination of findings from the research. The chapter concludes with a discussion of the results and their significance in relation to theoretically predicted changes in parent–child interactions during the early and midadolescent years.

METHOD

Sample

When first interviewed in 1989, the sample for these analyses consisted of 451 families. Only White families were studied because there were too few minority families in rural Iowa where the study took place to generate meaningful data for them. In these analyses, listwise deletion of missing data was used across three waves of data collection, leaving a total of 378 families for whom complete data were available. In most instances, missing data was produced by videotaping equipment failures that produced random rather than systematic data loss.

Each family included two parents, a seventh-grade adolescent (198 girls, 180 boys, average age = 12.6 years in 1989), and a sibling within 4 years of age of the seventh grader. Families lived in one of eight adjacent counties in Iowa in an area heavily dependent on agriculture. For the final sample of 378 families, 32% lived on farms, 12% lived in rural areas but not on a farm, and 56% lived in towns or small cities with a population under 6,500 (all but one of the towns was under 5,000). These families were selected to be representative of two-parent rural families living in northcentral Iowa. Participants were interviewed during the first 3 months of 1989, 1990, and 1991.

Family median income for these 378 families from all sources for the previous year in 1989 was $33,800, about $5,000 per year less than married couples with children in the United States as a whole. A total of 11.0% of the families ($N = 42$) had incomes below the federal poverty line, about twice the proportion (5.6%) for married-couple families nationally in 1988 (Bureau of the Census, 1989). Because of the sampling criteria, the average number of family members was 4.95. Per capita income ranged from a net loss of over $10,000 (a troubled farm family) to $51,800 in the last year, suggesting that the sample contains families with a broad range of sociodemographic characteristics. Occupational prestige scores (from 1 = least prestigious to

99 = most prestigious) for fathers (M = 42.75) and mothers (M = 33.66) indicate that fathers were generally skilled laborers or entrepreneurs and working mothers averaged less skilled occupations typically in the service sector of the economy. On average, these families could best be described as middle to lower middle class, ranging from household heads who are unskilled laborers (22.05) to those who are professionals (86.05; Nakao & Treas, 1990).

The retention rate at each wave of data collection was about 95%. Overall retention rate from 1989 (N = 451) to 1991 (N = 407) was 90%, although the final sample for these analyses was reduced to 378 (84% of the original sample) by listwise deletion for missing data. Families not included in the analyses did not have significantly lower incomes than those who remained in the sample, nor were they likely to demonstrate higher levels of emotional distress. However, parents not included in the final sample of 378 families were slightly less well educated. Fathers not in the analyses averaged 12.74 years of education compared to 13.57 years for those who remained in the study, a statistically significant difference ($p < .05$). For mothers, the mean years of education were 12.87 (missing subjects) and 13.31 (in the final sample), which was not a significant difference. These findings are consonant with those for other longitudinal studies of families and adolescents that also report greater attrition for less educated parents (e.g., Flanagan & Eccles, 1993). In 1989, fathers averaged 40 years of age, mothers 38 years.

Procedures

Families were recruited in 1989 through 34 public and private schools in the eight counties. Names and addresses of seventh-grade students and their parents were obtained from all schools in communities of 6,500 or less. Families were sent a letter explaining the project and were subsequently contacted by telephone and asked to participate. In 1989, 78.8% of the families agreed to be interviewed. Each family member was compensated at a rate of about $10 per hour for his or her time in the study.

Each year interviewers visited each family at home for approximately 2 hours on each of two occasions. During the first visit, each of the four family members completed a set of questionnaires focusing on individual family member characteristics, the quality of family relationships and interactions, and family demographic characteristics. During the second visit to the home, which occurred within 2 weeks of the first, the family members were video-taped as they engaged in several different structured interaction tasks. A trained interviewer began the session by asking each individual to complete independently a short questionnaire designed to identify issues of concern that led to disagreements in the family (e.g., chores, recreation, money, etc.). The family members were then gathered around a table and given a set of cards with questions for them to read and discuss. All four family members were involved in this first task, which lasted about 30 minutes. The cards for the first task asked general questions about family life, such as approaches to parenting, performance in school, household chores, and important family events.

After explaining the procedures, completing a practice card with the family, and checking the video-recording equipment for Task 1 (and each subsequent task), the interviewer left the room for another part of the house where she or he could not hear the discussion. The family members were asked to discuss among themselves each of the items listed on the cards and to continue talking until the interviewer returned. The video camera recorded the family's interaction around the issues raised by the task cards. After the first task was completed, the interviewer returned, stopped the discussion, and described the second task. The next tasks proceeded in a similar fashion.

The second interaction task, 15 minutes in length, also involved all four family members. For this task, the interviewer selected three topics based on the questionnaires completed at the beginning of the visit. The family members were asked to discuss and try to resolve the issue that they had identified as leading to the greatest conflict in their family. If they resolved this problem, they could go on to the second or even the third issue during the task. A third task involved only the two siblings and the fourth task included just the parents. Because we did not use data from these tasks in the present analyses, they are not described here.

Trained observers rated several dimensions of family interaction and family member characteristics from the videotapes. Observers received 2 months of training and had to pass extensive written and viewing tests before they could code videotapes. A separate, independent coder was used for each task. For approximately 12% of all tasks in 1989, and for 20% of all tasks in subsequent years, a second observer was randomly assigned to code independently family interactions so that interobserver reliability coefficients (an intraclass correlation) could be estimated. An observer rating manual with complete definitions for all rating scales and all task procedures is available from the first author.

Measures

As suggested by the title of this chapter, our focus of measurement involved behaviors by parents and adolescents indicative of either conflict or cohesion in interpersonal relations. If parents and adolescents actually increase their emotional distance from one another, as suggested by the theoretical perspectives reviewed earlier, then conflict should increase and cohesion decrease from the early to midadolescent period.

Typically, studies of parent–adolescent conflict examined the negative emotional tone that accompanies disagreements over specific conflict topics (e.g., Steinberg, 1988). Because we are less interested in particular domains of conflict and more interested in this affective dimension of conflict, in these analyses we define conflict as expressions of negative affect rated by trained observers of videotaped family interactions. The concept of cohesion parallels most closely the notion of emotional closeness, which has been shown by some research to decline at this stage of life (Paikoff & Brooks-Gunn, 1991; Steinberg, 1990). In this study, cohesion or emotional closeness was operationalized as observed positive affect or warmth and supportiveness in parent–adolescent interactions. Descriptions of the specific measures follow.

Observer Ratings of Conflict/Hostility.   Observers rated parent and adolescent behaviors on a 5-point scale with higher scores indicating higher levels of the attribute being assessed (1 = no evidence of the behavior, 5 = the behavior is quite frequent and/or quite intense). The measure of conflict/hostility was derived from the summation of three separate rating scales: hostility, antisocial behavior, and angry coercion. *Hostility* included behaviors that were angry, critical, disapproving, or rejecting of the other interactor's behaviors, actions, appearance, or personal characteristics. *Antisocial behaviors* involved actions that were self-centered, defiant, insensitive, or immature. Finally, expressions of *angry coercion* included attempts to change the other person's actions or thoughts in a hostile, threatening, or blaming manner.

Observers rated both parents and adolescents on hostile, antisocial, and angry coercive behaviors. Separate observers independently rated these behaviors for Task 1 (family discussion) and Task 2 (family problem-solving). Coefficients of internal consistency for the summed conflict/hostility construct were all above .80. Interobserver reliabilities were all above .70. The same observer rating procedures were followed in coding cohesive behaviors.

Observer Ratings of Cohesion/Warmth/Supportiveness.   The second construct was based on five different ratings of specific observed behaviors that were summed to create the more global construct, cohesion or warmth/support. The *communication* measure reflects the focal person's actions that convey needs, wants, ideas, and opinions in a clear, neutral, or positive manner. It involves verbal demonstrations of interest in the other's point of view and also responses appropriate to the conversation. The *warmth* rating reflects verbal and nonverbal expressions of caring, affection, affirmation, supportiveness, and positive emotional responsiveness shown toward the other person.

The rating of *assertiveness* assesses the degree to which the focal person shows self-confidence and forthrightness when expressing himself or herself in a clear, appropriate, and neutral or positive fashion. Assertive behaviors involve actions that are not threatening or defensive even when areas of disagreement are being discussed. *Prosocial* behaviors included the family member's tendency to relate to others in a cooperative, sensitive, helpful fashion and also reflected a willingness to comply with the wishes of the other interactor. Finally, the *listener responsiveness* rating indicates attention to, interest in, acknowledgment of, and validation of the verbalizations of the other person through both verbal and nonverbal means. Across both parents and children and across both tasks, the internal consistency coefficients for the cohesion construct were all above .80 and the interobserver reliabilities were all above .70.

RESULTS

As indicated in the section on study hypotheses, three theory-based predictions guided the present analyses. First, and most consistent with the social relations perspective, both parents and children were expected to demonstrate gradual increases in hostile/conflicting behaviors from Time 1 (seventh grade) to Time 3 (ninth grade). Second, emotional closeness, as evidenced by levels of cohesion or warmth and supportiveness, was expected to decline during this time period. Finally, and again consistent with the social relations model, earlier qualities of parent–child interaction were expected to be important predictors of changes in these interactional processes during the early to midadolescent period.

Table 9.1 provides the findings for adolescent behaviors toward their mothers and fathers. The first three columns of the table provide the results for Task 1 (family discussion). Consistent with study predictions, both girls and boys demonstrated increasing levels of hostility to both mothers and fathers over the 3-year period. For example, row 1 shows an average level of hostility to mothers for girls at Time 1 of 6.15, 7.13 at Time 2, and 7.80 at Time 3. The trend is similar for boys to mothers, from 5.44 to 6.72, and for both boys and girls to their fathers. In each case, the F tests for time indicate that there were significant increases in adolescent conflict/hostility over time (e.g., $F = 28.86$, $p < .01$ for girls' hostility to mothers, Task 1).

The results for Task 2 indicate that the Task 1 findings for hostility were replicated for a separate task scored by a second, independent observer. These results are especially important in that they demonstrate that the initial findings were not task dependent nor a function of one set of coders' unique responses to the videotaped materials. Interestingly, the results related to hostility show that girls, compared to boys, were significantly more hostile toward their parents (e.g., the F test for gender for hostility toward mother, Task 2, Time 3 was 15.74, $p < .01$). This trend in the data was more apparent for the Task 1 than Task 2 findings. These findings may result from the fact

TABLE 9.1

Mean Scores for Adolescents' Observed Hostility and Warmth Toward Fathers and Mothers

Adolescent Behavior	First Interaction Task				Second Interaction Task			
	Time 1	Time 2	Time 3	F for Time	Time 1	Time 2	Time 3	F for Time
Hostility to Mothers								
Girls:	6.15	7.13	7.80	28.86**	6.43	6.96	8.05	23.42**
Boys:	5.44	5.90	6.72	25.14**	5.98	6.45	6.76	6.20**
F for Gender:	8.46**	20.40**	13.17**		2.96	3.17†	15.74**	
Hostility to Fathers								
Girls:	5.94	6.67	7.21	18.51**	5.97	6.58	7.57	25.73**
Boys:	5.26	5.85	6.48	21.56**	5.62	6.10	6.55	8.99**
F for Gender:	8.33**	9.69**	6.11*		1.92	3.31†	9.97**	
Warmth to Mothers								
Girls:	12.89	12.51	11.51	19.83**	11.08	9.61	8.36	88.18**
Boys:	12.39	12.79	11.81	27.35**	10.86	9.51	8.53	63.93**
F for Gender:	3.52†	0.88	1.38		0.72	0.15	0.66	
Warmth to Fathers								
Girls:	12.72	12.34	11.91	20.86**	10.58	9.20	8.06	81.81**
Boys:	12.33	12.64	11.14	22.26**	10.51	9.34	8.47	49.68**
F for Gender:	2.04	1.06	0.03		0.06	0.39	4.14*	

Note: †p < .10; *p < .05; **p < .01

that girls mature more quickly than boys and may demonstrate changes in their relationships with parents at an earlier chronological age. However, no predictions were made regarding such gender differences, thus we do not want to overstate their significance.

The findings related to warmth and supportiveness or cohesion in Table 9.1 also were consistent with study hypotheses. For example, the scores for boys to fathers during Task 1 declined from 12.33 at Time 1 to 11.14 at Time 3 ($F = 22.26, p < .01$). Interestingly, boys actually demonstrated a slight increase in expressed warmth to mothers and fathers at Time 2, whereas girls showed the expected steady decline across time in warmth to both parents. The results for Task 2 again replicate those for Task 1; however, in this instance boys demonstrated the expected steady drop in warmth (e.g., scores of 10.86, 9.51, and 8.53 toward their mothers for Times 1, 2, and 3, respectively). There were no consistent differences between boys and girls in terms of their warmth to mothers and fathers.

Table 9.2 provides the findings regarding parents' hostility and warmth toward their children. A quick scan of the table, which has the same format as Table 9.1, shows that there were no consistent differences between mothers and fathers in terms of their behaviors toward their male and female children. The exact same trends of increasing hostility and conflict and declining warmth and support were present for parents, however, as were found for their children. And again, the findings replicate across two different tasks coded by independent observers. For example, the scores for fathers' hostility to girls during Task 1 were 5.48, 6.18, and 6.28 from Time 1 to Time 3; the equivalent scores for Task 2 were 5.63, 6.14, and 6.72.

In summary, the results from Tables 9.1 and 9.2 are consistent with theoretical expectations from a social relational perspective that changes in parent–adolescent interactions will be gradual, rather than demonstrating dramatic disjunctions from one time period to another. The findings are also supportive of theories that suggest that biological, social, and cognitive changes during this period of life will lead to emotional distancing between parents and children. The measured pace of these changes, however, suggests significant stability in the nature of parent–adolescent interactions over time.

That is, on average we would expect that parents and children who have a history of harmonious relations would demonstrate a great deal of consistency in these interaction styles during the early adolescent period. Similarly, parents and children embroiled in conflict and strife prior to early adolescence should be at greatest risk for experiencing increasing problems in their relationships. These expectations derive from a social relational perspective and from our third study hypothesis. The following four figures provide results from the path analyses conducted to evaluate these predictions. Maximum likelihood estimation was used to compute the path models (Joreskog & Sorbom, 1993). Because initial analyses showed no adolescent gender

TABLE 9.2

Mean Scores for Parents' Observed Hostility and Warmth Toward Boys and Girls

Adolescent Behavior	First Interaction Task				Second Interaction Task			
	Time 1	Time 2	Time 3	F for Time	Time 1	Time 2	Time 3	F for Time
Mother's Hostility to								
Girls:	5.26	6.24	6.72	43.38**	6.19	6.59	7.41	19.75**
Boys:	5.19	5.96	6.32	19.39**	6.41	7.03	7.29	9.79**
F for Gender:	0.12	1.45	1.65		0.86	3.36†	0.15	
Father's Hostility to								
Girls:	5.48	6.18	6.28	13.04**	5.63	6.14	6.72	16.59**
Boys:	5.48	6.15	6.46	12.41**	5.93	6.87	7.19	20.58**
F for Gender:	0.00	0.05	0.50		1.57	8.82**	3.11†	
Mother's Warmth to								
Girls:	17.36	16.34	15.22	38.98**	14.24	12.41	11.15	71.84**
Boys:	17.47	16.71	15.70	19.90**	14.19	12.30	10.99	86.05**
F for Gender:	0.93	1.95	1.95		0.03	0.12	0.35	
Father's Warmth to								
Girls:	15.71	14.88	13.43	43.52**	13.06	11.59	10.33	61.38**
Boys:	15.90	15.19	14.04	28.61**	13.70	11.65	10.49	77.29**
F for Gender:	0.33	0.77	3.54†		3.53+	.03	0.33	

Note: †$p < .10$; *$p < .05$; **$p < .01$

differences in the findings, the following models were estimated for the combined sample of boys and girls. In addition, for the remaining figures, behaviors are summed across Tasks 1 and 2 so as to retain as much information as possible.

The results in Fig. 9.1 for mothers and adolescents are consistent with the third study hypothesis. To begin with, the findings show that expressions of hostility are quite stable over time. For example, adolescent hostility at Time 1 predicts own hostility at Time 2 ($b^* = .47$). The t value for this coefficient (10.10) indicates that the finding is highly significant. Adolescent hostility at Time 1 also predicts Time 3 hostility ($b^* = .21$), as does Time 2 hostility ($b^* = .32$). The figure shows similar stabilities for maternal behavior. Thus, consistent with the social relations perspective, much of the hostility expressed between mothers and children during early to midadolescence results from earlier levels of hostility in these dyads.

Especially important, the findings in Fig. 9.1 also demonstrate that earlier levels of hostility help to account for change in hostile interactions over time. For example, adolescent hostility at Time 1 is significantly related mother hostility at Time 2 ($b^* = .11$, $p < .01$) controlling for Time 1 maternal behavior. This cross-lagged regression coefficient indicates that earlier adolescent hostility leads to an increase in the mother's hostile actions. As expected, all of the cross-lagged paths in the model are positive and statis-

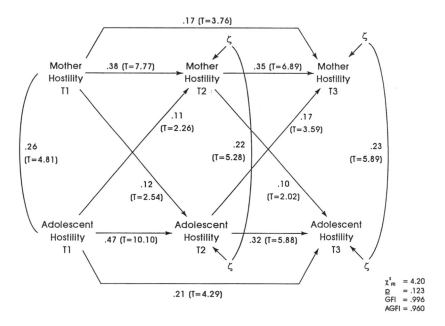

FIG. 9.1. The path model for mother and adolescent hostility, standardized regression coefficients.

tically significant. These results indicate that earlier hostile interactions between mothers and adolescents lead to relative increases in similar behaviors over time. Thus, those parent–child dyads who experienced a history of relatively greater conflict and hostility were at greatest risk for increasing negative affect during this life stage. These results are consistent with the third hypothesis. Finally, the adjusted-goodness-of-fit index in Fig. 9.1 indicates a good fit between the hypothesized model and the data (AGFI = .960).

Figure 9.2 provides the results for hostile interactions between fathers and their adolescent children. The findings are quite consistent with those reported in Fig. 9.1 for mothers and adolescents. Both father and adolescent hostility demonstrated a good deal of stability across time (e.g., b* = .41 for fathers' Time 1 to Time 2 hostility), and the cross-lagged coefficients indicated that earlier hostility generated increasing levels of negative interactions across the years of the study. Again, these findings are consistent with the third study hypothesis. Also important, the AGFI of .938 indicates that there was a good fit between the model and the data.

Figures 9.3 and 9.4 provide the findings for stability and change in warm and supportive behaviors between mothers and adolescents (Fig. 9.3) and between fathers and adolescents (Fig. 9.4). The format for these figures is the same as for Fig. 9.1 and Fig. 9.2. To begin with, the findings indicate a good fit between the hypothesized model and the data for both the mother

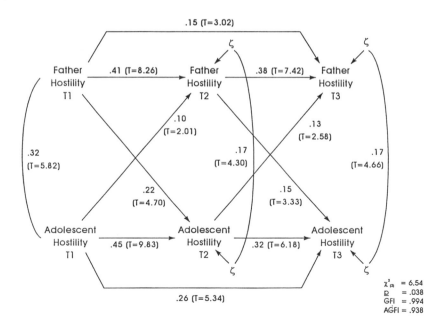

FIG. 9.2. The path model for father and adolescent hostility, standardized regression coefficients.

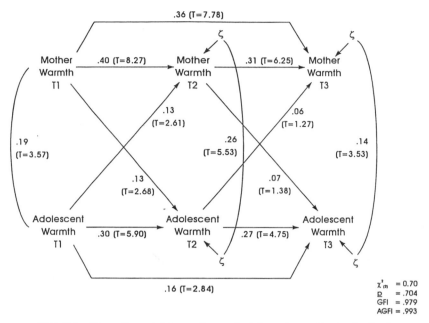

FIG. 9.3. The path model for mother and adolescent warmth, standardized regression coefficients.

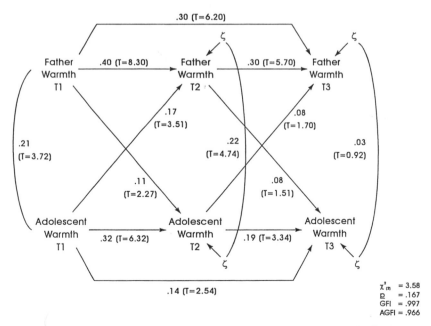

FIG. 9.4. The path model for father and adolescent warmth, standardized regression coefficients.

201

(AGFI = .993) and father (AGFI = .966) analyses. Moreover, the stability coefficients are similar to, but not quite as high as, the same values in Figs. 9.1 and 9.2 (e.g., $b^* = .32$ from adolescent warmth toward father at Time 1 to the same behavior at Time 2, see Fig. 9.4). In addition, all of the cross-lagged path coefficients are positive, as predicted. However, only the cross-lagged paths from Time 1 to Time 2 are statistically significant in every case (i.e., $t > 2.00$). The expected associations between earlier parent behavior and change in adolescent warmth, and vice versa, were most evident from Time 1 to Time 2. The paths from Time 2 to Time 3 were, at best, marginally significant, even though in the expected directions. Thus, the across-time findings for warmth are only partially supportive of the third study hypothesis.

DISCUSSION

Although most theoretical perspectives on parent–adolescent relations predict that the transition from early to midadolescence will be marked by emotional distancing between the two generations, inconsistent research findings and methodological limitations in earlier studies provided only limited empirical support for these perspectives (Laursen & Collins 1994; Paikoff & Brooks-Gunn, 1991). The present study sought to improve on earlier research efforts by investigating changes in parent–adolescent relations using research methodologies that reduced some of the weaknesses in the previous studies. More specifically, we (a) employed a longitudinal research design, (b) used a large, representative sample with limited participant attrition, (c) overcame problems of method variance confounds by relying on observer rather than family member reports of parent–adolescent interaction, and (d) focused on the affective dimensions of intergenerational relationships that are more closely tied to theoretical predictions than conflicts within a limited number of domains of possible disagreements between parents and their children.

Consistent with both biological and cognitive perspectives on interactional change during adolescence, we predicted that conflicts (operationalized as observed hostility or negative affect) would increase and cohesion (operationalized as warmth/support or positive affect) would decrease between parents and their early to midadolescents. Following the social relational model proposed by Laursen and Collins (1994), we also predicted that these changes in emotional expression would be gradual or incremental over time, rather than demonstrating sharp disjunctions from one year to the next. Finally, and also based on a social relations perspective, we hypothesized that the interactional history of the parent–child dyad would play an important role in determining the degree and type of change during the early to midadolescent transition. That is, we expected that parents and adolescents with a history of negative interactions would demonstrate relatively greater increases in conflict than those without such a history and that those with a history of low warmth and support would be at greater risk for experiencing decreasing cohesion during this time of life.

The study findings demonstrated the expected increases in conflict and hostility as well as the expected decreases in warmth and cohesion. These results are consistent with biological and cognitive theories that predict such changes in parent–child interactions during this life stage. They also are especially consistent with a social relations perspective in that the observed changes in emotional expression between parents and their children were incremental, increasing gradually and in fairly equal steps from one year to the next. Moreover, the results showed that adolescent girls expressed even greater hostility toward their parents than did boys, suggesting perhaps that their more rapid pubertal and social development led to higher levels of conflict at earlier ages. Similar gender differences were not observed for warmth and supportiveness, however, nor did parents appear to behave differently as a function of adolescent gender.

The findings also supported the prediction that the interaction histories of parents and children would play an important role in both continuity and change in emotional expression during the early to midadolescent period. Parent–adolescent dyads that had been high on conflict and hostility at Time 1 demonstrated the predicted relative increases in such behaviors during the second and third years of the study. Moreover, there was a great deal of continuity or stability as well as change in these behaviors over time. Those parents and adolescents who were high on warmth and support at Time 1 actually demonstrated relative increases in their emotional closeness over the following two years of the study; however, these findings were not as statistically robust as the results for expressions of negative affect. An interesting way to view these findings on warmth and supportiveness is to reverse the signs of the coefficients. That is, the results imply that parents and adolescents who were low on warmth and supportiveness at Time 1 were more likely to demonstrate relative declines in these behaviors over time. Because these results were replicates across two different tasks coded independently by different trained observers, we can have a great deal of confidence in the trends in the data.

The findings regarding change suggest that earlier social relations between parent–adolescent dyads play an important role in determining the impact of maturation on future interactions. Just as especially hostile parents and children may experience increases in this interactional quality under the pressure of the biological, cognitive, and social changes that occur during early to midadolescence, those parent–child dyads without such a history may actually decrease in their level of negative interactions during this time period. Such results would be predicted by a social relational perspective but not by biological or cognitive theories, which do not take interactional histories into account in their hypotheses (Laursen & Collins, 1994). Thus, we conclude that the findings reported here, although consistent with all theories that predict these interactional changes during this time period, are most consonant with social relations models that specifically take interactional histories into account in their predictions of later parent–adolescent relationships.

There are, of course, some other possible explanations for these findings, as well as limitations that need to be addressed in future research. The most compelling alternative explanation for the observed trends in emotional expression is an observer learning effect. That is, perhaps observers simply became more sensitive in their use of the rating scales and this sensitivity led to the coding of more hostility in parent–adolescent interactions over time. If this were true, however, we would expect a similar upward trajectory in the warmth and supportiveness ratings. Instead, the predicted decline in these behaviors occurred, a finding that seriously questions the possibility of an observer learning effect.

Another limitation in these findings involves the limited time frame for the analyses. Ideally, one would like to study these behavioral trends beginning in late childhood, before the onset of adolescence, and follow families forward in time through the adolescent years. Certainly, future studies are needed that can investigate this longer time span. In the meantime, the present results do help to correct for the frequent absence of longitudinal findings of any type in this area of inquiry. From that standpoint, they do help to advance the field. The sample in the present study also has significant limitations. It is confined to a rural location, intact families, and a single ethnic group. Future studies with more varied samples are needed to test the broader generality of these findings. Nevertheless, the participating families in this study were socioeconomically diverse, and this diversity helped to assure a range in the styles of social interactions likely to be observed between parents and children. This diversity may have helped to account for the consistency between the theoretical predictions and study findings.

Finally, the present study did not include measures of the specific dimensions of social, cognitive, and biological change hypothesized to lead to changes in parent–adolescent interactions over time. An important next phase in the current work will be to examine the ways in which these changing characteristics of adolescents combine with the passage of time to affect emotional expression between parents and their children. Despite all of these limitations, the methodological strengths of the present study help to increase confidence in the consistency between the findings and a number of theoretical perspectives on adolescent development. Based on these results, we conclude that the theories are probably more robust than many earlier studies suggest and that prior inconsistencies in empirical findings largely result from methodological limitations typical of earlier research.

Our perspective is similar to the position taken by Gecas and Seff (1990). They argue that the recent view that there is little change in parent–adolescent interactions from early to midadolescence is likely incorrect. They note evidence from parents who typically report that this is the most difficult period for childrearing. The present study provides important empirical support for this parental impression.

ACKNOWLEDGMENTS

Support for this research has come from multiple sources including the National Institute of Mental Health (MH00567, MH19734, MH43270, MH48165, MH51361), the National Institute on Drug Abuse (DA05347), the Bureau of Maternal and Child Health (MCJ-109572), the MacArthur Foundation Research Network on Successful Adolescent Development among Youth in High-Risk Settings, and the Iowa Agriculture and Home Economics Experiment Station (Project No. 3320).

REFERENCES

Blos, P. (1979). *The adolescent passage*. Madison, CT: International Universities Press.

Bureau of the Census. (1989). *Money income and poverty status in the United States: 1988* (Series P-60, No. 166, October). Washington, DC: U.S. Department of Commerce.

Flanagan, C. A., & Eccles, J. S. (1993). Changes in parents' work status and adolescents' adjustment at school. *Child Development, 64*, 246–257.

Furman, W., & Buhrmester, D. (1992). Age and sex differences in perceptions of networks of personal relationships. *Child Development, 63*, 103–115.

Galambos, N. L., & Almeida, D. M. (1992). Does parent–adolescent conflict increase in early adolescence? *Journal of Marriage and the Family, 54*, 737–747.

Gecas, V., & Seff, M. A. (1990). Families and adolescents: A review of the 1980's. *Journal of Marriage and the Family, 52*, 941–958.

Joreskog, K. G., & Sorbom, D. (1993). *LISREL 8 user's reference guide*. Chicago, IL: Scientific Software International.

Laursen, B., & Collins, W. A. (1994). Interpersonal conflict during adolescence. *Psychological Bulletin, 115*, 197–209.

Montemayor, R. (1983). Parents and adolescents in conflict: All families some of the time and some families most of the time. *Journal of Early Adolescence, 3*, 83–103.

Nakao, K., & Treas, J. (1990). *Computing 1989 occupational prestige scores*. General Social Survey Methodological Report No. 70. Chicago, IL: National Opinion Research Center.

Paikoff, R. L., & Brooks-Gunn, J. (1991). Do parent–child relationships change during puberty? *Psychological Bulletin, 110*, 47–66.

Smetana, J. G. (1988). Concepts of self and social convention: Adolescents' and parents' reasoning about hypothetical and actual family conflicts. In M. R. Gunner & W. A. Collins (Eds.), *Minnesota symposia on child psychology* (Vol. 21, pp. 79–122). Hillsdale, NJ: Lawrence Erlbaum Associates.

Smetana, J. G. (1989). Adolescents' and parents' reasoning about actual family conflict. *Child Development, 60,* 1052–1067.

Steinberg, L. (1981). Transformations in family relations at puberty. *Developmental Psychology, 17,* 833–840.

Steinberg, L. (1988). Reciprocal relations between parent–child distance and pubertal maturation. *Developmental Psychology, 24,* 122–128.

Steinberg, L. (1990). Autonomy, conflict, and harmony in the family relationship. In S. Feldman & G. Elliott (Eds.), *At the threshold: The developing adolescent* (pp. 255–276). Cambridge, MA: Harvard University Press.

Tein, J. Y., Roosa, M. W., & Micheals, M. (1994). Agreement between parent and child reports on parental behaviors. *Journal of Marriage and the Family, 56,* 341–355.

10

"Sometimes I Think That You Don't Like Me": How Mothers and Daughters Negotiate the Transition Into Adolescence

Julia A. Graber
Jeanne Brooks-Gunn
Teachers College, Columbia University

The period of adolescence poses unique challenges for adolescents and their parents as both work through the process of redefining roles and expectations in the family environment. These adaptations in the family have been identified as a source of increased conflict among adolescents and their parents; however, at the same time, warmth and closeness are not necessarily diminished in family relations, with these factors playing an important role in the individual's navigation of the adolescent decade (Collins, 1990; Hill, 1980, 1987; Paikoff & Brooks-Gunn, 1991). In other words, conflict and change occur, hopefully, in the context of love.

Biological and social transitions are important landmarks for defining the developmental transitions at either end of adolescence. That is, for biological transitions, entry into puberty and pubertal development defines the early adolescent transition, and starting a family of one's own or pregnancy is one transition that characterizes young adulthood (and midlife, given recent trends for pregnancy in some groups of women). In between these events, for most adolescents, is the entry into sexual activity. The experiences of puberty, sexual behavior, and ultimately parenthood are not limited to the biological or physical aspects of each transition, but also are experienced as social events and social transitions. For example, during or just after the pubertal transition, many adolescents make the transition from an elementary to a junior or middle school environment. Early adolescents also begin to pursue romantic relationships and seek more independence from parental control in their lives. Adolescents take on more adult roles, and others expect them to engage in more adult-typical activities commensurate with the more adult-like appearance adolescents are developing.

At the same time that adolescents are experiencing biological and social transitions, their mothers are also either in or approaching their own biological and psychosocial transition, menopause. Coupled with an interest in the literature on changing family relations during adolescence is an interest in how pubertal development intersects with adolescents' own social changes and those of their mothers. (See Paikoff & Brooks-Gunn, 1991, for a review of this literature.)

We take the approach, as have others (e.g., Rossi & Rossi, 1990; Silverberg, 1996), that adolescent transitions are interconnected with the life experiences of families. Adolescent transitions influence both the adolescents and their parents. The correspondences between reproductive and social transitions may be particularly salient in the lives of mothers and daughters. Specifically, reproductive transitions across the life span are potentially linked in at least two ways. First, puberty and menopause may be associated in the manner already described, with both mothers and daughters experiencing reproductive transitions at the same time; the psychological experience of each individual's transition may affect her perception of the other's transition. A second link between these transitions is the fact that physiologically they involve the same reproductive system.

Whereas puberty and menopause share physical commonalities, they also signal social changes and changes in self-perception for both mothers and daughters. Much as puberty is the process of activating the reproductive system, menopause is the process of deactivating this system. It has been suggested that puberty starts a process of gender intensification of gender roles (Brooks-Gunn & Matthews, 1979; Hill & Lynch, 1983), and menopause is characterized by a less gender stereotypic gender role identity (Gutmann, 1975). In addition, increased striving for autonomy that is subsequent to pubertal maturation may also serve as a stimulus to adolescent girls' mothers to redefine their concept of their maternal self and the behaviors and expectations that are appropriate for the mother of a more self-reliant child. Other reproductive transitions in women's lives are also linked to role changes. Notably, the transition to motherhood changes nearly every aspect of a woman's life and may also signal the role change from mother to grandmother for her own mother.

The focus in this chapter is on the role of biological and social transitions in the lives of women with specific interest in mother–daughter relationship changes during the adolescent period. The links between generations of women are also important in understanding the social impact that these transitions have on both generations, the adolescents and their mothers. We focus primarily on the social, biological, and psychological correlates of the pubertal transition, with an emphasis on mother–daughter relationships.

Mother–daughter conflict, cohesion, and discourse in mother–daughter relationships are discussed. Possible links between mother–daughter conflict and closeness in the early to midadolescent years, and adolescent sexuality and pregnancy in the late adolescent and young adult years, are considered, using illustrations from our adolescent research program.

MODELS AND ISSUES IN THE STUDY OF PUBERTAL TRANSITIONS

In this section, we present six models for studying reproductive transitions and brief examples of how these models apply to pubertal transitions, as this has been a focal point in research on adolescence (Graber, Brooks-Gunn, & Petersen, 1996). In addition, we describe the studies and issues that comprise the program of research on which we draw for the present discussion. (See Graber & Brooks-Gunn, 1996b, for a more complete discussion of these models.)

Models employed for studying reproductive transitions generally take into consideration the biological nature of the change as it interacts with psychological and social transitions, either causally linked to or in combination with the biological transition. Six models are relevant for discussion. The first centers on the **biological nature of the transition** and its influence on related psychological and social developmental processes. In particular, changes in mother–daughter relationships at puberty may be due to changes in increased emotionality of the adolescent associated with pubertal hormone increases (Buchanan, Eccles, & Becker, 1992) or may be related to psychological and social changes that puberty signals to the adolescent and her environmental context (Brooks-Gunn & Reiter, 1990). Such interactions are also likely at other transitions, as in the case of pregnancy and menopause. At these times, hormonal systems may affect moods and behavior directly or via indirect paths. In either path, social context also factors into relational changes at the time of transition.

A second model focuses on the **social context of the transition**, with less attention given to biological processes that may interact with social factors. Instead, emphasis is on identifying changing roles and responsibilities commensurate with the transition. The reproductive changes made in adolescence and the transition to adulthood—puberty, sexuality, pregnancy—are associated with changing status from childhood to adulthood with different social expectations in school, family, and peer domains. For example, teachers exhibit different grading practices between more and less pubertally advanced adolescents (Eccles et al., 1993), and parents of more physically mature girls are often more accepting of their dating behaviors than parents of same-age girls who are less mature (Stattin & Magnusson, 1990).

A third approach focuses on **self-definitional or intrapsychic changes** associated with the reproductive transition. In this case, the individual herself associates a specific meaning to making the transition. In line with the aforementioned examples, more physically developed adolescents are more likely to expect to be treated as adults (Hill & Lynch, 1983; Simmons & Blyth, 1987). Other transitions also involve self-definitional change; pregnancy involves the transition into viewing oneself as a parent in addition to the other roles the adolescent or woman may already have incorporated into her sense of self (Deutsch, Ruble, Fleming, Brooks-Gunn, & Stangor, 1988; Ruble et al., 1990).

Cumulative events models draw on the previous models but note that intrapsychic, social role and context, and biological changes are often happening at the same time and hence have a cumulative effect on the outcome (Simmons & Blyth, 1987). The importance of experiencing simultaneous or cumulative events during puberty without having time to cope with each successive change was linked to the development of depressive affect and depression in girls (Brooks-Gunn, 1991; Petersen, Sarigiani, & Kennedy, 1991). Cumulative models are not applied as often to other reproductive transitions, but it is this hypothesis that suggests that the reproductive transition is a time of increased vulnerability to multiple stressors. It was also demonstrated that stressors accumulate during these transitions.

An important corollary is that the **timing of the transition** influences how the reproductive transition is experienced. Timing refers to whether the individual experiences the event at about the same time, earlier, or later than other girls or women her age. Timing is a pervasive theme across most reproductive transitions studied. It is predictive of adjustment outcomes of puberty, onset of sexual behavior, pregnancy, and menopause (e.g., Bromberger & Matthews, 1994; Brooks-Gunn & Chase-Lansdale, 1995; Graber, Brooks-Gunn, Paikoff, & Warren, 1994; Graber et al., 1996). Timing effects themselves may be demonstrated biologically, psychologically, and socially, with most of the research identifying the effects of experiencing the transition off-time from a social perspective (Neugarten, 1979; Rossi, 1977). Interestingly, it is the experience of each transition—puberty, sexuality, pregnancy, and menopause—earlier than one's peers that is most often associated with negative outcomes for girls and women and potentially their families.

Finally, more recent interest in **family systems** (as exemplified by much of the work in the present volume) highlighted the intersection of the lives of adolescent girls and their mothers examining (a) the joint biological and intrapsychic changes, (b) the new social contexts and roles occurring for each individual, and (c) how adolescents' reproductive transitions impact on the lives of mothers and parents, in general. In this case, much of the research is in the area of the pregnancy transition, especially in the context of teen childbearing (Brooks-Gunn & Chase-Lansdale, 1995; Obeidallah & Burton, this volume), along with a few studies examining puberty and menopause conjointly (Paikoff, Brooks-Gunn, & Carlton-Ford, 1991; Powers, this volume).

Although these frameworks are easily applied to all reproductive transitions, most research on these models is on the pubertal transition. The body of literature on the pubertal transition is conducted on White, middle to upper-middle class adolescents and their families; thus, it is difficult to consider issues of diversity or generalizability across the range of adolescent experiences. Context of a transition is studied mostly vis-à-vis individual level (e.g., timing of and/or preparation for pubertal events) and family level factors (e.g., relationships, conflict). Less work is done on contexts such as neighborhoods, schools, and peer groups. (See Brooks-Gunn & Warren, 1985; Brooks-Gunn, Warren, Samelson, & Fox, 1986; Caspi, Lynam, Moffitt, & Silva, 1993; Eccles et al., 1993; Stattin & Magnusson, 1990; and Simmons & Blyth, 1987, for exceptions in studies of puberty, especially in the study of school and peer contexts.) In addition, this work typically is not intergenerational, and instead, focuses on the outcome of one person at a time, most often the girl as she goes through puberty. Much less studied is the intersection of mother and daughter lives vis-à-vis reproductive and role transitions. The effects of a daughter's pubertal changes (biological, psychological, and social) on the mother, or the effects of a mother's menopausal changes (again, biological, psychological, and social) on the daughter are rarely studied. (See Ryff and Seltzer, 1996, for a discussion of this issue in the study of midlife parental experiences.)

Although we subscribe to a more contextually rich and truly generational approach, the literature base is so sparse that we chose to present examples from our own collaborative research projects that mainly address adolescent outcomes. These examples are our initial investigations of mother–daughter relationships in the context of reproductive and role transitions and will be linked to suggestions for the direction of future research. We discuss mother–daughter relationships mainly in the context of the daughter's pubertal transition, with brief discussions of relationship changes around teenage pregnancy.

Puberty is the universal reproductive transition of adolescence, most commonly used as the signifier that the individual is moving out of late childhood and into adolescence. Pubertal development is comprised of a series of interrelated processes including maturation of the reproductive organs, growth spurt in height and weight, changes in composition and distribution of fat and muscle mass, development of the circulatory and respiratory systems resulting in increased endurance and strength, and finally changes in the central nervous system and endocrine systems that regulate and initiate the other pubertal changes. Most girls begin pubertal development around 10 years of age with breast budding followed shortly by the appearance of pubic hair (Marshall & Tanner, 1969). It takes 4 to 5 years for a girl to traverse the main developmental landmarks of puberty, with most girls reaching menarche around 12.5 years of age, fairly late in the developmental progression (Brooks-Gunn & Reiter, 1990). Notably, substantial variations exist in the timing of maturation such that reaching menarche anywhere between age 9.5 to 15.5 is considered well within normal range; hence, variations fall within biological constraints.[1]

Interest and issues in mother–daughter relationships during the pubertal transition span a range of perspectives as noted in the models already outlined. The specific questions of interest to us have come out of the Adolescent Study Program. Since the inception of this program 15 years ago, a series of studies of the biological and psychosocial aspects of adolescent development in girls was conducted. The specific studies of relevance here are the Late Adolescence Study, the Early Adolescence Study, and the Mother–Daughter Interactions Study. The Adolescent Study Program began with a large cross-sectional study of girls in Grades 5 through 12. Girls were drawn from private schools in a major metropolitan area and were from White, middle to upper-middle class, well-educated families. Girls and their mothers filled out questionnaires on a variety of measures tapping their feelings and behaviors. The Early and Late Adolescence Studies both were more intensive longitudinal examinations of girls who participated in the initial cross-sectional study.

The Late Adolescence Study is a longitudinal investigation of adolescent development in girls who were in Grades 7, 8, and 9 in the initial cross-sectional study. The primary focus of this investigation was the development of adjustment and psychopathology through midadolescence, late adolescence, and into young adulthood (Attie & Brooks-Gunn, 1989; Graber et al., 1994).

The Early Adolescence Study is a longitudinal study of development in adolescent girls who were in Grades 4, 5, and 6 in the initial cross-sectional study. Girls were seen annually for 4 consecutive years and with a final follow-up assessment 2 years later. This study focused intensely on the biological changes of puberty and the links to psychosocial development during the early adolescent period (Brooks-Gunn & Warren, 1988; Warren & Brooks-Gunn, 1989).

The Mother–Daughter Interactions Study was designed as an intensive examination of conflict resolution in mother–daughter discourse and the association between different patterns of conflictual interactions to pubertal and psychosocial development (Brooks-Gunn & Zahaykevich, 1989). This

---

[1]Several factors are known to influence the timing of puberty (Brooks-Gunn, 1988; Graber, Brooks-Gunn, & Warren, 1995). Both intense exercise and restricted food intake can result in delaying pubertal development (Warren, 1980), but, even then, menarche usually occurs by 17 or 18 years of age.

study did not draw on the same population of girls as the Early and Late Adolescence studies but was conducted under the aegis of the Adolescent Study Program incorporating similar measures and concepts. Ninety seventh and ninth graders and their mothers participated in this study; families were predominantly White and middle-class. Dyads were then videotaped as they engaged in 20-minute discussion sessions about two self-selected, real-life conflicts. Measures covered the domains of pubertal development, family relations, self-image and affective state, and ego development. Interactional changes around the pubertal transition were considered cross-sectionally.

Using these three investigations, we consider several aspects of mother–daughter relationships during adolescence. Our first focus is on the experience of conflict in this relationship and its correlates for adolescent development. In contrast to conflictual mother–daughter relations, the role of cohesion and closeness in mother–daughter relationships is also examined, identifying the daughter and mother perceptions of cohesion and the links between these perceptions and adjustment. Discourse between mothers and daughters is the final aspect of mother–daughter relationships at puberty to be considered. The investigation of discourse addresses the nature of changes in autonomy and reciprocity in the adolescent's relationship with her mother. Discourse is examined in relation to daughter's pubertal status and to adjustment.

THE EXPERIENCE OF MOTHER–DAUGHTER CONFLICT

Much of the literature on mother–daughter relationships focused on conflict in the early adolescent years. As such, we begin with an overview of the role of conflict during the adolescent transition, identifying the theoretical basis and nature of changes in family conflict at this time. Family relationships in families with adolescent offspring typically are studied under the rubric of the stressful nature of the transition for the adolescent, although other conceptual frameworks are appropriate and have been applied to studying family relationships at this time (e.g., family systems, psychodynamic, transactional approaches). Our premise is that conflict between mothers and daughters is normative in early adolescence, and that some conflict may be necessary for girls to become more autonomous. The question is when does conflict become maladaptive? In what circumstances is the balance between conflict and closeness disrupted?

The transition to adolescence has been characterized as stormy and stressful at least since the time of G. Stanley Hall (1904), the father of adolescent psychology. Much of the early research on adolescence conducted in the 1960s and 1970s focused on testing this commonly accepted premise. Somewhat surprisingly, most of the initial research did not focus on either the biological or social changes that accompany the adolescent transition as possible media-tors of tumultuous behavior or alterations in self-images (Brooks-Gunn, 1990; Brooks-Gunn & Reiter, 1990). Generally, these seminal, early studies did not substantiate either the belief in universal storm or a dramatic, discontinuous change in self-image during adolescence (Offer, 1987).

The initial characterization of storm and stress encompassed two over-lapping but not identical dimensions. The stress experienced by the young adolescent referred to the potentially stressful life events that characterize the transition from childhood to adolescence and that lead to alterations in mood and affect via cumulative event models as presented earlier (e.g., Simmons & Blyth, 1987). Storminess referred to moodiness, rapid shifts in moods, and outbursts of often short-lived negative behavior. Pubertal changes are usually mentioned as the most likely culprit, with hormones as the prime candidate of pubertal change to be nominated as the underlying cause of mood perturbations—given the deference paid to "raging hormones" in explanations for young adolescents' behavior (Buchanan et al., 1992). Indirect pathways are postulated indicating that hormonal changes of pu-berty lead to increased moodiness or lability, which subsequently exacerbates parent–child interactions and relationships.

Evidence that hormonal changes do influence moods and reactivity lend support to this hypothesis (Buchanan et al., 1992; Olweus, Mattsson, Schal-ling, & Low, 1988). For example, we found an increase in depressive symp-tomatology and aggressive feelings and behavior at the time that the hor-monal system is producing the fastest rise in gonadal hormones (Warren & Brooks-Gunn, 1989). Whether such feelings and behavior contribute to interactive behavior has not been studied, although Susman and her col-leagues (Susman et al., 1987) found effects of hormonal status on aggressive affect but not on actual behavior in parent–child interactions (Inoff-Germain et al., 1988). In looking at biological effects on parent–child interactions (or interactions between the adolescent and any other person more generally), not only do the behaviors or arousal systems affected need to be specified (and models tested), but the possibility of reciprocal effects between family interactions and biological changes must be considered.

As indicated previously, puberty may also influence relationships via the social stimulus value of the development of secondary sexual characteristics. As the external signs of development signal the incipient reproductive and social maturity of the child, an event laden with meaning for both parent and child, parent–child interactions may be influenced by both adolescent and parent responses to puberty. At the same time, since rapid rises in hormones occur at precisely the time that multiple social changes are en-countered, comparisons of relative effects of biological and social changes on moodiness and affective behaviors must be considered as an interactive system that accounts for rises in certain behaviors from about age 10 to age

15 (Brooks-Gunn, Graber, & Paikoff, 1994). Indeed, ample evidence indicates that certain behaviors do increase at this time; these include depressive symptomatology, eating problems, and aggressive behavior, as well as clinical forms of these problems, with increases in depressive and eating problems being more common in adolescent girls.

Perhaps the most colloquial use of storm and stress, however, arises in terms of adult–adolescent interchanges. Parental interchanges with young adolescents are almost always portrayed as conflictual (Steinberg, 1990). Personal experiences lend face validity to the characterization of conflict and strife, often impeding the study of parent–child relationships at this age. At the very least, belief in the pervasiveness of conflict hindered the search for mechanisms underlying conflict when it occurs. Conflict became reified vis-à-vis interactions between parents and young adolescents.

What does the research to date tell us about changes in relationships during the first half of adolescence? Conceptual models stress the transformations from unilateral authority to mutuality, from a more vertical to a somewhat more horizontal relationship. However, renegotiation models were not applied to the young adolescent or to the pubertal years directly, being used instead for older adolescents.

The indices used to study parent–child interactions at this time include time spent with parents, changing perceptions of relationships, emotional distance, and yielding to parents in decision making. All four decrease from early to middle adolescence. The most prevalent index of family relations is conflict. Conflict seems to be higher in early adolescence, although the frequency of conflict is similar in early and middle adolescence (Montemayor & Hanson, 1985). However, little comparative work exists looking at late childhood through late adolescence.

Smetana (1988b) describes these conflicts as "mild bickering, disagreements, and conflicts over everyday issues and emotional stress during early adolescence" (p. 79). Parents and children both report that their most frequent disagreements occur over rules and regulations regarding dress codes, dating, grades, and other personal management issues (as has been the case since the late 1920s; see Montemayor, 1983). Montemayor (1982) reported that, during midadolescence, parent–adolescent conflicts occurred approximately twice a week in a sample of 64 10th-grade girls—a high rate when compared to conflict in marital couples who are not distressed (Montemayor, 1986). Adolescents tend to report that conflicts occur more frequently than do parents. The conflict is not intense and does not necessarily presage a diminution of a strong bond between parents and children. Although mild, both parents and children agree that these conflicts are significant.

In studies of the cognitive understanding of changing social roles, Smetana (1988a, 1988b) finds that teenagers and parents disagree as to the legitimacy of parental authority in many situations. Teenagers tend to classify more situations as involving personal choice, and parents categorize more situations as involving social conventions. Although not addressing role change in relation to pubertal change per se, the greatest shift toward personal choice categorizations by children occurs in early adolescence. Parent–child disagreements are largest in the middle school years. It is important that many of the 7th and 8th graders understand, but reject, their parents' perspective for issues in which they believe personal jurisdiction is legitimate.

Of particular interest is evidence that conflict is more frequent in the mother–daughter dyad than in other family dyads (Hill, 1988; Montemayor, 1983; Smetana, 1988b). For this dyad, conflict peaks after midpuberty and only slowly tapers off until the transition out of the home (Papini, Datan, & McCluskey-Fawcett, 1988; Steinberg, 1987). Collins (1988, 1990) notes that transitional periods, in this case the reproductive transition of puberty, are times when families are less likely to share similar views about the family because such transitions usually indicate role change on the part of at least one family member.

Drawing from the Late Adolescence Study of the Adolescent Study Program, investigations of the role of conflict in the adolescent daughter–mother relationship were conducted. In the studies reviewed, 161 girls in 9th, 10th, or 11th grade (the midadolescent assessment point) were examined. Perceptions of family relations were measured using the Conflict and the Cohesiveness subscales of the Family Environment Scale (FES; Moos, 1974), which were completed by both daughters and mothers. Adjustment of daughters and mothers was assessed via reports of depressive affect and eating problems. The Center for Epidemiological Studies Depression Scale (CES–D; Radloff, 1977) tapped depressed affect, and dieting and bulimic behaviors were measured by the respective subscales of the EAT–26 (EAT; Garner & Garfinkel, 1979).

Do Mothers and Daughters Have Similar Perceptions of Family Conflict?

The first consideration was to determine the extent of similarity in the perceptions of family conflict held by adolescent girls and their mothers. In general in this study, mothers and daughters differed as to their ratings of family climate. Whereas mother and daughter reports of conflict were significantly associated with $r = .51$ (sharing about 25% of variance), daughters rated conflict higher than did mothers (Paikoff, Carlton-Ford, & Brooks-Gunn, 1994). The moderate level of shared variance indicates that substantial differences in perceptions of family conflict exist. Higher scores on the part of daughters may indicate that conflict is more salient to daughters, who are in the midst of working out autonomy issues. Alternatively, daughters may be more realistic than are the mothers in their respective ratings.

An opposing view holds that reports of family climate are only perceptions, and therefore realism or accuracy is a misguided notion. That mothers and daughters perceive the family climate somewhat differently is an important observation in itself. Such perceptions make up the dynamic family system, which is composed of the multitude of sometimes divergent beliefs and expectations held by various family members.

Are Perceptions of Conflict Linked to Daughter Adjustment?

A related objective was to understand whether differing perceptions of the family environment were linked to the emotional well-being of the daughter as indexed by depressive affect and dieting behaviors (Paikoff et al., 1994). It was hypothesized that disparate perceptions, either in absolute value or dependent on direction, may result in poorer adjustment outcomes for adolescents.

Interestingly, neither the mother's nor the daughter's perceptions of conflict were correlated with adolescent adjustment. Instead, the *discrepancy* as indicated by the absolute value of the difference between mother and daughter ratings of conflict was correlated with depressive symptomatology. Even though significant, the size of the correlation was small ($r = .15$). No associations between perceptions of conflict and dieting were found.

We suspect that such discrepancies are highlighting underlying tension in the family about how conflict is defined and possibly how different family members approach it. Discrepancies may indicate denial or a low level of awareness of conflict on the part of one member of the dyad (given that conflict had to do with *family* conflict, not *dyadic* conflict; high conflict scores could indicate high conflict among all family members or high conflict among only a few family members). However, it is not the case that discrepancies were only due to mothers reporting high conflict (perhaps with their spouses) that was being masked from the daughter. (See Carlton-Ford, Paikoff, & Brooks-Gunn, 1991, for a discussion of the analytic procedures for calculating and comparing discrepancy scores.)

Typically, such results would be interpreted as demonstrating that family conflict contributed to poor outcomes of the adolescent without taking the next step to assess whether these effects might be reciprocal. That is, families with more depressed daughters may over time become more conflictual. Analyses incorporating a prior time of measurement 2 years earlier (i.e., using cross-lagged panel analyses) suggest that effects may be bidirectional, in that families with more depressed daughters in middle school do in fact experience (or report) more conflict in high school (Carlton-Ford, Paikoff, Oakley, & Brooks-Gunn, 1996).

The influence of conflict on maternal adjustment was also assessed, although not as extensively as the effect on daughters. Examination of this question indicated that neither mother nor daughter perceptions of family conflict were related to a variety of indices of maternal adjustment (Paikoff et al., 1994). Links between discrepant perceptions of conflict and maternal adjustment were not studied in the present investigation, although such questions could be addressed, especially in relation to issues of the mother's role satisfaction as she attempts to devote time to both a career and her adolescent daughter. Related to this question is the issue of how reproductive transitions of both adolescent and mother may be influencing their reports on the family environment, specifically, conflict in the family.

Do Pubertal and Menopausal Transitions Have Effects on Both Mother and Daughter Adjustment?

We extended these analyses by adding reproductive transitions to the equation. We expected that the timing of daughter's maturation might influence family climate, given previous research. Since this sample was about 16 years of age, the late maturers would be completing their secondary sexual development. If, as Hill (1988) suggested, conflict peaks around the time of peak pubertal development, then more conflict might be expected for the late maturing girls. Of course, given that the sample was 16 years of age at the high school assessment point, it was also possible that puberty effects might have dissipated. Effects might be most pronounced for early maturing girls whose families may be less prepared for commensurate changes in adolescent roles and sense of self.

Psychodynamic theorists have talked about the mother's difficulty in accepting her daughter's reproductive maturity, when her own reproductive years are coming to an end. Taking seriously the notion that the changes in family conflict and other aspects of family climate are due to the parent as well as the teenager, the mother's reproductive status was also examined. It is possible that a greater proximity between daughters' onset of menarche and mothers' menopause would result in heightened conflict between mothers and daughters and, perhaps, in lowered levels of maternal well-being.

The interaction between mother and daughter reproductive status may also be understood under the framework of timing of reproductive transitions. The combination of maternal and daughter reproductive changes to produce "on-time" versus "off-time" parenting (Neugarten, 1979; Rossi, 1977) would be germane to an understanding of maternal well-being, with off-time parenting perhaps having negative consequences. In a recent survey, Rossi (personal communication) found that only 35% of married women in their 50s had a child living at home, whereas 81% of women in their 40s had one or more children residing with them. In the Late Adolescence Study, mothers who had experienced menopause might be considered off-time, as they are in their 50s and still have at least one child living at home. Alternatively, elements of self-definition and role change may be salient given that this was a highly professional sample and that childbearing was likely delayed in many families, resulting in an older normative age of having a teenage daughter; in this case, the older mothers may not perceive themselves to be off-time.

The effects of mother's reproductive status (menstruating vs. not menstruating) and daughter's menarcheal timing (early, on time, late) on mother and daughter reports of family functioning were tested. Daughter's pubertal timing was associated with maternal perceptions of family conflict. Specifically, mothers of late maturing girls reported more family conflict than did mothers of early maturing girls, although late maturing girls, themselves, did not perceive increased family conflict (Paikoff et al., 1991). These findings concur with the notion of a "temporary perturbation" as put forth by Hill (1988). Notably, this is the only study to look at girls late enough in the maturation process to demonstrate increased conflict for late maturers.

Daughter and mother well-being as indexed by depressive affect, dieting behaviors, and bulimic symptoms were also examined in association with reproductive transitions (Paikoff et al., 1991). Maternal reproductive status was associated with daughter's dieting behavior, via an interaction with daughter's menarcheal timing, and demonstrated a trend for association with mother's own dieting behavior ($p < .10$). Postmenopausal women had the tendency to engage in more dieting behaviors than premenopausal women. The highest dieting scores were reported by early maturing girls whose mothers were postmenopausal; much lower scores were seen for early maturing girls whose mothers were premenopausal. Maternal menopausal status did not influence the dieting scores of on-time and late maturing girls. This association did not disappear when analyses controlled for daughter or mother ponderal index (weight for height), ruling out weight as the mediating mechanism.

Perhaps girls whose mothers are postmenstrual are more conscious of possible weight gain (due to maternal concerns over this issue) and thus the girls engage in more dieting behavior. The mothers themselves may urge the girls to diet, more in response to their own weight gain (which often occurs after menopause); this would occur for early maturing girls because they are more likely than the later maturers of the same age to have the rounded contours of a woman.

However, no associations of maternal reproductive status on family climate were found. Our primary hypothesis, then, was not substantiated. What is interesting, however, is that reproductive status of the mother played a role in dieting behavior and body concerns, the arena in which changes are taking place for the adolescent.

In reflecting on our own studies and the majority of research examining the role of conflict in mother–daughter relationships at the time of puberty, all have similar constraints. Most research has been conducted on White, middle and upper-middle class, two-parent families (although exceptions exist as exemplified by the work of Hetherington, 1989 on family relations during divorce and remarriage). In most of these families, mothers were in their 20s when children were born. Hence, what is known about mothers and daughters at this phase in their respective lives is based on a very limited segment of the population. Whether effects such as those reported linking mother's assessment of family environment to daughter dieting and depressive affect would be found in mothers and daughters from different ethnic, racial, or income backgrounds is unclear. Mothers who are younger or single have different constraints on their own roles and different contexts for their own development and that of their daughters. Future research of conflict (and affective family environment, in general) must incorporate a more diverse subject pool of families in order to reflect accurately and generalize to more of the population of families.

In addition, research on mother–daughter relations and the influence on adjustment and well-being is also limited by several assessment issues. Whereas in the Late Adolescence Study mothers and daughters completed the same measures of family functioning and adjustment (at least for depressive affect and eating concerns), comparable measures for adults and adolescents are not available for all constructs that may be of interest in this research area. This is a challenge for developmental research in general because children of different ages have different response abilities and because the constructs themselves may change with development, making it unclear whether the same construct is still being measured. Another factor in the assessment of family influences on well-being is that the indicators of adjustment are limited. In our own research, we frequently focused on depressive affect and eating problems; hence, the findings reflect an emphasis on unhealthy adjustment rather than positive aspects of adjustment. This issue may be particularly salient in the subsequent discussion of family cohesion as cohesion might be more predictive of healthy rather than unhealthy development.

The Role of Family Conflict in the Timing of Pubertal Development

In the investigation of links between pubertal processes and family relations, we also studied more complex or bidirectional models of physical and psychological associations. Variations in pubertal timing, specifically age at menarche, are associated with several antecedents, both genetic and environmental. Recent research considered a broader range of environmental stressors and their influence on the development of the reproductive system (Moffitt, Caspi, Belsky, & Silva, 1992; Steinberg, 1989). Surbey (1990), in analyses of retrospective reports of stressful events and family structure, found that young women who grew up in father-absent homes had earlier ages of menarche than other women and that in two-parent households, greater numbers of stressful life events were also associated with earlier ages at menarche. Subsequent prospective examinations of the links between stress and timing of maturation indicated that family conflict was also predictive of earlier ages at menarche (Moffitt et al., 1992). Prior research was not able to control for responses of others (e.g., parents) to physical signs of development that may act as cues that precipitate behavioral change.

In our investigation (Graber, Brooks-Gunn, & Warren, 1995) conducted using a subsample of the Early Adolescence Study, the following possible antecedents were considered: (a) hereditary transmission, (b) absence or presence of the father in the household, (c) family warmth and acceptance as well as conflict, and (d) stressful life events. In hierarchical regression models, the strongest psychosocial predictors of age at menarche were the affective measures of the family (change in $R^2 = .15$, $p < .01$) such that more warmth and less conflict were associated with later ages at menarche. A comparable model that examined psychological stress as indexed by depressive affect, rather than by family relations, was also significant. As expected, breast development and weight were predictive of age at menarche. However, family relations continued to predict age at menarche even after accounting for the influence of breast development or weight (the external signs of development). Weight for height, presence of an adult male in the home, and stressful events were not predictive of age at menarche.

The complex interactions of biological and psychosocial development demonstrated here may account to some extent for the inter and intraindividual variation observed in pubertal development. Additionally, the association of family affective environment with timing of maturation, along with the existing literature on maturational timing effects on subsequent psychological adjustment, is the beginning for demonstrating the interactive nature of early adolescent development and for teasing apart developmental processes, in general. Our results are similar to those reported by Moffitt and her colleagues (1992). In our research (and that of others), family conflict and/or paternal absence seems to be associated with earlier puberty. Our study is the only one with longitudinal measures of family conflict *and* puberty, allowing us to control for initial pubertal status.

Although very few girls in our study did not live with their biological father, findings in other projects suggest that family structure may be an important factor (Moffitt et al., 1992; Surbey, 1990). Although mechanisms for such effects are still unclear, several possibilities exist. Biological explanations focused on animal models, which have found that presence of related males suppresses reproductive functioning whereas exposure to unrelated males stimulates functioning, presumably as a population control against inbreeding. An alternative hypothesis is that different family structures themselves can be a stressor. Certainly, research on divorce and remarriage patterns would fit this model for some girls and their mothers. This particular scenario has strong implications for the mother–daughter dyad because the resulting situation involves not only a key change in the mother's life (e.g., divorce or death of partner resulting in father absence for the daughter) but also acceleration of the pubertal process, itself altering their relationship at a time when it is already in flux. As yet, studies on mechanisms for effects and studies that follow these relationships through the periods of change still need to be conducted.

THE EXPERIENCE OF MOTHER–DAUGHTER CLOSENESS

Despite the tendency to focus on negative changes in parent–adolescent relationships, the literature also described positive dimensions of relational changes. Whereas the study of positive family relations is less extensive than the literature on conflict, we present analyses assessing the nature and influence of family closeness that have been conducted in the Late Adolescence Study. These analyses parallel the analysis of conflict previously described and hence, are covered more briefly. Specifically, closeness was studied in terms of both mothers' and daughters' perceptions of closeness and the links between these perceptions and adjustment outcomes for daughters, and to a lesser extent, the outcomes of mothers. Again, as we are interested in models for studying transitions that incorporate multiple facets of the transition (biological, social, and psychological) along with the intersection of daughters' and mothers' lives, we also report on the links between mother's menopause and daughter's puberty in predicting perceptions of closeness and adjustment outcomes for daughters.

Probably only a minority of all families with adolescents experiences a marked deterioration in parent–child relationships (Steinberg, 1990), suggesting that conflicts, or more specifically, the processes by which conflicts are resolved, contribute in positive ways to adolescent development. This may occur through greater individuation in the context of a warm parental relationship (Cooper, 1988; Hill, 1988; Steinberg, 1990). As such, family warmth and closeness may reflect somewhat different family relational processes.

Again, different perceptions of family closeness and cohesion are likely to be held by differing members of the family (Rossi & Rossi, 1990). Similar analytic strategies were employed to examine the role of closeness in mother–

daughter relationships as were applied to conflict. First, the extent of similarity or agreement in perceptions within the dyad was assessed, followed by testing the effect of perceptions on adolescent and mother well-being.

Do Mothers and Daughters Have Similar Perceptions of Family Closeness?

As indicated, mothers and daughters differed in their ratings of family environment. Both had higher overall scores for cohesion than conflict, providing supporting data for the premise that conflict and warm affective bonds coexist in most families (Paikoff et al., 1994). Aggregate scores for cohesion were more similar across dyad pairs than were scores for conflict; that is, mother and daughter reports of cohesion were not significantly different. However, the correlation between mother and daughter reports was in the moderate range ($r = .43$), suggesting that mothers and daughters do not rate cohesion the same within families.

Such reports are comparable to those of Rossi and Rossi (1990); in examination of the four adolescent–parent dyads, Rossi and Rossi report that mothers rated cohesion higher than fathers and daughters rated cohesion higher than sons, resulting in the mother–daughter dyad reporting the highest rates of cohesion. It is possible that women use a different response set when assessing cohesion than do men; as such, their scores are inherently more likely to be similar on this dimension than on other dimensions or between other dyads.

Are Perceptions of Closeness Linked to Daughter Adjustment?

Again, analyses were conducted to test whether differing perceptions of family cohesion related to the emotional well-being of the daughter as indexed by depressive affect and dieting behaviors (Paikoff et al., 1994). It was hypothesized that disparate perceptions, either in absolute value or dependent on direction, may result in poorer adjustment outcomes for adolescents.

In contrast to findings for conflict, discrepant perceptions of cohesion were not associated with depressive symptoms; however, the absolute value of the discrepancy in family cohesion was significantly correlated ($r = .24$, $p < .01$) with daughter dieting. Hierarchical regression models were used to test for the effects of either the difference score in perceptions of cohesion or the absolute value of the difference score after controlling for overall family cohesion. These analyses did not diminish the association between discrepancy scores and daughter dieting. Mothers' reports of cohesion (Attie & Brooks-Gunn, 1989), as well as discrepancy scores, were correlated with daughter eating problems, while daughters' reports were not (Paikoff et al.,

1994). In general, mothers' positive feelings about the family environment were associated with higher body image for daughters. Mother reports of poor cohesion in the family were also associated with increased disturbances in the eating habits of the daughter (e.g., dieting and bulimic symptoms).

These results are in line with those found in samples of eating disordered adolescent girls and their families. The clinical literature focuses on enmeshment and warmth. Families with eating disordered girls may exhibit less warmth and more distant parental behavior. (See reviews by Attie, Brooks-Gunn & Petersen, 1990; Attie & Brooks-Gunn, 1995). Some observers suggested that family conflict is suppressed, in order to maintain a perception of control within the family. However, the absence of conflict coupled with low warmth might also indicate the absence of any meaningful interaction.

Comparable analyses for maternal adjustment found that effects were limited to the mother's own reports of cohesion; that is, daughter's perceptions of the family were not linked to mother's adjustment (Paikoff et al., 1994). Instead, mother's feelings of family cohesion were related both to her depressive affect and to her body image, with better feelings about family warmth correlating with better adjustment (i.e., lower depressive affect, more positive body image).

Do Reproductive Transitions Have Effects on Mother and Daughter Perceptions of the Family?

Paralleling the analyses for conflict, family cohesion was examined by both daughter's menarcheal timing and mother's menstrual status in relation to family cohesion. No association was found between either mother's or daughter's reproductive transition on their perceptions of family cohesion (Paikoff et al., 1991). Effects of reproductive status on adjustment were discussed previously.

Overall, few associations were found between reports of family cohesion and reproductive transitions although, as indicated, cohesion was linked with dieting behavior and this association did not differ by reproductive status. Certainly, one consideration for interpreting these findings is that, in general, reports of family cohesion by both mothers and daughters were quite high in this sample. As already suggested, women may be predisposed to define relationships as close, dissociating negative aspects (e.g., conflict) from the sense of cohesion, at least in part. In fact, correlations between reports of cohesion and conflict were $-.56$ for daughters and $-.40$ for mothers, suggesting somewhat more dissociation between the two domains on the part of the mother. Another constraint in these analyses is that cohesion may be more strongly associated with positive aspects of daughter and mother development and adjustment rather than the presence or absence of depressive affect or eating problems. Such factors have not yet been analyzed.

THE EXPERIENCE OF MOTHER–DAUGHTER DISCOURSE

Interaction between mother and daughter is one of the venues in which an adolescent girl begins to assert the new images she has of herself and in which she attempts to have these new roles recognized. Through the study of adolescent and mother discourse, it is possible to ascertain how changes in self and role at the time of reproductive transitions is actually responded to by important others who help shape the outcome of the transition.

Taking the perspective that self-definitional changes are, in part, due to the meaning of pubertal changes, reorganization of self-definitions may be based on bodily changes and the social role alterations that accompany such bodily changes. However, the pubertal changes themselves may not be a comfortable topic for girls to discuss with family members, even mothers. The early studies in this area (Brooks-Gunn, 1987; Brooks-Gunn, Newman, Holderness, & Warren, 1994) reported a variety of emotional responses to puberty, specifically menarche. The general pattern reported across these investigations is a shifting of communication from the family to the peer environment with the transition into adolescence. Although almost all girls learn about pubertal changes, in particular menarche, from their mothers, they tend not to discuss their feelings with her, instead turning to girlfriends, with girls engaging in few discussions about puberty with their fathers (Brooks-Gunn & Ruble, 1982). In some cases, girls perceive their mothers and fathers as insensitive to the concerns about body changes. For example, 5th- and 6th-grade girls perceive their parents' comments about breast development as teasing (Brooks-Gunn, Newman, Holderness, & Warren, 1994). Anecdotal evidence indicates that parents do not see their comments in the same light.

Rather than direct discussions about pubertal development, presumably the self-definitional changes resulting from pubertal development stimulate other, often conflictual, discussions between mothers and daughters. From a psychodynamic perspective, such interactions stem from both the parents' need to recognize the separateness of their daughters and the daughters' need to be more autonomous (Blos, 1979; Brooks-Gunn & Zahaykevich, 1989; Hill, 1988). Drawing on psychodynamic perspectives, Josselson (1980) differentiated the process of individuation into phases. The practicing phase of individuation is characterized by a lack of ambivalence and an assertion of will. In early adolescence, bad objects are projected onto the parent as part of this process. Deutsch (1944) suggested that this process of projecting may be more characteristic of prepubertal girls who may be highly critical of their mothers. A rapprochement phase of individuation occurs when the pubertal adolescent has constructed enough of a sense of autonomy to allow a new reliance on the parent. At the same time, a mother's own satisfaction with her role as a parent and woman influences her response to her daughter's practicing and rapprochement behaviors (Chodorow, 1978); mothers who fear the loss of closeness with their daughters may seek to constrain their daughters' individuation behaviors.

As part of a pilot study of mother–daughter interactions, adolescent girls aged 12 to 17 and their mothers were asked to discuss a hypothetical conflict situation, as well as a situation that one or both of them chose to discuss that was relevant to their own interactions. Examples from these interactions demonstrate the range of interchanges that take place among different mother–daughter dyads. Responses to the hypothetical situation are included in order to highlight several themes that emerge in mother–daughter inter-actions. In the hypothetical scenario, mothers and daughters are given the following prompt: "Carol is in a bad mood and wants to spend the entire Saturday sitting alone in her room. Carol's mother asks her what the problem is, but Carol refuses to discuss it. Carol's mother then attempts to get Carol involved in some activity to get her out of her mood. This gets Carol even more upset, which further confuses her mother." This scenario elicited a range of responses. For some dyads, mothers clearly dominated discusion, whereas in others, both parties contributed more equally; in only a few cases did daughters seem to dominate the discourse. Mothers and daughters also expressed different emotion "projections" to the characters in the scenario, with some mothers relating to the hypothetical mother's confusion and another mother chastising the hypothetical mother for not acknowledging that adolescent girls may need time alone. A few excerpts are included to demonstrate some of this variation.

The following mother–daughter exchange provides an example of a mother who may be trying to fill the role of the "secure base" as a parent. In this case, the mother seeks to explain to her daughter why the hypothetical mother behaves as she does, providing reasons for why mothers want to help in these situations. The interaction can also be characterized by the equality of participation, with both participants expressing their interpretations of the situation and responding to the other person's thoughts on it. (The daughter is 15 years old.)

Daughter: Well, I think that if you're in a bad mood then you should first figure out what it is by yourself first. You know, just go over what might have happened and figure it out yourself. And then you know, if you want to tell someone, you can tell them. And if it's someone who will listen to you it's better, you know, that's good that they'll listen to you and maybe help you out. But otherwise, I think that most of the time since *you* know what happened and *you* know exactly how *you* feel that you can usually figure it out—if you really think about it you can figure it out for yourself.

Mother: I know, but sometimes mothers want to . . . they want to share some of these concerns that you might have. And this is probably where some of the conflict comes in because sometimes you think I am very nosey because I ask you questions. It's really not that at all. I think it has a lot to do with the mother being very concerned about the welfare of the child. This is part of the maternal instinct, you know, that we have. And maybe someday you'll have the same feelings.

Daughter: Yeah, I'm sure I'll probably do the same thing if I have a daughter. I'll ask her how she's doing and what the problem is, but at this point right now I just think that if I was in a bad mood I'd rather be left alone just so I can think it over myself.

Mother: And I would . . . as I do with you . . . I would just leave you alone. I would check in on you every few hours like I do [laughing] and say, "[Tamara]²—is everything alright?"

Daughter: That's right, knock on the door. Don't just open the door and walk in. Knock on the door first . . .

The mother in the next exchange had a different response to the hypothetical situation. In this case, she relates to the hypothetical mother's experience of feeling confused. She experiences frustration that her own daughter does not seem to be interested in talking to her. Whereas both members of the dyad in the prior example expressed an opinion or interpretation of the hypothetical situation, the exchange of the following dyad is characterized by less communication by the daughter (age 14). In this exchange, she makes no interpretation of the situation and provides only minimal response to her mother's statements.

Mother: How many times have I tried to go upstairs to talk to you, and you wouldn't tell me why you were crying or something, right? And see . . . it confused the mother [in the hypothetical situation]. That's what you do to me—you confuse me.

Daughter: [laughs]

Mother: Don't you think I get confused enough without that?

Daughter: I like keep things to myself, thank you.

Mother: Well, you shouldn't have to. You should be able to talk 'em out. No, really, because when you keep a problem to yourself it gets bigger. When you talk to someone and open it up and let it out into the air, it's not as big as you thought it was. It

---

²In order to maintain confidentiality, identifying information has been changed.

gets a lot smaller. And sometimes you even find a solution to it. And see how this girl [character in hypothetical situation] went ahead and discussed it with her mom? And maybe it was something dumb, or maybe it was a big problem, you know. But her mother doesn't know. And you know, I love you. And I don't like to see you like this. I like to see you go ahead and be able to talk to me and tell me things, and I like to be able to sit down and talk to you and tell you things without you saying, "Oh, that's so boring mom." I don't consider myself an idiot, and I can talk about just about anything to you. Right or wrong?

Daughter: Mmmmm-hmmmm

Mother: So, I mean I think maybe we ought to try sitting down and discussing something once in a while. It would never hurt. You name the subject, we talk about it. Okay?

The next exchange is between an older adolescent (age 17) and her mother. In this situation, the mother and daughter do not seem to find the scenario personally relevant. Instead, the two discuss the situation with both providing their impressions of what would be the best thing for the hypothetical mother to do in this situation. Moreover, the mother asserts that adolescent girls need time alone.

Daughter: . . . well, Carol's just mad at the world (laughs).

Mother: Right. And her mother doesn't sound like a very perceptive woman. I mean the best thing to do with someone who is in a mood is to leave them alone.

Daughter: Right (laughs).

Mother: No matter how old or young they are. If somebody is a pickle, let them stew for a while.

Daughter: I would ask her what the problem is, but if they don't want to discuss it, that's fine . . . I would leave them alone.

Mother: Yeah, I mean, it's alright to display some interest, but sometimes people are just in moods. There's no problem— they're just moody. Although I think that the deeper thing here is that they just don't seem to get along. You sort of get that feeling.

Daughter: But we don't know what caused Carol to be in a bad mood . . .

Mother: Well, I think we just have the idea here that whatever Carol's problem is, her mother is a nag.

Daughter: I don't know . . .

Mother: Well, she asked what the problem is. And Carol refused to discuss it. So you would think, leave her alone for a while—let her get over the mood, or at least let her, you know, let some time pass. And then ask her again. Because if someone's in a mood, it's certainly . . . I think it's futile to attempt to get them involved in something else.

Daughter: Hmm.

Mother: And some things just have to run their course.

The Mother–Daughter Interactions Study was conducted for the purpose of understanding some of these issues. As indicated, mothers and daughters discussed and attempted to resolve conflict situations experienced in their relationship during videotaped interactions. Each utterance made by mothers and daughters was then coded as to how it contributed to each person's claim in the disagreement. The four categories of maternal speech were (a) legitimatizing arguments, (b) other-centered speech, (c) dogmatic speech, and (d) projecting speech. Daughter's speech was coded as (a) legitimatizing arguments, (b) compliance, (c) other-centered, (d) active opposition, and (e) passive negativism. (See Table 10.1 for descriptions of these codes.) This study is particularly relevant to the nature of interactions between mothers and daughters during early adolescence and speaks to psychodynamic approaches to understanding mother–daughter conflict. The psychological correlates (e.g., depressive affect) of each member of the dyad were studied in relation to the behavior exhibited in a conflict resolution task. In addition, this study tested whether the nature of interactions differed depending on the maturational level of the daughter (i.e., pre- or postmenarcheal).

The following is an excerpt of a mother–daughter dyad; again excerpts were drawn from the pilot study of the project. In this dyad, the daughter is premenarcheal. The mother chose the conflictual situation that was discussed by the dyad. The mother often makes statements indicative of the projecting argumentation strategy; that is, she uses covert control as demonstrated via preferential claims that are not substantiated by generalizable justification and relies on guilt as a justification for her position by referring to her hard work and exhaustion after long days.

Mother: We've been on the go, doing so many things, and when it comes to the end of the day, I'm really ready to quiet down, and I really do not like what you are doing. . . . . causing [Susie], getting her riled up, interrupting her practicing. . . . . putting me in a position where. . . .

Daughter: [interrupts] But its fun.

TABLE 10.1
Mother–Daughter Argumentation Codes

Mother Speech	Definition
Legitimatizing	Statement is made to persuade the other of the validity of one's claim. Appeals to generalizable principles, such as adherence to a specific set of rules or conventions, are used to provide backing for claims made during conflictual situations.
Dogmatic	Statements of overt control are made that assumes the absolute authority of a behavioral convention, accusation of the daughter of transgressing a behavioral convention, negation of the daughters' argument, and/or rejection of daughters' requests aimed to resolve the conflict.
Projecting	Covert control is made via statements of preferences alone, with no attempt to provide any generalizable justification for the preferential claim; using guilt by referring to mother's hard work, suffering, or sacrifice; using projection by reference to a trait or ability that the mother once wanted or possessed and now wants the daughter to possess; and/or using coercive attribution by referring to positive attributes of the daughter in order to obtain her compliance to do something the daughter is opposed to doing.
Other-centered	These statements consist of acknowledging the daughters' argument, presenting additional data or evidence to support the daughters' argument, emotionally supporting daughters, and complying with daughters' requests aimed to resolve the conflict.

Daughter Speech	
Legitimatizing Arguments	Coded the same as for mothers.
Compliance	These statements consist of concurrence with mother and requests to resolve conflicts.
Other-centered	This code was comparable to the code for mothers with a focus on acknowledgment of the mothers' argument, but the code did not include statements of daughters' emotional support of mothers.[a]
Active Opposition	These speeches directly attacked, derided, or blamed the mother, such as statements of accusation, criticism, mimicry, and sarcasm.
Passive Negativism	These statements were characterized by daughters' refutation of the mothers' argument without a launching of a counterargument, rejection of mothers' requests, and negation of and indifference to the mothers' argument.

[a]Because daughters rarely emotionally supported their mothers during argumentation, this variable was not included in daughters' other-centered speech.

Mother: [interrupts] Putting me in a position where I have to holler at both of you. I'm hearing this, I'm hearing an undercurrent of fighting and silliness, and it's really coming at a time when I'm too tired to cope with it. I've put my best into the day, and at the end. . . . . I've prepared dinner. I've cleared it away—everything that has to be taken care of with food preparation, and I'm ready to put my feet up and relax on those few nights that we are at home. I really find myself asking, "why is [Jennifer] doing this?!" I know that [Susie] has a part in this, but. . . . . I'm just not looking forward to dealing with this.

Daughter: But when you or [Susie] interrupt my practicing, that's all fine and good. She just gets away with murder!

Mother: [interrupts] But if that is the case. . . . . well, you know it's the end of my day. . . . .

Daughter: [interrupts] And she comes into my room when I'm getting dressed, just to get socks or something. . . . . It's no big thing. I'll just stop bothering her.

Mother: I know that it's fun for you, but I'm really wrapping up the day, you know I have tons to do with our usual, busy schedule and it really puts pressure on me.

Separation–Individuation in Mother–Daughter Interactions

In examination of discussions about conflictual situations in this sample, mothers clearly exhibited differing levels of acceptance of their daughters' assertion of increased independence (Brooks-Gunn & Zahaykevich, 1989). Some mothers had difficulty accepting their daughters' legitimate requests in discussions and were less likely to provide models of negotiation and legitimation than were other mothers. Less accepting maternal behaviors influenced daughters' emotional well-being such that girls whose mothers were less likely to accept their arguments and claims as legitimate had lower ego development scores, as well as higher anxiety and depressive affect (Brooks-Gunn & Zahaykevich, 1989). Daughters of mothers who project their feelings (and claims) onto their daughters were also more likely to show poorer psychological functioning than were daughters whose mothers did not use projection during discussions about disagreements.

As separation–individuation, in the psychodynamic sense, is a two-way street, mothers can either facilitate or block their daughters' moves toward more autonomous functioning. In this sense, the *process* by which conflicts are negotiated in families is more important than the frequency, severity, or content of conflict (Grotevant & Cooper, 1985; Hauser et al., 1984).

The following excerpt (again, from the pilot study) was taken from discussions between a mother and her postmenarcheal daughter. As in our previous example, the conflict being discussed was chosen by the mother. In this case, the daughter engages in more legitimatizing arguments to assert the validity of her claims for greater autonomy from her mother.

Mother: Ok, what I want to say first is that I do not think we have a basic personality difference. I don't think that's the issue because that was running through my mind—that there was a basic personality conflict. But there seems to me to always be a repeat—a repetition of the same thing happening. For example, I seem to want to talk to you and be with you and you reject me. I feel a lot of times that you . . . . don't want me around.

Daughter: Well, it's not that I don't want you around or anything, it's just that it's the constant nagging or questioning—repeating the same thing, asking me the same thing time after time, and it just gets to a point where I'm just like, "just shut up." You know, I'll just start being obnoxious to you or whatever just to let you know I don't approve of what you're doing.

Mother: But it comes out of caring and concern . . .

Daughter: [interrupts] Well, I obviously realize that.

Mother: And the other thing is that I would like you to tell me more things—to be friendlier and more open . . .

Daughter: [interrupts] Mom, I have been so open in the past. I mean, to compare . . . just to compare us to other, you know, friends of mine and their mothers, we're like the closest mother and daughter that I know. So, I think I tell you and I am as open to you as a mother and daughter should be. And there always has to be something that I'm gonna keep from you. I mean, I can't tell you everything.

Mother: Why is that? Why is there a limit?

Daughter: Because I mean there are obviously things I don't want you to know and I'm sure there are things that you don't want me to know. And for us to . . . for us to know everything about each other or to know everything that the other is doing, I don't think that's a right relationship. I think there always should be something that, you know, you're always questioning or wondering about—just like a curiosity inside. Like it's sort of like a relationship wouldn't be the same if you don't fight. If you're always getting along so well then how good can that relationship be? So there are going to be things that I'm not going to tell you, and you're just going to have to accept that.

Mother: I guess I don't want to make excuses for myself but, um, one thing I think I do is ask you the same question over and over again. I know I do that. Now, I wasn't even aware that I did that—and it's not senility I don't think at this point.

Daughter: I don't know about that . . .

Mother: I think that I try to make conversation with you—that I . . .

Daughter: [interrupts] I don't mind talking—I don't mind making conversation if it's something different. But if you're going to ask me the same question that you just asked me five minutes ago, I don't know if it's that you don't listen, you don't hear, or you just . . . I don't know what it is, but it bothers me and I obviously let you know that just by responding in an obnoxious or hostile way.

Mother: Yeah, so then sometimes I think you just don't like me (laughs) . . . that you don't like me. And you're mean sometimes.

Daughter: Well, you have to accept that. I'm a teenager. I mean, if you walk into . . . if you think we're bad . . . just to compare us to the [Turner]'s . . . if you walk into their household, the whole thing is [Rachel]'s mother will walk up to her and [Rachel] will scream, "Get away from me! Don't touch me!" And like, they just have these constant . . . just out and out . . . yelling and screaming at each other for no reason. And, I mean, I just wish you could see that to realize that what we have, I think, is more or less just normal or average. I don't think it's anything to . . . you know . . .

Mother: [interrupts] Yeah. Another thing which all of this reminds me of is how much I want you to have a good life. I'm very into . . . I'm very wrapped up in your life and your future and I think maybe that causes conflict.

Daughter: You just want to make sure I'm always doing the right thing, and there's nothing that I'm doing that would get you mad or would upset you. You'll just have to have faith in me.

Role of Puberty in Separation-Individuation Processes

Of additional interest is the role of puberty in signaling the initiation of a change in mother–daughter interchanges. Examinations of this question indicated that pubertal development appeared to be a transition point in interactions. Changes based on daughter's menarcheal status occurred in both the content of the conflicts most frequently reported by mothers and daughters and in the type of dyadic interaction (Brooks-Gunn & Zahaykevich, 1989). Younger girls and their mothers argued about clothes and appearance more often than did older girls and their mothers. More importantly, premenarcheal girls exhibited more active opposition to their mothers during the conflict resolution task, whereas postmenarcheal girls, especially those in ninth grade, were more likely to move from more aggressive to more passive modes of resisting maternal control (Brooks-Gunn & Zahaykevich, 1989). Mothers also

TABLE 10.2
Means, Standard Deviations, and F-tests of
Averaged Mother and Daughter Speeches

	Grade 7 Premenarcheal		Grade 7 Postmenarcheal		Grade 9 Postmenarcheal		
	Mean[a]	SD	Mean	SD	Mean	SD	F^b
Mother Speeches							
Legitimation	.12	.11	.12	.11	.14	.11	
Other-centered	.24	.11	.17	.10	.22	.11	2.93*
Dogmatic	.23	.14	.21	.13	.18	.12	
Projection	.10	.09	.18	.10	.16	.12	3.36*
Daughter Speeches							
Legitimation	.06	.06	.08	.07	.21	.12	16.16***
Other-centered	.20	.15	.18	.10	.18	.10	
Compliant	.06	.05	.04	.05	.04	.05	
Oppositional	.15	.11	.06	.05	.08	.06	7.97***
Negativistic	.18	.10	.28	.13	.20	.13	5.32**

[a]All speech means represent an average of speech proportions from the two conflict discussions.
[b]Only significant F-values are reported. $*p < .05$, $**p < .01$, $***p < .001$.

attempted more covert means of control with premenarcheal than post-menarcheal daughters. (See Table 10.2 for means, standard deviations, and results of analysis of variance by menarcheal status group.)

These findings suggest that relationships do change at the time of puberty. Changes may be interpreted as increased bids for autonomy by daughters. These bids are met by some parental resistance. Individual differences in interaction patterns are critical to examine, as they allow for an understanding of the ways in which families facilitate girls' movement to more autonomous functioning and more advanced ego development. These initial results highlight the continual changes and renegotiations that occur in mother–daughter relationships during adolescence. How these behavioral patterns relate to the psychological well-being of the adolescent girls is still under investigation.

IMPLICATIONS FOR SUBSEQUENT REPRODUCTIVE TRANSITIONS

How and to what extent conflict is resolved by mothers and daughters may have implications for the subsequent reproductive transitions that adolescent girls or young adult women make. Prolonged or high levels of conflict may have lasting influences on girls' behavior or adjustment. One result of highly conflictual relationships may be earlier entry into sexual behavior potentially when girls are less prepared for the challenges incurred through these behaviors. Earlier engagement in intercourse is linked with engagement in unprotected sexual situations and the experience of unplanned pregnancies (Zabin & Hayward, 1993). In the most recent follow-up of the Late Adolescence Study, when the participants were about 22 years of age, young women were asked about their reproductive history. To reiterate, this study consisted of girls from middle to upper-middle class, White families originally seen in young adolescence (M age = 14.3), midadolescence (M age = 16.0) and most recently in young adulthood.

In young adulthood, 15% (N = 24) of the young women indicated that they had been pregnant. All pregnancies occurred between 16 and 24 years of age (M age = 20.2, SD = 2.26). What is interesting about this information is that only one woman reported having a child; two reported miscarriage and the remaining young women had abortions. Thus, for this sample of young women, most unplanned pregnancies occurred in the college years rather than during high school. Also, almost exclusively these young women chose not to continue the pregnancy. This is likely due to the fact that young women in college perceive greater opportunities in their lives and may be less willing to have an unplanned child when they are still in school. In fact, most of the young women in our study expected to have their first child around the age of 30, about 2 years after getting married, and about 6 years after starting their first full-time job (Graber & Brooks-Gunn, 1996a).

Because young women in the Late Adolescence Study reported pregnancies almost exclusively during the college years, it was possible to examine the familial precursors to these pregnancies. Using information from the midadolescent assessment, we examined whether getting pregnant in the college years was associated with family relations by comparing girls who did and did not go on to get pregnant in later adolescence. Girls who later got pregnant had, in midadolescence, lower family cohesion, more family conflict, and a more controlling family environment than girls who did not become pregnant. In young adulthood when parent–child relationships were assessed separately by parent, conflict with father was associated with prior pregnancy such that young women who had been pregnant had more conflict with their fathers than young women who had not as yet been pregnant. Conflict with mother in young adulthood was not associated with pregnancy history. Interestingly, young women who had been pregnant also reported higher depressed affect in young adulthood than those who had not become pregnant by this time. Neither mothers' feelings about the family environment or mothers' depressive affect were related to whether or not their daughters subsequently became pregnant.

Overall, our analyses suggest that pregnancy is a problem for some young women from middle and upper middle class backgrounds. Such young women choose to terminate the pregnancy rather than alter their education and career paths. Interestingly, these young women would have more resources for caring for a child (at least financial and educational resources) than most single women who decide to continue their pregnancies and have children in their late teens and in young adulthood, but it is exactly these women who do not want to have a child before completing their educational plans. Whereas the present sample is unusual in comparison to the majority of unmarried women who become pregnant, this study provides an interesting prospective examination of predictors of pregnancy in a group of adolescents and young women whose pregnancies have been relatively unstudied. The present investigation identifies a potential course of events in which family relationships defined by lower cohesion, higher conflict, and higher control precede late adolescent pregnancy that in turn leads to increased depressive affect. How poor family relations predispose young women to become pregnant earlier than their peers is undetermined. Young women may become depressed while trying to cope with the strain of pregnancy (and potentially the subsequent abortion), especially in the absence of a supportive family environment. Poorer family relations appear to be confined to the relationship between father and daughter rather than with mother. As yet, the processes that link these events have not been ascertained but merit further study with adolescents and young women who give birth and keep their children, as well as with young women who terminate their pregnancies.

CONCLUSION

Each reproductive and role transition is in some sense shared by mothers and daughters inasmuch as the progression of one member of the dyad through the transition influences and is influenced by the response of the other member. Developmental study necessitated a focus on continuity and change over the course of the life span. Reproductive and role transitions may be discontinuous periods that set individuals on different mental and physical health trajectories (Graber & Brooks-Gunn, 1996b). As we tried to demonstrate, the navigation of a reproductive transition is influenced by numerous individual and contextual factors. This is also true for nearly all transitions, although this perspective is most often applied to the study of adolescence. (See Graber et al., 1996, for exemplars.)

Clearly, the pubertal transition is a period of change and, at least initially, conflict for mothers and daughters. This transition has demonstrated influence on both the girls experiencing it as well as their mothers; however, girls' experiences have been studied more extensively. Maternal characteristics influence how mothers interact with their daughters as well as with daughters' outcome (e.g., Paikoff et al., 1994). How a girl's puberty influences her mother's adjustment and role change requires further investigation. Notably in the findings reviewed, there was a sparsity of effects of mother–daughter relationship variables on mothers' well being. Lack of effects may be due to a variety of unexplored causes. Potentially, mother's well-being may not be as affected by the relationship changes as is daughter's well-being. This would be in sharp contrast to the hypothesis that separation is a difficult developmental task and that autonomy issues often are enacted in the context of mother–daughter interactions. Due to the centrality of puberty to the adolescent, the challenges of early adolescence may have primary impact on the adolescent herself, with the mother being more capable to reflect objectively rather than internally on the redefinition of roles. Given that mothers (and daughters) continue to report closeness in the relationship, the conflict may be less salient.

Alternatively, puberty may not be the reproductive transition of the daughter that proves the most stressful for the mother. Later occurring adolescent transitions such as becoming sexually active, pregnant, or a young mother may be more relevant to the mother–daughter relationship and to the mother's realignment or new definition of self in response to the daughter's transition. A further consideration is the spacing of these transitions. Mothers and daughters may experience more individual and dyadic upheaval if the daughter makes several of these transitions in rapid succession before role integration and coping have occurred.

One challenge to studies of biological and social transitions will be to understand better the nature of individual differences in response to the transition and how different contexts interact with these differences. For several of the reproductive transitions, research has been limited to how a particular segment of the population makes the transition and the effect this has on their families (or how the families influence the transition). Once we understand how these processes are similar and different for other groups of adolescent girls and their mothers, better predictions can be made about whose transitional experience is likely to have negative health outcomes.

Notably, studies have not examined the interconnection of the transitions themselves; that is, if the pubertal transition has negative effects on an adolescent and her mother, will the daughter's pregnancy also produce negative effects on both members of the dyad? If consistent responses to the challenge of navigating a reproductive transition are exhibited by a dyad or consistently by one member of a dyad, then stress during reproductive transitions could be intensified and accumulate over the life course. Studies of conflict and autonomy around puberty often assume that once mothers and daughters come to terms with the effects of puberty on each of their lives and on their relationship, the dyad experiences improvements in the relationship. But, will the same process begin again with the advent of sexual behavior or pregnancy? As studies of intergenerational developmental processes progress, identifying consistency and change becomes increasingly complex, but hopefully more enlightening.

ACKNOWLEDGMENTS

Portions of this chapter were also published as Graber, J. A., & Brooks-Gunn, J. (1996). Reproductive transitions: The experience of mothers and daughters. In C. D. Ryff & M. M. Seltzer (Eds.), *The parental experience in midlife* (pp. 255–299). Chicago: The University of Chicago Press.

The authors were supported by a grant from the National Institute of Child Health and Human Development (NICHD) during the writing of this chapter. Studies conducted under the Adolescent Study Program were supported by grants from the W. T. Grant Foundation and NICHD. The authors also wish to acknowledge the influence of Michelle P. Warren, the co-director of the Adolescent Study Program; Marta Zahaykevich for her work on the Mother–Daughter Discourse Study; Andrea Archibald and Jessica Auth for their assistance with transcription of videotape data; Roberta Paikoff for her work on the Late-Adolescence Study; Richard Fox for his work on data analysis; Karen Matthews, Judith Rodin, Nancy Adler, Joyce Bromberger, Judy Cameron, Ralph Horowitz, Bruce McEwen, Anne Petersen, Marielle Rebuffe-Scrive, and Elizabeth Susman, members of the Reproductive Transitions Working Group of the John D. and Catherine T. MacArthur Foundation Research Network on Health-Promoting and Disease-Preventing Behaviors, in some of the ideas presented; and the National Institute of Mental Health Family Research Consortium.

REFERENCES

Attie, I., & Brooks-Gunn, J. (1989). The development of eating problems in adolescent girls: A longitudinal study. *Developmental Psychology, 25*(1), 70–79.

Attie, I., & Brooks-Gunn, J. (1995). The development of eating regulation across the lifespan. In D. Cicchetti & D. J. Cohen (Eds.), *Developmental psychopathology* (Vol. 2, pp. 332–368). New York: Wiley.

Attie, I., Brooks-Gunn, J., & Petersen, A. C. (1990). The emergence of eating problems: A developmental perspective. In M. Lewis & S. Miller (Eds.), *Handbook of developmental psychopathology* (pp. 409–420). New York: Plenum.

Blos, P. (1979). The second individuation process. In P. Blos (Ed.), *The adolescent passage: Developmental issues at adolescence* (pp. 141–170). New York: International University Press.

Bromberger, J. T., & Matthews, K. A. (1994, May). *Does stress accelerate the cessation of menses in middle-aged women?* Paper presented at the APA conference, "Psychosocial and behavioral factors in women's health: Creating an agenda for the 21st century," Washington, DC.

Brooks-Gunn, J. (1987). Pubertal processes: Their relevance for psychological research. In V. B. Van Hasselt & M. Hersen (Eds.), *The handbook of adolescent psychology* (pp. 111–130). New York: Pergamon.

Brooks-Gunn, J. (1988). Antecedents and consequences of variations in girls' maturational timing. *Journal of Adolescent Health Care, 9*(5), 365–373.

Brooks-Gunn, J. (1990). Overcoming barriers to adolescent research on pubertal and reproductive development. *Journal of Youth and Adolescence, 19*(5), 425–440.

Brooks-Gunn, J. (1991). How stressful is the transition to adolescence in girls? In M. E. Colten & S. Gore (Eds.), *Adolescent stress: Causes and consequences* (pp. 131–149). Hawthorne, NY: Aldine de Gruyter.

Brooks-Gunn, J., & Chase-Lansdale, P. L. (1995). Adolescent parenthood. In M. H. Bornstein (Ed.), *Handbook of parenting: Vol. 3. Status and social conditions of parenting* (pp. 113–149). Mahwah, NJ: Lawrence Erlbaum Associates.

Brooks-Gunn, J., Graber, J. A., & Paikoff, R. L. (1994). Studying links between hormones and negative affect: Models and measures. *Journal of Research on Adolescence, 4*(4), 469–486.

Brooks-Gunn, J., & Matthews, W. (1979). *He and she: How children develop their sex-role identity.* Englewood Cliffs, NJ: Prentice-Hall.

Brooks-Gunn, J., Newman, D., Holderness, C., & Warren, M. P. (1994). The experience of breast development and girls' stories about the purchase of a bra. *Journal of Youth and Adolescence, 23* (5), 539–565.

Brooks-Gunn, J., & Reiter, E. O. (1990). The role of pubertal processes in the early adolescent transition. In S. Feldman & G. Elliott (Eds.), *At the threshold: The developing adolescent* (pp. 16–53). Cambridge, MA: Harvard University Press.

Brooks-Gunn, J., & Ruble, D. N. (1982). The development of menstrual-related beliefs and behaviors during early adolescence. *Child Development, 53,* 1567–1577.

Brooks-Gunn, J., & Warren, M. P. (1985). The effects of delayed menarche in different contexts: Dance and nondance students. *Journal of Youth and Adolescence, 14*(4), 285–300.

Brooks-Gunn, J., & Warren, M. P. (1988). The psychological significance of secondary sexual characteristics in 9- to 11-year-old girls. *Child Development, 59,* 1061–1069.

Brooks-Gunn, J., Warren, M. P., Samelson, M., & Fox, R. (1986). Physical similarity of and disclosure of menarcheal status to friends: Effects of age and pubertal status. *Journal of Early Adolescence, 6*(1), 3–14.

Brooks-Gunn, J., & Zahaykevich, M. (1989). Parent-child relationships in early adolescence: A developmental perspective. In K. Kreppner & R. M. Lerner (Eds.), *Family systems and life-span development.* Hillsdale, NJ: Lawrence Erlbaum Associates.

Buchanan, C. M., Eccles, J. S., & Becker, J. B. (1992). Are adolescents the victims of raging hormones: Evidence for activational effects of hormones on moods and behavior at adolescence. *Psychological Bulletin, 111,* 62–107.

Carlton-Ford, S., Paikoff, R. L., & Brooks-Gunn, J. (1991). Methodological issues in the study of divergent views of the family. In R. L. Paikoff (Ed.), *New directions for child development: Shared views in the family during adolescence.* San Francisco: Jossey-Bass.

Carlton-Ford, S., Paikoff, R., Oakley, J., & Brooks-Gunn, J. (1996). A longitudinal analysis of depressed mood, self-esteem and family processes during adolescence. *Sociological Focus, 29,* (2), 135–154.

Caspi, A., Lynam, D., Moffitt, T. E., & Silva, P. A. (1993). Unraveling girls' delinquency: Biological, dispositional, and contextual contributions to adolescent misbehavior. *Developmental Psychology, 29,* 19–30.

Chodorow, N. (1978). *The reproduction of mothering: Psychoanalysis and sociology of gender.* Berkeley, CA: University of California Press.

Collins, W. A. (1988). Research on the transition to adolescence: Continuity in the study of developmental processes. In M. R. Gunnar & W. A. Collins (Eds.), *Development during transition to adolescence: Minnesota symposia on child psychology, Vol. 21* (pp. 1–15). Hillsdale, NJ: Lawrence Erlbaum Associates.

Collins, W. A. (1990). Parent–child relationships in the transition to adolescence: Continuity and change in interaction, affect, and cognition. In R. Montemayor, G. Adams, & T. Gullotta (Eds.), *Advances in adolescent development: Vol.2, The transition from childhood to adolescence* (pp. 85–106). Newbury Park, CA: Sage.

Cooper, C. R. (1988). Commentary: The role of conflict in adolescent–parent relationships. In M. R. Gunnar & W. A. Collins (Ed.), *Development during transition to adolescence: Minnesota symposia on child psychology, Vol. 21* (pp. 181–187). Hillsdale, NJ: Lawrence Erlbaum Associates.

Deutsch, H. (1944). *The psychology of women: A psychoanalytic interpretation.* New York: Grune & Stratton.

Deutsch, F. M., Ruble, D. N., Fleming, A., Brooks-Gunn, J., & Stangor, C. (1988). Information-seeking and self-definition during the transition to motherhood. *Journal of Personality and Social Psychology, 55*(3), 420–431.

Eccles, J. S., Midgley, C., Wigfield, A., Buchanan, C. M., Reuman, D., Flanagan, C., & MacIver, D. (1993). Development during adolescence: The impact of stage-environment fit in young adolescents' experiences in schools and in families. *American Psychologist, 48*, 90–101.

Garner, D. M., & Garfinkel, P. E. (1979). The Eating Attitudes Test: An index of the symptoms of anorexia nervosa. *Psychological Medicine, 9*, 1–7.

Graber, J. A., & Brooks-Gunn, J. (1996a). Expectations for and precursors of leaving home in young women. In W. Damon (Series Ed.), J. A. Graber & J. S. Dubas (Vol. Eds.), *New directions for child development: Vol. 71. Leaving home: Understanding the transition to adulthood* (pp. 21–38). San Francisco: Jossey-Bass.

Graber, J. A., & Brooks-Gunn, J. (1996b). Transitions and turning points: Navigating the passage from childhood through adolescence. *Developmental Psychology, 32* (4), 768–776.

Graber, J. A., Brooks-Gunn, J., Paikoff, R. L., & Warren, M. P. (1994). Prediction of eating problems: An eight year study of adolescent girls. *Developmental Psychology, 30* (6), 823–834.

Graber, J. A., Brooks-Gunn, J., & Petersen, A. C. (Eds.). (1996). *Transitions through adolescence: Interpersonal domains and context.* Mahwah, NJ: Lawrence Erlbaum Associates.

Graber, J. A., Brooks-Gunn, J., & Warren, M. P. (1995). The antecedents of menarcheal age. *Child Development, 66*, 346–359.

Grotevant, H. D., & Cooper, C. R. (1985). Patterns of interaction in family relationships and the development of identity exploration in adolescence. *Child Development, 56*, 415–428.

Gutmann, D. (1975). Parenthood: A key to the comparative study of the life cycle. In N. Datan & L. Ginsberg (Eds.), *Life Span Developmental Psychology.* New York: Academic Press.

Hall, G. S. (1904). *Adolescence: Its psychology and its relations to physiology, anthropology, sociology, sex, crime, religion, and education.* New York: Appleton.

Hauser, S. T., Powers, S. I., Noam, G. G., Jacobson, A. M., Weiss, B., & Follansbee, D. J. (1984). Familial contexts of adolescent ego development. *Child Development, 55*, 195–213.

Hetherington, E. M. (1989). Coping with family transitions: Winners, losers, and survivors. *Child Development, 60*, 1–14.

Hill, J. P. (1980). The family. In M. Johnson (Ed.), *Toward adolescence: The middle school years. The seventy-ninth yearbook of the National Society for the Study of Education* (pp. 32–55). Chicago: University of Chicago Press.

Hill, J. P. (1987). Research on adolescents and their families: Past and prospect. In C. E. Irwin (Ed.), *Adolescent social behavior and health: Vol. 37, New directions for child development* (pp. 13–31). San Francisco, CA: Jossey-Bass.

Hill, J. P. (1988). Adapting to menarche: Familial control and conflict. In M. R. Gunnar & W. A. Collins (Ed.), *Development during transition to adolescence: Minnesota symposia on child psychology, Vol. 21* (pp. 43–77). Hillsdale, NJ: Lawrence Erlbaum Associates.

Hill, J. P., & Lynch, M. E. (1983). The intensification of gender-related role expectations during early adolescence. In J. Brooks-Gunn & A. C. Petersen (Eds.), *Girls at puberty: Biological and psychosocial perspectives* (pp. 201–228). New York: Plenum.

Inoff-Germain, G., Arnold, G. S., Nottelmann, E. D., Susman, E. J., Cutler, G. B., & Chrousos, G. P. (1988). Relations between hormone levels and observational measures of aggressive behavior of young adolescents in family interactions. *Developmental Psychology, 24*(1), 129–139.

Josselson, R. L. (1980). Psychodynamic aspects of identity formation in college women. *Journal of Youth and Adolescence, 2,* 3–52.

Marshall, W. A., & Tanner, J. M. (1969). Variations in the pattern of pubertal changes in girls. *Archives of Disease in Childhood, 44,* 291–303.

Moffitt, T. E., Caspi, A., Belsky, J., & Silva, P. A. (1992). Childhood experience and the onset of menarche: A test of a sociobiological model. *Child Development, 63,* 47–58.

Moos, R. H. (1974). *Family Environment Scale.* New York: Consulting Psychologists Press.

Montemayor, R. (1982). The relationship between parent–adolescent conflict and the amount of time adolescents spend alone and with parents and peers. *Child Development, 53,* 1512–1519.

Montemayor, R. (1983). Parents and adolescents in conflict: All families some of the time and some families most of the time. *Journal of Early Adolescence, 3,* 83–103.

Montemayor, R. (1986). Family variation in parent–adolescent storm and stress. *Journal of Adolescent Research, 1,* 15–31.

Montemayor, R., & Hanson, E. (1985). A naturalistic view of conflict between adolescents and their parents and siblings. *Journal of Early Adolescence, 5,* 23–30.

Neugarten, B. L. (1979). Time, age and life cycle. *American Journal of Psychiatry, 136,* 887–894.

Offer, D. (1987). In defense of adolescents. *Journal of the American Medical Association, 257,* 3407–3408.

Olweus, D., Mattsson, A., Schalling, D., & Low, H. (1988). Circulating testosterone levels and aggression in adolescent males: A casual analysis. *Psychosomatic Medicine, 50,* 261–272.

Paikoff, R., & Brooks-Gunn, J. (1991). Do parent–child relationships change during puberty? *Psychological Bulletin, 110*(1), 47–66.

Paikoff, R. L., Brooks-Gunn, J., & Carlton-Ford, S. (1991). Effect of reproductive status changes upon family functioning and well-being of mothers and daughters. *Journal of Early Adolescence, 11*(2), 201–220.

Paikoff, R. L., Carlton-Ford, S., & Brooks-Gunn, J. (1994). Mother–daughter dyads view the family: Associations between divergent perceptions and daughter well-being. *Journal of Youth and Adolescence, 22* (5), 473–492.

Papini, D. R., Datan, N., & McCluskey-Fawcett, K. A. (1988). An observational study of affective and assertive family interactions during adolescence. *Journal of Youth and Adolescence, 17,* 477–482.

Petersen, A. C., Sarigiani, P. A., & Kennedy, R. E. (1991). Adolescent depression: Why more girls? *Journal of Youth and Adolescence, 20,* 247–271.

Radloff, L. S. (1977). The CES-D scale: A self-report depression scale for research in the general population. *Applied Psychological Measurement, 1,* 385–401.

Rossi, A. S. (1977). A biosocial perspective on parenting. *Daedalus, 106,* 1–31.

Rossi, A. S., & Rossi, P. H. (1990). *Of human bonding.* New York: Aldine de Gruyter.

Ruble, D. N., Brooks-Gunn, J., Fleming, A. S., Fitzmaurice, G., Stangor, C., & Deutsch, F. (1990). Transition to motherhood and the self: Measurement, stability, and change. *Journal of Personality and Social Psychology, 58*(3), 450–463.

Ryff, C. D., & Seltzer, M. M. (1996). The uncharted years of midlife parenting. In C. D. Ryff & M. M. Seltzer (Eds.), *The parental experience in midlife* (pp. 3–25). Chicago: The University of Chicago Press.

Silverberg, S. B. (1996). Parents' well-being at their children's transition to adolescence. In C. D. Ryff & M. M. Seltzer (Eds.), *The parental experience in midlife* (pp. 215–254). Chicago: The University of Chicago Press.

Simmons, R. G., & Blyth, D. A. (1987). *Moving into adolescence: The impact of pubertal change and school context.* New York: Aldine.

Smetana, J. G. (1988a). Adolescents' and parents' conceptions of parental authority. *Child Development, 59,* 321–335.

Smetana, J. G. (1988b). Concepts of self and social convention: Adolescents' and parents' reasoning about hypothetical and actual family conflicts. In M. R. Gunnar & W. A. Collins (Eds.), *Development during transition to adolescence: Minnesota symposia on child psychology* (Vol. 21, pp. 79–122). Hillsdale, NJ: Lawrence Erlbaum Associates.

Stattin, H., & Magnusson, D. (1990). *Paths through life: Vol. 2. Pubertal maturation in female development.* Hillsdale, NJ: Lawrence Erlbaum Associates.

Steinberg, L. (1987). Impact of puberty on family relations: Effects of pubertal status and pubertal timing. *Developmental Psychology, 23,* 451–460.

Steinberg, L. (1989). Pubertal maturation and parent–adolescent distance: An evolutionary perspective. In G. R. Adams, R. Montemayor, & T. P. Gullotta (Eds.), *Biology of adolescent behavior and development* (pp. 71–97). Newbury Park, CA: Sage.

Steinberg, L. (1990). Autonomy, conflict, and harmony in the family relationship. In S. Feldman & G. Elliott (Eds.), *At the threshold: The developing adolescent* (pp. 255–276). Cambridge, MA: Harvard University Press.

Surbey, M. K. (1990). Family composition, stress, and the timing of human menarche. In T. E. Ziegler & F. B. Bercovitch (Eds.), *Socioendocrinology of primate reproduction* (pp. 11–32). New York: Wiley.

Susman, E. J., Inoff-Germain, G. E., Nottelmann, E. D., Cutler, G. B., Jr., Loriaux, D. L., & Chrousos, G. P. (1987). Hormones, emotional dispositions, and aggressive attributes in early adolescents. *Child Development, 58,* 1114–1134.

Warren, M. P. (1980). The effects of exercise on pubertal progression and reproductive function in girls. *Journal of Clinical Endocrinology and Metabolism, 51,* 1150–1157.

Warren, M. P., & Brooks-Gunn, J. (1989). Mood and behavior at adolescence: Evidence for hormonal factors. *Journal of Clinical Endocrinology and Metabolism, 69*(1), 77–83.

Zabin, L. S., & Hayward, S. C. (1993). *Adolescent sexual behavior and childbearing.* Newbury Park, CA: Sage.

Mother–Daughter Interactions and Adolescent Girls' Depression[1]

Sally I. Powers
University of Massachusetts at Amherst

Deborah P. Welsh
University of Tennessee at Knoxville

One relatively brief period of the life span, adolescence, contains the first expressions of two of the most significant aspects of depression noted around the world: the strikingly high level of prevalence and the "gender switch" in incidence. The dramatic rise in rates of depressive symptoms and diagnoses begins in early adolescence and quickly reaches the same high rates that characterize adulthood (Brooks-Gunn & Peterson, 1991; Fleming & Offord, 1990; Gotlib & Hammen, 1992; Kashani et al., 1987a, 1987b; McFarlane, Bellissimo, Norman, & Lange, 1994; Monck, Graham, Richman, & Dobbs, 1994a; Nolen-Hoeksema, Girgus, & Seligman, 1991; Petersen, Sarigiani, & Kennedy, 1991; Rutter, 1986). Early adolescence is also the period in which girls begin to outnumber boys by three to one in the incidence of depression. Prior to adolescence, boys have either equal or higher rates of depression than girls (Anderson, Williams, McGee, & Silva, 1987; Kandel & Davies, 1982; Lewinsohn, Hops, Roberts, Seeley, & Andrews, 1993; Nolen-Hoeksema, 1987, 1990; Nolen-Hoeksema & Girgus, 1994; Nolen-Hoeksema, Girgus, & Seligman, 1992; Petersen et al., 1991; Reinherz et al., 1989). As the

---

[1]The term *depression* refers to many different constructs in the theoretical and research literature, encompassing dysphoric mood, depressive symptoms, depressive and internalizing syndromes, and clinical diagnoses of major depression and dysthymia (Compas, Ey, & Grant, 1993; Petersen et al., 1993). In this chapter, our discussion of the theoretical relation of interaction processes to adolescent depression is applicable to all these manifestations. The empirical results we report in this chapter pertain specifically to depression as evidenced through the behavioral syndrome of internalizing.

period of origin of both the rise in prevalence and the gender switch, adolescence is a uniquely important life-span period in which to investigate the causes and consequences of depression (Allgood-Merten, Lewinsohn, & Hops, 1990; Gjerde & Block, 1991; Petersen et al., 1993).

Several factors have been proposed as contributing to the rise in prevalence of depression for girls in adolescence. Among these, the influence of sociocultural forces such as societal roles, social stressors, socialization practices, and social relationships have received substantial research attention (discussed later in this chapter). Remarkably, although interpersonal interactions are the behavioral processes that constitute these sociocultural constructs, observational investigations of the relation of interpersonal behaviors in families to adolescent depression are rare. We located only four published studies that assess the relation of observed family interactions to adolescent depression (Allen, Hauser, Eickholt, Bell, & O'Connor, 1994; Dadds, Sanders, Morrison, & Rebgetz, 1992; Ge, Lorenz, Conger, Elder, & Simons, 1994; Sanders, Dadds, Johnston, & Cash, 1992). In this chapter we provide data to examine two models of the temporal relation of adolescent girls' depression to their interpersonal interactions with their mothers. Our study investigates the relation of six interpersonal behaviors (support, conflict, submission, humor, sarcasm, and misunderstanding) to girls' depression. We expect these behaviors to be relevant to the onset and maintenance of depression in adolescent girls because these behaviors are integrally involved in girls' attempts to undertake the fundamental adolescent task of individuation. We hypothesize that (a) girls' depression in adolescence leads to mother–daughter interactions that are suggested by theory to inhibit individuation, and (b) these inhibiting interactions, in turn, lead to increases in girls' depression, beyond that predicted by prior levels of depression.

Three of the four studies that analyzed the connection between family interactions and adolescent depression were unable to examine this relation separately for girls and boys, due to sample size (Allen et al., 1994b; Dadds et al., 1992; Sanders et al., 1992). Separate examination is important because depression is more prevalent for girls than boys in adolescence, girls exhibit interpersonal attributes likely to impede individuation (Allgood-Merten et al., 1990; Brooks-Gunn & Peterson, 1991; Nolen-Hoeksema, 1987, 1990, 1994; Nolen-Hoeksema & Girgus, 1994), and interpersonal behaviors have different patterns of predicting mental health for adolescent girls and boys (Cooper, Grotevant, & Condon, 1983; Gjerde, Block, & Block, 1988; Gjerde & Block, 1991; Grotevant & Cooper, 1985; Welsh & Powers, 1991). Thus, we focus on individual differences in adolescent girls' interpersonal interactions and depression.

A second focus of our investigation is the subjective understanding that girls and their mothers have regarding their interactions. Our method of assessing subjective understanding of interpersonal behavior uses girls' and mothers' ratings of their videotaped interactions. Our emphasis on subjective understanding is motivated by the expectation that the meaning that interpersonal interactions have for girls and their mothers is a crucial element in determining the impact of those behaviors on mental health, psychopathology, and developmental processes (Powers, Welsh, & Wright, 1994).

THE RELEVANCE OF THE DEVELOPMENTAL TASK OF INDIVIDUATION FOR ADOLESCENT DEPRESSION

Developmental psychopathologists suggest that an important contributing cause of dysfunctional affect and behavior is an individual's failure to achieve essential developmental tasks (Cicchetti, 1984; Cicchetti & Toth, 1995; Kovacs, 1989; Sroufe, 1992). In this chapter we examine the related proposition (Allen et al., 1994b; Barber, Olsen, & Shagle, 1994; Gjerde & Block, 1991; Kobak, Ferenz-Gillies, Everhart, & Seabrook, 1994) that adolescent depression is associated with difficulties with interpersonal skills necessary for the central developmental task of adolescence: the task of negotiating greater autonomy from parents while still maintaining closeness and intimacy (Grotevant & Cooper, 1985; Hill & Holmbeck, 1986; Laursen & Collins, 1994; Steinberg, 1990). This task of negotiating increased separateness and simultaneously nurturing connection to parents is typically referred to as achieving *mutuality* (Youniss & Smollar, 1985) or *individuation* (Grotevant & Cooper, 1985). Achievement of individuation supports the achievement of other developmental tasks of adolescence and young adulthood, such as establishment of romantic relationships and identity, and is positively associated with several dimensions of mental health (Allen, Hauser, Bell, & O'Connor, 1994a; Campbell, Adams, & Dobson, 1984; Collins, 1990; Grotevant & Cooper, 1985; Hill & Holmbeck, 1986; Steinberg, 1990).

Individuation is a process of interpersonal negotiation and occurs through parent–adolescent interactions. Several interpersonal skills are required of families in order to provide a context for successful individuation (Powers, Hauser, & Kilner, 1989). First, families must be able to tolerate at least moderate levels of conflict (Baumrind, 1987; Cooper, 1988; Cooper et al., 1983; Holmbeck, 1996; Holmbeck & Hill, 1988; Montemayor, 1983; Powers, 1988, 1989; Powers et al., 1989; Powers, Schwartz, Hauser, Noam, & Jacobson, 1983; Steinberg, 1990; Yau & Smetana, 1996). A child's transition into adolescence is usually accompanied by increases in assertions of personal autonomy (Smetana & Asquith, 1994) that lead to moderate increases in conflict with parents and decreased submission of the adolescent (Montemayor, 1983).[2] With the rise in conflict and lessening of submissive behavior comes a rise in the adolescent's power. This rise in power is typically at the expense of the mother's, whose power decreases (Steinberg, 1981, 1990). Parent–adolescent conflict signals the need for negotiation. At this point in an adolescent's development, either an absence of conflict or levels of conflict that are too high interfere with this task. Intolerance of conflict allows no forum for the adolescent to negotiate new patterns of independence and mutuality with parents. Parents (particularly mothers, who may have the most to lose) must make room in their relationship for conflict. If adolescents are too submissive and give in too readily to the parents' point of view, negotiation is foreclosed. On the other hand, conflict that is too extreme may force parents and adolescents to seek escape and relief by cutting off continued negotiation and sharing of independent viewpoints. In this study we assessed levels of mothers' and daughters' conflictual interactions as they discussed real-life issues on which they disagreed. Because extreme levels of conflict do not facilitate the developmental task of individuation, levels of conflict that were either unusually low or unusually high could be associated with daughters' depression. We also hypothesized that daughters' depression would be positively associated with daughters' submissive behaviors. These hypotheses are supported by findings from the only investigation thus far to examine the relation of adolescent depression to family behaviors coded for their relevance to individuation (Allen et al., 1994b). Allen and his colleagues coded family behaviors as inhibiting of relatedness, autonomous-related, or inhibiting of autonomy. They found that adolescent depression was predicted by family interactions that were less inhibiting of relatedness (less hostile), less autonomous-related, and more inhibiting of autonomy. Thus, families of depressed adolescents were less tolerant of conflict and avoided active negotiation of differences. Allen et al. concluded that "adolescent depressed affect is linked to a particular type of failure . . . best characterized as avoidance of autonomy . . ." (p. 548).

In addition to the ability to tolerate moderate levels of conflict, parents and adolescents must be able to communicate clearly with one another. Family members must be able to express their differences, as well as their closeness, in a manner that is not misunderstood by others. As an indication of communication clarity, we assessed mothers' and daughters' levels of misunderstanding of each other. We expected that both mothers' and daughters' misunderstanding would be positively related to daughters' depression.

---

[2]See Laursen and Collins (1994) for a different view. They argue that level of interpersonal conflict is consistent from childhood through adolescence, but varies among different types of relationships. Whatever the view toward the amount of change in conflict from childhood to adolescence, investigators of adolescence agree on the importance of moderate levels of conflict for healthy parent–adolescent relationships.

A third type of interpersonal behavior suggested as crucial for individuation is parental support (Hauser, Powers, & Noam, 1991; Powers et al., 1989). Supportive interactions provide an atmosphere that allows adolescents to fully participate in difficult interpersonal negotiations. Ge and his colleagues (Ge et al., 1994) examined the relation of adolescent boys' and girls' depression to observers' ratings of mothers' and fathers' supportive behaviors. Significant results were found only for mothers and daughters. Maternal support for daughters was shown to protect girls from depression by attenuating the association between stressful life events and depression. Our investigation assessed mothers' and daughters' supportive interactions, and we hypothesized that mothers' support would be negatively associated with daughters' depression.

DEPRESSIVE INTERPERSONAL BEHAVIORS OF ADULTS

Our hypotheses thus far were derived from theoretical considerations regarding the importance of developmentally appropriate interpersonal interactions for girls in adolescence. These hypotheses were also supported by the few studies that investigated the association of adolescent depression with observed family behaviors. We turn now to findings from interaction research with depressed adults to provide additional clues as to how interpersonal behaviors may be related to adolescents' depression. Researchers of adult depression have investigated the relation of interpersonal behavior to depression with direct observation methods for two decades, but this research has remained largely unconnected to theoretical and empirical studies of adolescent depression. At present, it is unclear whether depressed adolescents exhibit "depressive interpersonal behaviors" similar to those observed with depressed adults and whether others react to these behaviors in similar ways. If similarities are found, it is possible that these depressive behaviors would produce difficulties for depressed adolescents in negotiating individuation. Major findings from adult studies that are relevant to adolescent depression and the task of individuation are summarized next.

The proposition that adolescent depression is associated with difficulties in interpersonal behaviors that facilitate individuation is consistent with the interactional perspective of adult depression, introduced by Coyne (1976a, 1976b) and by Lewinsohn (1974) in the 1970s. These investigators suggested that depressed persons' symptoms of helplessness and negative affect provoke negative moods in others and, over time, depressed persons experience more hostility and little positive reinforcement from others. This interactive pattern then leads to increased or prolonged depression. Several recent reviews of research on the interactional perspective concluded that depressed adults are less involved and responsive (or are more passive) with others, as well as exhibiting more hostility, irritability, and negative affect (Downey & Coyne, 1990; Segrin & Abramson, 1994; Segrin & Dillard, 1992).

Reactions to Adults' Depressive Interpersonal Behaviors

The majority of studies on reactions to depressed adults' social interactions describe the reactions of strangers. Although studies with depressed adults interacting with strangers fail to show that depressed adults cause negative moods in others, depressed adults do reliably receive rejection from those in their social environment. In contrast to studies with strangers, research with married couples (Biglan et al., 1985; Biglan, Rothlind, Hops, & Sherman, 1989; Nelson & Beach, 1990) shows that depressed persons are often "rewarded" by their spouses for emitting depressive behaviors. That is, depressive behaviors often inhibit the hostile and irritable behaviors of the spouse. In similar fashion, children of depressed mothers tend to suppress their own frustration and tension (Cole, Barrett, & Zahn-Waxler, 1992; Cummings & Davies, 1994).

Adult studies lead us to expect that depression in adolescents will be associated with three types of interpersonal behaviors: (a) passivity, nonresponsiveness, and submissiveness; (b) sadness and negativity, and (c) irritability, hostility, and criticism. These are behaviors that we would expect to handicap an adolescent when facing the challenge of negotiating individuation. In particular, the autonomy dimension of individuation seems to be most threatened by this triad of depressive interpersonal behaviors. Negotiating with parents for a greater level of autonomy requires active, self-assertive interactions, in contrast to the submissive behaviors associated with depression. When differences need to be negotiated with a parent, healthy adolescents' self-efficacious behaviors work best in an interpersonal context that allows moderate levels of conflict. This is in contrast to high levels of conflict that are likely to be engendered by the irritability, hostility, and criticism associated with depression. Although these depressive interpersonal behaviors may hinder the negotiation of autonomy in adolescence, we do not know the extent to which these findings with adults are generalizable to depressed adolescents and to those that interact with them.

Successful negotiation of autonomy may be further threatened by parents' responses to these depressive interpersonal behaviors. Studies with adults leave us unclear, however, as to whether to expect parents' responses to adolescents to be more negative and rejecting (like the responses of strangers to depressed adults) or whether parents negative behaviors will be inhibited (like the responses of spouses to their depressed partners).

THE ROLE OF SUBJECTIVE UNDERSTANDING
OF BEHAVIOR

An additional concern of our investigation was to examine the role of mothers' and daughters' subjective understanding of their behaviors. In an earlier article (Powers et al., 1994), we argued that "an adolescent's subjective understanding of his or her family's behaviors is an important determinant of the way that adolescent responds to those behaviors. Differences in adolescents' responses to family behaviors may then be reflected in differences in psychosocial outcomes [such as depression] . . ." (p. 588). We expect that examining adolescents' and mothers' subjective understanding of their interpersonal behaviors may be particularly useful in illuminating new relations between behaviors and depression because their subjective understanding of those behaviors is based on the history of the mother–daughter relationship, the immediate interpersonal context, individual differences in personality and development, and their own cultural norms.

THE IMPORTANCE OF AN INDIVIDUAL DIFFERENCES
APPROACH

Although gender differences in the prevalence of depression are well documented, clearly not all adolescent girls become depressed. Current research on the causes and consequences of girls' depressive symptoms and disorders in this period of life focuses primarily on searching for etiological factors that differentiate boys from girls. While this course of investigation is undoubtedly important, it is equally critical to investigate factors that exhibit a wide range of individual differences among girls—factors that may increase girls' vulnerability to depression (Nolen-Hoeksema, 1990).

Three factors that may make adolescent girls especially vulnerable to depression are relevant to the hypothesis that girls are susceptible to difficulties with interpersonal behaviors necessary for establishing autonomy. First, girls view themselves as less instrumental and more passive in how they cope with stress and solve problems (Allgood-Merten et al., 1990; Compas, Malcarne, & Fondacaro, 1988; Craighead & Green, 1989; Hill & Lynch, 1983; Horwitz & White, 1987; Huselid & Cooper, 1994; Nolen-Hoeksema, 1994). This passivity leaves girls vulnerable to feelings of helplessness and hopelessness when facing developmental challenges (Nolen-Hoeksema, 1994). It is argued that such a lack of instrumentality can be both a reaction to existing depression and a cause of increased or prolonged depression (Allgood-Merten et al., 1990; Craighead & Green, 1989; Horwitz & White, 1987; Huselid & Cooper, 1994; Nolen-Hoeksema, 1994).

A second factor discussed as contributing to some girls' vulnerability to depression and that may also be associated with a vulnerability to difficulties in the interpersonal negotiation of autonomy is a preoccupation with interpersonal issues (Compas, Ey, & Grant, 1993; Petersen et al., 1991). Adolescent girls experience "interpersonal depressive preoccupations" more often than do boys (Leadbeater, Blatt, & Quinlan, 1995) and have a more difficult time balancing a need for positive social interchange with autonomy (Baron & Campbell, 1993).

A final factor posited as contributing to girls' risk for depression that is also relevant to girls' difficulty with interpersonal behaviors signifying autonomous negotiation is the notion that depressive affect and lack of autonomous behaviors may be perceived by girls and their parents as gender syntonic. Parents hold increasingly gender-stereotyped expectations for their children as they enter adolescence, and girls begin to fear social rejection if they do not act in accordance with gender-stereotyped behavior patterns (Hill & Lynch, 1983; Nolen-Hoeksema, 1990, 1994).

This chapter focuses exclusively on the relation of interpersonal behaviors signifying difficulties with autonomy and adolescent girls' depression. Our primary hypothesis is that interpersonal behaviors that signify difficulties with negotiating autonomy are related to depression in adolescent girls. If confirmed, an association of depression with difficulties in the individuation process for girls could contribute to explanations of the dramatic rise in girls' depression in adolescence.

TEMPORAL MODELS OF THE RELATION OF INDIVIDUATION TO DEPRESSION

The general hypothesis that difficulties with individuation (specifically negotiating autonomy) are related to depression for adolescent girls does not specify the direction of effects between individuation difficulties and depression. At least two simple models of the relation of individuation processes to girls' depression are possible: the reactive model and the causative model. The two models are not competing, but each clarifies a different aspect of the temporal relation between individuation and depression. The reactive model proposes that difficulties in the individuation process will be a reaction to girls' depressive symptoms. To the extent that difficulties in individuation are expressed in interactions, both girls and their mothers should react with observable behaviors to the girls' depressive symptoms. The causal model proposes that difficulties in the individuation process of adolescents will predict increases in adolescents' depressive symptoms, over and above that predicted by adolescents' prior levels of depression.

This chapter explicitly examines both the reactive and the causal model of the relation of individuation processes to adolescent girls' symptoms using

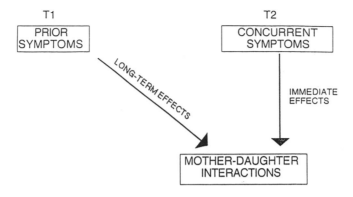

FIG. 11.1a.   The Reactive Model.

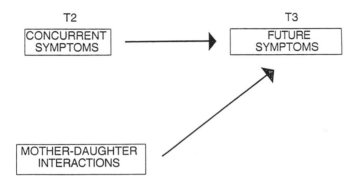

FIG. 11.1b.   The Causal Model.

longitudinal data. Figure 11.1 illustrates the variables and time points in-cluded in our analyses of each model. All analyses are correlational and are not based on an experimental design. Results from our analyses, therefore, are "tests" of each model only in the sense that they can provide data that are consistent or inconsistent with the proposed models. They cannot rule out alternative models. With regard to the reactive model, our specific hypotheses are that girls' symptoms at T1 and at T2 (1 year later) will be associated with interpersonal behaviors at T2 in the following ways: (a) symptoms will be significantly associated with girls' and mothers' conflict behaviors; (b) symptoms will be positively associated with girls' submission to mothers; (c) symptoms will be positively associated with girls' and mothers' misunderstanding of one another; and (d) symptoms will be negatively as-sociated with mothers' support.

Our hypotheses regarding the causal model are that interpersonal behav-iors at T2 will predict girls' symptoms at T3 (1 year later), after controlling for girls' symptom levels at T2. Specifically, we hypothesize that: (a) girls' and mothers' conflict will be associated with girls' symptoms; (b) girls' submission to mothers will be associated with increases in girls' symptoms; (c) girls' and mothers' misunderstanding of one another will be associated with increases in girls' symptoms; and (d) mothers' support will be associated with decreases in girls' symptoms.

In addition to the behaviors of conflict, submission, misunderstanding and support, we also examine the relation of humor and sarcasm to girls' depression. We propose no hypotheses regarding these behaviors, however, as they were not examined in previous studies of adolescent depression and family behaviors.[3]

OUTLINE OF ANALYTIC STRATEGY

Before testing our major hypotheses regarding the relation of mother–daughter behaviors to daughters' symptoms, it is useful to establish whether there are gender differences in adolescent symptoms in the population from which our family sample was drawn and, if so, whether the gender differences were maintained throughout the 3 years of data collection. Although the focus of our analyses of the relation of mother–daughter interactions to daughters' symptoms is on examining individual differences within girls rather than on examining gender differences, our findings regarding girls in this rural sample are less likely to be atypical if adolescents in this sample exhibit the gender differences in symptoms that are so well established in other samples. Thus, our first step was to examine the means of our symptom scale for gender differences. Gender differences in symptoms were examined in three nested samples: a large cross-sectional community sample, a longitudinal community subsample assessed at two time points, and a smaller subsample of intensively studied families of adolescents assessed at three time points.

Second, we used the intensive family subsample to test the hypotheses associated with the reactive model and causal models, using hierarchical regression analyses. Because of the number of regressions computed, we

---

[3]Dadds (Dadds et al., 1992), Sanders (Sanders et al., 1992), and their colleagues observed family behaviors of 14 depressed children and early adolescents (ages 7 to 14 years) in two different interaction sessions: a mother–child discussion of real-life conflicts, and family dinner conversations. Although they did not assess humor or sarcasm, they did assess family members' sad, angry, critical, and happy affect (Sanders et al., 1992) and family members' smiling and frowning behaviors (Dadds et al., 1992). Sanders et al. report that depressed children expressed more sad affect during the interaction session than did conduct-disordered children or nondiagnosed children. On the other hand, Dadds et al. report that depression was positively associated with family members' smiling and negatively associated with their frowning. Allen et al. (1994b) included hostility in their code for "inhibiting relatedness" and found that inhibiting relatedness was negatively associated with adolescent depressed affect. The only other study of adolescent depression and observed family interactions (Ge et al., 1994) did not report assessments of observed affect. At this point, the role of expressed affect in the family interactions of depressed adolescents is unclear.

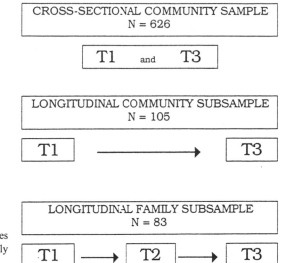

FIG. 11.2.   Three Nested Samples of the Rural Adolescent and Family Study.

discuss significance of the betas of individual variables only when the multiple R for a final equation showed significance ($p \leq .05$) or a strong trend toward significance ($p < .10$) (Cohen & Cohen, 1983). Finally, we discuss the relative importance of adolescents' vs. mothers' subjective interpretation of the meaning of the observed behaviors for each set of analyses.

METHODS

Participants

Figure 11.2 shows an overview of the design of our three nested samples.

Cross-Sectional Community Sample (N = 626).   The U.S. Census Bureau definition of rural (town population of 2,500 or less) was used to select nine northeastern rural towns for sampling. In 1991 and 1993, we administered questionnaire measures assessing dimensions of community life, social relationships, and individual differences in personality, attitudes, and mental health of adolescents to two cohorts of adolescents between the ages of 14 and 19 in all nine communities. As there were no substantive changes in the demographic, economic, or political life of the communities between the two administrations, data from the two cohorts were combined to form the "cross-sectional community sample."[4] The sample was primarily working class

---

[4]Data for the second wave of assessment were not included for subjects who were tested at both time points in order to maintain independence among cases.

and nearly all Caucasians of European descent and included over 95% of all the adolescents living in these nine towns at each administration. Both adolescents in high school and those who had dropped out of high school participated.

Longitudinal Community Sample (N = 105).   A subsample of participants from the first administration of the cross-sectional assessment also participated in the second administration 2 years later The cross-sectional community sample and the longitudinal community subsample are used in this chapter to examine prevalence and gender differences in adolescent symptoms in the rural community from which our longitudinal family subsample was drawn.

Longitudinal Family Sample (N = 83).   Data were collected from the family subsample at three time points, each a year apart. Complete data for the variables examined in this chapter were collected from 43 girls at Time 1 (T1) and Time 2 (T2) and from 35 girls at Time 3 (T3). When we compared data from families who participated at all three time points to families who did not participate at Time 3 on the variables of interest in this chapter, no significant differences were found. Families in this subsample participated in 6 hours of data collection in their homes and in our laboratory and were paid $165.

To examine whether families in this subsample differed from the families of adolescents in our larger cross-sectional community sample, we compared data from adolescents in the family subsample to data from adolescents in the first administration of the community survey on sociodemographic variables, family variables, and personality variables. Adolescents in the family subsample differed significantly from adolescents in the larger community sample in only one of 55 comparisons after a Bonferroni correction: Adolescents in the family subsample worked fewer hours in jobs outside school.

Measures

Assessment of Symptoms.   As noted, the term *depression* can signify a wide variety of constructs in the theoretical and empirical literature and is assessed by a correspondingly diverse array of methods. In studies of childhood and adolescence, researchers often study depressive symptoms as a subset of symptoms characterized more broadly as "internalizing." We chose to examine girls' internalizing in our investigation because it is the more inclusive construct in the adolescent literature, and the phenomena of dramatic increases in prevalence and the gender switch in adolescence hold true for this broader internalizing syndrome.

Internalizing symptoms were assessed for all adolescents at T1, T2, and T3 by the Youth Self Report form (YSR; Achenbach, 1991). The YSR is a 102-item checklist of behavioral symptoms of the adolescent in the past 6 months. The YSR identifies eight syndromes that make up two broadband syndromes of internalizing and externalizing symptoms. The broadband syndrome of internalizing consists of the three narrower syndromes of anxious/depressed, withdrawn, and somatic complaints. Achenbach (1991) reports extensive data on the YSR, including test–retest reliability and stability, criterion and discriminant validity, and normative data. Comparison of our rural cross-sectional community sample to Achenbach's (1991) nationally representative, normative sample of 1,315 adolescents indicates that both boys and girls in our rural community sample score higher than the national norm (see Table 11.1).

Assessment of Family Behaviors. Four discussion tasks were videotaped in the adolescent's home at T2: two discussions took place between the adolescent and mother and two discussions between the adolescent and father (Powers et al., 1994). These discussions were designed to elicit interactions that were pertinent to the developmental task of individuation. The first discussion involved negotiating ways of being close and maintaining relatedness. This task was modeled on the "plan a vacation" task of Grotevant and Cooper (Grotevant & Cooper, 1985). The second discussion task required negotiating areas of conflict. For this task, adolescents and their parents independently filled out a Topics Checklist (Prinz, Foster, Kent, & O'Leary, 1979), noting issues they had discussed in the past 4 weeks and rating the intensity of the discussion. Only issues that were designated by both the parent and adolescent were discussed. Mother–daughter interactions in the conflictual task are examined in this chapter because of the theoretical relevance of conflict negotiation for internalizing symptoms.

A primary goal of data collection with the family subsample was to assess both mothers' and adolescents' independent understanding of their dyadic interactions. We employed the video-mediated recall procedure, a method used primarily in research with married couples to assess spouses' subjective understanding of their behaviors (Gottman & Levenson, 1985; Levenson & Gottman, 1983, 1985; Margolin, 1987; Weiss, 1984), although it has been used with children and adolescents in three instances (Beaumont, 1996; Callan & Noller, 1986; Sanders et al., 1992). With this method, participants

TABLE 11.1
Mean Internalizing Scores For Boys and Girls in the Rural Community
Sample and National Norms

	Boys			Girls		
Sample	n	M	(SD)	n	M	(SD)
Rural Community Sample	273	11.9	(9.1)	312	17.9	(9.6)
National Norms (Achenbach, 1991)	637	10.5	(7.0)	678	12.9	(8.5)

in the study describe their understanding of their interpersonal behaviors while watching a videotape of their interaction session.

Support for this method as a valid assessment of participants' subjective understanding of behavior comes from evidence that depressed children and their mothers differ from conduct-disordered children and nondiagnosed children and their mothers in their ratings of their behaviors (Sanders et al., 1992), distressed and nondistressed couples differ in their ratings of their behaviors (Notarius, Benson, Sloane, Vanzetti, & Hornyak, 1989), couples' ratings are significantly associated with current and future marital satisfaction (Gottman & Levenson, 1985; Margolin, 1987; Markman, 1981; Weiss, 1984), and couples physiological responses (heart rate, pulse transmission time to the finger, skin conductance level, and general somatic activity) change at the same time points when viewing the videotape of the interaction as they did when they were in the original interaction (Gottman & Levenson, 1985).

Mothers and adolescents came to our university laboratory within a few days of participating in the original home interaction tasks to view the videotape of their interaction. We conducted three procedures to assess different dimensions of subjective understanding: semi-structured interviews, rating scales, and manipulation of a computer joystick indicating continuous positive–negative affect (Powers et al., 1994). In each procedure, investigators asked subjects to give information about their experience in the original interaction and not about their experience of watching themselves on video-tape. Results from the rating scale procedure are presented in this chapter.

Mothers and adolescents used six Likert-type rating scales to describe their understanding of the purpose or intent of behaviors in the conflict negotiation discussion. The challenge in using the video-mediated recall method with adolescents and their parents was to develop rating procedures that allowed participants to convey significant aspects of their understanding of their behaviors without becoming tired or confused. Adolescents and mothers had to be able to understand the ratings and the rating procedure with minimal instructions, learning the procedure with only a 2-minute training session. The number of ratings had to be limited so that the entire procedure was not too time-consuming. In the first viewing, adolescents and mothers rated the extent to which their own behaviors were supportive, conflictual, humorous, submissive (giving in), and sarcastic. After each 15-second portion, a computer paused the tape for 15 seconds, and participants completed the rating scales, considering the full 15-second segment of the discussion. Subjects rated 32 such segments, for a total of 8 minutes of interaction. Subsequently, the mothers and adolescents again viewed the same 8-minute portion of videotape and repeated the procedure, this time rating the extent to which the behaviors of the family member with whom they were interacting indicated support, conflict, humor, submission, and misunderstanding. Adolescents' and mothers' ratings for themselves and for

TABLE 11.2
Intercorrelations Among Self-Ratings of Behaviors ($N = 48$)

Behavior	1	2	3	4	5
1. Support	—	−.04	.26	.10	−.03
2. Conflict	−.17	—	.25	.29*	.53**
3. Submission	−.11	.72**	—	.20	.33*
4. Humor	.06	.33*	.43**	—	.50***
5. Sarcasm	−.23	.55***	.52***	.50***	—

Note: Correlations for daughters' ratings are above the diagonal and correlations for mothers' ratings are below the diagonal.
  ***$p \leq .001$ **$p \leq .01$ *$p \leq .05$

each other were separately aggregated into a total score for each behavior. Table 11.2 shows the correlation matrix of self-ratings for each of these behaviors for mothers and daughters. For both mothers and daughters, the behaviors that are significantly correlated are conflict, humor, sarcasm, and submission. Humor and support are very weakly related. This gives some indication that conflict is negotiated through sarcasm and humor for mothers and daughters in our sample. Table 11.3 shows the correlations for mothers' and daughters' ratings, indicating the degree of similarity in mothers' and daughters' ratings. Submissive behaviors are the behaviors that are perceived most differently by mothers and daughters.

RESULTS

Gender Differences in Internalizing

Significant gender differences were found in the cross-sectional community sample, $t(583) = -7.79$, $p < .001$ (means for boys and girls were previously

TABLE 11.3
Correlations Between Mothers' and Daughters'
Ratings of Behaviors ($N = 48$)

Behavior	Mothers' Behaviors	Daughters' Behaviors
Support	.56***	.66***
Conflict	.34*	.48***
Submission	.13	.31*
Humor	.48***	.52***

Note: Sarcasm was only rated for the self, and misunderstanding was only rated for the interaction partner.
  ***$p \leq .001$
  **$p \leq .01$
  *$p \leq .05$

TABLE 11.4
Mean Internalizing Scores for Boys and Girls in the
Longitudinal Community and Family Subsamples

Sample	Time 1			Time 2			Time 3		
	n	M	(SD)	n	M	(SD)	n	M	(SD)
Longitudinal Community									
Boys	40	10.35	(8.18)	—		—	36	9.22	(6.28)
Girls	61	18.12	(10.46)	—		—	61	16.31	(9.04)
Longitudinal Family									
Boys	28	11.43	(8.96)	26	12.39	(8.19)	15	9.47	(8.00)
Girls	43	17.42	(10.83)	44	17.84	(8.42)	35	14.20	(9.52)

shown in Table 11.1) and at both time points assessed (T1 and T3) in the longitudinal community subsample, [T1: $t(99) = -3.97$, $p < .001$; T3: $t(95) = -4.54$, $p < .001$; see Table 11.4 for means]. We examined gender differences at all three time points within the smaller family subsample (see Table 11.4). At T1, girls had higher levels of internalizing than boys, $t(69) = -2.43$, $p < .02$. One year later, at T2, girls continued to show higher levels of internalizing, $t(68) = -2.65$, $p < .01$. At T3, the internalizing scores of both boys and girls had lowered and the gender difference had narrowed, $t(48) = -1.68$, $p < .10$.

The Reactive Model: Family Behaviors as Reactions to Internalizing Symptoms

Girls Behaviors as Expressions of Internalizing Symptoms. To test our hypothesis that daughters' symptoms are expressed behaviorally, we conducted hierarchical regression equations in three steps. In the first step, we regressed girls' or mothers' subjective understanding of the behaviors of girls on linear terms for T1 and T2 symptoms. Including both time points allowed us to distinguish the long-term association of prior symptoms to behavior (controlling for concurrent symptoms) from the immediate association of concurrent symptoms to behavior (controlling for prior symptoms). In a second step, we forced the quadratic terms for T1 and T2 symptoms into the equation in a block, allowing us to examine whether symptoms were associated with behaviors in a curvilinear fashion. If the quadratic terms did not explain a significant amount of variance beyond the linear terms, we did not include them in the final equations. A third step was included for every equation in which the quadratic terms of the second step were not significant. In this third step, we forced in a term for the interaction between T1 and T2 symptoms. This allowed us to examine whether T1 symptoms moderate the relation of T2 symptoms to behaviors. Again, if the interaction terms did not explain a significant amount of variance beyond the linear terms, they are not included in the table reporting the final equations All initial terms were centered before entering either quadratic or interaction terms to eliminate multicollinearity problems (Jaccard, Turrisi, & Wan, 1990).[5]

These regressions allowed us to test our general hypothesis that girls' internalizing symptoms would predict their negotiation behavior, as well as test our three hypotheses regarding specific types of behaviors: (a) Girls' internalizing at T1 and T2 will be associated their conflict behavior at T2; (b) Girls' internalizing at T1 and T2 will be positively associated with girls' submission to mothers at T2; and (c) Girls' internalizing at T1 and T2 will be positively associated with girls' misunderstanding of their mothers at T2.

As shown in Table 11.5, girls' internalizing significantly predicted four of the six behavior categories: conflict, submission, misunderstanding, and humor. The equations for girls' humor and misunderstanding contained significant quadratic terms (mothers' ratings: β for humor = .56; β for misunderstanding = .34), signifying curvilinear relations between internalizing and these behaviors. Scatterplots showed that girls with either very low or very high levels of internalizing were perceived by their mothers as using more humor and also misunderstanding their mothers more. The interaction term was significant for conflict (girls' rating: β = .32) and submission (girls' rating: β = .31), showing that T1 symptoms moderate the relation of T2 symptoms to girls' conflictual and submissive behaviors. To clarify the interpretation of these interactions, we divided the girls into two groups: those scoring above the mean on T1 symptoms and those scoring below the mean on T1 symptoms. Correlations between T2 symptoms and each category of girls' behavior were then obtained for each of the two groups of girls (see Table 11.6). These correlations indicate that for girls with high levels of T1 symptoms, T2 symptoms strongly and positively predict girls' conflict and submission, whereas the prediction is less strong if girls had low levels of symptoms at T1.

Consideration of the differences in mothers' and daughters' subjective understanding of their behaviors adds another dimension to our findings. Strikingly, daughters' symptoms are associated in very different ways to their own understanding of their behaviors than to mothers' understanding of the daughters' behaviors. A daughter's chronic level of internalizing (high levels at both T1 and T2) predicts her understanding of herself as both more conflictual and more submissive toward her mother: a discomforting scenario for successfully dealing with the developmental task of negotiating differences. In contrast, the mother's perception of the chronically internalizing

---

[5]We allowed quadratic terms entry into the equations before interaction terms because of the assumption that quadratic terms are a more parsimonious explanation of the data (Darlington, 1990). All results of nonsignificant quadratic and interaction terms and equations may be obtained from the first author on request.

TABLE 11.5

Summary of Hierarchical Regression Analyses for Variables Predicting Girls' Interpersonal Behaviors

Daughters' Symptoms	Support	Conflict	Submission	Humor	Sarcasm	Misunderstanding
			Adolescent Rating			
			(βs shown for Final Step in Equations)			
Prior (Linear)	.08	.12	.24^t	.21	.06	—
Concurrent (Linear)	.07	.22	.28^t	.03	.15	—
Prior (Quadratic)	—	—	—	—	—	—
Concurrent (Quadratic)	—	—	—	—	—	—
Interaction term	—	.32*	.31*	.29^t	—	—
Final Step: ΔR^2	.01	.10	.09	.08	.02	—
Final Step: ΔF	.18	4.31*	4.49*	3.32^t	.74	—
Final Multiple R	.12	.45*	.55**	.38	.17	—
Final R^2	.02	.20	.30	.15	.03	—
			Mother Rating			
Prior (Linear)	-.11	-.26	.06	-.14	—	.07
Concurrent (Linear)	.02	.07	-.06	-.05	—	-.23
Prior (Quadratic)	—	—	—	.26	—	-.20
Concurrent (Quadratic)	—	—	—	.56***	—	.34*
Interaction term	—	—	—	—	—	—
Final Step: ΔR^2	.00	.01	.00	.36	—	.12
Final Step: ΔF	.01	.20	.15	9.55***	—	2.36^t
Final Multiple R	.11	.26	.08	.61**	—	.38
Final R^2	.01	.07	.01	.37	—	.14

Note: ***$p \leq .001$ **$p \leq .01$ *$p \leq .05$ $^t p \leq .10$

TABLE 11.6
Correlations of Girls' T2 Symptoms with Girls' T2 Behaviors for Two
Groups: High T1 Symptoms and Low T1 Symptoms

Girls' Behaviors	T1 Symptom Groups	
Self-Ratings	High Group	Low Group
Conflict	.65**	.13
Submission	.50*	.27

Note: **p < .01
*p < .05

daughter is as more humorous, although somewhat more misunderstanding of the mother. These are seemingly very different views of how a girl's internalizing is related to her behavior. From the daughter's point of view, negotiation of autonomy appears difficult. From the mother's point of view, this may be a fairly comfortable scenario for dealing with differences.

Mothers' Behaviors as Reactions to Daughters' Internalizing Symptoms. Thus far, our findings speak to how adolescent girls' internalizing predicts their interpersonal behaviors. To test our hypotheses that mothers also react behaviorally to daughters' internalizing symptoms, we conducted hierarchical regression equations in three steps, as in the prior analyses. Our three hypotheses were: (a) Daughters' internalizing at T1 and T2 will be associated with mothers' conflict behavior at T2; (b) Daughters' internalizing at T1 and T2 will be positively associated with mothers' misunderstanding of their daughters' at T2; and (c) Daughters' Internalizing at T1 and T2 will be negatively associated with mothers' support of daughters at T2.

As shown in Table 11.7, results substantiate our general hypothesis that girls' internalizing predicts their mothers' behavior. Internalizing predicted four of the six behavior categories of mothers: conflict, humor, sarcasm, and misunderstanding. In three of the four significant equations (conflict, humor, and sarcasm) the quadratic term for concurrent symptoms was significant, indicating that daughters' T2 symptoms (controlling for her T1 symptoms) were related to mothers' behaviors in a curvilinear manner (mothers' ratings: β for conflict = .47; β for humor = .48; β for sarcasm = .41). This partially confirmed our hypothesis regarding mothers' conflictual behaviors. Scatterplots reveal that high levels of daughters' T2 symptoms predicted higher levels of mothers' conflict, but, interestingly, low levels of daughters' T2 symptoms also predicted higher levels of mothers' conflict.

Besides these quadratic effects, one interaction term was significant, showing that T1 symptoms moderate the relation of T2 symptoms to mothers' misunderstanding of their daughters (girls' rating: β = .46). The correlation between T2 internalizing symptoms and mothers' misunderstanding for girls

TABLE 11.7

Summary of Hierarchical Regression Analyses for Variables Predicting Mothers' Interpersonal Behaviors

Daughters' Symptoms	Support	Conflict	Submission	Humor	Sarcasm	Misunderstanding
			Adolescent Rating			
			(βs shown for Final Step in Equations)			
Prior (Linear)	.03	.06	.24	.10	—	.16
Concurrent (Linear)	.05	.12	.09	-.04	—	-.06
Prior (Quadratic)	—	—	—	—	—	—
Concurrent (Quadratic)	—	—	—	—	—	—
Interaction term	—	—	—	—	—	.46**
Final Step: ΔR^2	.00	.01	.01	.00	—	.21
Final Step: ΔF	.08	.49	.28	.05	—	9.67**
Final Multiple R	.06	.14	.28	.10	—	.50*
Final R^2	.00	.02	.08	.01	—	.25
			Mother Rating			
Prior (Linear)	-.14	-.29	-.05	-.04	-.16	—
Concurrent (Linear)	.09	-.01	-.12	-.04	-.14	—
Prior (Quadratic)	—	.01	—	.18	.11	—
Concurrent (Quadratic)	—	.48**	—	.49**	.42*	—
Interaction term	—	—	—	—	—	—
Final Step: ΔR^2	.01	.21	.02	.25	.17	—
Final Step: ΔF	.29	4.73*	.55	5.86**	3.56*	—
Final Multiple R	.15	.51*	.14	.52*	.42	—
Final R^2	.02	.26	.02	.27	.18	—

Note: ***$p \leq .001$ **$p \leq .01$ *$p \leq .05$ ᵗ$p \leq .10$

whose T1 internalizing was high was .59 and for girls whose T1 internalizing was low was −.29. Therefore, prior internalizing moderates the relation between a girl's current symptoms and her mother's misunderstanding of her in the following manner: if a girl has shown early internalizing, her subsequent internalizing predicts a higher level of misunderstanding by her mother. If a girl has shown no early signs of internalizing, then new signs of internalizing predict lower levels of misunderstanding by her mother. In other words, chronically internalizing girls are more likely to be misunderstood, whereas girls with a recent onset of symptoms are less likely to be misunderstood.

With subjective understanding, it is most often mothers' perceptions of their own behaviors (rather than daughters' perceptions of their mothers) that are predicted by daughters' symptoms. Daughters' internalizing positively predicted mothers' subjective understanding of their own conflict, humor, and sarcasm. In contrast, only one category of daughters' perceptions of mothers' behaviors (misunderstanding) is predicted by daughters' symptoms.

The Causal Model: Family Behaviors as Causes of Internalizing Symptoms

The causal model suggests that interpersonal behaviors indicative of difficulties in the negotiation of autonomy contribute to increases in girls' internalizing symptoms. To test our hypotheses that daughters' and mothers' behaviors predict changes in daughters' symptoms, we again conducted hierarchical regression equations with three steps. In the first step, we regressed girls' T3 symptoms on the linear terms for their T2 symptoms and girls' or mothers' perceptions of their behaviors. (Including T2 symptoms in the equation allowed us to determine the unique contribution of behavior to predicting T3 symptoms.) In a second step, we forced the quadratic terms for girls' or mothers' behaviors into the equation. This step allowed us to examine whether behaviors were associated with change in symptoms in a curvilinear fashion. As in earlier analyses, if the quadratic term did not explain a significant amount of variance beyond the linear terms, we did not report it in the table of the final significant equations. The third step was included for every equation in which the quadratic term of the second step was not significant. In this third step, we forced in a term for the interaction between T2 symptoms and girls' or mothers' behaviors. Again, if the interaction term did not explain a significant amount of variance beyond the linear terms, we did not include it in the table reporting the final equations. As in previous analyses, all initial terms were centered before entering either quadratic or interaction terms (Jaccard et al., 1990).

With these regressions, we tested our general hypothesis that girls' behaviors would predict changes in their internalizing symptoms. Our hypotheses regarding specific behaviors were: (a) girls' conflictual behaviors at T2 will be associated with girls' T3 internalizing, controlling for T2 internalizing; (b) girls' submissive behaviors at T2 will be positively associated with girls' T3 internalizing, controlling for T2 internalizing; and (c) girls' misunderstanding of their mothers at T2 will be positively associated with girls' T3 internalizing, controlling for T2 internalizing.

Girls' Behavior as Causes of Internalizing Symptoms. As shown in Table 11.8, the results confirm our general hypothesis that girls' behaviors at T2 explain a significant amount of variance in symptoms at T3, above and beyond the variance explained by symptoms at T2. Four of the six behavior categories significantly predicted future internalizing: conflict, submission, humor, and sarcasm. Two of our three hypotheses regarding the specific behaviors of conflict, submission, and misunderstanding were confirmed. First, girls' conflictual behaviors did predict their T3 internalizing symptoms, and this relation was moderated by the level of internalizing at T2 (i.e., the interaction term was significant). Indeed, girls' T2 symptoms moderated the relation of girls' perceptions of themselves as conflictual, humorous, and sarcastic to their T3 symptoms (β for conflict = .42; β for humor = .54; β for sarcasm = .48). To interpret these interaction effects, we obtained correlations between girls' behaviors and T3 symptoms for girls who were above the mean on T2 internalizing (High Group) and girls who were below the mean on T2 internalizing (Low Group; see Table 11.9). T2 symptoms moderate the relation between girls' behaviors and their T3 symptoms in the following manner: When girls who were already experiencing high levels of internalizing negotiate interpersonal differences with high levels of conflict, humor, and sarcasm, it predicts future internalizing. In contrast, for girls who had few T2 symptoms, the negotiation of interpersonal differences with high levels of conflict, humor, and sarcasm negatively predict T3 symptoms.

Second, as expected, the girls' ratings of their own submissive behaviors predicted their T3 symptoms, over and above the effect of T2 symptoms. Together, T2 symptoms and submissive behavior explained 47% of the variance in girls' T3 symptoms. It appears that a combination of high conflict and high submission is a risky one for girls. We saw from the results from the reactive model that this interpersonal pattern may be a response to internalizing, but it appears from the causal model analyses that this behavioral response then carries its own risk for future internalizing, over and above the risk of prior symptoms.

Third, our hypothesis that girls' misunderstanding of their mothers would predict increases in internalizing was not confirmed.

Reviewing the role of subjective understanding, we note that it is most often girls' perceptions of their own behaviors (rather than mothers' perceptions) that predict girls' future symptoms. Girls' subjective understanding of

TABLE 11.8
Summary of Hierarchical Regression Analyses for Girls' T2 Symptoms and Girls' T2 Behaviors Predicting Girls' T3 Symptoms

Type of T2 Behavior in Equation	T2 Symptom	T2 Behavior (Linear)	T2 Behavior (Curvilinear)	T2 Symptom/ T2 Behavior Interaction	ΔR^2 Final Step	ΔF Final Step	Multiple R Final Step	R^2 Final Step
			Adolescent Rating					
			(βs shown for Final Step in Equations)					
Girls'								
Support	.45**	.07	—	—	.01	.18	.46*	.21
Conflict	.52**	.24	—	.42**	.15	7.07**	.61**	.37
Submission	.28^t	.54***	—	—	.26	14.79***	.69****	.47
Humor	.36*	.04	—	.54***	.29	16.68***	.71****	.50
Sarcasm	.40**	.10	—	.48**	.23	12.34**	.67***	.45
			Mother Rating					
Girls'								
Support	.46**	-.15	—	—	.02	.84	.48*	.23
Conflict	.45**	-.15	—	—	.02	.88	.48*	.23
Submission	.45**	-.04	—	—	.00	.04	.46*	.21
Humor	.47**	-.38*	—	—	.14	6.61*	.59**	.35
Misunderstanding	.46**	-.00	—	—	.00	.00	.46*	.21

Note: ****$p \le .0001$ ***$p \le .001$ **$p \le .01$ *$p \le .05$ $^t p \le .10$

TABLE 11.9
Correlations of Girls' T2 Behavior With Girls' T3 Symptoms in Two
Groups: High T2 Symptoms and Low T2 Symptoms

Girls' Behavior	Groups	
Self-Ratings	High T2 Symptoms	Low T2 Symptoms
Conflict	.24	−.19
Humor	.30	−.25
Sarcasm	.37	−.26

four out of five categories of their behavior positively predicted their T3 symptoms. In contrast, mothers' perceptions of only one category of their daughters' behaviors (humor) predicted their daughters' future symptoms. Mothers' perceptions of their daughters' humorous behaviors were negatively predictive of the daughters' T3 symptoms.

Mothers' Behavior as Causes of Internalizing Symptoms. As shown in Table 11.10, results indicate that mothers' behaviors at T2 do predict their daughters' symptoms at T3. Three of the six maternal behavior categories significantly predicted daughters' future symptoms (controlling for prior daughters' symptoms): conflict, humor, and sarcasm. Two additional categories, misunderstanding of daughter and submission to daughter, showed a trend toward predicting daughters' future symptoms. All of these effects were above the ability of daughters' T2 symptoms to predict their T3 symptoms. In all equations, T2 symptoms significantly predicted T3 symptoms.

Our specific hypothesis regarding conflict was confirmed. The quadratic term for mothers' conflict was significant (mothers' rating: $\beta = .51$), as well as for humor (girls' rating: $\beta = .63$ and sarcasm (mothers' rating: $\beta = .93$), indicating that these behaviors were related to daughters' T3 symptoms (controlling for T2 symptoms) in a curvilinear manner. Scatterplots of the relation between mothers' behaviors and daughters' T3 symptoms reveal that higher levels of daughters' symptoms were predicted when mothers' conflict, humor, and sarcasm were either too high or too low. These behaviors explained an additional 11% to 21% of variance in T3 internalizing scores, beyond the amount explained by T2 internalizing scores.

Our hypothesis regarding mothers' misunderstanding received weak support: A linear trend was found for girls' rating of their mothers' misunderstanding to positively predict girls' T3 symptoms ($\beta = .27$; controlling T2 symptoms). Our hypothesis regarding the negative association of mothers' support to daughters' internalizing was not confirmed.

Although no hypotheses were made regarding mothers' submissive behavior with their daughters, we did analyze the relation of this behavior to changes in daughters' internalizing. We found that, for both daughters' and mothers' ratings of mothers' submission, girls' T2 symptoms moderated the

TABLE 11.10
Summary of Hierarchical Regression Analyses for Girls' T2 Symptoms and Mothers' T2 Behaviors Predicting Girls' T3 Symptoms

Type of T2 Behavior in Equation	T2 Symptom	T2 Behavior (Linear)	T2 Behavior (Curvilinear)	T2 Symptom × T2 Behavior Interaction	ΔR^2 Final Step	ΔF Final Step	Multiple R Final Step	R^2 Final Step
			Adolescent Rating					
			(βs shown for Final Step in Equations)					
Mothers'								
Support	.42**	.20	—	—	.04	1.57	.50**	.25
Conflict	.46**	.04	—	—	.00	.07	.46*	.21
Submission	.43**	.24^t	—	.40**	.16	8.13**	.65***	.44
Humor	.39*	-.56*	.63*	—	.13	5.45*	.58**	.33
Misunderstanding	.46**	.27^t	—	—	.07	2.95^t	.53**	.28
			Mother Rating					
Mothers'								
Support	.47*	-.10	—	—	.01	.38	.47*	.22
Conflict	.36**	-.46^t	.51*	—	.11	4.48**	.56**	.32
Submission	.44**	.01	—	.27^t	.07	2.91^t	.53*	.28
Humor	.44**	-.46**	—	—	.21	11.04**	.67***	.42
Sarcasm	.35*	-.88**	.93**	—	.21	10.63**	.65***	.43

Note: ***$p \leq .001$ **$p \leq .01$ *$p \leq .05$ $^t p \leq .10$

relation of mothers' submission to girls' T3 symptoms (daughters' rating: β = .40; mothers' rating: β = .27). For daughters with high levels of T2 symptoms, the correlations between mothers' submission and daughters' T3 symptoms were .48 (daughters' ratings) and .15 (mothers' ratings). The correlations for daughters with low levels of T2 symptoms were −.11 (daughters' ratings) and −.42 (mothers' ratings). This pattern of correlations indicates that for girls who were experiencing high levels of internalizing at T2, mothers' submission to these girls predicts increases in girls' internalizing at T3 (particularly if it was daughters' perception that the mother was submissive). For girls who had low levels of symptoms at T2, mothers' submission predicted decreases in girls' symptoms at T3.

Reviewing the role of subjective understanding, we note that *both* girls' and mothers' perceptions of mothers' behaviors were important predictors of girls' future symptoms. Girls' perceptions of three of their mothers' behaviors (submission, humor, and misunderstanding) and mothers' perceptions of four of their own behaviors (conflict, submission, humor, and sarcasm) predicted girls' future symptoms at significant or trend levels.[6]

DISCUSSION

Current theories seeking to explain the increased prevalence of depression for girls emphasize the role of sociocultural factors (such as gender roles, gender stereotypes, socialization practices, and norms for social relationships) that place girls at particular risk during adolescence. Very few studies examine the relation of girls' actual social interactions to symptoms in adolescence, and none investigate both reactive and causal models of this relation with longitudinal data. The purpose of our study was to examine these models with respect to clarifying the relation of mother–daughter interactions to daughters' internalizing symptoms. We examined both mothers' and daughters' perceptions of their observed interpersonal behaviors. The types of behavior we investigated were indicative of difficulties with one of the primary developmental tasks of adolescence, the negotiation of autonomy. Our major hypotheses were that: (a) daughters and mothers would exhibit interpersonal behaviors that indicated difficulties in negotiating autonomy as reactions to daughters' internalizing symptoms (the reactive model), and (b) these interpersonal behaviors, in turn, would predict increases in daughters' internalizing symptoms 1 year later (the causal model). These general hy-

---

[6]A strong negative linear relation between mothers' own rating of their humor to daughters' T3 symptoms was found, in contrast to the curvilinear relation of mothers' own ratings of her conflict and sarcasm and daughters' ratings of mothers' humor (β = −.46). Mothers' perception of themselves as less humorous predicted increases in their daughters' symptoms.

potheses were confirmed. Findings regarding our more specific hypotheses of the relation of girls' internalizing to specific behaviors are discussed next.

CONFLICT AND SUBMISSION

The Reactive Model

Girls' Behaviors. Girls' internalizing symptoms positively predicted girls' perceptions of their conflictual and submissive behaviors, with chronically high levels of symptoms most strongly predictive of these behaviors. This pattern of results suggests that girls react to chronic internalizing symptoms with high levels of both conflict and submission, a behavioral combination unlikely to be successful in negotiating more autonomous relations with their mothers. We label this combination of behaviors as "agitated submission." Agitated submission may be the behavioral expression of socialization practices that have encouraged girls to be less assertive and aggressive (Block, 1983; Eron, 1980; Gjerde & Block, 1991; Radloff, 1980; Radloff & Rae, 1979) and more passive in coping and problem solving (Gore, Aseltine, & Colten, 1993; Nolen-Hoeksema, 1987). Girls may encounter particular difficulties in trying to abide by these socialized norms when undertaking the essential developmental tasks of adolescence—tasks that require active negotiation on behalf of the self. Sheldon (1992) showed that when negotiating conflict, female children have a tendency to be less direct and are more likely to be oriented to the other's agenda as well as to their own agendas. Our results suggest that girls with chronically higher levels of internalizing symptoms exhibit more vacillation between conflictual and submissive behaviors in a negotiation situation. These results are consistent with results from observational studies of adults that show that depressed women are more submissive in disagreements with their husbands (Merikangas, Ranelli, & Kupfer, 1979) and are more likely to be dominated by their husbands in decision making (Hoover & Fitzgerald, 1981).

These findings regarding daughters' ratings of their own behaviors contrast with findings using mothers' perceptions of their daughters' behaviors. A curvilinear pattern of association revealed that girls' very low and very high levels of concurrent symptoms predicted mothers' perceptions that their daughters were more humorous and somewhat more misunderstanding of their mothers. Apparently, the behaviors that internalizing daughters use to negotiate difficult issues with their mothers are interpreted differently by these daughters and their mothers. Internalizing daughters see themselves as engaging in conflict but also giving in to their mothers. Mothers of these daughters do not interpret their daughters' behaviors as conflict or as submission, but instead as humorous. Such different interpretations of internalizing girls' behaviors may make it less likely that mothers can identify their daughters' difficulties with negotiating autonomy or their daughters' behavioral signs of internalizing. The perception that one's daughter is dealing with interpersonal differences with humor is not likely to be interpreted by mothers as a sign of risk for their daughters. It may well signal risk, however, if the daughters' perception is that she handles interpersonal differences with high levels of conflict and submission.

Mothers' Behaviors.   Daughters' internalizing was associated in a curvilinear manner to mothers' conflict (as well as to mothers' humor and sarcasm), indicating that daughters' very low and very high levels of symptoms predicted these maternal behaviors. Mothers' conflictual, humorous, and sarcastic behaviors were highly correlated, suggesting that mothers in our sample tend to negotiate conflict with humor and sarcasm. Higher levels of conflict combined with humor and sarcasm might be mothers' response to their nonsymptomatic daughters' developing autonomy, evidenced in the finding that nonsymptomatic girls show fewer submissive behaviors to their mothers. This may be a developmentally necessary and appropriate interchange with a daughter who is negotiating her autonomy with less submissiveness. These daughters apparently use humor to interact with their conflictual, humorous, and sarcastic mothers and do not feel the need to be highly conflictual in return. Mothers of symptomatic daughters also interact using high levels of conflict, humor, and sarcasm, but in this case chronically symptomatic girls seem to be overpowered and submit. Mothers may have trouble recognizing and responding to their daughters' difficulty maintaining and defending a point of view. This difficulty recognizing daughters' ineffectiveness may very well be facilitated by societal messages that lead some mothers to accept the submissive behaviors of their adolescent daughters as natural.

The Causal Model

Girls' Behaviors.   Girls that perceive themselves as exhibiting high levels of submission to their mothers are at risk for increased internalizing 1 year later. In addition, the initial level of girls' internalizing moderates the relation of her perceived conflictual (as well as humorous and sarcastic) behaviors to her subsequent internalizing. That is, if a girl is already experiencing internalizing symptoms (and, therefore, sees herself as submissive), she is at risk for increased internalizing in the future if she also experiences herself as showing higher levels of conflict, humor, and sarcasm with her mother. We saw with the reactive model that the combination of high conflict and high submission (agitated submission) may be a response to internalizing, but it appears from our results with the causal model that this behavioral combination then carries its own risk for future internalizing, over and above the risk of prior symptoms.

Mothers' Behaviors. Mothers' conflict, humor, and sarcasm were related in a curvilinear fashion to daughters' future symptoms, indicating that daughters' symptoms were predicted when mothers' conflict, humor, and sarcasm were either too low or too high. These results support the notion that it is developmentally important for mothers of adolescent girls to be able to tolerate a moderate degree of conflict.

The relation of both girls' and mothers' perceptions of mothers' submission to girls' future symptoms was moderated by girls' prior symptoms. If the daughter was symptomatic at the time of the interaction session and the mother exhibited submissive behaviors to her daughter, then higher levels of daughters' internalizing were predicted in the future. If the daughter was not symptomatic at the time of the interaction and the mother exhibited submissive behaviors to her daughter, then lower levels of daughters' internalizing were predicted in the future. This finding is consistent with Hops and Biglans' (Biglan et al., 1985; Biglan et al., 1989; Hops et al., 1987) conclusion, based on observations of interaction in marital couples with a depressed member, that if depressive behaviors inhibit the assertive behaviors of others, the depressive behaviors are reinforced and maintained. It is possible that when mothers submit to their highly internalizing daughters, this reinforces the daughters' depressive behavioral patterns and maintains her internalizing symptoms. In contrast, mothers' responding to the more autonomous, self-efficatious behaviors of nonsymptomatic girls by submitting is rewarding to the girl, reinforces these behaviors, and lessens the girls' risk of developing internalizing symptoms in the future.

The role of humor and sarcasm in the interactions of persons with depressive or internalizing symptoms was unclear in previous work (Dadds et al., 1992; Sanders et al., 1992), but our findings suggest that for girls and their mothers, humor and sarcasm are closely linked to conflictual behaviors. These females may negotiate conflict in this way to "soften the blow" of their conflictual behaviors.

MISUNDERSTANDING

In analyses of the reactive model, daughters' symptoms predicted both mothers' and daughters' perceptions of the other as misunderstanding. These results are consistent with our findings that when daughters have higher levels of internalizing symptoms, mothers' and daughters' view their interactions quite differently. Differences in subjective understanding of interpersonal behaviors may result in misunderstanding. Misunderstanding was only weakly related, however, to daughters' internalizing in analyses of the causal model.

SUPPORT

Contrary to our hypothesis, mothers' supportive behaviors were not associated with their daughters' symptoms in either the reactive model or the causal model. This is consistent with Dadds' observational research (Dadds et al., 1992) that showed that positive family behaviors do not differentiate depressed samples from nondepressed samples as well as aversive family behaviors. Studies that assess family support, closeness, and cohesion using questionnaire methods, however, found that these variables were protective against depressive symptoms (Feldman, Rubenstein, & Rubin, 1988; Garrison, Jackson, Marsteller, McKeown, & Addy, 1990; Gore et al., 1993). We believe that substantial differences in the way support is assessed in questionnaire studies and observational studies contribute to the discrepancies in findings regarding the role of parental support in child and adolescent depression. Support was assessed as a global concept in questionnaire studies that found a significant relation between support and depressive symptoms In contrast, Dadds et al. (1992) assessed specific positive behaviors within 20-second intervals, and we asked mothers and daughters to rate the extent to which their interactions were supportive within 15-second intervals. It is possible that support is too general a construct to be accurately assessed in such minute periods of time and linked to specific, discrete behaviors.[7] Our rating procedure seemed to be effective for other constructs that are more easily linked to specific behaviors, such as conflict, humor, and submission.

SUBJECTIVE UNDERSTANDING

In this study, mothers' and daughters' viewed their interactions on videotape and rated their understanding of the meaning of their behaviors. Mothers' and daughters' interpretations of their behaviors were related in very different ways to daughters' symptoms. Daughters' internalizing both predicted and is predicted by the daughters' view of herself as conflictual and submissive. In contrast, daughters' internalizing predicted and is predicted by the mothers' perception of the daughters' humor. Our findings support previous research that showed that discrepancies between depressed patients' perceptions of the family environment and those of other family members can be an important indicator of problems, such as increased suicide attempts (Keitner, Miller, & Furrzetti, 1987).

Family members' subjective understanding of their behaviors are informed by the interpersonal history of their relationships with one another. Obtaining

---

[7]The one observational study that did find a significant association between parental support and adolescent depression (Ge et al., 1994) assessed support with a global rating of the amount of warmth and support during an entire interaction session and then averaged scores across several years.

these informed perceptions helps us identify links between interpersonal behaviors and symptoms that might be invisible if we rely only on outside observers' interpretations of family behaviors (Kowalik & Gotlib, 1987). These informed perceptions may be particularly important for investigation of the interpersonal behaviors associated with girls' internalizing if, as Gjerde and Block (1991) suggested, girls' internalizing symptoms are "less straightforwardly recognizable to others via behavior" than are boys' symptoms.

Our findings suggest that mothers of internalizing daughters may not be able to perceive their daughters' struggle with issues of interpersonal power and autonomy. If mothers do not sense their daughters' difficulties, it is unlikely that mothers will feel the need to help their daughters develop more successful interpersonal negotiation strategies or sense their daughters' vulnerability to increased symptoms of internalization.

LIMITATIONS

Generalizability

Sample. This study is based on a European-American, working class, rural sample, which, although extending the literature to this understudied population, nevertheless limits the generalizability of these findings to other groups of adolescents. Additionally, this study focused on examining individual differences in mother–daughter interpersonal behaviors and how girls' internalizing symptoms were associated with these differences. Associations of father–daughter, mother–son, and father–son behavior patterns to adolescent symptoms are also clearly important (Ge, Conger, Lorenz, Shanahan, & Elder, 1995), but are expected to be different because socialization norms for behavior differ. In ongoing analyses, we are examining mother–son and father–adolescent interpersonal behaviors and the relation of these behaviors to adolescent internalizing. We focus on the mother–daughter relationship for this chapter because prior research most often showed significant associations between depression and aspects of the relationship with the mother (Allen et al., 1994b; Ge et al., 1994), most adolescents in our sample spent considerably more time with their mothers, and mothers in our sample had the primary responsibility for childcare in the family.

Raters of Behavior. Assessing the subjective understanding of participants regarding their interpersonal behaviors was an important aspect of this study and allowed us to note that mothers' and daughters' interpretations of their behaviors had different implications for the daughters' symptoms. This emphasis on subjective understanding, however, precluded presenting analyses of observers' ratings of participants' behaviors. By stressing that family members' subjective understanding of their behaviors may play an important role in fully understanding the impact of those behaviors on adolescent internalizing, we do not want to suggest that the standardized meanings that observers from outside the family ascribe to family behaviors are unimportant. Our project also included observers' ratings of families (Welsh, Vickerman, & Powers, 1997). Cognitive theories of depression clearly assert that depressed mood makes negative thoughts more accessible and salient and thereby leads to more negative interpretations of events (Abramson, Seligman & Teasdale, 1978). Evidence from numerous research studies supports this view (Forgas & Bower, 1987; Forgas, Bower, & Krantz, 1984; Peterson & Seligman, 1984; Pietromonaco, 1985; Pietromonaco, Rook, & Lewis, 1992; Teasdale, 1983, 1988; Teasdale & Fogarty, 1979). Examining differences in observer versus participant ratings allow us to understand whether internalizing girls' perceptions of their behaviors are subject to a cognitive bias (Nolen-Hoeksema et al., 1991; Sanders et al., 1992). If so, this underscores the need for assessment of the internalizing person's subjective understanding of interpersonal interactions, in addition to observer ratings.

Interpersonal Situation. Results of this study are also limited to understanding the relation of internalizing to interpersonal behaviors in situations that demand negotiation of differences. Our choice of this situation was prompted by theoretical concerns that focused on adolescent girls' needs to successfully cope with these negotiations, but we do not know the extent to which our results are generalizable to other, less conflictual situations. It is possible that girls' internalizing symptoms would be unrelated to mother–daughter interactions in situations that call for developing and maintaining intimacy and closeness.

Symptom Specificity. We do not know if these findings are specific to internalizing symptoms as assessed by the YSR (Achenbach, 1991). As discussed, internalizing symptoms include depressive symptoms, as well as other symptoms that are found to be difficult to empirically distinguish from depressive symptoms in childhood and adolescence (Achenbach, 1991). Futher studies are required to determine whether our findings regarding the subjective understanding of girls' interpersonal behaviors are relevant to depressive symptoms and diagnoses as assessed by other methods. In addition, it is possible that difficulties with autonomous interpersonal behaviors could be related to externalizing symptoms as well as internalizing symptoms (although Allen et al.'s 1994b study suggests otherwise).

Correlational Analyses. All results in this chapter were based on correlational analyses. We used correlational techniques of hierarchical multiple regression to examine whether findings were consistent with a model of mother–daughter behavioral reactions to daughters' symptoms (the reactive model) and a model of how mother–daughter interactions cause daughters' symptoms (the causal model). Of course, proof of reactive or causal connections between variables requires an experimental design and, although our study had the advantage of yielding longitudinal data, the design was nonexperimental. When research findings from a variety of studies yield consistent empirical relations between family behaviors and internalizing symptoms, it will be crucial to conduct experimental intervention research with families of depressed adolescents to more adequately examine these reactive and causal models. In addition, our findings raise questions regarding the sequencing of mother–daughter interactions. For example, the submissive behavior of internalizing daughters may be a response to mothers' high levels of conflictual behaviors or, daughters' submissive behaviors may be an immediate response of daughters to *their own* perceived expressions of conflict—self-monitoring attempts to dilute the impact of their assertive interactions. These questions are best addressed with conditional probability analyses in which the sequential nature of mother–daughter interactions could be examined.

Variables Not Included in the Model. Our analyses were restricted to examining the relation of participants' subjective understanding of interpersonal behaviors to internalizing symptoms. In an earlier article (Powers et al., 1994), we proposed that subjective understanding would be moderated by a wide range of individual differences variables (such as level of social-cognitive reasoning or temperament) and environmental variables (such as social class or parental symptomatology). We expect to examine the role of these moderating variables in subsequent analyses. Although we expect moderating variables to strengthen the models presented in this chapter, it is important to note that our findings for the simple models examined here were quite strong, with results for the reactive model explaining from 14% to 37% of the variance in behavior and results for the causal model explaining from 28% to 50% of the variance in internalizing symptoms.

ACKNOWLEDGMENTS

This research was funded by the National Science Foundation. We thank Kristen Pollack and Virginia Wright for their coordination of the data collection and management for this project and for their participation in discussions regarding the ideas presented in this chapter.

REFERENCES

Abramson, L. Y., Seligman, M. E. P., & Teasdale, J. (1978). Learned helplessness in humans: Critique and reformulation. *Journal of Abnormal Psychology, 87,* 49–74.
Achenbach, T. M. (1991). *Manual for the Youth Self-Report and 1991 profile.* Burlington, VT: University of Vermont.

Allen, J. P., Hauser, S. T., Bell, K. L., & O'Connor, T. G. (1994a). Longitudinal assessment of autonomy and relatedness in adolescent–family interactions as predictors of adolescent ego development and self-esteem. *Child Development, 65*, 179–194.

Allen, J. P., Hauser, S. T., Eickholt, C., Bell, K. L., & O'Connor, T. G. (1994b). Autonomy and relatedness in family interactions as predictors of expressions of negative adolescent affect. *Journal of Research in Adolescence, 4*, 535–552.

Allgood-Merten, B., Lewinsohn, P. M., & Hops, H. (1990). Sex differences and adolescent depression. *Journal of Abnormal Psychology, 99*, 55–63.

Anderson, J. C., Williams, S., McGee, R., & Silva, P. A. (1987). DSM–III disorders in preadolescent children. *Archives of General Psychiatry, 44*, 69–76.

Barber, B. K., Olsen, J. E., & Shagle, S. C. (1994). Associations between parental psychological and behavioral control and youth internalized and externalized behaviors. *Child Development, 65*, 1120–1136.

Baron, P., & Campbell, T. L. (1993). Gender differences in the expression of depressive symptoms in middle adolescents: An extension of earlier findings. *Adolescence, 28*(112), 903–911.

Baumrind, D. (1987). Developmental perspectives on adolescent risk-taking in contemporary America. In C. E. Irwin (Ed.), *Adolescent social behavior and health* (pp. 93–125). San Francisco: Jossey-Bass.

Beaumont, S. (1996). Adolescent girls' perceptions of conversations with mothers and friends. *Journal of Adolescent Research, 11*(3), 325–346.

Biglan, A., Hops, H., Sherman, L., Friedman, L. S., Arthur, J., & Osteen, V. (1985). Problem-solving interactions of depressed women and their husbands. *Behavior Therapy*, 431–451.

Biglan, A., Rothlind, J., Hops, H., & Sherman, L. (1989). Impact of distressed and aggressive behavior. *Journal of Abnormal Psychology, 98*, 218–228.

Block, J. H. (1983). Differential premises arising from differential socialization of the sexes: Some conjectures. *Child Development, 54*, 1335–1354.

Brooks-Gunn, J., & Peterson, A. C. (1991). Studying the emergence of depression and depressive symptoms during adolescence. *Journal of Youth and Adolescence, 20*, 115–119.

Callan, V. J., & Noller, P. (1986). Perceptions of communicative relationships in families of adolescents. *Journal of Marriage and the Family, 48*, 813–820.

Campbell, E., Adams, G. R., & Dobson, W. R. (1984). Familial correlates of identity formation in late adolescence: A study of the predictive utility of connectedness and individuality in family relations. *Journal of Youth and Adolescence, 13*, 509–525.

Cicchetti, D. (1984). The emergence of developmental psychopathology. *Child Development, 55*, 1–7.

Cicchetti, D., & Toth, S. L. (1995). Developmental psychopathology and disorders of affect. In D. Cicchetti & D. J. Cohen (Eds.), *Developmental psychopathology: Risk, disorder, and adaptation* (pp. 369–420). New York: Wiley.

Cohen, J., & Cohen, P. (1983). *Applied MRC analysis for the behavioral sciences.* (2nd ed.). Hillsdale, NJ: Lawrence Erlbaum Associates.

Cole, P. M., Barrett, K. C., & Zahn-Waxler, C. (1992). Emotion displays in two-year-olds during mishaps. *Child Development, 63*, 314–324.

Collins, W. A. (1990). Parent–child relationships in the transition to adolescence: Continuity and change in interaction, affect, and cognition. In R. Montemayor, G. R. Adams, & T. P. Gullotta (Eds.), *From childhood to adolescence: A transitional period?* (Vol. 2, pp. 85–106). Newbury Park, CA: Sage.

Compas, B. E., Ey, S., & Grant, K. E. (1993). Taxonomy, assessment, and diagnosis of depression during adolescence. *Psychological Bulletin, 114*, 323–344.

Compas, B. E., Malcarne, V. L., & Fondacaro, K. M. (1988). Coping with stressful events in older children and young adolescents. *Journal of Consulting and Clinical Psychology, 56*, 405–411.

Cooper, C. (1988). Commentary: The role of conflict in adolescent–parent relationships. In M. R. Gunnar & W. A. Collins (Eds.), *21st Minnesota symposium on child psychology* (pp. 181–187). Hillsdale, NJ: Lawrence Erlbaum Associates.

Cooper, C. R., Grotevant, H. D., & Condon, S. M. (1983). Individuality and connectedness in the family as a context for adolescent identity formation and role-taking skill. In H. D. Grotevant & C. R. Cooper (Eds.), *Adolescent development in the family* (pp. 43–59). San Francisco: Jossey-Bass.

Coyne, J. C. (1976a). Depression and the response of others. *Journal of Abnormal Psychology, 85*, 186–193.

Coyne, J. C. (1976b). Toward an interactional description of depression. *Psychiatry, 39*, 28–40.

Craighead, L. W., & Green, B. J. (1989). Relationship between depressed mood and sex-typed personality characteristics in adolescents. *Journal of Youth and Adolescence, 18*, 467–474.

Cummings, E. M., & Davies, P. T. (1994). Maternal depression and child development. *Journal of Child Psychology and Psychiatry, 35*(1), 73–112.

Dadds, M. R., Sanders, M. R., Morrison, M., & Rebgetz, M. (1992). Childhood depression and conduct disorder: II. An analysis of family interaction patterns in the home. *Journal of Abnormal Psychology, 101*(3), 505–513.

Downey, G., & Coyne, J. C. (1990). Children of depressed parents: An integrative review. *Psychological Bulletin, 108*, 50–76.

Eron, L. D. (1980). Prescription for reduction of aggression. *American Psychologist, 35*, 244–252.

Feldman, S. S., Rubenstein, J. L., & Rubin, C. (1988). Depressive affect and restraint in early adolescents: Relationships with family structure, family process and friendship support. *Journal of Early Adolescence, 8*, 279–296.

Fleming, J. E., & Offord, D. R. (1990). Epidemiology of childhood depressive disorders: A critical review. *Journal of American Academy of Child and Adolescent Psychiatry, 29*, 571–580.

Forgas, J. P., & Bower, G. H. (1987). Mood effects on person–perception judgments. *Journal of Personality and Social Psychology, 53*, 53–60.

Forgas, J. P., Bower, G. H., & Krantz, S. E. (1984). The influence of mood on perception of social interactions. *Journal of Experimental Social Psychology, 20*, 497–513.

Garrison, C. Z., Jackson, K. L., Marsteller, F., McKeown, R., & Addy, C. (1990). A longitudinal study of depressive symptomatology in young adolescents. *Journal of the American Academy of Child and Adolescent Psychiatry, 29*, 581–585.

Ge, X., Conger, R. D., Lorenz, F. O., Shanahan, M., & Elder, G. H. (1995). Mutual influences in parent and adolescent psychological distress. *Developmental Psychology, 31*, 406–419.

Ge, X., Lorenz, F. O., Conger, R. D., Elder, G. H., & Simons, R. L. (1994). Trajectories of stressful life events and depressive symptoms during adolescence. *Developmental Psychology, 30*, 467–483.

Gjerde, P., Block, J., & Block, J. H. (1988). Depressive symptoms and personality during late adolescence: Gender differences in the externalization–internalization of symptom expression. *Journal of Abnormal Psychology, 97*, 475–486.

Gjerde, P. F., & Block, J. (1991). Preadolescent antecedents of depressive symptomatology at age 18: A prospective study. *Journal of Youth and Adolescence, 20*, 217–223.

Gore, S., Aseltine, R. H., & Colten, M. E. (1993). Gender, social–relational involvement, and depression. *Journal of Research in Adolescence, 3*(2), 101–125.

Gotlib, I. H., & Hammen, C. L. (1992). *Psychological aspects of depression*. New York: Wiley.

Gottman, J. M., & Levenson, R. W. (1985). A valid procedure for obtaining self-report of affect in marital interaction. *Journal of Consulting and Clinical Psychology, 53*, 156–160.

Grotevant, H. D., & Cooper, C. R. (1985). Patterns of interaction in family relationships and the development of identity exploration in adolescence. *Child Development, 56*, 415–428.

Hauser, S. T., Powers, S. I., & Noam, G. G. (1991). *Adolescents and their families: Paths of ego development*. New York: Free Press.

Hill, J. M., & Lynch, M. E. (1983). The intensification of gender-related role-expectations during early adolescence. In J. Brooks-Gunn & A. C. Petersen (Eds.), *Girls at puberty: Biological and psychosocial perspectives* (pp. 201–228). New York: Plenum.

Hill, J. P., & Holmbeck, G. N. (1986). Attachment and autonomy during adolescence. *Annals of Child Development, 3*, 145–189.

Holmbeck, G. N. (1996). A model of family relational transformations during the transition to adolescence: Parent–adolescent conflict and adaptation. In J. A. Graber, J. Brooks-Gunn, & A. C. Petersen (Eds.), *Transitions through adolescence: Interpersonal domains and context* (pp. 167–199). Mahwah, NJ: Lawrence Erlbaum Associates.

Holmbeck, G. N., & Hill, J. P. (1988). Conflictive engagement, positive affect, and menarche in families with seventh-grade girls. *Child Development, 62*, 1030–1048.

Hoover, C. F., & Fitzgerald, R. G. (1981). Dominance in the marriage of affective patients. *Journal of Nervous and Mental Disease, 169*, 624–628.

Hops, H., Biglan, A., Sherman, L., Arthur, J., Friedman, I., & Osteen, V. (1987). Home observations of family interactions of depressed women. *Journal of Consulting and Clinical Psychology, 55*, 341–346.

Horwitz, A. V., & White, H. R. (1987). Gender role orientations and styles of pathology among adolescents. *Journal of Health and Social Behavior, 28*, 158–170.

Huselid, R. F., & Cooper, M. L. (1994). Gender roles as mediators of sex differences in expressions of pathology. *Journal of Abnormal Psychology, 103*, 595–603.

Jaccard, J., Turrisi, R., & Wan, C. K. (1990). *Interaction effects in multiple regression* (Vol. 72). Newbury Park, CA: Sage Publications.

Kandel, D. B., & Davies, M. (1982). Epidemiology of depressive moods in adolescence. *Archives of General Psychiatry, 39*, 1205–1212.

Kashani, J. H., Beck, N. C., Hoeper, E. W., Fallahi, C., Corcoran, C. M., McAllister, M. A., Rosenberg, T. K., & Reid, J. C. (1987a). Psychiatric disorders in a community sample of adolescents. *American Journal of Psychiatry, 144*, 584–589.

Kashani, J. H., Carlson, G. A., Beck, N. C., Hoeper, E. W., Corcoran, C. M., McAllister, M. A., Fallahi, C., Rosenberg, T. K., & Reid, J. C. (1987b). Depression, depressive symptoms, and depressed mood among a community sample of adolescents. *Journal of Child Psychology and Psychiatry, 23*, 437–457.

Keitner, G. I., Miller, I. W., & Furzzetti, A. E. (1987). Family functioning and suicidal behavior in psychiatric inpatients with major depression. *Psychiatry, 50*, 242–255.

Kobak, T., Ferenz-Gillies, T., Everhart, E., & Seabrook, L. (1994). Maternal attachment strategies and emotion regulation with adolescent offspring. *Journal of Research in Adolescence, 4*(4), 553–566.

Kovacs, M. (1989). Affective disorders in children and adolescents. *American Psychologist, 44*, 209–215.

Kowalik, D. L., & Gotlib, I. H. (1987). Depression and marital interaction: Concordance between intent and perception of communication. *Journal of Abnormal Psychology, 96*, 127–134.

Laursen, B., & Collins, W. A. (1994). Interpersonal conflict during adolescence. *Psychological Bulletin, 115*, 197–209.

Leadbeater, B. J., Blatt, S. J., & Quinlan, D. M. (1995). Gender-linked vulnerabilities to depressive symptoms, stress, and problem behaviors in adolescents. *Journal of Research on Adolescence, 5*, 55–70.

Levenson, R. W., & Gottman, J. M. (1983). Marital interaction: Physiological linkage and affective exchange. *Journal of Personality and Social Psychology, 45*, 587–597.

Levenson, R. W., & Gottman, J. M. (1985). Physiological and affective predictors of change in relationship satisfaction. *Journal of Personality and Social Psychology, 49*, 85–94.

Lewinsohn, P. M. (1974). A behavioral approach to depression. In R. J. Friedman & M. M. Katz (Eds.), *The psychology of depression: Contemporary theory and research* (pp. 157–178). Washington, DC: Winston-Wiley.

Lewinsohn, P. M., Hops, H., Roberts, R. E., Seeley, J. R., & Andrews, J. A. (1993). Adolescent psychopathology: I. Prevalence and incidence of depression and other DSM-III-R disorders in high school students. *Journal of Abnormal Psychology, 102,* 133–144.

Margolin, G. (1987). Participant observation procedures in marital and family assessment. In T. Jacobs (Ed.), *Family interaction and psychopathology: Theories, methods, and findings* (pp. 391–426). New York: Plenum.

Markman, H. J. (1981). Prediction of marital distress: A 5 year follow-up. *Journal of Consulting and Clinical Psychology, 49,* 760–762.

McFarlane, A. H., Bellissimo, A., Norman, G. R., & Lange, P. (1994). Adolescent depression in a school-based community sample: Preliminary findings on contributing social factors. *Journal of Youth and Adolescence, 23,* 603–620.

Merikangas, K. R., Ranelli, C. J., & Kupfer, D. J. (1979). Marital interactions in hospitalized depressed patients. *Journal of Nervous Mental Disease, 167,* 689–695.

Monck, E., Graham, P., Richman, N., & Dobbs, R. (1994a). Adolescent girls: I. Self-reported mood disturbance in a community population. *British Journal of Psychiatry, 165,* 760–769.

Montemayor, R. (1983). Parents and adolescents in conflict: All families some of the time and some families most of the time. *Journal of Early Adolescence, 5,* 23–30.

Nelson, G. M., & Beach, S. R. H. (1990). Sequential interaction in depression: Effects of depressive behavior on spousal aggression. *Behavior Therapy, 21,* 167–182.

Nolen-Hoeksema, S. (1987). Sex differences in unipolar depression: Evidence and theory. *Psychological Bulletin, 101,* 259–282.

Nolen-Hoeksema, S. (1990). *Sex differences in depression.* Stanford, CA: Stanford University Press.

Nolen-Hoeksema, S. (1994). An interactive model for the emergence of gender differences in depression in adolescence. *Journal of Research in Adolescence, 4*(4), 519–534.

Nolen-Hoeksema, S., & Girgus, J. S. (1994). The emergence of gender differences in depression during adolescence. *Psychological Bulletin, 115,* 424–443.

Nolen-Hoeksema, S., Girgus, J. S., & Seligman, M. E. P. (1991). Sex differences in depression and explanatory style in children. *Journal of Youth and Adolescence, 20,* 233–245.

Nolen-Hoeksema, S., Girgus, J. S., & Seligman, M. E. P. (1992). Predictors and consequences of childhood depressive symptoms: A five-year longitudinal study. *Journal of Abnormal Psychology, 101,* 405–422.

Notarius, C. I., Benson, P. R., Sloane, D., Vanzetti, N. A., & Hornyak, L. M. (1989). Exploring the interface between perception and behavior: An analysis of marital interaction in distressed and nondistressed couples. *Behavioral Assessment, 11,* 39–64.

Petersen, A. C., Compas, B. E., Brooks-Gunn, J., Stemmler, M., Ey, S., & Grant, K. E. (1993). Depression in adolescence. *American Psychologist, 48,* 155–168.

Petersen, A. C., Sarigiani, P. A., & Kennedy, R. E. (1991). Adolescent depression: Why more girls? *Journal of Youth and Adolescence, 21,* 247–271.

Peterson, C., & Seligman, M. E. P. (1984). Causal explanations as a risk factor for depression: Theory and evidence. *Psychological Review, 91,* 347–374.

Pietromonaco, P. R. (1985). The influence of affect on self-perception in depression. *Social Cognition, 3*(1), 121–134.

Pietromonaco, P. R., Rook, K. S., & Lewis, M. A. (1992). Accuracy in perceptions of interpersonal interaction: Effects of dysphoria, friendship, and similarity. *Journal of Personality and Social Psychology, 63*(2), 247–259.

Powers, S. I. (1988). Moral judgment development in the family. *Journal of Moral Education, 17*(2), 209–219.

Powers, S. I. (1989). Individual development through the lifespan: Family constellations of development, meaning, and behavior. In K. Kreppner & R. M. Lerner (Eds.), *Family systems throughout the lifespan.* Hillsdale, NJ: Lawrence Erlbaum Associates.

Powers, S. I., Hauser, S. T., & Kilner, L. (1989). Adolescent mental health. *American Psychologist, 44*(2), 200–208.

Powers, S. I., Schwartz, J., Hauser, S. T., Noam, G. G., & Jacobson, A. M. (1983). Adolescent ego development and family interaction: A structural-developmental perspective. In H. D. Grotevant & C. R. Cooper (Eds.), *Adolescent development in the family* (pp. 5–25). San Francisco: Jossey-Bass.

Powers, S. I., Welsh, D. P., & Wright, V. (1994). Adolescents' affective experience of family behaviors: The role of subjective understanding. *Journal of Research on Adolescence, 4*, 585–600.

Prinz, R. J., Foster, S., Kent, R. N., & O'Leary, K. D. (1979). Multivariate assessment of conflict in distressed and nondistressed mother–adolescent dyads. *Journal of Behavior Analysis, 12*, 691–700.

Radloff, L. S. (1980). Risk factors for depression. What do we learn from them? In M. Guttentag, S. Salasin, & D. Belle (Eds.), *The mental health of women*. New York: Academic Press.

Radloff, L. S., & Rae, D. S. (1979). Susceptibility and precipitating factors in depression: Sex differences and similarities. *Journal of Abnormal Psychology, 88*, 174–181.

Reinherz, H. Z., Stewart-Berghauer, G., Pakiz, B., Frost, A., Moeykens, B. A., & Holmes, W. M. (1989). The relationship of early risk and current mediators to depressive symptomatology in adolescence. *Journal of the American Academy of Child Psychiatry, 28*, 942–947.

Rutter, M. (1986). The developmental psychopathology of depression: Issues and perspectives. In M. Rutter, C. E. Izard, & P. B. Read (Eds.), *Depression in young people*. New York: Guilford.

Sanders, M. R., Dadds, M. R., Johnston, B. M., & Cash, R. (1992). Childhood depression and conduct disorder: I. Behavioral, affective and cognitive aspects of family problem-solving interactions. *Journal of Abnormal Psychology, 101*(3), 495–504.

Segrin, C., & Abramson, L. Y. (1994). Negative reactions to depressive behaviors: A communication theories analysis. *Journal of Abnormal Psychology, 103*, 655–668.

Segrin, C., & Dillard, J. P. (1992). The interactional theory of depression: A meta-analysis of the research literature. *Journal of Social and Clinical Psychology, 11*, 43–70.

Sheldon, A. (1992). Conflict talk: Sociolinguistic challenges to self-assertion and how young girls meet them. *Merrill-Palmer Quarterly, 38*(1), 95–116.

Smetana, J., & Asquith, P. (1994). Adolescents' and parents' conceptions of parental authority and personal autonomy. *Child Development, 65*, 1147–1162.

Steinberg, L. (1981). Transformations in family relations at puberty. *Developmental Psychology, 17*, 833–840.

Steinberg, L. (1990). Interdependency in the family: Autonomy, conflict, and harmony. In S. Feldman & G. Elliot (Eds.), *At the threshold: The developing adolescent* (pp. 255–276). Cambridge, MA: Harvard University Press.

Sroufe, L. A. (1992). Considering normal and abnormal together: The essence of developmental psychopathology. *Development and Psychopathology, 2*, 335–347.

Teasdale, J. D. (1983). Negative thinking in depression: Cause, effect or reciprocal relationship. *Advances in Behavior Research and Therapy, 5*, 3–26.

Teasdale, J. D. (1988). Cognitive vulnerability to persistent depression. *Cognition and Emotion, 2*, 247–274.

Teasdale, J. D., & Fogarty, S. J. (1979). Differential effects of induced mood on retrieval of pleasant and unpleasant events from episodic memory. *Journal of Abnormal Psychology, 88*, 248–257.

Weiss, R. L. (1984). Cognitive and behavioral measures of marital interaction. In N. S. Jacobson & K. Hahlweg (Eds.), *Marital interaction: Analysis and modification*. New York: Guilford.

Welsh, D. P., & Powers, S. I. (1991). Gender differences in parent–child interactions. In R. M. Lerner, A. Petersen, & J. Brooks-Gunn (Eds.), *The encyclopedia of adolescence*. New York: Garland.

Welsh, D. P., Vickerman, R., & Powers, S. I. (1997). *Divergent realities and perceived inequalities: Adolescents', mothers', and observers' perceptions of family interactions and adolescent psychological functioning.* Manuscript submitted for publication.

Yau, J., & Smetana, J. (1996). Adolescent–parent conflict among Chinese adolescents in Hong Kong. *Child Development, 67*(3), 1262–1275.

Youniss, J., & Smollar, J. (1985). *Adolescent relations with mothers, fathers, and friends.* Chicago: University of Chicago Press.

12

▼▼▼▼▼▼▼

Conflict and Cohesion
in Rhesus Monkey Family Life

Stephen J. Suomi
National Institute of Child Health and Human Development

Much of human social activity involves interactions among kin. Although precise definitions of family often can differ both between and within cultures, few would deny that family life is a central feature of every culture. Virtually every human infant born into any society spends its initial weeks and months of life in the close presence of some family member or members for at least several hours each day, and many spend most of this time with their mothers. The majority of children in most societies grow up in the primary care and oversight of family members, and most retain some sort of family ties during and after adolescence, if not throughout the rest of their lives (Whiting & Whiting, 1975). Family interactions clearly represent a fundamental aspect of human social life.

Of course, humans do not have a monopoly on family interactions. Kin-specific activities are seen in almost all social animals (a fundamental tenet of sociobiology), especially in mammals and particularly in most other primate species, for which extensive and extended family interactions are almost always the norm. Although no other species of primate shows the remarkable diversity of different modal social systems that characterize different human cultures, virtually all monkeys and apes have species-normative patterns of social organization that center in large part around multigenerational family relationships (Smuts, Cheney, Seyfarth, Wragham, & Struhsaker, 1987).

Consider the case of rhesus monkeys (*Macaca mulatta*). Although rhesus monkeys are clearly not our closest phylogenetic relatives (that role falls to chimpanzees and bonobos), in evolutionary terms they are probably our most *successful* fellow primates. Next to humans, rhesus monkeys live over a wider geographic range (essentially the whole of the Indian subcontinent), encompassing a broader mix of climatic and habitat variation, than any other primate species (Lindburg, 1991). Whereas many nonhuman primate species are currently classified as endangered or threatened, rhesus monkeys are actually expanding local populations in some parts of their extensive range (Malik, Seth, & Southwick, 1984; Richard, Goldstein, & Dewar, 1989). They generally thrive when introduced to new settings (e.g., tropical Caribbean islands or arid Texas plains), and they readily adapt to a wide variety of captive environments (Sameroff & Suomi, 1996).

Wild rhesus monkeys naturally reside in large, socially complex communities known as *troops*. Although troops can vary widely in size, ranging from a few dozen to several hundred individual members each, the basic social structure of each troop is remarkably similar from setting to setting. Rhesus monkey troops are always organized around multigenerational matrilines, that is, female-headed extended families. All troops, large and small alike, are comprised of several separate families, each typically encompassing three or more generations of close female kin (Lindburg, 1971). The long-term stability of these matrilineal families (and indeed, of the troop as a distinctive whole) derives from the fact that every female remains in her natal troop throughout her entire lifetime, whereas virtually every male emigrates from his natal troop around the time of puberty, never to return. After leaving home, most adolescent males first briefly congregate in all-male gangs, then attempt to join other established troops. Some of the males who are successful in these efforts remain in their adoptive troop for the rest of their lives, whereas others stay no more than a few years and then leave to seek membership in another established troop, sometimes repeating this pattern several times throughout their adult years (Berard, 1989).

Thus, adult females and their female progeny are the ones who provide the long-term foundation for rhesus monkey communities. To be sure, every rhesus monkey troop contains numerous males of all ages—but whereas troop membership for any one male is typically transitory, it is always lifelong for every female. This is not to say that males play no significant roles in rhesus monkey social group life; to the contrary, their presence is essential for the long-term survival of the troop as a whole. Nevertheless, it is the female-headed families around which most of the social activities of the troop are organized and the underlying social structure of the troop is defined and maintained (Nicolson, 1987). This particular form of social organization is relatively common among different species of Old World monkeys, whereas communities based on nuclear families characterized by long-term monogamous relationships are essentially nonexistent in these species (Fedigan, 1982).

Within each rhesus monkey troop, the constituent families interact extensively with one another in complex but largely predictable ways. For example, there is a clear-cut linear dominance hierarchy among the troop's different families, such that all members of the highest ranking matriline, including infants, are socially dominant over all members of the second-ranking matriline, including adults, who in turn outrank all members of the third-ranking matriline, etc. This protypical hierarchy can be maintained as long as relevant family members consistently support any other family member being challenged by monkeys from lower-ranking matrilines, such as when adult members of a high-ranking matriline immediately come to the defense of one of their infants if it is being threatened or attacked by anyone outside of the family (Bernstein, 1971).

On the other hand, squabbles between rhesus monkey families quickly vanish in the face of major threat, challenge, or danger to the troop as a whole. Rhesus monkey troops become remarkably cohesive, coordinated, and arguably purposeful with respect to specific actions of individuals and interactions among families when predators are detected, when challenged by neighboring troops, or when experiencing an ecological catastrophe such as a major hurricane. Indeed, the speed at which dramatic transformations of troop activity from petty infighting to concerted community effort can transpire is simply breathtaking to behold. Clearly, a rhesus monkey troop reflects considerably more substance and complexity than the individual activities of its constituent families, just as each rhesus monkey family represents much more than a mere collection of matrilineal kin.

The complex familial and dominance relationships that characterize rhesus monkey troops seemingly require that every troop member have some knowledge of every other member's specific kinship and dominance status—and utilize such knowledge—in order to survive, let alone thrive, in everyday family and troop life. How might such knowledge be acquired, maintained, and utilized in generation after generation of monkeys born into the troop? An impressive body of both laboratory and field data strongly suggests that it is an emergent property of the species-normative pattern of socialization that virtually all rhesus monkeys experience as they are growing up in their respective families (Sameroff & Suomi, 1996).

DEVELOPMENTAL ASPECTS OF RHESUS MONKEY SOCIALIZATION

Every rhesus monkey infant begins life completely dependent on its biological mother, and it spends virtually all of its initial postnatal weeks in physical contact with or within arm's reach of her. The mother, in turn, provides her newborn with essential nourishment, physical and psychological warmth, and protection from the elements, potential predators, and even other troop members, including pesky older siblings (Harlow, Harlow, & Hansen, 1963). During this time, a strong and enduring social bond inevitably develops between mother and infant, recognized by Bowlby to be basically homologous with the mother–infant attachment relationship universally seen in all human cultures, the product of diverse evolutionary pressures over millions of years (Bowlby, 1969).

Rhesus monkey infants are inherently curious (Harlow, 1953), and like human infants, once they become attached to their mother they quickly learn to use her as a secure base from which to organize the exploration of their immediate environment, which often includes contact with older siblings and other family members. As they grow older, most monkey infants become able and willing to spend increasing amounts of time at increasing distances from their mother, apparently confident that they can return to her protective care without interruption or delay on her part whenever they tire or become hungry or frightened. The presence of such a psychologically secure base clearly promotes exploration of both the physical and social aspects of their ever-expanding world. On the other hand, when rhesus monkey infants develop less than optimal attachment relationships with their mothers, their subsequent exploratory behavior is often compromised, just as Bowlby and other attachment theorists described for human infants and young children (Suomi, 1995).

During the course of their excursions away from their mother rhesus monkey infants inevitably come in contact not only with siblings and other matrilineal kin, but also with members of other families, including infants of similar age and comparable physical, cognitive, and social capabilities as themselves. Most soon come to prefer to interact with others their age, related or not, than to interact with older relatives. Consequently, interactions with agemates occur with increasing frequency in the third and fourth months of life, and by the time of weaning, most rhesus monkey youngsters already spend several hours each day playing with same-age peers. These peer interactions continue to increase in both frequency and complexity throughout the rest of the monkeys' first year, and they remain at high levels essentially until the onset of puberty (Ruppenthal, Harlow, Eisele, Harlow, & Suomi, 1974). During this time, the play patterns that dominate peer interactions become increasingly gender specific and sex segregated (i.e., males tend to play more with males and females with females); they also incorporate behavioral sequences that increasingly resemble adult patterns of interaction (Harlow & Lauersdorf, 1974). By the end of their third year, rhesus monkey juveniles have had ample opportunity to develop, practice, and perfect behavioral routines that will be crucial for normal functioning when they become adults. Among the most important lessons learned through play with peers is the appropriate expression—and control—of emerging aggressive capabilities, as well as knowledge about and respect for the various dominance hierarchies within the troop (Suomi, 1979).

Puberty typically begins for females around the end of their third year, when they have their initial menses (and regular 28-day menstrual cycles thereafter), and the start of the fourth year for males, when their testes enlarge and begin producing viable sperm. Adolescence in rhesus monkeys is associated not only with pronounced growth spurts and other marked physical changes, but also with major social changes for both sexes (Suomi, Rasmussen, & Higley, 1992). Males experience the most dramatic changes: during adolescence, they sever all ties with their matriline and emigrate out of their natal troop. Most of these males soon join "gangs" comprised of other adolescent and young adult males and remain in these all-male groups for a period ranging from several months to a year or more before attempting to join another monkey troop. Field data clearly show that the process of natal troop emigration represents an exceedingly dangerous transition for adolescent males: the mortality rate for these males from the time they leave their natal troop until they successfully join another approaches 50% (Dittus, 1979). Recent field studies also indicate that there are major individual differences in both the timing of male emigration and the basic strategy followed in attempting to join an unfamiliar troop. Moreover, as mentioned earlier, some surviving males remain in their adoptive troop for the rest of their lives, whereas others subsequently switch troops, often several times, although they never return to their natal troop (Berard, 1989).

Females, by contrast, never leave the natal troop. Puberty for rhesus monkey females is instead associated with increases in social activities directed toward their matrilinear kin, typically at the expense of interactions with peers. Family interactions are heightened even more when these young females begin to have offspring of their own (Digregorio, Suomi, Eisele, & Chapman, 1987). Indeed, the birth of a new infant (especially to a new mother) has the effect of invigorating the matriline, drawing its members closer both physically and socially and, conversely, providing a buffer from external threats and stressors for mother and infant alike. Rhesus monkey females continue to be actively involved in matrilineal social affairs for the rest of their lives, even after they cease having infants of their own.

CONFLICTS WITHIN RHESUS MONKEY FAMILIES

The fact that rhesus monkey females are extensively involved in family affairs virtually every day of their lives (and, for males, every day until adolescence) does not mean that all this involvement is uniformly positive and pleasant. To the contrary, within-family conflicts are frequent and often predictable, if not inevitable, occurances in everyday rhesus monkey social life. Such conflicts can involve any and all possible combinations of kin.

Consider, for example, the developing relationship between a mother and her infant. Sociobiologists have long argued that although mothers and infants share many genes and (therefore) many long-term goals, their short-term interests are not always mutual and hence periodic conflict is inevitable (Trivers, 1974). Whether this view is valid or not, an obvious instance of parent–offspring conflict occurs for virtually every rhesus monkey infant at around 20 weeks of age, when its mother begins to wean it from her own milk to solid food. Whether this process begins because the mother "wants" her infant to cease nursing (so she can stop lactating, begin cycling, and be able to produce another offspring, as the sociobiologists would have it), because she "knows" that she cannot continue to produce enough milk to sustain her infant's rapidly growing energy requirements, or because her infant's erupting teeth make nursing increasingly uncomfortable is certainly open to question. What *is* clear is that weaning is almost always associated with significant changes in the nature of mother–infant interactions, and those changes are seldom placid in nature (Hinde & White, 1974).

Mothers, for their part, make increasingly frequent efforts to deny their infants access to their nipple(s), albeit with considerable variation in the precise form, timing, and intensity of their weaning behavior, ranging from the exquisitely subtle to bordering on abuse. Infants, on the other hand, dramatically increase their efforts to obtain and maintain physical contact with their mother, even when nipple contact is not attainable. As with mothers, there is substantial variation in the nature, intensity, and persistence of the infants' efforts to prevent or at least delay the weaning process (Berman, Rasmussen, & Suomi, 1993). Moreover, in virtually all cases, an infant's newfound preoccupation with maintaining maternal contact clearly inhibits its exploratory behavior and noticeably alters and diminishes its interactions with peers (and often other kin) as well. Indeed, it usually takes a month or more (if at all) before those interaction patterns return to some semblance of normalcy (Hinde & White, 1974).

Postweaning "normalcy" for a young rhesus monkey seldom lasts for more than a few additional weeks before a second form of conflict with its mother typically arises. Most mothers return to reproductive receptivity around the time that their infants are 6 to 7 months old, at which point they begin actively soliciting selected adult males for the next 2 or 3 months (rhesus monkeys are seasonal breeders in nature). Throughout this period, they may enter into consort relationships with several different males, typically lasting 1 to 3 days each. During this time, a female and her chosen partner usually leave the main body of the troop for most (if not all) of the time they are together, often seeking relative seclusion to avoid harassment or other interruptions from other troop members (Manson & Perry, 1993). At the same time, her offspring from the previous year's consort tends to be ignored, actively avoided, or even physically rejected by both the mother and her current mate (Berman, Rasmussen, & Suomi, 1994).

Not surprisingly, most rhesus monkey yearlings become quite upset in the face of such functional maternal separations; indeed, a few actually develop dramatic behavioral and physiological symptoms that parallel Bowlby's descriptions of separation-induced depression in human infants and young children (Suomi, 1995). Most of their cohorts likewise exhibit an initial period of protest following loss of access to their mother but soon begin directing their attention elsewhere. Interestingly, female offspring "left behind" by their mothers during consorts tend to seek out other family members during their mother's absence, whereas young males are more likely to increase interactions with peers while their mother is away (Berman, Rasmussen, & Suomi, 1994). These gender differences in the protypical response to maternal separation at 6 to 7 months of age thus appear to presage the much more dramatic gender differences in life course that emerge during adolescence and continue throughout adulthood.

It would seem that a rhesus monkey mother would always have the upper hand in these conflicts with her offspring during both weaning and breeding periods, given her great size and strength advantage over even the most persistent 5- to 7-month-old infant. However, a number of research findings suggest that infants bring resources of their own into these conflicts. For example, Simpson, Simpson, Hooley, and Zunz (1981) reported that infants who remained in physical contact with their mothers more and explored less during the preweaning months were more likely to delay the onset of weaning by several weeks and in some cases even preempt their mothers' cycling during the normal breeding season; this pattern was especially clear for male infants. More recently, Berman, Rasmussen, and Suomi (1993) found that infants who achieved the most frequent nipple contacts with their mothers during the breeding season had mothers who were least likely to conceive, even if they engaged in multiple consorts during that period. The end result in both cases was that these infants could, by their own actions, "postpone" their mother's next pregnancy for another year, thus gaining additional opportunities for unfetttered access to her not shared by agemates whose mothers had become pregnant during the same period. In the process, they were also able to postpone by at least a year the appearance of a new source of conflict—that of "rivalry" with their mother's next infant.

The birth of a new sibling has major consequences for a yearling rhesus monkey. From that moment on, its relationship with its mother is altered dramatically, if not largely preempted. No longer is a yearling the primary focus of its mother's attention. Instead, many of its attempts to use her as a source of security and comfort are often ignored or rebuffed, especially when its newborn sibling is nursing or merely clinging to the mother's ventrum. Moreover, whenever the yearling tries to push its younger sibling off the mother, obstruct its access to her, or disrupt its activity when it moves away from her, the mother's most likely response is to physically punish the yearling quickly, without warning, and often with considerable severity. On the other hand, the mother seldom if ever punishes the younger sibling when it interrupts the yearling's attempts to interact with her or otherwise disrupts the yearling's activities (Berman, 1992).

It does not take long for most rhesus monkey infants to learn that because their mother will consistently support them if they make a sufficient fuss, they can literally push their yearling brother or sister around at will without much fear of retaliation by the older sibling. Moreover, in these situations other family members seldom, if ever, intervene on the yearling's behalf. Thus, from very early in life onward a rhesus monkey infant becomes socially dominant over its yearling sibling, even though the yearling is physically much bigger and stronger. In addition, not only is this dominance relationship clearly observed and usually respected by members of other families in the troop, but it also tends to be maintained as the infant and yearling grow older, such that future conflicts between the two are typically settled in the younger sibling's favor, even when the mother is not immediately available to support it (Berman, 1982). Of course, the younger sibling's special status with its mother lasts only until the birth of her next infant, after which it, too, becomes subordinate.

Thus, the overall pattern of dominance relationships within rhesus monkey families, namely that younger siblings tend to outrank older siblings, appears to be initially enforced by the mother and subsequently reinforced or at least maintained by other family members and even troop members outside the matriline. This general pattern seems to hold for male offspring until puberty, at which point they rapidly drop to the very bottom of their family hierarchy and ultimately emigrate out of not only their matriline but the troop as a whole. Indeed, some authors suggested that a primary motivation for male emigration is this sudden loss of status, marked by increasingly frequent and intense physical conflict with other family members (Higley, Linnoila, & Suomi, 1994). In contrast, dominance relationships among female siblings tend to remain quite stable (following the "younger outranks older" rule) not only during their infant and juvenile years but throughout the rest of their adult lives as well, even after their mother has died. Moreover, there is evidence that this dominance pattern tends to hold across generations, such that offspring of younger adult females usually come out ahead in conflicts with their older sisters' offspring of comparable age (Suomi & Levine, 1998).

It should be pointed out that conflicts within individual rhesus monkey matrilines—be they between mothers and infants, older and younger siblings, first and second cousins, or other sets of relatives—tend to be relatively mild by rhesus monkey standards. Most of these conflicts, especially those between adult family members, involve little or no overt physical aggression and instead consist largely of bluffs, facial threats, and harsh vocalizations, and as a result actual wounding is rare. Within-family conflicts also tend to be brief, typically lasting only a few seconds per episode. Moreover, although these various family conflicts are usually much more frequent (and more predictable) than are those between members of different matrilines, they are generally less intense and more likely to be followed by various forms of reconciliation behavior (e.g., mutual grooming) than are most between-family conflicts (deWaal & Yoshirara, 1983).

FACTORS INFLUENCING THE RELATIVE "CLOSENESS" OF RHESUS MONKEY FAMILY TIES

Clearly, much of rhesus monkey social life involves interactions with close matrilineal kin. In general, members of any given matriline spend more time in physical proximity with one another, they typically groom each other more frequently and for longer periods, and they even tend to have more conflicts (albeit of shorter duration and less intensity) than they do with members of the other matrilines in their troop, as well as with resident adult males and monkeys from neighboring troops. Yet the relative "closeness" of individual family members to one another, both in the physical and the psychological sense, as well as the degree to which their activities appear to be coordinated, can vary substantially among different family members, across situations, and over time as a function of a number of different variables.

The extent to which the relative closeness of particular individuals to other family members family is systematically related to age and gender differences was already discussed at some length. Newborn infants obviously have "closer" relationships with their biological mother than with anyone else in the family or troop, but in subsequent months they broaden their social horizons to include other family members and, increasingly, peers. During their childhood years, these peer relationships tend to become sex-segregated, and with the onset of puberty, males sever all family ties, whereas females strengthen theirs, largely at the expense of existing relationships with unrelated peers, and they subsequently spend the rest of their life in the presence of their female relatives. Indeed, these matrilineal relationships tend to intensify, if anything, throughout adulthood (Suomi, Novak, & Well, 1997).

The relative closeness of family members to one another also varies systematically in a circadian fashion. Family members tend to sleep huddled together as a large mass of bodies, not only during the night but also during periodic nap times throughout the day. On the other hand, they tend to spead out physically when the troop is on the move, although even then individual family members generally stay closer to one another than to members of other matrilines. The same is true during the several hours each day they usually must spend foraging for food, although after they finish eating, the adults typically regroup for extended bouts of mutual grooming while their offspring play nearby. There is also systematic variation in the nature of family and nonfamily interactions as a function of time of year. Not surprisingly, rhesus monkey families tend to be most scattered during breeding season, whereas the period when infants are born represents the time of the year when family relationships are at their closest, especially for adolescent females and grandmothers, who seem to be attracted to the new infants as if they were some kind of powerful social magnet.

Perhaps the most dramatic examples of the extent to which rhesus monkey families become cohesive and coordinated occur in the face of outside threats or challenges to someone in the family. Individual rhesus monkeys often get into conflicts not only with their own kin but also with monkeys from other families. Whereas in-family conflicts are largely limited to brief spats and squabbles that result in little more than injured pride on the part of the loser, fights between members of different matrilines, although also typically brief and usually inconsequential, can in some cases rapidly escalate into serious, full-fledged brawls in which the participants are capable of inflicting serious physical injury on one another. Most of these interfamily conflicts initially involve only two or three individuals, such as when a play bout among juveniles begins to get a bit rough or when an adolescent female from one family gets too close to an exploring infant from another. A single scream from any one of the participants can bring other family members to the scene within seconds; this action, in turn, may serve to recruit immediate reinforcements from the other matriline, and a major aggressive encounter may then ensue. These episodes usually last less than 5 seconds, ending as abruptly as they began, or they may go on for a minute or more, sometimes drawing in additional participants who are not part of either matriline, for example, resident adult males. Generally speaking, the longer a major bout of aggression continues, the greater the probability that one or more of the participants may suffer serious injury (Higley, Linnoila, & Suomi, 1994). Eventually, one side or the other backs down and retreats, although it may be some time before tension levels among participants and bystanders abate.

Between-family conflicts such as these are essentially a normal part of everyday life in a rhesus monkey troop. What is truly remarkable about them is how quickly family members of all ages are capable of responding to the plight of an embattled relative, and how well coordinated the responses appear to be. In some cases, monkeys who are 50 or more yards away from the point of initial encounter and seem to be preoccupied with other activities can appear on the scene within seconds. How can such a rapid response actually take place? One possible explanation lies in the nature of the calls emitted by the initial contestants at the start of the episode. Gouzoules, Gouzoules, and Marler (1984) found that these calls, termed *recruitment screams*, exhibited systematic variation in their acoustic characteristics that appeared not only to identify who the caller was, but also to convey important information regarding both the family membership and the relative dominance status of the caller's antagonist. Basically, any monkey hearing such a call could tell whether the caller was a member of its own family and also whether the caller was likely to be outmatched (i.e., in a fight with a more dominant individual) or not. Gouzoules et al. (1984) showed that the probability and magnitude of response by other family members was systematically related to the specific type of recruitment scream initially emitted. Essentially, monkeys were far more likely to come to the aid of a member of their own matriline than was anyone else. Family members were also more likely to be recruited when the vocalizing monkey was subordinate to its antagonist (and presumably in need of aditional support)—but much less so when the matriline to which the antagonist belonged was dominant to their own, suggesting that they might be aware of the potential risk involved when taking on multiple members of a more powerful family.

What factors might be responsible for one matriline being dominant over another? One factor that might seem obvious is the relative size of the matriline—presumably a larger matriline could provide any member being attacked with greater numbers of potential recruits in any fight. But in many troops, the highest ranking matriline is not the largest in size, so other factors must also be in play (Rasmussen, Timme, & Suomi, 1997). Indeed, it appears that the relative closeness and cohesiveness of a matriline may be at least as important to its status in the overall troop hierarchy as is its number of family members. Matrilines that are able to respond quickly and effectively as a group when any one member is threatened or attacked usually triumph in a disproportionate number of agonistic exchanges, and, over time, members of other matrilines may become reluctant to support any relative that tries to challenge monkeys who have such potential back-up support.

Evidence that the relative strength of family ties may be a crucial determinant of the relative dominance of a matriline comes from two sources. First, there appears to be an inverse relationship between the amount of within-family conflict and the status of the family within the troop; that is, families that fight a great deal among themselves are seldom at the top of the troop's hierarchy. This finding suggests that the relative aggressiveness of family members per se may be less important than low levels of within-family conflict for achieving and sustaining high family social status. Second, several investigators have documented cases in which high ranking families that lost a prominant family member quickly fell in rank. Indeed, such events were often followed by renewed challenges from other families just below them in rank, almost as if members of the challenging matrilines were detecting a new vulnerability in the once-dominant family. These reports imply that members of different matrilines may be paying close attention to the activities and interactions of other families. There is good reason to believe that mothers with newborns might be especially interested in such "outside" activities.

MATERNAL BEHAVIOR, FAMILY RELATIONSHIPS, AND TROOP DEMOGRAPHICS

Numerous studies over the past 30 years demonstrated that rhesus monkey mothers are highly sensitive to those aspects of their immediate physical and social environment that pose a potential threat to their infants' well-being, and most appear to adjust their maternal behavior accordingly. For example, both laboratory and field studies have consistently shown that low-ranking mothers tend to be much more restrictive of their infants' exploratory efforts than are high-ranking mothers, whose own maternal style has been termed "laissez-faire." The standard interpretation of these findings is that low-ranking mothers risk reprisal from others if they try to intervene whenever their infant is threatened, so they minimize such risk by restricting their infant's exploration. High-ranking mothers have no such problem; hence, they can afford to let their infant explore as it pleases.

Other studies have found that mothers generally become more restrictive and increase their levels of infant monitoring when their immediate social environment becomes less stable, such as when major changes in interfamily dominance hierarchies take place or when alien males try to join the troop. Changes in various aspects of the physical environment, such as the food supply becoming less predictable, have also been associated with increases in maternal restriction of early infant environmental exploration (Andrews & Rosenblum, 1991). For infants whose opportunities to explore are chronically limited during their first few months of life, development of species-normative relationships with others in their social group, especially peers, can be compromised, often with long-term consequences for both the infants and their social group (Suomi, 1997).

The extent to which mothers' rearing styles can affect not only their offspring but also other family members and the troop as a whole can be seen in a long-term study (Berman, Rasmussen, & Suomi, 1997) of free-ranging troops of rhesus monkeys living on Cayo Santiago, an island off the eastern coast of Puerto Rico, where rhesus monkeys were first introduced over 50 years ago and have thrived ever since (Kessler & Berard, 1989). This particular population, like many on the Indian subcontinent, has steadily increased in number over the past few decades, an increase that is reflected by the tendency of individual troops to increase in number of residents over time—but only up to a point, after whch each troop typically fissions into several smaller "splinter" troops (Rawlins & Kessler, 1986).

Berman et al. (1997) found that, in small troops, mothers generally tended to be laissez-faire in their maternal style relative to mothers living in troops with larger populations. Mothers in small troops rarely restricted their infants' early exploratory efforts, seldom intervened in their infants' social activities, and indeed spent relatively little time monitering their behavior. In turn, their infants actively sought out peers from neighboring matrilines and spent increasing amounts of time in mutual play bouts as they were growing up. As a result, they established strong, basically positive social relationships with these nonkin peers prior to puberty, and those positive relationships tended to be maintained, at least among the females, throughout adolescence and into adulthood. Perhaps not surprisingly, Berman et al. (1997) found these small troops to be relatively peaceful, at least with respect to relations between matrilines within each troop.

However, in suceeding years most of these small troops increased in population, resulting in an increase in the relative density of nonkin, that is, members of other matrilines, within each mother's effective social "space" (which Berman et al. operationally defined as activity within a 5-meter radius of the mother, a well-established metric in the rhesus monkey field literature). As the ratio of nonkin to kin within this space increased, so did these mothers' tendency to restrict their infants' exploration, intervene in their social activities, and indeed moniter their every move. As a result, these infants had fewer opportunities to seek out agemates from other matrilines, and when they did manage to interact with those nonkin peers, their play bouts were often truncated by their mothers' interventions. The play bouts that did occur tended to be less frequent, briefer in duration, and less affectively positive than had been the case when the troop was smaller. These young monkeys thus did not have the same opportunities to develop extensive social relationships with peers from other families prior to puberty as did cohorts from previous years. Moreover, their interactions with nonkin peers did not improve much with age, remaining infrequent and often hostile throughout adolescence and into adulthood. Not surprisingly, Berman et al. (1997) found that the general atmosphere within these now-larger troops was considerably more tense and involved less cooperation between matrilines than in previous years when the troops had been smaller.

As these troops continued to grow in population, the presence of nonkin within most mothers' effective social space likewise increased, and the mothers tended to become even more diligent in restricting their infants' opportunities to explore and interact with nonkin peers, to the point where almost all of their offsprings' play and affiliative behaviors were limited to partners from within their matriline. The few interactions that these young monkeys had with peers from other families were mostly negative in nature, with aggression the rule rather than the exception it had been when the troops were smaller. These negative relations with nonkin peers continued into adulthood, generally adding to the overall tension and lack of cohesion characteristic of the larger troops.

Berman et al. (1997) also found that over time these large troops eventually broke up, usually splintering after a long episode of particularly intense interfamily aggression. The breakups always occurred along matrilines, resulting in several small "splinter" troops that quickly developed their own distinctive identity. Of special interest was the finding that in each new splinter group, the ratio of nonkin to kin within each mother's effective social space dropped to levels comparable to that of the original troop back in the days when it had been relatively small. As before, mothers in these new small troops tended to be laissez-faire in their respective maternal styles, and once again their offspring developed extensive positive play partnerships with peers from other families. However, as these small splinter groups started expanding in population themselves, the mothers once more began restricting their infants' social world, thus beginning the cycle anew.

The findings of the Berman et al. (1997) study provide compelling evidence that rhesus monkey mothers are indeed capable of adjusting their maternal style to deal with changes in their troop's social demographic characteristics. However, the larger lesson from this study is that the mothers' adaptations had long-term consequences not only for their offspring and their larger family, but also for the basic identity of the troop as a whole. This case demonstrates that although changes at the "community" level can affect how a mother raises her infants, changes in those individual dyadic relationships can ultimately influence the very nature of the troop itself. Thus, individual relationships, family allegiances, and troop characteristics appear to be inextricably linked in a system involving long-term reciprocal feedback.

COMMENTARY

This chapter has focused on various aspects of family life observed in one highly adaptive nonhuman primate species. Rhesus monkey families encompass multiple generations of matrilineal kin embedded in larger social groupings that have some degree of distinctiveness and permanence. Within each family, infants grow up in the care of their mothers and the close presence of relatives, and although they subsequently expand their social world to include peers and others in the larger community and beyond, they continue to retain strong family ties throughout adolescence (for males) and indeed for the rest of their lives (for females). There are plenty of conflicts within every rhesus monkey family, but there are also many strong and lasting ties among family members. Rhesus monkey families differ in relative status within their community-like troops, and these differences can have long-term consequences for individuals within each family. Yet there is also evidence that changes in within-family relationships, particularly those between mothers and offspring, can eventually lead to changes in the basic nature of the troop itself. What implications might these findings have for advancing our understanding of human families and the various ties, as well as the conflicts, that characterize them?

To be sure, rhesus monkeys are certainly not furry little humans with tails, but instead are only close phylogenetic relatives who share much of our genetic heritage but clearly lack certain capabilities, such as spoken and written language, that make us uniquely human. Moreover, fathers are not active participants in rhesus monkey family life, whereas they typically are in most human families around the world. Nevertheless, there *are* striking parallels between many aspects of rhesus monkey families and those of humans. The presence of these parallels suggests, at the very least, that one should be cautious when attributing certain features of human family processes and relationships exclusively to current cultural conditions. The rhesus monkey data suggest that some more basic evolutionary factors might be operating as well.

REFERENCES

Andrews, M. W., & Rosenblum, L. A. (1991). Security of attachment in infants raised in variable- or low-demand environments. *Child Development, 62,* 686–693.

Berard, J. (1989). Male life histories. *Puerto Rico Health Sciences Journal, 8,* 47–58.

Berman, C. M. (1982). The ontogeny of social relationships with group companions among free-ranging infant rhesus monkeys. II. Differentiation and attractiveness. *Animal Behavior, 30,* 163–170.

Berman, C. M. (1992). Immature siblings and mother–infant relationships among free-ranging rhesus on Cayo Santiago. *Animal Behavior, 44,* 247–258.

Berman, C. M., Rasmussen, K. L. R., & Suomi, S. J. (1993). Reproductive consequences of maternal care patterns during estrus among free-ranging rhesus monkeys. *Behavioral Ecology and Sociobiology, 32,* 391–399.

Berman, C. M., Rasmussen, K. L. R. , & Suomi, S. J. (1994). Responses of free-ranging rhesus monkeys to a natural form of social separation: I. Parallels with mother–infant separation in captivity. *Child Development, 65,* 1028–1041.

Berman, C. M., Rasmussen, K. L. R., & Suomi, S. J. (1997). Group size, infant development, and social networks: A natural experiment with free-ranging rhesus monkeys. *Animal Behavior, 53,* 405–421.

Bernstein, I. S. (1971). Primate status hierarchies. In L. A. Rosenblum (Ed.), *Primate behavior: Developments in field and laboratory research* (Vol. 1, pp. 71–111). New York: Academic Press.

Bowlby, J. (1969). *Attachment.* New York: Basic Books.

deWaal, F. B. M., & Yoshihara, D. (1983). Reconciliation and redirected aggresion in rhesus monkeys. *Behaviour, 85,* 224–241.

Digregorio, G., Suomi, S. J., Eisele, C. D., & Chapman, S. A. (1987). Reactions of nuclear family reared rhesus macaques to the birth of younger siblings. *American Journal of Primatology, 13,* 231–253.

Dittus, W. P. J. (1979). The evoiution of behaviours regulating density and age-specific sex ratios in a primate population. *Behaviour, 69,* 265–302.

Fedican, L. (1982). *Primate paradigms: Sex roles and social bonds.* Toronto: Eden Press.

Gouzoules, S., Gouzoules, H., & Marler, P. (1984). Rhesus monkey (*Macaca mulatta*) scream vocalizations: representational signalling in the recruitment of agonistic aid. *Animal Behavior, 32,* 182–193.

Harlow, H. F. (1953). Mice, monkeys, men, and motives. *Psychological Review, 60,* 23–35.

Harlow, H. F., Harlow, M. K., & Hansen, E. W. (1963). The maternal affectional system of rhesus monkeys. In H. L. Rheingold (Ed.), *Maternal behavior in mammals* (pp. 254–281). New York: Wiley.

Harlow, H. F., & Lauersdorf, H. E. (1974). Sex differences in passion and play. *Perspectives in Biology and Medicine, 17,* 348–360.

Higley, J. D., Linnoila, M., & Suomi, S. J. (1994). Ethological contributions. In R. T. Ammerman (Ed.), *Handbook of aggressive and destructive behavior in psychiatric patients* (pp. 17–32). New York: Raven Press.

Hinde, R. A., & White, L. E. (1974). The dynamica of a relationship—rhesus monkey ventro–ventro contact. *Journal of Comparative and Physiological Psychology, 86,* 8–23.

Kessler, M. J., & Berard, J. (1989). A brief description of the Cayo Santiago rhesus monkey colony. *Puerto Rico Health Sciences Journal, 8,* 55–59.

Lindburg, D. G. (1971). The rhesus monkey in North India: An ecological and behavioral study. In L. A. Rosenblum (Ed.), *Primate behavior: Developments in field and laboratory research* (Vol. 2, pp. 1–106). New York: Academic Press.

Lindburg, D. G. (1991). Ecological requirements of macaques. *Laboratory Animal Science, 41,* 315–322.

Malik, I., Seth, P. K., & Southwick, C. H. (1984). Population growth of free-ranging rhesus monkeys at Tughlaqabad, northern India. *American Journal of Primatology, 7,* 311–321.

Manson, J. H., & Perry, S. E. (1993). Inbreeding avoidance in rhesus macaques: whose choice? *American Journal of Physical Anthropology, 90,* 335–344.

Nicolson, N. A. (1987). Infants, mothers, and other females. In B. B. Smuts, D. L. Cheney, R. M. Seyfarth, R. W. Wrangham, & T. T. Struhsaker (Eds.), *Primate societies* (pp. 330–342). Chicago: University of Chicago Press.

Rasmussen, K. L. R., Timme, A., & Suomi, S. J. (1997). Comparison of physiological measures of Cayo Santiago rhesus monkey females within and between social groups. *Primate Reports, 47,* 49–55.

Rawlins, R. G., & Kessler, M. J. (1986). Demography of free-ranging Cayo Santiago macaques, 1976–1983. In R. G. Rawlins & M. J. Kessler (Eds.), *The Cayo Santiago macaques: History, biology, and behavior* (pp. 47–72). Albany, NY: SUNY Press.

Richard, A. F., Goldstein, S. J., & Dewar, R. E. (1989). Weed macaques: the evolutionary implications of macaque feeding ecology. *International Journal of Primatology, 10,* 569–594.

Ruppenthal, G. C., Harlow, M. K., Eisele, C. D., Harlow, H. F., & Suomi, S. J. (1974). Social development of infant monkeys reared in a nuclear family environment. *Child Development, 45,* 670–682.

Sameroff, A. J., & Suomi, S. J. (1996). Primates and persons: A comparative developmental understanding of social organization. In R. B. Cairns, G. H. Elder, & E. J. Costello (Eds.), *Developmental science* (pp. 97–120). New York: Cambridge University Press.

Simpson, M. J. A., Simpson, A. E., Hooley, J., & Zunz, M. (1981). Infant-related influences on birth intervals in rhesus monkeys. *Nature, 290,* 49–51.

Smuts, B. B., Cheney, D. L., Seyfarth, R. M., Wragham, R. W., & Struhsaker, T. T. (Eds.), *Primate societies.* Chicago: University of Chicago Press.

Suomi, S. J. (1979). Peers, play, and primary prevention in primates. In M. Kent & J. Rolf (Eds.), *Primary prevention of psychopathology, Vol. 3: Social competence in children* (pp. 127–149). Hanover, NH: New England Universities Press.

Suomi, S. J. (1995). Influence of Bowlby's attachment theory on research on nonhuman primate biobehavioral development. In S. Goldberg, R. Muir, & J. Kerr (Eds.), *Attachment theory: Social, developmental, and clinical perspectives* (pp. 185–201). Hillsdale, NJ: The Analytic Press.

Suomi, S. J. (1997). Early determinants of behaviour: evidence from primate studies. *British Medical Bulletin, 53,* 170–184.

Suomi, S. J., & Levine, S. (1998). Psychobiology of intergenerational effects of trauma: Evidence from animal studies. In Y. Daniele (Ed.), *International handbook of multigenerational legacies of trauma* (pp. 623–637). New York: Plenum.

Suomi, S. J., Novak, M. A., & Well, A. (1996). Aging in rhesus monkeys: Different windows on behavioral continuity and change. *Developmental Psychology, 32,* 1116–1128.

Suomi, S. J., Rasmussen, K. L. R., & Higley, J. D. (1992). Primate models of behavioral and physiological change in adolescence. In E. R. McAnarney, R. E. Kriepe, D. P. Orr, & G. D. Comerci (Eds.), *Textbook of adolescent medicine* (pp. 135–139). Philadelphia: Saunders.

Trivers, R. L. (1974). Parent–offspring conflicts. *American Zoologist, 14,* 249–264.

Whiting, B. B., & Whiting, J. W. M. (1975). *Children of six cultures.* Cambridge, MA: Harvard University Press.

The Effects of Psychiatric Disorders on Family Formation and Stability

Ronald C. Kessler
Harvard Medical School

Melinda S. Forthofer
University of South Florida

The past decade saw a growing interest in the social consequences of psychiatric disorders (e.g., Clark, 1994; Kouzis & Eaton, 1994; Rice, Kelman, Miller, & Dunnmeyer, 1990), fueled in part by the social policy debate concerning society's ability to afford the inclusion of mental health care coverage in universal health insurance (Mechanic, 1993; Weil, 1991). Studies in this area show that psychiatric disorders often have substantial personal and social costs (e.g., Kouzis & Eaton, 1994) and that the current role impairment associated with these disorders can be as great as that associated with serious chronic physical illnesses (Wells et al., 1989).

Most research on the social consequences of psychiatric disorders focused on short-term financial implications. However, equally important is research on broader social outcomes. In an effort to expand the assessment of the social consequences of psychiatric disorders, we initiated a program of research that used epidemiologic data to evaluate the life course effects of psychiatric disorders on a series of important role transitions. Our work to date documented that early-onset psychiatric disorders have powerfully adverse effects on educational attainment (Kessler, Foster, Saunders, & Stang, 1995) and are associated with a substantially increased risk of teenage childbearing (Kessler, Foster, Saunders, & Stang, 1996). This chapter considers the possibility that psychiatric disorders may also affect probability of marriage, marital timing, and marital stability.

Marriage is an important outcome to consider because of considerable evidence that married people enjoy better mental health than their unmarried counterparts (e.g., Gove, 1972; Kessler & McRae, 1984). Moreover, marriage is associated with many other advantages, including financial security and social support. Longitudinal research (Aseltine & Kessler, 1993; Booth & Amato, 1991; Mastekaasa, 1992) provides some evidence that psychological well-being may be an important determinant of both marriage and marital stability. However, these previous studies did not consider the effects of a comprehensive set of rigorously defined psychiatric disorders. This is the goal of the present chapter. Specifically, we present data from a large-scale national survey of the extent to which 14 DSM-III-R psychiatric disorders affect the probability and timing of marriage and marital stability. Because previous research suggested that associations between psychopathology and marriage may be contingent on marital timing (e.g., Booth & Edwards, 1985; Teti, Lamb, & Elster, 1987), gender (Gotlib & McCabe, 1990), type of disorder (Rosenfield, 1982), and birth cohort (Warner, Kessler, Hughes, Anthony, & Nelson, 1995; Wittchen, Zhao, Kessler, & Eaton, 1994), specifications on the basis of these variables are considered along with total sample analyses.

Based on the results of previous research, our analyses began with the hypothesis that prior psychiatric history would be associated with both a decreased probability of becoming married and an increased probability of divorce. However, based on evidence that first marriage during the early and middle teens is associated with negative social consequences (Booth & Edwards, 1985; Teti et al., 1987) and the fact that we had previously documented effects of early-onset psychiatric disorders on increased probability of teenage childbearing (Kessler et al., 1996), we also hypothesized that young people who suffered from certain psychiatric disorders, especially those associated with externalizing problems, would be more likely than others to become married as teenagers, even though probability of later marriage would be inversely related to psychiatric disorder.

METHODS

Sample

The data used in this study come from the National Comorbidity Survey (NCS; Kessler et al., 1994), a nationally representative general population survey of persons in the age range 15 to 54 designed to examine the prevalences, risk factors, and consequences of psychiatric morbidity and comorbidity in the United States. The NCS was fielded between September 1990 and March 1992 and consisted of face-to-face, in-home interviews averaging somewhat more than 2 hours to complete, with a sample of 8,098 respondents in the household population, including a supplemental sample of students living in campus group housing. More details about the NCS design and data collection methods are reported elsewhere (Kessler et al., 1994; Kessler, Little, & Groves, 1995).

The results reported in this chapter are based on the Part II NCS sub-sample of 5,877 respondents made up of all NCS respondents who screened positive for any lifetime diagnosis in the first half of the interview, all other respondents in the age range 15 to 24, and a random subsample of the remaining respondents. The data were weighted to correct for the differential probabilities of selection into Part II as well as for weights for differential probabilities of within-household selection and differential nonresponse. These weights are described in detail elsewhere (Kessler, Little, & Groves, 1995). Comparisons of the Part II NCS demographic distributions with census data show that the sample is highly representative of the U.S. population in the age range 15 to 54 (Kessler et al., 1994).

Measures

Marital Transitions. Questions that assessed whether respondents had ever married, their age at first marriage, ages of subsequent marital transitions, and reasons for these transitions (widowhood vs. divorce) were used to construct variables representing timing of first and subsequent marriages and marital terminations. Widowhoods were excluded from the analyses of marital terminations so that the focus was exclusively on divorce. Consistent with previous research (Lamb & Teti, 1989), early marriage was defined as marriage prior to age 19 in order to evaluate the hypothesis that prior psychiatric disorders are positively related to chances of early marriage but negatively related to chances of later marriage.

Diagnostic Assessment. A total of 14 psychiatric diagnoses are considered in the analyses reported in this chapter. These diagnoses are based on the DSM-III-R diagnostic system (American Psychiatric Association, 1987) and were generated from a modified version of the Composite International Diagnostic Interview (CIDI; World Health Organization, 1990). The CIDI is a fully structured psychiatric diagnostic interview designed to be used by trained interviewers who are not clinicians. World Health Organization Field Trials of the CIDI documented good reliability and validity of all the diagnoses used here (Wittchen, 1994). The latter include mood disorders (major depression, dysthymia, mania), anxiety disorders (panic disorder, generalized anxiety disorder, phobias, and posttraumatic stress disorder), conduct disorder, adult antisocial behavior, and addictive disorders (alcohol abuse and dependence, drug abuse and dependence).

Control Variables. We developed control models that included constructs found in previous research to predict marriage, marital timing, and marital termination (Axinn & Thornton, 1992; Marini, 1984, 1985) and that might also be considered possible causes of mental disorders. Three of these assessed the socioeconomic status of the respondent's family of origin (education of the chief breadwinner of the respondent's family of origin; the Duncan SEI score of the chief breadwinner of the respondent's family of origin; and the relative socioeconomic position of the respondent's family of origin compared to other families). Three other control variables assessed family of origin demography (number of siblings; number of older siblings; and mother's age when the respondent was born). An additional construct assessed family of origin intactness. Four constructs assessed geographic factors associated with differential access to marital partners and differential norms concerning marital timing (number of times the family of origin moved during the respondent's childhood; whether the respondent's childhood was spent mostly in a city, suburb, medium-sized town, small town, or rural area; urbanicity of residence after leaving the family of origin; and region of residence—northeast, midwest, south, west). Two additional controls differentiated among non-Hispanic Whites, non-Hispanic Blacks, Hispanics, and others, and between respondents who were born in the U.S. and those who were not. Additional controls of a time-varying nature were also used. Information about being pregnant at the time of marriage and having previous children were used as predictors of marriage and remarriage, and information about having children in the current marriage was used as an additional predictor of marital termination. Number, ages, and sex of children were included in all these analyses based on evidence that these are important determinants of either marriage (Axinn & Thornton, 1992; Marini, 1984, 1985) or marital termination (Booth & Edwards, 1992; Heaton, Albrecht, & Martin, 1985; Keith & Finlay, 1988; Morgar & Rindfuss, 1985).

Analysis Procedures

The analyses were based on discrete-time survival models (Allison, 1984) using a person-year data structure. This was done by creating separate observational records for each year of each respondent's life beginning with age 15 (the earliest age at which a meaningful proportion of respondents reported a marriage) and combining all these records into a single data file. Respondents who married for the first time prior to or at their current age contributed one record (person-year) for each year between age 15 and their age at first marriage. Respondents who were never married contributed one record for each year of their lives beginning with age 15. Data on the age-of-onset of each NCS/DSM-III-R disorder were used to define a series of variables in each observational record for whether or not the respondent had a history as of the age in the person-year of each of the 14 disorders.

The data in this file were analyzed with a series of logistic regression equations in which the variables that defined prior history of each NCS/DSM-III-R disorder were treated as predictor variables, controlling for cohort, person-year, and the sociodemographic control variables. The outcomes were defined either as a dichotomous measure of whether the respondent became married in a given year (in the subsample of years that included years of not being married plus years in which marriage occurred) or became divorced in a given year (in the subsample of years that included years of being married plus years in which marital termination occurred). The logistic regression coefficients generated by these models are equivalent to discrete-time survival coefficients (Allison, 1984). For ease of interpretation, these coefficients were exponentiated and interpreted as odds ratios.

In addition to conventional logistic regression analysis, we carried out simulations to evaluate the social policy significance of the effects we documented. This was done in four steps. In the first step, we created a new person-year file in which each respondent was allotted as many person-years as his or her current age, regardless of whether he or she was ever married or divorced. In the second step, we estimated separate summary models, one for the predictors of marriage and the other for the predictors of divorce, in each of which we included terms for the effects of separate classes of psychiatric disorders (e.g., affective disorders), comorbidities among the disorders, and control variables. In the third step, predicted probabilities of becoming married and of becoming divorced were calculated for each person-year of each respondent, based on these summary models. The predicted probabilities were generated several different times, using different subsets of coefficients in the models. One set of predicted probabilities was based on the full model; others set the coefficients for one particular class of disorders to zero before computing the predicted probabilities; yet another set all the disorder coefficients to zero and predicted entirely on the basis of the coefficients associated with the control variables. In the fourth step, we generated the cumulative predicted probability of marriage and the cumulative probability of divorce for each respondent for each of the prediction sets and compared the sum of these cumulations across all respondents in order to simulate the effects of each class of disorders on the population proportions of marriage and divorce.

Due to the complex sample design and weighting of the NCS, standard errors of the discrete-time survival coefficients and the attributable proportions were estimated using the method of Balanced Repeated Replications (BRR) in 44 design-based balanced subsamples (Kish & Frankel, 1970). The survival coefficients were exponentiated and are reported next in the form of odds ratios with 95% confidence intervals that were adjusted for design effects.

When we speak of a result as being "significant," we are referring to statistical significance rather than substantive significance, and all tests are based on two-tailed, design-based tests evaluated at the .05 level of significance.

RESULTS

The Distribution of First Marriages

Cumulative probability curves for age at first marriage were estimated separately for men and women, and significance tests for the difference in these curves (Lee & Desu, 1972) showed, consistent with census population data (U.S. Bureau of the Census, 1992), that there was a significant intercohort increase over time in the age distribution of first marriage for both men (X^2_3 = 171.1, $p < .05$) and women (X^2_3 = 174.2, $p < .05$) across the four 10-year birth cohorts included in the NCS. A comparison of results across the two figures also showed that women tended to marry at earlier ages than men throughout the 40-year time period retrospectively covered in the NCS. This pattern, which is consistent with census population data (U.S. Bureau of the Census, 1992), is statistically significant in each of the four cohorts (X^2_1 = 94.9, 96.2, 130.8, and 54.73, respectively, from earliest to most recent cohort, each significant at $p < .05$).

The Gross Effects of Psychiatric Disorders in Predicting Onset of Marriage

As described in more detail elsewhere (Forthofer et al., 1996), the gross effects of psychiatric disorders were estimated with 18 different survival equations (yielding 20 coefficients): one for each of the 14 DSM-III-R disorders; one for each of three broad classes of disorders (any anxiety disorder, any affective disorder, any addictive disorder); and an overall summary equation for the effects of total number of disorders. Sociodemographic control variables were included in all these models. Each model was estimated for early (15–18), on-time (19–25), and late (26+) marriage in three slightly different forms. First, we evaluated the significance of the gender difference in the impact of psychiatric disorders on marriage and found significant differences no more often than would be expected by chance. Subsequent models were then estimated with men and women combined. Second, we tested for cohort differences in the effects of the disorders on marriage. No significant cohort differences were found in predicting either early or late marriage. Two significant cohort differences were found in predicting on-time marriage, but more detailed analyses revealed that these differences were due to outliers rather than to systematic trends. Subsequent models were then estimated for all cohorts combined. Third, we examined the effects of psychiatric disorders on marriage in models that included main effects for gender and cohort.

The estimated effects of the disorders obtained in the third set of models are presented in the first three columns of Table 13.1. These odds ratios (ORs) can be interpreted as the relative odds of marriage in a single year associated with the existence of a prior lifetime history of a single disorder or class of disorders. As shown in the table, these effects differ depending on age at marriage. For early marriage, 16 of the 20 coefficients are greater than 1.0 and two are significant at the .05 level, which means that adolescents with a history of these disorders are more likely than others to marry by age 18. In comparison, the coefficients are consistently less than 1.0 for on-time (18 of 20) and late (16 of 20) marriage. Eight of the on-time marriage coefficients and three of the late marriage coefficients are significant at the .05 level, meaning that respondents who did not marry by the age of 18 were less likely to marry later if they had a history of one or more of the significant psychiatric disorders. The results in the last two columns of Table 13.1 disaggregate the effects of psychiatric disorders on subsequent on-time and late marriages into the effects on first marriage and on remarriage. Early marriages were not disaggregated into first marriages and remarriages, because virtually all early marriages were first marriages. The results show that the effects of prior disorders on decreased odds of marriage are largely confined to first marriages.

Proportions of First Marriages Associated With Psychiatric Disorders

The results in Table 13.1 are based on equations in which the disorders are considered individually. We also evaluated their joint effects in a series of multivariate equations for the individual disorders having significant effects in Table 13.1, variables defining various combinations of comorbid disorders, and sociodemographic control variables. As described in the section on Analysis Procedures, the results of these models were used to estimate the proportion of early, on-time, or late marriages attributable to psychiatric disorders using simulation methods. The results suggest that 11.7% of early first marriages among men and 9.0% of those among women were associated with prior psychiatric disorders. If these results were interpreted in causal terms, they would indicate that the prevalence of early first marriages would be reduced by these proportions if previous onsets of psychiatric disorders were prevented. Given the proportions of NCS respondents who married by age 18 (6% of men and 25% of women), approximately 2.3 million early marriages (0.5 among men and 1.8 among women) would be attributable to psychiatric disorders, according to this interpretation. The results show that prior psychiatric disorders are associated with a reduction in on-time first

TABLE 13.1
Effects of Psychiatric Disorders in Predicting Onset of Marriage, Controlling for Sociodemographic Predictors

| | Marital Timing | | | | | Marital Sequence | | | |
| | Early[d] | | On-Time | | Late | | First Marriage | | Remarriage | |
	OR	(95% CI)	OR	(95% CI)	OR	(95% CI)	OR	(95% CI)	OR	(95% CI)
A. Anxiety Disorders										
Agoraphobia	1.08	0.69 - 1.68	0.76	0.50 - 1.15	0.79	0.39 - 1.63	0.68*	0.50 - 0.93	1.10	0.41 - 2.93
Panic Disorder	0.89	0.36 - 2.20	0.47*	0.27 - 0.80	0.88	0.45 - 1.70	0.81	0.51 - 1.30	0.54	0.18 - 1.61
Social Phobia	0.99	0.77 - 1.28	0.97	0.77 - 1.22	0.87	0.55 - 1.38	0.84	0.66 - 1.07	1.48	0.71 - 3.06
GAD[a]	1.43	0.86 - 2.38	0.77	0.46 - 1.30	0.93	0.46 - 1.90	0.76	0.52 - 1.10	1.28	0.58 - 2.82
Simple Phobia	1.28	0.93 - 1.76	1.06	0.76 - 1.47	1.02	0.53 - 1.96	1.01	0.79 - 1.30	1.20	0.43 - 3.31
PTSD[b]	1.15	0.89 - 1.49	0.72	0.49 - 1.04	1.14	0.65 - 1.98	0.82	0.59 - 1.14	1.02	0.51 - 2.02
Any Anxiety	1.22	0.96 - 1.55	0.90	0.70 - 1.14	0.93	0.63 - 1.37	0.88	0.72 - 1.08	1.05	0.51 - 2.14
B. Affective Disorders										
Major Depression	0.93	0.62 - 1.36	0.53*	0.38 - 0.74	0.76	0.53 - 1.09	0.56*	0.45 - 0.69	1.05	0.64 - 1.74
Dysthymia	1.32	0.72 - 2.44	0.70	0.43 - 1.14	0.49*	0.29 - 0.85	0.68*	0.51 - 0.92	0.52	0.18 - 1.54
Mania	1.84	0.87 - 3.89	1.00	0.43 - 2.33	0.41	0.12 - 1.40	0.69	0.33 - 1.46	0.65	0.16 - 2.63
Any Affective	1.07	0.75 - 1.54	0.53*	0.38 - 0.73	0.67*	0.46 - 0.96	0.55*	0.46 - 0.67	0.81	0.46 - 1.41

C. Addictive Disorders

Alcohol Abuse	1.27	0.93 - 1.74	0.82*	0.68 - 0.98	0.79	0.58 - 1.07	0.83*	0.70 - 0.98	0.67	0.35 - 1.27
Drug Abuse	1.19	0.85 - 1.64	0.72*	0.55 - 0.95	1.05	0.70 - 1.56	0.75*	0.61 - 0.93	0.99	0.51 - 1.91
Alcohol Dependence	0.90	0.54 - 1.51	0.74*	0.56 - 0.99	0.79	0.51 - 1.20	0.79*	0.65 - 0.96	0.71	0.35 - 1.44
Drug Dependence	1.21	0.74 - 1.98	0.77	0.52 - 1.13	1.01	0.66 - 1.54	0.78	0.60 - 1.01	0.87	0.40 - 1.87
Any Substance	1.12	0.83 - 1.52	0.78*	0.66 - 0.92	0.76	0.56 - 1.03	0.82*	0.70 - 0.97	0.58	0.32 - 1.05

D. Other Disorders

Conduct Disorder	1.54*	1.19 - 1.98	0.85	0.68 - 1.06	0.88	0.58 - 1.34	0.75*	0.61 - 0.92	1.06	0.50 - 2.27

E. Comorbidity

1 Disorder[c]	1.45*	1.13 - 1.87	0.88	0.73 - 1.05	0.63*	0.43 - 0.92	0.94	0.79 - 1.11	0.38*	0.16 - 0.90
2 Disorders	1.39	0.92 - 2.12	0.84	0.66 - 1.07	0.84	0.53 - 1.34	0.83*	0.69 - 0.99	0.77	0.28 - 2.14
3+ Disorders	1.16	0.82 - 1.65	0.72*	0.56 - 0.94	0.72	0.50 - 1.03	0.71*	0.55 - 0.90	0.70	0.35 - 1.42

Note: Reproduced, in part, from Forthofer et al. (1996).

*Significant at the .05 level, two-tailed test.

[a]Generalized Anxiety Disorder.

[b]PostTraumatic Stress Disorder.

[c]Variables representing exactly one disorder, exactly two disorders, and three or more disorders were included in the same model.

[d]More than 99.5% of early marriages are first marriages.

[e]Sequence is only studied in the subsample of on-time and late marriages, as virtually all early marriages in the sample were first marriages.

marriages of 7.5% among men and 3.2% among women and a reduction in late first marriages of 3.9% among men and 5.3% among women. Because the number of people who marry in these age ranges is large, these small proportions translate into large raw numbers: 4.3 million on-time marriages (2.3 among men and 1.0 among women) and 0.9 million late marriages (0.5 among men and 0.4 among women). Cohort-specific analyses show a general trend for the proportions of first marriages associated with prior disorders to increase in more recent cohorts. This is because the prevalences of almost all of the disorders considered here are higher in recent cohorts than in earlier cohorts (Warner et al., 1995; Wittchen et al., 1994).

The Distribution of Divorce

Cumulative probability curves for age at divorce were estimated separately for men and women by age at first marriage and cohort. Results for the age analysis showed that early marriages are much more likely to end in divorce than on-time or late marriages among both men ($X^2_2 = 5358.7$, $p < .05$) and women ($X^2_2 = 4282.8$, $p < .05$). In the subsample of early marriages, furthermore, a significant cohort effect was found that documented an increasing prevalence of divorce in more recent cohorts among both men ($X^2_3 = 591.2$, $p < .05$) and women ($X^2_3 = 2385.1$, $p < .05$). Similar results were found in separate analyses of on-time and late marriage. Furthermore, it was found that the cumulative probability of divorce differs substantially for first marriages and remarriages among men ($X^2_1 = 563.0$, $p < .05$) but not women ($X^2_1 = 10.6$, $p < .05$), with a cross in the male curve at about 20 years of marriage indicating that men who are remarried are more likely than men in their first marriages to become divorced in the first two decades of the marriage, but less likely than men in their first marriages to become divorced once the marriage goes beyond 20 years. Based on these results, subsequent analyses of the effects of psychiatric disorders on marital dissolution were estimated separately for first marriages and remarriages and for recent cohorts (ages 15–34 at interview) and older cohorts (ages 35–54 at interview).

The Gross Effects of Psychiatric Disorders on Divorce

As described in more detail elsewhere (Kessler, Walters, & Forthofer, 1998), the gross effects of psychiatric disorders on divorce were estimated with the same 18 different survival equations as described in the analysis of marriage. However, unlike the results of the marriage models, we found that the ORs differed significantly by sex in predicting divorce. The results of the analyses are consequently reported separately for men and women. As shown in the first column of Table 13.2, the associations of prior psychiatric disorders and divorce from first marriage among men are generally positive (20 of 20

TABLE 13.2

Effects of Psychiatric Disorders in Predicting Onset of Divorce, Controlling for Sociodemographic Predictors Among Men

	Marital Sequence				Cohort			
	First Marriage		Remarriage		15–34 at Interview		35–54 at Interview	
	OR	(95% CI)	OR	(95% CI)	OR	(95% CI)	OR	(95% CI)
A. Anxiety Disorders								
Agoraphobia	1.54	0.84 - 2.85	0.52*	0.08 - 3.34	2.73	0.94 - 7.93	0.50	0.26 - 0.95
Panic Disorder	2.06*	1.03 - 4.10	0.63	0.15 - 2.66	7.10*	1.87 - 26.99	0.48	0.18 - 1.28
Social Phobia	1.19	0.84 - 1.68	0.35*	0.14 - 0.88	1.44	0.65 - 3.20	0.44	0.25 - 0.79
GAD[a]	2.40*	1.52 - 3.79	1.34	0.24 - 7.34	4.55*	2.02 - 10.29	0.74	0.36 - 1.53
Simple Phobia	1.79*	1.30 - 2.47	0.72	0.27 - 1.88	2.01*	1.09 - 3.70	0.85	0.45 - 1.60
PTSD[b]	1.99*	1.11 - 3.58	4.54*	1.30 - 15.82	3.10*	1.61 - 5.95	2.64	0.89 - 7.81
Any Anxiety	1.49*	1.13 - 1.97	1.05	0.35 - 3.15	1.61	0.85 - 3.08	1.09	0.49 - 2.43
B. Affective Disorders								
Major Depression	2.08*	1.56 - 2.78	0.95	0.37 - 2.40	2.57*	1.31 - 5.06	0.94	0.50 - 1.78
Dysthymia	1.54	0.86 - 2.75	1.71	0.66 - 4.43	1.79	0.50 - 6.47	1.09	0.54 - 2.21
Mania	4.43*	2.77 - 7.06	0.54	0.01 - 21.34	3.63	0.31 - 42.23	0.76	0.31 - 1.87
Any Affective	1.97*	1.48 - 2.63	1.10	0.46 - 2.71	2.60*	1.36 - 4.98	0.96	0.52 - 1.77

(Continued)

TABLE 13.2
(Continued)

| | Marital Sequence | | | | Cohort | | | |
| | First Marriage | | Remarriage | | 15–34 at Interview | | 35–54 at Interview | |
	OR	(95% CI)	OR	(95% CI)	OR	(95% CI)	OR	(95% CI)
C. Addictive Disorders								
Alcohol Use	1.20	0.89 - 1.60	0.83	0.31 - 2.21	1.11	0.67 - 1.85	0.96	0.46 - 1.99
Drug Abuse	1.52*	1.12 - 2.06	0.81	0.32 - 2.09	1.36	0.71 - 2.63	0.91	0.48 - 1.73
Alcohol Dependence	1.40*	1.03 - 1.89	1.12	0.46 - 2.72	1.43	0.76 - 2.69	1.18	0.56 - 2.46
Drug Dependence	1.60*	1.10 - 2.32	0.88	0.34 - 2.27	1.67	0.80 - 3.50	0.84	0.41 - 1.74
Any Substance	1.25	0.95 - 1.66	0.77	0.29 - 2.07	1.10	0.62 - 1.95	0.94	0.45 - 1.99
D. Other Disorders								
Conduct Disorder	1.48*	1.11 - 1.96	0.18*	0.07 - 0.45	1.16	0.69 - 1.95	0.45	0.20 - 0.98
E. Comorbidity								
1 Disorder[c]	1.29	0.93 - 1.79	0.78	0.09 - 6.98	0.88	0.41 - 1.90	1.01	0.31 - 3.28
2 Disorders	1.41	0.92 - 2.15	0.60	0.08 - 4.34	0.83	0.38 - 1.82	0.92	0.28 - 3.01
3+ Disorders	1.81*	1.28 - 2.57	0.51	0.16 - 1.63	1.82	0.82 - 4.06	0.73	0.29 - 1.86

Note: *Significant at the .05 level, two-tailed test.
[a]Generalized Anxiety Disorder.
[b]PostTraumatic Stress Disorder.
[c]Variables representing exactly one disorder, exactly two disorders, and three or more disorders were included in the same model.

coefficients) and statistically significant (13 of 20 coefficients). The results in the second column show that most of the associations of prior disorders with divorce from remarriages among men are negative (14 of 20 coefficients). The results in the third and fourth columns show that whereas most of the ORs are positive among men in more recent cohorts (18 of 20 coefficients, 6 of them significant), most of the coefficients are negative (15 of 20 coefficients, although none of them is significant) in the older cohorts.

The results for women in Table 13.3 show very similar patterns. All 20 of the coefficients in predicting divorce from first marriage are positive and 14 are significant, but 11 of 20 are negative (none significant) in predicting divorce from remarriage. All 20 coefficients in the more recent cohorts are positive (8 of them significant), whereas 10 of the 20 are negative in the older cohorts (2 significant, both associated with positive coefficients).

Proportions of Divorce Associated With Psychiatric Disorders

Simulations from a series of multivariate equations for the joint effects of the individual disorders estimated that 20.5% of first divorces among men and 16.5% of those among women were associated with prior psychiatric disorders. These proportions are equivalent to 2.6 million divorces among men and 3.6 million among women. Among men and women alike, there was consistent evidence that these proportions were larger in more recent cohorts, consistent with the increasing prevalences of these disorders among younger respondents and with the stronger ORs for divorce in the younger cohorts.

DISCUSSION

Limitations

Two limitations of the preceding analysis must be recognized. First, the NCS sample probably contains a lower proportion of respondents with a history of psychiatric disorders than the population because the sampling frame was incomplete (excluding the homeless, residents of institutional settings and group housing, and persons who were deceased), the response rate was less than 100%, and available evidence suggests that nonrespondents had higher rates of disorder than did respondents (Kessler, Little, & Groves, 1995). This could have led to bias in the estimated effects of psychiatric disorders. Second, the validity of the results is contingent on respondent recall of lifetime psychiatric disorders and ages of onset. We attempted to address this problem by using a variety of memory priming techniques (Kessler, Mroczek, & Belli,

TABLE 13.3

Effects of Psychiatric Disorders in Predicting Onset of Divorce, Controlling for Sociodemographic Predictors Among Women

| | Marital Sequence | | | | Cohort | | | |
| | First Marriage | | Remarriage | | 15–34 at Interview | | 35–54 at Interview | |
	OR	(95% CI)	OR	(95% CI)	OR	(95% CI)	OR	(95% CI)
A. Anxiety Disorders								
Agoraphobia	1.71*	1.33 – 2.20	2.32	0.68 - 7.88	1.40*	1.02 – 1.91	2.53*	1.13 - 5.64
Panic Disorder	1.45	0.96 - 2.19	1.30	0.28 - 6.07	1.99*	1.09 – 3.62	1.38	0.55 - 3.45
Social Phobia	0.96	0.74 - 1.25	1.44	0.54 - 3.86	1.15	0.80 - 1.64	1.23	0.66 - 2.30
GAD[a]	2.14*	1.52 - 3.02	2.05	0.44 - 9.62	1.68	0.88 - 3.20	2.31	0.86 - 6.20
Simple Phobia	1.06	0.78 - 1.44	1.22	0.45 - 3.36	1.06	0.71 - 1.60	1.27	0.59 - 2.73
PTSD[b]	2.04*	1.48 - 2.79	0.66	0.16 - 2.66	1.68*	1.09 – 2.60	1.08	0.54 - 2.15
Any Anxiety	1.34*	1.07 - 1.69	1.28	0.58 - 2.83	1.42*	1.02 – 1.98	1.53	0.96 - 2.43
B. Affective Disorders								
Major Depression	1.74*	1.37 - 2.19	0.69	0.29 - 1.64	1.36	0.89 – 2.08	0.96	0.51 - 1.80
Dysthymia	1.73*	1.32 - 2.26	0.32	0.06 - 1.90	1.35	0.75 – 2.45	0.79	0.33 - 1.92
Mania	2.21*	1.36 - 3.59	—	—	3.49*	1.18 - 10.33	0.46	0.10 - 2.23
Any Affective	1.76*	1.45 - 2.15	0.59	0.26 - 1.37	1.49*	1.07 – 2.08	0.88	0.48 - 1.61

C. Addictive Disorders							
Alcohol Use	1.60*	1.23 - 2.09	0.52	0.15 - 1.76	1.26	0.81 - 1.94	0.99	0.46 - 2.11
Drug Abuse	1.28	0.76 - 2.16	0.38	0.08 - 1.76	1.25	0.71 - 2.22	0.69	0.27 - 1.74
Alcohol Dependence	1.84*	1.31 - 2.58	0.41	0.10 - 1.60	1.38	0.75 - 2.56	0.84	0.29 - 2.44
Drug Dependence	1.66*	1.02 - 2.69	0.24	0.03 - 2.01	1.48	0.86 - 2.55	0.54	0.16 - 1.78
Any Substance	1.45*	1.07 - 1.98	0.48	0.14 - 1.60	1.28	0.85 - 1.92	0.95	0.46 - 1.96
D. Other Disorders							
Conduct Disorder	1.20	0.88 - 1.63	0.35	0.02 - 7.83	1.72*	1.26 - 2.36	0.61	0.23 - 1.63
E. Comorbidity							
1 Disorder[c]	1.32	0.95 - 1.85	1.60	0.54 - 4.68	1.12	0.65 - 1.91	1.67	0.95 - 2.95
2 Disorders	1.57*	1.09 - 2.26	1.56	0.69 - 3.51	1.45	0.69 - 3.03	2.13*	1.15 - 3.95
3+ Disorders	1.64*	1.24 - 2.17	0.66	0.23 - 1.94	1.65*	1.10 - 2.49	1.19	0.62 - 2.29

Note: *Significant at the .05 level, two-tailed test.

[a]Generalized Anxiety Disorder.

[b]Post-Traumatic Stress Disorder.

[c]Variables representing exactly one disorder, exactly two disorders, and three or more disorders were included in the same model.

in press). However, despite these precautions, errors in recall could have led to bias in the estimated effects of prior disorders on subsequent marriage and/or to the appearance of higher prevalences in more recent cohorts (Simon & Von Korff, 1992).

Conclusions

Within the constraints of those limitations, the results suggest that psychiatric disorders are significantly associated with the subsequent probability and timing of marriage and marital dissolution. The research design does not permit these associations to be interpreted as causal. However, such an interpretation is certainly plausible. The positive associations of prior disorders with early marriage is consistent with evidence that distressed adolescents may marry early in order to escape stressful childhood environments (Brown & Harris, 1993; Quinton & Rutter, 1988). One possible contributing factor is that psychiatric disorders are positively associated with teenage pregnancy (Kessler et al., 1996), and early marriage may be a consequence of premarital pregnancy (among NCS respondents, no more than 28% of early marriages were preceded by premarital pregnancies). The negative associations of prior disorders with on-time and late first marriage could reflect the operation of mechanisms that treat psychiatric disorders as handicaps in the marriage market, an interpretation consistent with evidence that psychiatric disorders are recognized as undesirable (Link, Cullen, Frank, & Wozniak, 1987; Mechanic, 1975), and that they are often associated with rejection in social situations (e.g., Nieradzik & Cochrane, 1985). This interpretation is also consistent with evidence that other undesirable personal characteristics, such as physical deformity and low earnings, influence chances of marriage (Becker, 1981; Bergstrom & Bagnoli, 1993; Oppenheimer, 1988). A similar interpretation can be made for the positive associations between prior disorders and divorce, emphasizing the fact that psychiatric disorders are often associated with the kinds of interpersonal difficulties that are known to promote marital disruption.

All of these associations can be seen as leading to increased exposure to adverse life experiences among people with histories of psychiatric disorders. There is considerable evidence that married people enjoy advantages in health, social support, and financial security compared to both the never married and the previously married (Aseltine & Kessler, 1993; Booth & Amato, 1991; Mastekaasa, 1992). To the extent that psychiatric disorders are associated with a decreased chance of marriage and an increased chance of marital dissolution, they reduce access to those resources. In addition, there is good evidence that early marriage, in comparison with on-time marriage, is associated with subsequent life adversities, including increased marital instability, limited access to economic resources, restricted educational attainment, and heavy child-care burdens (Booth & Edwards, 1985; Teti et al., 1987). Some of these effects endure throughout the life course. For example, early-married couples are at greater risk for divorce than those who married later, even after controlling for the duration of the marriage (Booth & Edwards, 1985). In addition, the lower socioeconomic resources associated with early marriage, as opposed to on-time or later marriage, controlling for socioeconomic origins, persist throughout life (Teti et al., 1987). Therefore, to the extent that early-onset psychiatric disorders are associated with an increased chance of early rather than on-time or later marriage, they lead to greater exposure to a variety of life adversities.

As noted in the introduction, the investigation of these consequences is part of a larger program of research aimed at documenting the social consequences of psychiatric disorders for purposes of informing the current social policy debate on mental health insurance coverage. Although the majority of people with psychiatric disorders in the United States do not seek professional treatment even when they have insurance (Kessler et al., 1994), payers and some health policy analysts are reluctant to expand coverage because of concerns that it may lead to profligate use (Frank, Goldman, & McGuire, 1994; Frank & McGuire, 1986). An implicit assumption in these positions is that the total societal costs of treating these disorders are greater than the costs of not treating them. The results reported here add to a growing body of evidence that this assumption is incorrect; that psychiatric disorders have a great many hidden costs that would more than offset the direct costs of interventions if effective prevention and treatment programs were made widely available.

It is relevant to this social policy debate that the costs of the adversities associated with psychiatric disorders are borne not only by the individuals who suffer from these disorders but also by the larger society. Regarding the marital effects examined in this report, there are costs to every taxpayer associated with the financial maintenance of Aid to Families with Dependent Children (AFDC) recipients who might otherwise have entered more successful and stable marriages, postponed childbearing, or continued their schooling rather than entered early marriages, were it not for their psychiatric disorders. Furthermore, there is evidence in the current report as well as elsewhere (Kessler, Foster, Saunders, & Stang, 1995, 1996) that these costs are increasing in recent cohorts due to both an increase in the prevalence of psychiatric disorders and an influence of these disorders on important aspects of role functioning. The current policy debate concerning our society's ability to pay for universal preventive and treatment services for the mentally ill needs to consider these costs in evaluating policies either to provide funding for programs or to allow these disorders to develop and go untreated.

ACKNOWLEDGMENTS

Portions of the data reported here were previously reported in Forthofer, Kessler, Story, and Gotlib (1996), and Kessler and Forthofer (in press). These data were collected with support from the National Institute of Mental Health (Grants R01 MH46376 and R01 MH49098) with supplemental support from the National Institute of Drug Abuse (through a supplement to R01 MH46376) and the W.T. Grant Foundation (Grant 90135190). Preparation of this report was also supported by a Research Scientist Award to Ronald Kessler (Grant K05 MH00507), a predoctoral trainship to Melinda Forthofer (Grant T32 MH16806), and an education grant from the Glaxo Research Institute. The authors thank David Almeida, Larry Bumpass, Mike Hughes, Chris Nelson, and Arland Thornton for helpful feedback on earlier drafts of this paper.

REFERENCES

Allison, P. D. (1984). *Event history analysis*. Beverly Hills, CA: Sage.

American Psychiatric Association. (1987). *Diagnostic and Statistical Manual of Mental Disorders* (3rd ed.-rev.). Washington, DC: American Psychiatric Association.

Aseltine, R. H., & Kessler, R. C. (1993). Marital disruption and depression in a community sample. *Journal of Health and Social Behavior, 34*, 237–251.

Axinn, W. G., & Thornton, A. (1992). The influence of parental resources on the timing of the transition to first marriage. *Social Science Research, 21*, 261–285.

Becker, G. S. (1981). *A treatise on the family*. Cambridge, MA: Harvard University Press.

Bergstrom, T. C., & Bagnoli, M. (1993). Courtship as a waiting game. *Journal of Political Economy, 101*(11), 185–202.

Booth, A., & Amato, P. R. (1991). Divorce and psychological stress. *Journal of Health and Social Behavior, 32*, 396–407.

Booth, A., & Edwards, J. N. (1985). Age at marriage and marital instability. *Journal of Marriage and the Family, 47*, 67–75.

Booth, A., & Edwards, J. N. (1992). Starting over: Why remarriages are more unstable. *Journal of Family Issues, 13*(2), 179–194.

Brown, G. W., & Harris, T. O. (1993). Aetiology of anxiety and depressive disorders in an inner city population—1: Early adversity. *Psychological Medicine, 23*, 143–154.

Clark, R. E. (1994). Family costs associated with severe mental illness and substance abuse. *Hospital and Community Psychiatry, 45*(8), 808–813.

Forthofer, M. S., Kessler, R. C., Story, A. L., & Gotlib, I. H. (1996). The effects of psychiatric disorders on the probability and timing of first marriage. *Journal of Health and Social Behavior, 37*, 121–132.

Frank, R. G., Goldman, H. H., & McGuire, T. G. (1994). Who will pay for health reform? Consequences of redistribution of funding for mental health care. Special Section: Health reform and mental health care. *Hospital & Community Psychiatry, 45*, 906–910.

Frank, R. G., & McGuire, T. G. (1986). A review of studies of the impact of insurance on the demand and utilization of specialty health services. *Health Services Research, 21*, 241–265.

Gotlib, I. H., & McCabe, S. B. (1990). Marriage and psychopathology. In F. Fincham & T. Bradbury (Eds.), *The Psychology of marriage: Basic issues and applications* (pp. 226–255). New York: Guilford.

Gove, W. R. (1972). Sex, marital status and suicide. *Journal of Health and Social Behavior, 13,* 204–213.

Heaton, T. B., Albrecht, S. L., & Martin, T. K. (1985). The timing of divorce. *Journal of Marriage and Family, 47,* 631–639.

Keith, V. M., & Finlay, B. (1988). The impact of parental divorce on children's educational attainment, marital timing, and likelihood of divorce. *Journal of Marriage and Family, 50,* 797–809.

Kessler, R. C., Berglund, P. A., Foster, C. L., Saunders, W. B., Stang, P. E., & Walters, E. E. (1997). The social consequences of psychiatric disorders. II. Teenage childbearing. *American Journal of Psychiatry, 154,* 1405–1411.

Kessler, R. C., Foster, C. L., Saunders, W. B., & Stang, P. E. (1995). The social consequences of psychiatric disorders: I. Educational attainment. *American Journal of Psychiatry, 152,* 1026–1032.

Kessler, R. C., Little, R. J. A., & Groves, R. M. (1995). Advances in strategies for minimizing and adjusting for survey nonresponse. *Epidemiologic Reviews, 17,* 192–204.

Kessler, R. C., McGonagle, K. A., Zhao, S., Nelson, C. B., Hughes, M., Eshleman, S., Wittchen, H.-U., & Kendler, K. S. (1994). Lifetime and active prevalence of DSM-III-R psychiatric disorders in the United States: Results from the National Comorbidity Survey. *Archives of General Psychiatry, 51,* 8–19.

Kessler, R. C., & McRae, J. A. (1984). A note on the relationships of sex and marital status to psychological distress. *Research in Community and Mental Health, 4,* 109–130.

Kessler, R. C., Mroczek, D. K., & Belli, R. F. (in press). Retrospective adult assessment of childhood psychopathology. In D. Shaffer & J. Richters (Eds.), *Assessment in child and adolescent psychopathology.* New York: Guilford.

Kessler, R. C., Walters, E. E., & Forthofer, M. S. (1998). The social consequences of psychiatric disorders: III. Probability of marital stability. *American Journal of Psychiatry.*

Kish, L., & Frankel, M. R. (1970). Balanced repeated replications for standard errors. *Journal of the American Statistical Association, 65,* 1071–1094.

Kouzis, A. C., & Eaton, W. W. (1994). Emotional disability days: Prevalence and predictors. *American Journal of Public Health, 84*(8), 1304–1307.

Lamb, M., & Teti, D. M. (1989). Socioeconomic and marital outcomes of adolescent marriage, adolescent childbirth, and their co-occurrence. *Journal of Marriage and the Family, 51,* 203–212.

Lee, E., & Desu, M. M. (1972). A computer program for comparing K samples with right-censored data. *Computer Programs in Biomedicine, 2,* 315–321.

Link, B. G., Cullen, F. T., Frank, J., & Wozniak, J. F. (1987). The social rejection of former mental patients: Understanding why labels matter. *American Journal of Sociology, 92*(6), 1461–1500.

Marini, M. M. (1984). The order of events in the transition to adulthood. *Sociology of Education, 57*(2), 63–84.

Marini, M. M. (1985). Determinants of the timing of adult role entry. *Social Science Research, 14*(4), 309–350.

Mastekaasa, A. (1992). Marriage and psychological well-being: Some evidence on selection into marriage. *Journal of Marriage and the Family, 54,* 901–911.

Mechanic, D. (1975). Sociocultural and social–psychological factors affecting personal responses to psychological disorder. *Journal of Health and Social Behavior, 16*(4), 393–404.

Mechanic, D. (1993). Mental health services in the context of health insurance reform. *Milbank Quarterly, 71*(3), 349–364.

Morgar, S. P., & Rindfuss, R. R. (1985). Marital disruption: Structural and temporal dimensions. *American Journal of Sociology, 90*(5), 1055–1077.

Nieradzik, K., & Cochrane, R. (1985). Public attitudes towards mental illness: The effects of behavior, roles and psychiatric labels. *International Journal of Social Psychiatry, 31*(1), 23–33.

Oppenheimer, V. K. (1988). A theory of marriage timing. *American Journal of Sociology, 94*(3), 563–591.

Quinton, D., & Rutter, M. (1988). *Parenting breakdown: The making and breaking of inter-generational links.* Brookfield, VT: Gower.

Rice, D. P., Kelman, S., Miller, L. S., & Dunnmeyer, S. (1990). *The economic costs of alcohol and drug abuse and mental illness: 1985.* Rockville, MD: Alcohol, Drug Abuse and Mental Health Administration.

Rosenfield, S. (1982). Sex roles and societal reactions to mental illness: The labeling of "deviant" deviance. *Journal of Health and Social Behavior, 23,* 18–24.

Simon, G. E., & Von Korff, M. (1992). Reevaluation of secular trends in depression rates. *American Journal of Epidemiology, 135,* 1411–1422.

Teti, D. M., Lamb, M. E., & Elster, A. B. (1987). Long-range socioeconomic and marital consequences of adolescent marriage in three cohorts of adult males. *Journal of Marriage and the Family, 49,* 499–506.

U.S. Bureau of the Census. (1992). *Marital status and living arrangements: March 1991.* (Current Population Reports, Series P-20, No. 461). Washington, DC: U.S. Government Printing Office.

Warner, L. A., Kessler, R. C., Hughes, M., Anthony, J. C., & Nelson, C. B. (1995). Prevalence and correlates of drug use and dependence in the United States: Results from the National Comorbidity Survey. *Archives of General Psychiatry, 52,* 219–229.

Weil, T. P. (1991). Mental health services under a U.S. National Health Insurance Plan. *Hospital & Community Psychiatry, 42*(7), 695–700.

Wells, K., Stewart, A., Hays, R., Burnam, M., Rogers, W., Daniels, M., Berry, S., Greenfield, S., & Ware, J. (1989). The functioning and well-being of depressed patients: Results from the Medical Outcomes Study. *Journal of the American Medical Association, 262,* 914–919.

Wittchen, H.-U. (1994). Reliability and validity studies of the WHO Composite International Diagnostic Interview (CIDI): A critical review. *Journal of Psychiatric Research, 28,* 57–84.

Wittchen, H.-U., Zhao, S., Kessler, R. C., & Eaton, W. W. (1994). DSM-III-R Generalized Anxiety Disorder in the National Comorbidity Survey. *Archives of General Psychiatry, 51,* 355–364.

World Health Organization. (1990). *Composite International Diagnostic Interview (CIDI, Version 1.0).* Geneva: World Health Organization.

14

▼▼▼▼▼▼▼

Perspectives on Conflict
and Cohesion in Families

Martha J. Cox
University of North Carolina at Chapel Hill

Jeanne Brooks-Gunn
Teachers College, Columbia University

Blair Paley
University of California, Los Angeles
Neuropsychiatric Institute and Hospital

In this concluding chapter, in line with our goal of understanding individual development in the context of relationships in the family, we discuss the importance of: (a) more specific definitions of family conflict and cohesion for advancing the study of critical family processes; (b) a more nuanced and less deficit-driven model of family conflict; (c) a better understanding of bidirectional influences of family relationships and individual development; (d) more information concerning the relations between relationships in the family; (e) a more contextualized look at diverse family constellations; (f) understanding how different family relationships come into being; and (g) moving the study of the family from exclusive use of small samples to use of large national data sets as well. In this discussion, we reflect on the contributions in this volume, integrate the insights gained from this research, discuss implications for perspectives on mental health and development, and highlight issues that remain to be addressed.

THE NEED FOR MORE SPECIFIC DEFINITIONS
OF FAMILY CONFLICT AND COHESION

Often the advancement of a research area is limited by problems in definition, with similar construct names used for widely different constructs, or insufficient specificity in constructs. This is the case for the constructs of conflict and cohesion. Imprecision in definitions led to confusion and lack of clarity about the roles of these constructs in family development and functioning.

Regarding cohesion, Barber and Buehler (1996) noted that confusion results from the fact that the construct is sometimes used to refer to warmth and closeness in families (where one presumes that more is better). In other cases, it is assumed that at the extreme, cohesion becomes "enmeshment," a set of family relationships detrimental for individual growth and development (e.g., Epstein, Bishop, & Baldwin, 1982; Olson, Russell, & Sprenkle, 1983). Barber and Buehler (1996) asserted that the two are separate aspects of family functioning. *Family cohesion* is more appropriately defined as shared affection, support, helpfulness, and caring among family members, and *enmeshment* refers to family patterns that facilitate psychological and emotional fusion among family members, "potentially inhibiting the individuation process and maintenance of psychosocial maturity" (p. 433). They asserted that the predictors of each construct and the mechanisms by which families come to show patterns characterized by each construct are different. Therefore, treating these as the same phenomena, with enmeshment representing an extreme case of cohesion or closeness, does not help clarify the processes through which families come to be characterized as either cohesive or enmeshed. Cohesion represents positive, supportive interaction among family members, similar to the notions of "closeness" and "warmth" and is linearly related to individual and family functioning (Maccoby & Martin, 1983). Enmeshment is not an element of supportive relationships; instead it involves controlling and constraining interaction patterns that inhibit individual psychological autonomy (Barber & Buehler, 1996).

Data that Barber and Buehler (1996) collected on 470 adolescents support this contention. First, adolescents' reports of cohesion and enmeshment in their families were unrelated to each other. Moreover, cohesion and enmeshment were associated differently with adolescent internalizing and externalizing behavior problems, and the two constructs interacted differently with other measures. As expected, cohesion was positively and linearly associated with positive outcomes, whereas enmeshment had consistently positive associations with adolescent difficulties, especially internalizing behavior problems.

In line with Barber and Buehler, we define family cohesion as positive, supportive interaction among family members, closeness, and warmth; we consider "enmeshment" a separate construct, not part of the continuation of cohesion. Findings from several contributions to this volume (i.e., Graber & Brooks-Gunn; Forgatch & DeGarmo; Powers & Walsh; Conger & Ge) point to the positive role that cohesion plays in the family.

Similarly, lack of specificity of definition hindered our understanding of family conflict and its implications in the family. Margolin (1988) noted that imprecision in the definition of conflict led to several areas of confusion. First, the term *conflict* is used when what is really meant is *destructive conflict*.

As discussed in the next paragraph, it is important that destructive conflict be differentiated from benign or even constructive conflict. Second, in the marital literature, *conflictual relationship* sometimes is used interchangeably with *distressed marriage*. This leads to the mistaken conclusion that all distressed marriages are conflicted and that all conflicted marriages are distressed. Finally, Margolin noted that the term "conflicted" itself is problematic in that calling some families conflicted suggests that there are families without conflict. In any close knit group, conflicts over resources and power are inherent, and the implication that there are family relationships without some conflict is probably misleading. Thus, a set of more specific descriptors is needed to differentiate conflict that is detrimental to the development and functioning of individuals in families and conflict that is benign or perhaps even positive in families. Clearly, there is a need for a more nuanced and less deficit-driven view of conflict in family relationships.

A MORE COMPLEX VIEW OF CONFLICT: CONSTRUCTIVE VERSUS DESTRUCTIVE CONFLICT

Many years ago Deutsch (1969) distinguished between destructive and constructive conflict. Destructive conflict was described as an interpersonal process in which there is escalation beyond the initial issue and reliance on threats and coercion as strategies. Constructive conflict, on the other hand, was characterized as issue-focused and involving negotiation and mutual problem solving.

In line with the notion that there is *constructive* as well as *destructive* conflict, Shantz and Hobart (1989) proposed that conflict is a process that contributes to social development, and that the study of conflict can help shed light on the dynamics of the development of individuals and their social relationships. Shantz and Hobart mostly referred to child–child conflict, but Katz and Gottman (this volume) also suggest that conflict may be a process that contributes to the maintenance of closeness and intimacy in couple relationships. This more subtle view of conflict stands in contrast to a view of conflict as completely negative and something that must be avoided, with harmony as the ideal state for families (Shantz & Hobart, 1989).

Shantz and Hobart contended that the establishment of individuation and connectedness are two major lifelong goals that are not entirely distinct. How one individuates and defines oneself is related to experiences in close relationships, and the types of connections or closeness one has with others are influenced by one's degree of individuation and self-definition. They considered the role conflict might have in establishing and maintaining individuation and connectedness in suggesting that "everyday give-and-take, the minor and major conflicts with parents, siblings, and peers also contribute to individuation—precisely because such conflicts highlight, at the moment they occur, one's differences from others" (p. 89). Thus, they suggested that conflict may be important in the service of individual development that favors individuation and that individuation may make closeness or cohesion more likely. In this way, the two qualities of family are not antithetical, but may even serve to support the development and maintenance of the other. This view of conflict can be seen in the contributions by Graber and Brooks-Gunn and by Powers and Walsh in this volume.

THE NEED TO UNDERSTAND HOW FAMILY RELATIONSHIPS AND INDIVIDUAL DEVELOPMENT ARE MUTUALLY INFLUENTIAL

As we noted in the introduction, a common thread in current perspectives on individual development is that development is seen as occurring in the context of relationships. As a result, there is recognition that the way in which we define healthy or disturbed relationships for children in families must take into account the way that the relationships serve a child with respect to critical developmental issues (Sroufe, 1989). Although this perspective is gaining acceptance, more research is needed that takes this focus. In order to understand how family relationships influence individual development, we need to understand the intersection between qualities of family relationships and how these qualities relate to parenting that is responsive to the developmental needs of the child. Contributions to this volume help make these connections. For example, Forgatch and DeGarmo (this volume) note the importance of cohesive parent–child relationships in fostering the collaboration needed for good parental supervision of young adolescents. Supervision as an aspect of parenting in adolescence is key to the prevention of delinquent behavior. How relationships serve the important adolescent process of individuation is another example. Powers and Walsh (this volume) suggest that parent–child relationships in which a certain amount of negative affect can be tolerated may better serve the process of individuation.

There is growing understanding of how family relationships influence (and are influenced by) individual development. Several chapters in this volume contribute to that literature. In this section, we discuss marital conflict and individual development as well as conflict with parents and individuation of adolescents.

Marital Conflict and Individual Development

Much of the research on conflict in families focused on marital conflict, especially on the impact of marital conflict on the development of children. Two decades of research on the effects of divorce and discord on children (see reviews by Emery, 1982; Grych & Fincham, 1990) highlighted the negative effects of exposure to angry conflict between adults on children's emotional regulation and competence. However, this research also resulted in a growing recognition of the need for a more complex understanding of the association between conflict in marital relationships and children's adaptation (Cummings & Davies, 1994a). Conflict, whether marital or parent–child or sibling, is a fact of family life, and it may have constructive as well as destructive effects on the development of children. The contribution of Cummings and Wilson (this volume) is significant in elucidating when marital conflict may be more benign or even may be constructive and have positive effects on children and when it may be more destructive. They report that resolutions of conflict and explanations of resolution seem to allay children's distress due to exposure to adults' conflicts. Children seem to appraise information about conflict, and their response to conflict is dependent at least partially on those appraisals. Thus, resolutions of conflict and explanations parents provide to children about the conflict, and even partial resolution, progress toward resolution, and explanation that it is okay to disagree seem to decrease the negative effect of conflict. Cummings and Wilson interpret these findings in light of their "emotional security hypothesis," which states that a major avenue through which marital conflict negatively impacts a child is through the threat to the child's emotional security. Thus, resolutions or explanations that serve to decrease the perception of threat have positive effects on children.

Katz, Wilson, and Gottman (this volume) also extend our understanding of the way in which specific forms of emotional communication in marriage differentially predict internalizing and externalizing behavior in children. They provide evidence that "parental meta-emotion philosophy" impacts parenting behavior and child regulation and is also related to marital satisfaction and stability, conflict resolution in marriage, and to the couple's philosophy of marriage. *Parental meta-emotion philosophy* refers to the parents' philosophy about emotion and emotion expression. Parents who are "emotion-coaching" provide a safe environment for the expression of thoughts, feelings, and concerns. This, in turn, is related to the child's regulatory physiology, which suggests that coaching the child's emotions may have an effect on the child's ability to self-soothe, regulate negative emotions, and focus attention. Parents who are emotion-coaching are more likely to be in marriages in which the couple believes in the importance of discussing emotional issues with each other and believes that marital conflict is worth the struggle. The willingness to tolerate and accept some negative affect in family relationships may be an important common element associated with good outcome for family members.

Conflict and Cohesion in Unmarried Couples

The research presented in this volume is paradigmatic of how relationships between mothers and fathers are being studied and conceptualized. Conflict and cohesion between parents is termed *marital conflict* and *marital cohesion*.

However, one third of all births in the United States today are to mothers who are not married. Unwed parenthood is not only limited to teenage mothers—it has become common in parents who are in their 20s as well. Indeed, that one of three births occurs out-of-wedlock (a term that is beginning to be seen as quaint) renders its relative invisibility in the field of family research disquieting. Unmarried parenthood occurs across ethnic and social class lines. Ironically, more attention has been paid to unwed mothers who are African American and teenagers than any other demographic group. As Burton and her colleagues point out (Obeidallah & Burton, this volume), the study of parenthood (family formation and parenting behavior) must be contextualized. Family research on married, middle class, White couples is not necessarily relevant for African American, poor, teenage, unwed mothers. Perspectives on parenting in married couples also might need modification when studying unmarried couples, poor and middle class, White and Black.

Interestingly, a relatively large number of unwed parents are cohabitating (perhaps between one quarter and one third of all unwed parents). A large number of those who are not cohabitating still have weekly involvement, meaning that perhaps more than one half of all unwed fathers are fulfilling a major aspect of the fathering role (i.e., consistent and frequent participation in the child's life). However, we know little about these families, termed *fragile families* by McLanahan and Garfinkel (McLanahan, Garfinkel, Brooks-Gunn, & Hongxin, 1998). What are the characteristics of fathers and mothers who, although unwed, cohabitate or have some form of shared parenting? How do we define different aspects of paternal involvement in these fragile families? Do emotional, time, and financial aspects of involvement tend to co-occur? What roles do parental conflict and closeness play in whether, and to what extent, fathers continue to be involved in their children's lives? Should conflict and closeness be operationalized differently in unwed than in married couples? And, do conflict and closeness influence child wellbeing in similar ways across different family types? We need to understand the dynamics of family relationships in the variety of family forms that children actually experience. This is clearly still a major challenge for the family research field.

Conflict With Parents and Individuation of Adolescents

Several chapters in this volume contribute to understanding the role of parent–child conflict in the process of adolescent individuation. Because adolescence is a time when the task of individuating from parents is particularly salient, it has been suggested that conflicts between parents and adolescent children increase with the onset of puberty, peak during early to midadolescence, and decrease after the adolescent years (Conger & Ge, this volume). However, little empirical evidence exists to document these changes in emotional expression between parents and children. Conger and Ge (this volume), theorizing from a social relational perspective, propose that changes in parent–adolescent relations derive not only from biological and cognitive changes in the adolescent, which result in increases in conflict (overt hostility and negative affect) and decreases in cohesion (observable warmth and support or positive affect) in parent–child relationships, but also from the social interactional histories of parents and adolescence. The earlier affective tone of the parent–child relationship is expected to predict the affective tone during adolescence. Using a longitudinal approach in which a large, carefully defined and enlisted sample of children and families was observed on three occasions when the adolescents were in the seventh, eighth, and ninth grades, this work represents a methodological improvement over much of the previous research. Their study supports their propositions in that findings demonstrate the expected increases in conflict and hostility as well as decreases in warmth or cohesion. The results show even greater hostility among adolescent girls toward their parents than among boys, reflecting perhaps the more rapid pubertal and social development of girls during that age period. Additionally, their findings support their prediction that the earlier interactional histories of parents and children predict the emotional quality of the interactions at adolescence. Those parents and children who were higher on warmth and support at an earlier time increased their emotional closeness over time, whereas those who were low on warmth and supportiveness showed declines over time. They conclude that earlier social relations between parents and their adolescents play an important role in determining the impact of biological and cognitive maturation on future interactions.

Graber and Brooks-Gunn (this volume) further illuminate the factors that affect the mother–daughter relationship during adolescence by considering conflict resolution in mother–daughter discourse and the association of different patterns of conflict interaction with pubertal and reproductive status for daughters and mothers. They note that conflict between mothers and daughters is likely to be normative, and some conflict may be necessary for girls to become more autonomous. They ask the question, "When does conflict become maladaptive, and when is the balance between conflict and closeness disrupted?" They note that there is an increase in depressive symptoms and aggressive feelings and behavior in young women at the time the hormonal system is producing the fastest rise in gonadal hormones. Thus, the physical changes associated with puberty could provide some stimulus for the increased conflict between mothers and daughters. Moreover, psychodynamic theorists have suggested that mothers may have difficulty accepting their daughters' reproductive maturity because their own reproductive years are coming to an end. These changes in both mother and daughter, in some families, may set the stage for increased conflict. But understanding these associations is complicated by the fact that Graber, Brooks-Gunn, and

Warren (1995) found that warmth and less conflict in the family is associated with later ages of menarche, so there are clearly complex interactions of biological and psychosocial development in pubertal development. The Graber and Brooks-Gunn work (this volume) demonstrates that there is much to be done to uncover the intricacies of developmental pathways through adolescence. However, several findings from their studies point in important directions.

First, they find that closeness and conflict coexist in most families, and, consequently, the balance between the two may be important for the adolescent daughter's development. Second, in this longitudinal work they find that mother–daughter relationships do change at the time of puberty. There are increased bids for autonomy by daughters, and individual differences in the extent to which these bids are met by parental resistance. These patterns of interaction seem to have long-term implications. They found that in their relatively advantaged sample, a pregnancy during the daughters' college years was predicted by lower family cohesion, more family conflict, and a more controlling family environment than for girls who did not become pregnant as early as the college years. Interestingly, it is conflict with fathers that predicted the early pregnancy, rather than conflict with mothers. These findings from the Graber and Brooks-Gunn research are provocative, but as they note, more needs to be done to understand the specific pathways by which family relationships during the adolescent years lead to variation in young adult adjustment. Also missing is an understanding of how cultural or socioeconomic context may alter the patterns of family influences.

Powers and Welsh (this volume) further extend understanding of the development of young women during the adolescent years by considering the relation of mother–daughter interactions to daughters' symptoms of depression. They found that mothers and daughters show difficulties in negotiating autonomy when daughters have high internalizing symptoms, and that these interpersonal behaviors indicative of difficulty in negotiating autonomy predict further increases in daughters internalizing symptoms. Their work clearly demonstrates the reciprocal nature of effects that make understanding these pathways to young adulthood so difficult. Specifically, they found that chronic internalizing symptoms in girls lead to high levels of both conflict and submission. Conflict and submission occurring together constitute a behavioral combination that is unlikely to lead to success in negotiating more autonomous relations with mothers. Mothers' conflict, humor, and sarcasm were related curvilinearly to daughters' future symptoms, such that daughters showed higher future symptoms when mothers' conflict, humor, and sarcasm were either too high or too low. Powers and Walsh suggest that these results support the idea that it is developmentally important for mothers of adolescent girls to tolerate a moderate degree of conflict. Again, the idea emerges that tolerance of a certain amount of negative emotion in family relationships may be important for a healthy outcome.

Thus, these contributions in this volume suggest that there are distinct changes in the parent–adolescent relationships during adolescence and that the history of and current interactions with parents characterized by closeness and conflict may be important for the adolescent's outcome in the negotiation of the parent–adolescent relationship.

THE NEED TO BETTER UNDERSTAND THE RELATIONS BETWEEN RELATIONSHIPS IN THE FAMILY

We need to know more about how relationships in the family influence each other. Models that view the child as a social being, forming part of a network of relationships (Hinde & Stevenson-Hinde, 1987), suggest the importance of understanding how this network of interpersonal relationships operates, as such relationships constitute a crucially important part of the child's environment. Of particular interest is the way in which the marital relationship influences other relationships in the family, especially the parent–child relationship (Cox, 1985; Cox & Paley, 1997), but also sibling–sibling relationships.

A general hypothesis was that the negative impact of marital conflict on child development is at least partially mediated by the negative impact of marital conflict on parenting or the parent–child relationship (see Crockenberg & Covey, 1991). A meta-analysis of 68 studies (Erel & Burman, 1995) found support for a "spillover" hypothesis, specifically that negative affect in the marital relationship "spills over" into the parent–child relationship. Again, however, we see the importance of precise definition of conflict. Destructive conflict in families, according to Deutsch (1969), involves conflict that goes beyond the original issue. Margolin, Christenson, and John (1996) report interesting findings that for "distressed" couples (those who scored as distressed on screening instruments and desired treatment for their difficulties), as compared to nondistressed couples, there was greater continuity of marital tensions from one day to the next and greater spillover of tensions from the marital relationship to the parent–child relationship. This spillover effect also was replicated with respect to marital attributions spilling over into parenting practices with young adolescents (Brody, Arias, & Fincham, 1996). It may be the ongoing tension in the marital relationship and the failure to resolve conflicts, rather than the frequency of conflict or negative affect, that is most detrimental to parenting.

In line with this reasoning, Cox, Paley, Payne, and Burchinal (this volume) report on data from a longitudinal study of the transition to parenthood. In that study, it was withdrawal from the partner in a marital interaction involving a current source of disagreement, rather than the amount of disagreement and negative affect, that predicted more negative interactions months later with infants. These findings were particularly strong for mothers. Women who were more withdrawn in their interactions with their husbands were later more likely to be flat and disengaged in interactions with their infants, especially with sons, than were women who were not withdrawn during marital interactions. This effect occurred even after controlling for mothers' depressive symptoms, mothers' education, and the child's negative affect in the interaction with the mother. Withdrawal in the marital interaction also predicted father's flat, disengaged parenting, but fathers were especially flat in affect and disengaged when they showed both withdrawal and angry, conflicted behavior in interaction with their wives.

We need to understand more about when conflict and tensions in the marital relationship spill over into other family relationships. It is clear that the avoidance of conflict that accompanies withdrawn marital behavior can be as detrimental to parent–child relationships as angry arguing. Conflict may serve a constructive function in marital relationships in some cases. A similar argument might be made for the role of conflict in marriages as is made for the role of conflict in adolescent development. That is, conflict can highlight the individual differences, needs, desires, and goals of each partner. Ideally, making those individual needs an understood part of the couple dialogue and planning would allow the marriage to stay close and the partners to stay connected. This quality of marriage has not been sufficiently explored. It is important to understand the mechanisms through which some marriages stay close and vibrant for couples, whereas others result in distance, estrangement, and withdrawal, and the way in which these aspects of marriage influence other relationships in the family.

Although the work on the link between marital processes and parent–child relationships is important, it has serious limitations. Much of the current work is confined to observations of the marriage and the parent–child relationships on tasks that the investigators construct. Clearly, more goes on in families than these tasks can represent. For example, work by McHale and colleagues (McHale, Kuerston, & Lauretti, 1996) alerts us to the fact that marital communication or relationships may have many implications in the family. Not only may the overt and readily observable parental behavior with the child be affected, but also more covert parent-to-child communication about the other parent. Additionally, they note that when marriages do not involve good communication, child-rearing agendas and goals are typically not discussed. Parenting then may become another area of marital contention or at least a place where children are getting different messages from parents and may find it necessary to align with one parent or the other. Thus, rather than just looking for the way interaction in one dyad is related to interaction in another when considering the impact of relationships on relationships, a broader view needs to be taken.

We know very little about how marital relationships are associated with the relationships between siblings. Some studies show that marital conflict is related to differential treatment of siblings (Deal, 1996). Differential treatment of siblings in families is likely to be problematic for individual development; Vandell and Bailey (1992) summarized studies that show that differential treatment of siblings is associated with poor outcome for the favored as well as the less favored sibling. This seems to be due to the fact that differential treatment is associated with destructive conflict in sibling relationships, marked by hostility and anger between siblings. Vandell and Bailey (1992) noted that the sibling relationship can be a place where constructive conflict can lead to psychological growth and emotional expression, as children learn competent ways of opposing, disagreeing, compromising, and conciliating with their siblings. Consequently, children in sibling relationships compromised by marital conflict and differential treatment of siblings may be deprived of the opportunity to learn ways of adaptively resolving conflict that could generalize to other important relationships in life (e.g., peer relationships).

BETTER UNDERSTANDING OF DIVERSE FAMILY CONSTELLATIONS AND FAMILY CONTEXTS

We know little about how the neighborhood, community, or cultural context of families influences the kinds of family relationships that develop and what aspects of relationships are associated with better outcome for individuals. The chapter by Obeidallah and Burton (this volume) challenges the assumption that current theories regarding individuation processes and mother–daughter relationships, developed mainly in considering middle class mothers and daughters, apply when generalized to female-headed families in high risk environments characterized by low resources. The work of Obeidallah and Burton suggests that the imperative for increased autonomy among adolescent girls may not be universal, and that context may play an important role. They note that many aspects of the situations of low income, African American families differ from those of more educated families who typically were studied with regard to family interactions and adolescent autonomy issues. Inner-city African American families may experience age-condensed generations such that the generational boundaries are not as clear. Because the boundaries between the roles of mothers and daughters may be blurred, the need for a struggle over autonomy issues may be less salient because the authority differences were never as strong. Additionally, autonomy issues may not be as pressing in a context characterized by preoccupations with physical survival amid low resources. Among some low income, African American adolescents, the desire may be to increase rather than decrease the ties with mothers. Increasing autonomy from the parent may not have the same valence when fewer chances for advanced education, gainful employment, and marriage exists. In contrast to the Graber and Brooks-Gunn study in which the young women who became pregnant during college years tended to terminate these pregnancies so that career plans would not be derailed, the poor adolescent mothers in the Burton study intended generally to have and keep their babies.

Clearly, little is known about what family relationships are critical in which contexts. For example, Forgatch and DeGarmo (this volume) find that cohesion in parent–child relationships is an important predictor of decreased "wandering" in a group of boys at high risk for antisocial behavior and delinquency, whereas conflict is not. Wandering is an intermediary child outcome that seems to mediate parental supervision and more serious adjustment outcomes, such as antisocial behavior and delinquency. Cohesion in the parent–child relationship may set the stage for the collaboration necessary for good parental supervision, but it may be particularly important in the context of growing up in neighborhoods with high delinquency and crime rates.

Suomi (this volume) highlights the importance of context in maternal behavior and in relationships both within and between family groups among rhesus monkeys in the wild. In reporting recent research, Suomi notes that in the context of small as opposed to large troops, mothers were less restrictive and provided less supervision of their infants' social activities. This resulted in infants playing more with agemate peers from other family groups (matrilines) and in infants developing generally positive relationships with those peers, relationships that persisted over time. However, as the size of the troop increased such that the density of nonkin in close proximity increased, mothers became much more restrictive with their infants. Infants did not have the same opportunities to develop social relationships with peers from other family groups as did cohorts from previous years when the troop was smaller. As a result, interactions with nonkin peers were more hostile throughout adolescence and adulthood, and the general atmosphere of the larger troop was more tense and less cooperative than in previous years when the troop was smaller. This work demonstrates how changes at the "community" level can affect how a mother raises her infant and how changes in individual dyadic relationships can influence the nature of the "community" and is important in suggesting processes to explore in "human communities."

The way in which context influences outcome for individuals as mediated by family processes is understudied. Patterson (this volume) notes, for example, the extent to which context (i.e., poverty and unemployment) disrupts family processes and that this process is important in understanding the effects of poverty and unemployment on juvenile offending. The effects of contextual factors such as parent criminality and social disadvantage have an indirect effect on juvenile crime mediated through disrupted parenting practices. Patterson points to the need to test models asking whether social disorganization variables contribute directly to societal rates of juvenile offending or whether these variables are mediated through their disrupting effect of family relationships. Models designed to account for individual differences in such events as early arrests may be helpful in the task of accounting for aggregate rates in that it is the interaction between macro-characteristics and family breakdown that determines crime rates. The family processes are key as mediators between context and outcome for individuals and in terms of aggregate indices of problematic behaviors.

HOW DIFFERENT FAMILY RELATIONSHIPS COME INTO BEING

One of the difficulties in studying the impact of family conflict or family cohesion is that both are associated with many other qualities of individuals and families that are also linked to the development of individuals within families. For example, parents who are involved in marital conflict also are likely to be depressed (Cummings & Davies, 1994b), and depression is associated with problems in parenting and poor outcome in children (Downey & Coyne, 1990). For this reason, we need to ask how well-functioning versus poorly functioning families come to be. Kessler and Forthofer (this volume) provide data from the National Comorbidity Study (NCS) showing that psychiatric disorders are significantly associated with the subsequent probability and timing of marriage and marital dissolution. Distressed adolescents appear to marry early to escape stressful home environments. Early marriage is associated with a higher probability of marital distress and dissolution. Psychiatric disorder is positively associated with teenage pregnancy and early marriage may be a consequence of premarital pregnancy. Individuals with histories of psychiatric disorders are at increased risk for exposure to adverse life circumstances. Thus, we see that a number of variables related to poor family relationships and child outcome tend to co-occur.

STUDYING THE FAMILY: LEVELS OF ANALYSES

The research in this volume highlights the importance of considering family relationships at various levels of analysis. The decision to study families at a particular level of analysis always involves trade-offs, vis-à-vis the questions that can be answered and the richness of data that are collected on various individuals and relationships. We wish to highlight the fact that families may be profitably studied in the context of larger samples and studies than are usually considered in family research. Some of the longitudinal, often nationally representative, studies have much to offer to the study of families (Brooks-Gunn, Phelps, & Elder, 1991). This section is framed not only in terms of levels of analyses, but the choices that are made in terms of whether to study (a) individuals or couples, (b) couples or families, (c) two generations or three generations of families, and (d) families as they split off to form their own families.

Individuals Versus Couples

Most large-scale studies focus on individuals, rather than couples. This volume portrays research that looks at mothers and fathers (Cox et al., this volume; Katz et al., this volume; Patterson, this volume) and demonstrates the value of looking at "relationships." One example of large-scale studies focusing on couples is the Adolescent Health Study, directed by Richard Udry, a large nationally representative study of youth. In this study, data are collected for a subsample of subjects on the romantic partners of individuals as well as on friends of individuals (Resnick et al., 1997; Udry, in press). This study may be the first systematic attempt to look at dyadic relationships in adolescence, as they influence health behavior. Another example is the Fragile Family Project, directed by McLanahan and Garfinkel. Unwed couples are identified in the hospital, after the birth of a child. Both mother and father are followed over the first 3 to 4 years of the child's life, in order to chart the adult relationship from both the mother's and the father's perspectives, as well as their relationship with the child. This is the first study to focus on a large nationally representative sample of unwed parents (McLanahan et al., 1998). A final example is the National Comorbidity Study in which couples filled out weekly diaries on their interactions and relationships (Almeida & Kessler, in press; Kessler & Forthofer, this volume).

Couples Versus Families

The work of this volume and of the Family Research Consortium generally highlights the value of looking at both parents and children when trying to understand family influences on children (see the following volumes: Cowan & Hetherington, 1991; Hetherington & Blechman, 1996; Patterson, 1990). A few large-scale studies employ this approach. An example is the Panel Study of Income Dynamics (PSID)–Child Supplement, directed by Sandra Hofferth. In this study, 2500 families from the 30-year PSID are being seen—mothers, fathers, and children are being assessed; children's ages range from birth to age 12. The Fragile Families Project (McLanahan et al., 1998) also is assessing mothers, fathers, and children. Given the sampling frame at birth, all of the children will be in the infancy, toddler, and preschool life phases. The National Evaluation of the Early Head Start Program, directed by John Love, Jeanne Brooks-Gunn, and Ellen Kisker, also is using a family-oriented data collection plan. Between 2,400 and 3,000 poor families will be seen across 17 sites. Mothers, children, and fathers are assessed. Additionally, videotaped observations of mother and child and father and child are being included in the Early Head Start Study (Berlin, O'Neal, & Brooks-Gunn, 1998).

Two Generations Versus Three Generations of Families

Even less work was conducted on relationships among grandparents, parents, and children. Linda Burton, Lindsay Chase-Lansdale, and their colleagues made a compelling case for the importance of examining child and parental wellbeing in the context of relationships with grandparents (Chase-Lansdale, Brooks-Gunn, & Zamsky, 1994; Chase-Lansdale, Gordon, Coley, Wakschlag, & Brooks-Gunn, in press; Obeidallah & Burton, this volume; Wakschlag, Chase-Lansdale, & Brooks-Gunn, 1996). This work focused, to a large extent, on teenage childbearers and their offspring. This is in part because generations are compressed in these families and in part because young mothers are more likely to live and/or engage in shared caregiving with their own mothers than are older mothers (Brooks-Gunn & Chase-Lansdale, 1995; Gordon, Chase-Lansdale, Matjasko, & Brooks-Gunn, 1997).

Another body of work illustrating the three-generational approach involves the 30-year follow-ups of several local, and relatively small, samples of families. These include the Baltimore Study of Teenage Motherhood (Furstenberg, Brooks-Gunn, & Morgan, 1987; Furstenberg, Levine, & Brooks-Gunn, 1990), the Woodlawn Study in Chicago (Ensminger, Lamkin, & Jacobson, 1996; Kellam, Ensminger, Branch, Brown, & Fleming, 1984), and the Children of Kauai Study (Werner, Bierman, & French, 1971; Werner, Honzik, & Smith, 1968). Additionally, several studies are following youth that were originally studied as they form families of their own, including the Iowa Youth and Families Project (Conger & Elder, 1994); and the Carolina Longitudinal Study (Cairns & Cairns, 1994). Two current studies are taking advantage of the Perinatal Collaborative Study of 50,000 births in the early 1960s. Families from the Providence and the Baltimore samples are being seen 30 years later (Hardy, Shapiro, Mellitts, Skinner, & Astone, 1996). Several thousand families are being followed from the Baltimore and Providence birth cohorts; additionally, data have been collected on parents and their offspring at the same age point (age 8) in the Baltimore study (Brooks-Gunn, Zhao, Singer, & McLanahan, in press).

This focus on multiple generations in the family also may tell us about couple and family formation: the parents of young adults are likely to play a role in family decisions such as whether or not to cohabitate or get married following a pregnancy. A young woman's decision to marry, cohabitate, or stay in her mother's home is likely to be influenced by the amount of support (emotional and financial) and the availability of space that her mother and other kin can provide (Brooks-Gunn & Chase-Lansdale, 1995). If this support is contingent on limiting interaction with the father of the child, then grandmothers and kin are part of the decision process (Chase-Lansdale et al., in press). Likewise, the father's kin might influence his decisions regarding marriage and cohabitation, vis-à-vis the availability of support and residence (since unwed young fathers are likely to live with their kin). Relationships with one's own parents might affect the decision of unwed fathers regarding continued involvement with their child. Such questions are just beginning to be addressed.

Families as Members of One Household Versus Multiple Households

Although family members in one household are typically the unit of analysis, behavioral scientists also followed family members as they move from one household to another. The most common example is the work on divorced couples and their children (Hetherington, 1989; Prado & Markman, this volume). Some of the national longitudinal data sets continue following household members after they leave the original household, irrespective of the reasons for the move. For example, the Panel Study of Income Dynamics (mentioned earlier), which began 30 years ago and is a representative sample of families from the original time period, continues to see all household members. Couples who are divorced or separated are followed. As children move out and form their own households, they continue to be in the sample. Such data are invaluable in terms of charting changes in relationships and in the formation of households. These data have not been exploited to any degree with regard to questions centering on family relationships.

Target Child Versus Siblings

Another unit-of-analysis issue has to do with the number of children that are seen in any one family. Most of the research presented in this volume looks at effects of family or parental relationships on an individual child. The target child is often chosen based on a particular interest in specific developmental transitions or ages. However, such designs preclude examining sibling relationships or differential parental relationships for various children in the same family. Many large-scale longitudinal studies include all children in the family to be assessed, or include two or three children per family. Examples include the National Longitudinal Study of Youth (the original 1979 sample), the National Longitudinal Study of Youth—Child Supplement (children of the females in the 1979 sample; assessment of their offspring began in 1986), the Panel Study of Income Dynamics (original sample and the Child Supplement), and the Adolescent Health Study, to name the most prominent (Brooks-Gunn, Brown, Duncan & Moore, 1995).

Developmental scholars typically used sibling study designs in order to examine the contributions of genetics and environment to an individual's functioning. Economists and sociologists are employing the national studies with sibling to control for selection bias. As an example, when attempting to estimate the effect of income poverty upon a specific child outcome or on parenting behaviors within a family, regression models are constructed that include a variety of social, economic, and demographic family characteristics associated with income poverty. The hope is that inclusion of such variables will help isolate the effect of poverty (ignoring for the moment interaction effects). In a recent volume on the consequences of growing up poor (Duncan & Brooks-Gunn, 1997), a dozen scholars estimated models using the same set of family characteristics as controls. For child achievement and verbal test scores, for example, the effect sizes for income were one fourth to one third of a standard deviation—a large effect in social science (Duncan, Brooks-Gunn, & Klebanov, 1994; Smith, Brooks-Gunn, & Klebanov, 1997). However, the fact remained that unmeasured family characteristics could have accounted for the income effect (Brooks-Gunn & Duncan, 1997). But how do we identify those critical characteristics? Even if we had more variables at our disposal, would some of the important ones remain unmeasured? To address this problem, behavioral scholars turned to sibling models. Income fluctuates within families to a large extent, so that one sibling might have experienced poverty at age 3, whereas the next child did not live in poverty at age 3. Looking at effects of income upon siblings' outcomes when they are the same age is a good way to attempt to control for unmeasured family characteristics (whether they are genetic or environmental). When using the Panel Study of Income Dynamics to estimate such fixed effects models, Duncan and Brooks-Gunn find that income or poverty effects on school attainment (high school graduation and number of years of completed schooling) are found in individual analyses and in sibling analyses (Duncan & Brooks-Gunn, in press). Our point is that sibling data in the national data sets may be used in several ways and that family researchers might find these data valuable.

CONCLUSION

The contributions of this volume point to many areas for further investigation concerning family processes and individual development. Four are highlighted here, including (a) more about conflict and its meaning in families, particularly with regard to the conditions under which conflict may actually strengthen or enhance family functioning; (b) more about individual qualities of family members and how those interact with family processes; (c) more about the strengths of families; and (d) more about the benefits and limitations of different approaches to the study of individuals and families.

The Meaning of Conflict

There is a growing recognition of the need for a more complex understanding of the relation between conflict and children's adaptation in families (Cummings & Davies, 1994a), and for additional focus on constructive interaction (Easterbrook, Cummings, & Emde, 1994). It is important to recognize that conflict, whether marital or parent–child or sibling, is a fact of family life and that conflict may have constructive as well as destructive effects on the development of children. Markman and colleagues (Prado & Markman, this volume) made the point that it is not conflict specifically that is problematic, but the way in which conflict is handled that spells trouble. In fact, avoidance of conflict, particularly in the form of withdrawal from interaction, is a marker of poor marital relationships (Cox et al., this volume). Conflict between marital partners may be necessary to stimulate the adjustments needed to keep a marriage intimate and satisfying (Katz, Wilson, & Gottman, this volume). Furthermore, constructive conflict in the marital relationship may provide children with models of effective strategies for conflict resolution (Easterbrook et al., 1994). Conflict between parents and children, when handled appropriately, may be critical to the necessary development of a child's autonomy (Graber & Brooks-Gunn, this volume; Powers & Walsh, this volume). However, we know little about responses to marital conflict and individual differences in reactivity to marital discord.

Understanding more specifically the patterns of family conflict and cohesion that are related to outcomes for individuals is important for interventions with couples. It is unlikely that one therapeutic approach will work for all couples; it is necessary to understand the variations in patterns and their import for families (Margolin, 1988).

Qualities of Individuals

The qualities of individuals that may influence family processes are not well studied. For example, male and female children may not only differ in the frequencies of certain behaviors, but also in the patterning of relationship between variables. Marital distress may play out more clearly in the parenting of opposite gender children, that is, mothers with sons (Cox et al., this volume) and fathers with daughters (Cowan, Cowan, & Kerig, 1993). Additionally, Conger and his colleagues (Ge, Conger, Lorenz, Shanahan, & Elder,

1995) report that distress (hostile, anxious, depressed mood) experienced by parents and adolescents is most strongly associated for mothers and sons during early adolescence, whereas fathers and daughters show a similar pattern especially toward midadolescence.

The same family circumstances may have different influences on the course of male and female development. Suomi (this volume) notes that in rhesus monkeys, gender differences in response to maternal separation occur when mothers return to reproductive receptivity around the time the infants are 6 to 7 months old and actively avoid and ignore the infant. Female offspring tend to seek out other family members during their mother's absence, whereas males are more likely to increase interactions with peers. These gender differences in response to maternal separation foreshadow much more dramatic gender differences in life that emerge in adolescence and continue in adulthood for rhesus monkeys. Not all studies in humans support different patterns by gender, but in general we know little about factors like community or cultural context that may support different patterns for males and females. The general conclusion is that we should look at gender interactions or we should look at gender separately to consider whether different paths are found for male and female children.

It is likely that other individual factors are also important in understanding family relationships and individual development. Parents with more problems in regulating emotions (those who are depressed or hostile) may be more affected by ongoing destructive marital conflict in their treatment of children than parents with fewer problems. Children with difficulty regulating emotion may be more severely affected by destructive marital conflict and rejecting, power assertive behaviors in parents. Opposite gender children may be more likely the target of a parent's rejecting behavior, whereas same gender children may be sought as allies and confidants (also to their detriment). These intricacies in family processes need to be elucidated.

Strengths of Families

After many years of research, little is known about the strengths of families. Egeland, Carlson, and Sroufe (1993) noted that resilience is not best conceived as a childhood given, but rather a capacity that develops over time in the context of person–environment interactions. Although a fair amount is known about how families fail under conditions of severe or pervasive adversity, little is known about the many families whose children show successful adaptation, positive functioning, and competence despite conditions of adversity. We know little about families that successfully negotiate risk conditions, although we know that many of these families exist. We know that what we consider typical risk factors, such as poverty and low education, do not operate in the same way in all contexts, but we are only beginning to understand why this is so (Duncan & Brooks-Gunn, 1997).

New Approaches to the Study of Individuals and Families

Most of the work in developmental psychology, as well as in sociology and economics, uses a variable-oriented approach. Even event history analyses look at aggregates of individuals as well as factors that predict differences among individuals. However, few studies follow individuals specifically, or consider the different pathways through which individuals manage to reach outcomes, or even explicate the various pathways through which subsets of individuals transverse. Person-oriented approaches, as advocated by scholars such as Singer and Ryff (Singer, Ryff, Carr, & Magee, in press) and Magnusson and Bergman (Bergman & Magnusson, 1997; Magnusson & Bergman, 1988), would be welcome additions to our research on families. Indeed, it is somewhat surprising that such approaches are not taken, given the clinical flavor of much of the family research. Person-oriented approaches often take the form of cluster analyses. However, Singer and his colleagues argued that using clustering approaches is only a partial solution to studying individual lives through time. They advocate using Boolean and classification approaches to identify individual pathways to specific outcomes. Additionally, they propose ways to prepare narratives from longitudinal survey data, in order to characterize individuals (see Brooks-Gunn, Zhao, Singer, & McLanahan, in press, for an exemplar using the National Longitudinal Study of Youth–Child Supplement in which various pathways through which children of teenage mothers who exhibit high achievement test scores or low behavior problems traverse to reach these outcomes).

In sum, although the contributions in this volume add greatly to our knowledge of family processes and individual development, there is still an ambitious agenda ahead. This agenda includes clearer definitions of our constructs; a clearer understanding of the effects of cultural, neighborhood, and community contexts; expansion of our investigations of family relationships to include all relationships and multiple generations; the use of new methodologies and analyses; and the expansion of research on relationships into large nationally representative data sets.

ACKNOWLEDGMENTS

Partial support for preparation of this chapter for Martha Cox was provided by Department of Education Grant R307A60004 (for the National Center for Early Development and Learning) and by the National Institute of Mental

Health Grant P50MH52429 (for the Center for Developmental Science Research).

REFERENCES

Almeida, D., & Kessler, R. (in press). Everyday stressors and gender differences in daily distress. *Journal of Personality and Social Psychology.*

Barber, B. K. & Buehler, C. (1996). Family cohesion and enmeshment: Different constructs, different effects. *Journal of Marriage and the Family, 58,* 433–441.

Bergman, L. R., & Magusson, D. (1997). A person-oriented approach in research on developmental psychopathology. *Development and Psychopathology, 9*(2), 291–319.

Berlin, L. J., O'Neal, C. R., & Brooks-Gunn, J. (1998). What makes early intervention programs work?: The program, its participants, and their interaction. In L. J. Berlin (Ed.), Opening the black box: What makes early child and family development programs work? [Special Issue]. *Zero to Three,* 18, 4–15.

Brody, G. H., Arias, I., & Fincham, F. D. (1996). Linking marital and child attributes to family processes and parent–child relationships. *Journal of Family Psychology, 10,* 408–421.

Brooks-Gunn, J., Brown, B., Duncan, G., & Moore, K. A. (1995). Child development in the context of family and community resources: An agenda for national data collection. In National Research Council Institute of Medicine, *Integrating federal statistics on children: Report of a workshop* (pp. 27–97). Washington, DC: National Academy Press.

Brooks-Gunn, J., & Chase-Lansdale, P. L. (1995). Adolescent parenthood. In M. H. Bornstein (Ed.), *Handbook of parenting: Volume 3. Status and social conditions of parenting* (pp. 113–149). Mahwah, NJ: Lawrence Erlbaum Associates.

Brooks-Gunn, J., & Duncan, G. J. (1997). The effects of poverty on children. *Futures of Children, 7*(2), 55–71.

Brooks-Gunn, J., Phelps, E., & Elder, G. H. (1991). Studying lives through time; Secondary data analyses in developmental psychology. *Developmental Psychology, 27*(6) 899–910.

Brooks-Gunn, J., Zhao, H., Singer, B., & McLanahan, S. (in press). A person-oriented approach to assessing longitude survey data: The care of risk and resilience in children of teenage mothers. *Wik's Castle Symposium: Developmental science and the holistic approach.* Swedish Royal Academy of Sciences, May 24–28, 1997.

Cairns, R. B., & Cairns, B. D. (1994). *Lifelines and risks: Pathways of youth in our times.* New York: Cambridge.

Chase-Lansdale, P. L., Brooks-Gunn, J., & Zamsky, E. S., (1994). Young African-American multigenerational families in poverty: Quality of mothering and grandmothering. *Child Development, 65*(2), 373–393.

Chase-Lansdale, P. L., Gordon, R. A., Coley, R. L., Wakschlag, L. S., & Brooks-Gunn, J. (in press). Young African-American families in poverty: The contexts, exchanges, and processes of their lives. In E. M. Hetherington (Ed.), *Coping with divorce, single parenting and remarriage: A risk and resilience perspective.* Mahwah, NJ: Lawrence Erlbaum Associates.

Conger, R. D., & Elder, G. H. (1994). *Families in troubled times: Adapting to changes in rural America.* New York: Aldine de Gruyter.

Cowan, P. A., Cowan, C. P., & Kerig, P. K. (1993). Mothers, fathers, sons, and daughters: Gender differences in family formation and parenting style. In P. A. Cowan, D. Field, D. A. Hansen, A. Skolnick, & G. E. Swanson (Eds.), *Family, self, and society: Toward a new agenda for family research* (pp. 165–195). Hillsdale, NJ: Lawrence Erlbaum Associates.

Cowan, P. A. & Hetherington, E. M. (Eds.) (1991). *Family transitions.* Hillsdale, NJ: Lawrence Erlbaum Associates.

Cox, M. J. (1985). Progress and continued challenges in understanding the transition to parenthood. *Journal of Family Issues, 6*(4), 395–408.

Cox, M. J., & Paley, B. (1997). Families as systems. *Annual Review of Psychology, 48,* 243–267.

Crockenberg, S., & Covey, S. L. (1991). Marital conflict and externalizing behavior in children. In D. Cicchetti & S. L. Toth (Eds.), *Rochester symposium on developmental psychopathology: Models and integrations* (Vol. 3, pp. 235–260). Rochester, NY: University of Rochester Press.

Cummings, E. M., & Davies, P. (1994a). *Children and marital conflict.* New York: Guilford.

Cummings, E. M., & Davies, P. (1994b). Maternal depression and child development. *Journal of Child Psychology and Psychiatry, 35,* 73–112.

Deal, J. E. (1996). Marital conflict and differential treatment of siblings. *Family Process, 35,* 333–346.

Deutsch, M. (1969). Conflicts: Productive and destructive. *Journal of Social Issues, 25,* 7–14.

Downey, G., & Coyne, J. C. (1990). Children of depressed parents: An integrative review. *Psychological Bulletin, 108,* 50–76.

Duncan, G. J., & Brooks-Gunn, J. (1997). Income effects across the life span: Integration and interpretation. In G. J. Duncan & J. Brooks-Gunn (Eds.), *Consequences of growing up poor* (pp. 596–610). New York: Russell Sage Foundation Press.

Duncan, G. J., & Brooks-Gunn, J. (in press). Welfare reform, poverty, and child development. *Issues in Science and Technology.*

Duncan, G. J., Brooks-Gunn, J., & Klebanov, P. K. (1994). Economic deprivation and early-childhood development. *Child Development, 65*(2), 296–318.

Easterbrook, M. A., Cummings, E. M., & Emde, R. N. (1994). Young children's responses to constructive marital disputes. *Journal of Family Psychology, 8*(2), 160–169.

Egeland, B., Carlson, E., & Sroufe, L. A. (1993). Resilience as process. *Development and Psychopathology, 5,* 517–529.

Emery, R. E. (1994). Foreword. In E. M. Cummings & P. Davies, *Children and marital conflict.* New York: Guilford.

Ensminger, M. E., Lamkin, R. P., & Jacobson, N. (1996). School leaving: A longitudinal perspective including neighborhood effects. *Child Development, 67,* 2400–2416.

Epstein, N. B., Bishop, D. S., & Baldwin, L. M. (1982). McMaster model of family functioning: A view of the normal family. In F. Walsh (Ed.), *Normal family processes* (pp. 115–141). New York: Guilford.

Erel, O., & Burman, B. (1995). Interrelatedness of marital relations and parent–child relations: A meta-analytic review. *Psychological Bulletin, 118*(1), 108–132.

Furstenberg, F. F., Jr., Brooks-Gunn, J., & Morgan, S. P. (1987). Adolescent mothers later in life. *Family Planning Perspectives, 19*(4), 142–151.

Furstenberg, F. F., Jr., Levine, J. A., & Brooks-Gunn, J. (1990). The children of teenage mothers: Patterns of early childbearing in two generations. *Family Planning Perspectives, 22*(2), 54–61.

Ge, X., Conger, R. D., Lorenz, F. O., Shanahan, M., & Elder, G. H. (1995). Mutual influences in parent and adolescent psychological distress. *Developmental Psychology, 31,* 406–419.

Gordon, R., Chase-Lansdale, P. L., Matjasko, J., & Brooks-Gunn, J. (1997). Young mothers living with grandmothers and living apart: How neighborhood and household contexts relate to multigenerational coresidence in African American families. *Applied Developmental Science, 1* (2), 89–106.

Graber, J. A, Brooks-Gunn, J., & Warren, M. P. (1995). The antecedents of menarcheal age. *Child Development, 66,* 346–359.

Grych, J. H., & Fincham, F. D. (1990). Marital conflict and children's adjustment: A cognitive–contextual framework. *Psychological Bulletin, 108,* 267–290.

Hetherington, E. M. (1989). Coping with family transitions: Winners, losers, and survivors. *Child Development, 60,* 1–14.

Hetherington, E. M., & Blechman, E. A. (1996). *Stress, coping, and resiliency in children and families.* Mahwah, NJ: Lawrence Erlbaum Associates.

Hinde, R. A., & Stevenson-Hinde, J. (1987). Interpersonal relationships and child development. *Developmental Review, 7*(1), 1–21.

Kellam, S. G., Ensminger, M. E., Branch, J. D., Brown, C. H., & Fleming, J. P. (1984). The Woodlawn mental health longitudinal epidemiological project. In S. A. Mednick, M. Harway, & K. M. Finello (Eds.), *Handbook of longitudinal research, Vol. Two: Teenage and Adult cohorts* (pp. 197–207). New York: Praeger.

Maccoby, E., & Martin, J. (1983). Socialization in the context of the family: Parent–child interaction. In E. M. Hetherington (Ed.), *Handbook of child psychology: Vol. 4. Socialization, personality, and social development* (pp. 1–101). New York: Wiley.

Magnusson, D., & Bergman, L. R. (1988). Individual and variable-based approaches to longitudinal research on early risk factors. In M. Rutter (Ed.), *Studies of psychosocial risk: The power of longitudinal data* (pp. 45–61). Cambridge, MA: Cambridge University Press.

Margolin, G. (1988). Marital conflict is not marital conflict is not marital conflict. In R. DeV. Peters & R. J. McMahon (Eds.), *Social learning and systems approaches to marriage and to family* (pp. 193–216), New York: Brunner/Mazel.

Margolin, G., Christenson, A., & John, R. S. (1996). The continuance of spillover of everyday tensions in distressed and nondistressed families. *Journal of Family Psychology, 10,* 304–321.

McHale, J. P., Kuersten, R., & Lauretti, A. (1996). New directions in the study of family-level dynamics during infancy and early childhood. In J. P. McHale & P. A. Cowan (Eds.) *Understanding how family-level dynamics affect children's development: Studies of two-parent families* (pp. 5–26). New York: Jossey-Bass.

McLanahan, S., Garfinkel, I., Brooks-Gunn, J., & Hongxin, Z. (1998). *Unwed fathers and fragile families.* Presented at Population Association of America Annual Meeting, May, 1998. Chicago, IL.

Olson, D. H., Russell, C. S., & Sprenkle, D. H. (1983). Circumplex model of marital and family systems: VI. Theoretical update. *Family Process, 22,* 69–83.

Patterson, G. R. (Ed.) (1990). *Depression and aggression in family interactions.* Hillsdale, NJ: Lawrence Erlbaum Associates.

Resnick, M. D., Bearman, P. S., Blum, R., Bauman, K. E., Harris, K. M., Jones, J. (1997). Protecting adolescents from harm. *Journal of the American Medical Association, 278*(10), 823–832.

Shantz, C. U., & Hobart, C. J. (1989). Social conflict and development: Peers and siblings. In T. J. Berndt & G. W. Ladd (Eds.), *Peer relationships in child development* (pp. 71–94). New York: Wiley.

Singer, B., Ryff, C. D., Carr, D., & Magee, W. J. (in press). Linking life histories and mental health: A person-centered strategy. In A. Raftery (Ed.), *Sociological methodology.* Washington, DC: American Sociological Association.

Smith, J. R., Brooks-Gunn, J., & Klebanov, P. K. (1997). The consequences of living in poverty for your children's cognitive and verbal abilities and early school achievement. In G. J. Duncan & J. Brooks-Gunn (Eds.), *Consequences of growing up poor* (pp. 132–189). New York: Russell Sage Foundation Press.

Sroufe, L. A. (1989). Relationships and relationship disturbances. In A. J. Sameroff & R. N. Emde (Eds.), *Relationships disturbances in early childhood: A developmental approach* (pp. 97–124). New York: Basic Books.

Udry, J. R. (in press). Integrating biological and sociological models of adolescent problem behaviors. In R. Ketterlinus & M. Lamb (Eds.), *Adolescent problem behaviors.* Mahwah, NJ: Lawrence Erlbaum Associates.

Vandell, D. L., & Bailey, M. D. (1992). Conflict between siblings. In C. U. Shantz & W. W. Hartup (Eds.), *Conflict in child and adolescent development* (pp. 242–269). New York: Cambridge University Press.

Wakschlag, L. S., Chase-Lansdale, P. L., & Brooks-Gunn, J. (1996). Not just "Ghosts in the Nursery": Contemporary intergenerational relationships and parenting in young African-American families. *Child Development, 67*(5), 2131–2147.

Werner, E. E., Bierman, J. M., & French, F. E. (1971). *The children of Kauai: A longitudinal study from the prenatal period to age 10.* Honolulu: University of Hawaii Press.

Werner, E. E., Honzik, M. P., & Smith, R. S. (1968). Prediction of intelligence and achievement at ten years from 20 months pediatric and psychological examinations. *Child Development, 39*, 1063–1075.

Author Index

Subject Index

A

Academic achievement, 132, 144, 145, 157
Adolescent development, parental relationship
    and, *see also* Delinquency;
    Mother-daughter relationship, adolescent
    transition and; Mother-daughter relation-
    ship, teen depression and;
    Mother-daughter relationship, teen
    parenting and
  and cohesion decrease, 185, 186, 187
  and conflict increase, 185, 186, 187, 188,
    195–205
  gender differences, 195, 197, 203
  and interaction history, 185, 186–187,
    195, 203–204
  research limitations, 185–186, 187–190,
    204
  study hypotheses, 186–187
  study measures, 193–195
    assertiveness, 194–195
    cohesion/warmth/support, 194–195,
      195–205
    communication, 194
    conflict/hostility, 194, 195–205
    listener responsiveness, 195
    prosocial behavior, 195
  study methodology, 190–195
    strengths of, 190–191, 202
  study participants, 191–192
  study procedures, 192–193
  study results, 195–205
  theoretical perspectives
    cognitive-developmental, 186, 197,
      202
    psychoanalytic, 186
    social relations, 186–187, 195, 197,
      202–203

    sociobiological, 186, 197, 202
    time dimension in, 186, 197, 203
Adolescent Health Study, 334, 337
Adolescent Study Program, 212–213, 216
Affectional system, 147
African Americans, *see also* Mother-daughter
    relationship, teen parenting and
  and delinquency, 11, 13, 18–19
Age issues
  and children, 113–114, 117–124, 125
  mother-daughter relationship, 38, 39, 42,
    43, 45, 46–47
Anger
  and marital conflict, 90, 100–101
  and meta-emotion philosophy, 134, 135,
    147
Antisocial behavior and delinquency
  antisocial parents, 20, 27–28
  antisocial trait, 27–29
  and wandering male children, 168,
    169–170, 171, 178,179–180
    antisocial parents, 171, 178, 179–180
Attachment theory, 137–138
Authoritarian parenting, 137
Authoritative parenting, 137
Autonomy
  and mother-daughter relationship
    adolescent transition, 207–208,
      225–226, 231–234
    teen depression, 245–247, 248,
      249–250
    teen parenting, 40, 46
  and wandering male children, 167–168

C

Center for Epidemiological Studies Depres-
    sion Scale (CES–D), 216

Please remember that this is a library book,
and that it belongs only temporarily to each
person who uses it. Be considerate. Do
not write in this, or any, library book.